NEW INTRODUCTION

When *The Journal of a Disappointed Man* was first published in March 1919, it caused a literary sensation. Its reception by the press was, for the most part, eulogistic: 'One of the most remarkable human documents of the generation', 'the record of a brilliant youth', 'there is fantastic stuff in it', 'hectic energy', 'abandoned sensuousness'; there was only the occasional howl of dissension: 'The dreariest book it has ever been our misfortune to handle . . . in parts it is disgusting.' Readers were intrigued to know the author's identity. There was 'a certain mystification' about W. N. P. Barbellion and some reviewers suggested that H. G. Wells, who had provided the generous introduction, might have 'faked' the *Journal*. In a letter to the *Westminster Gazette*, Wells denied that he was 'a quarter clever enough' to have 'forged the entire diary' and said that he had only written the introduction at the request of the dying author.

The *Journal* ends with an editorial parenthesis, '(Barbellion died on December 31)'. A late review in the *New Statesman* contained the intriguing information that Barbellion was not 'really dead'. He had killed himself off at the end of the *Journal* 'for the sake of an artistic finish'. Taxed with his fictitious death, Barbellion made light of it. 'The fact is,' he said, 'no man dare remain alive after writing such a book.' He died, a few months later than expected, on 22 October, shortly before his thirty-first birthday. He had been suffering from multiple sclerosis, a disease even less understood then than it is now.

A Last Diary, the continuation of the *Journal*, appeared posthumously in 1920; it had been prepared for publication in accordance with Barbellion's instructions by his brothers. It too was to become a subject of controversy. In April 1921, the historian A. F. Pollard launched a savage attack on the authenticity of the Barbellion diaries. Writing in *History*, of which he was then editor, Pollard demonstrated that any chronicler who relied on the diaries for historical accuracy would be misled: Zeppelin raids were misdated; where Greenwich observed sun, Barbellion recorded thunder; and Sundays were forever playing leapfrog with Mondays. He tried to resuscitate the issue of Wells's authorship (this, at a time when Barbellion's real identity was public knowledge), and he suggested that Barbellion's brothers had partly concocted *A Last Diary* after his death. The obtuseness of some of Pollard's observations, coupled with his obvious hostility to Barbellion, discredits the few minor points he made which would have required explanation had not Barbellion himself already demolished the premise of Pollard's 'exercise' by freely admitting to 'bowdlerising' his *Journal*. The suggestion that Barbellion, a trained scientist, was 'imagining his observations' of natural phenomena, is patently absurd. Even Pollard had to admit, 'There is genius in the *Journal*'.

The only other book written by Barbellion is *Enjoying Life and Other Literary Remains*, a collection of extracts which had to be excluded from the *Journal* for lack of space, together with some published essays and two short stories.

'W. N. P. Barbellion' was the pseudonym of Bruce Frederick Cummings. The initials stood for the world's three greatest failures – Wilhelm, Nero and Pilate. 'Barbellion', came from a confectioner's shop in Bond Street; Cummings thought it sounded 'appropriately inflated'.

Unlike the majority of people for whom a state of health is the norm, Barbellion was 'chronically sub-normal'; he inhabited what he termed that big, dirty city of ill-health, and his brief escapes from it were periods of intense euphoria. His brother, Arthur Cummings, attributed Barbellion's poor health to an attack of pneumonia in infancy. The youngest of six children, Barbellion was a 'puny, under-sized child, nervously shy, with a tiny white face and large brown melancholy eyes'. The *Journal* begins when he is thirteen and already passionately interested in natural history. For much of his reading he had to rely on the local library in his home town of

Barnstable, North Devon. 'His importunities resulted in a building up of the nucleus of a modern collection of scientific books out of all proportion to the size of the town and the tastes of its people.'

The facts of Barbellion's life are recorded in his *Journal*: his struggle to win a post at the British Museum; his marriage to 'E' (Eleanor Benger, a talented fashion designer); his discovery of the nature of his illness; his physical decline. His colossal ambition – one of the main themes of the *Journal* – focused at first on zoology. Later, in London, it became diffused. His colleague and friend 'R' (Guy Robson), introduced him to art and classical music. In 1914 he wrote to his brother Arthur, 'Life is extraordinarily distracting. At times Zoology melts from my purview . . . If I go to a sculpture gallery, the continued study of entomology appears impossible – I will be a sculptor. If I go to the opera, then I am going to take up music seriously . . . Life is a series of wrenches, I tremble for the fixity of my purposes . . . ' Before he ever entered the British Museum, Barbellion had contemplated 'large literary schemes'. Commenting on Wells's introduction to the *Journal*, he said, that Wells 'concentrates on me as a biologist whereas I like to look at myself posthumously as a writer.'

As early as December 1914, Barbellion is listing among 'Projects in view': 'To prepare and publish a volume of this Journal'. The volume he was contemplating would probably have corresponded to *Enjoying Life* rather than the *Journal* as it subsequently appeared. His death sentence, delivered in 1915, altered all his schemes. Realizing that his time was up, Barbellion decided to make the *Journal* his one bid for fame. In February 1917 he is 'busy re-writing, editing and bowdlerising my journals for publication against the time when I shall have gone the way of all flesh'. His wife and child, threatened with poverty, were an added incentive. In a letter to his brother Hal he writes: 'If . . . you can gain access to Arnold Bennett, he might be persuaded to assist in finding a publisher for my Journal – in some respects a remarkable book – edited, typed and anonymous. There might be a little money in it.'

Hal Cummings showed the typescript to his colleague on the

Manchester Guardian, George Mair. Mair placed it with Collins who began setting it up and then got cold feet; they feared the book might tarnish their reputation as publishers of school text books. The *Journal* passed to Chatto & Windus and was accepted by Frank Swinnerton. Barbellion was understandably nervous, 'Have Chatto & Windus definitely accepted? Mair should be careful carrying the M. S. He might be killed by a motor car, or Chatto & Windus burnt down.'

A Last Diary is a continuation of the *Journal* after a gap of several months. It was resumed when Barbellion found that 'the relief it affords could not be refused any longer'. The act of writing was difficult, at times impossible, and parts had to be dictated to his wife or sister. Hal Cummings believed that, 'any impression of Barbellion that is formed without taking *A Last Diary* into account is bound to be out of focus.' To come across this gentle coda after the turmoil of the earlier volume is to experience the same sense of relief that an impressionable child feels in the theatre when the slain hero rises reassuringly at the curtain call to take his bow: we breathe again. Much of *A Last Diary* is reflective, the events in the life of a bed-ridden man being limited. The tone has mellowed, the ebullience has given way to a serene lyricism. In the final entries, after the enthusiastic reception of the *Journal,* we witness Barbellion tasting 'the delicious honey of kindly recognition' and licking his lips gratefully. With recognition came the comforting knowledge that he had provided for his widow and daughter. In addition to whatever money the *Journal* might make, a trust fund was organised by Wells, Bennett and Galsworthy to supplement his meagre Civil Service pension. Barbellion was flattered.

It was in keeping that the end of *A Last Diary* should not be quite as conclusive as it appears. Barbellion wished it to end: 'To-morrow I go to another nursing home. E. came down and decided the place here was impossible.' Barbellion's brothers lopped off the last sentence, leaving him eternally *en route.* In fact he died in the cottage at Gerrard's Cross that had been his home for the last few years of his life.

Barbellion described his *Journal* as a 'self-portrait in the nude'. Afterwards he said, 'I made myself worse than I was.' To get an idea of how he appeared to his contemporaries, we must look outside his own writing. Edward Shanks, in an appreciation written for the *London Mercury*, said, 'he was, it is agreed by all who knew him, a man of enormous, almost daemonic force of character.' His brother Arthur has given us a lovingly detailed description of him in his preface to *A Last Diary*:

...he was more than six feet in height, and as thin as a rake, and he looked like a typical consumptive...His appearance, notwithstanding his emaciation, was striking...A head of noble proportions was crowned by a thick mass of soft, brown hair tumbling carelessly about his brow. Deep-set, lustrous eyes, wide apart and aglow with eager life, lighted up a pale, sharply pointed countenance with an indescribable vividness of expression. His nose, once straight and shapely, owing to an accident was irregular in its contour, but by no means unpleasing in its irregularity, for it imparted a kind of rugged friendliness to the whole face; and he had a curious habit in moments of animation of visibly dilating the nostrils, as if unable to contain his excitement. His mouth was large, firm, yet mobile, and his chin like a rock. He had a musical voice, which he used without effort; and when he spoke, especially when he chose to let himself go on any subject that had aroused his interest, the energetic play of his features, the vital intensity which he threw into every expression, had an irresistible effect upon his friends. His hands were strong and sensitive, with a remarkable fineness of touch very useful to him in the laboratory; and it was always a pleasure to watch them at work upon a delicate dissection. His hands and arms were much more active members than his legs. In conversation he tried in vain to control a lifelong and amusing habit of throwing them out and beating the air violently to emphasise a point in argument. But he moved and walked languidly, like a tired man, as indeed he was...He had a real capacity for friendship, and his affections, once they were engaged, were deep and abiding; but he could be impishly provoking to an acquaintance, and he suffered fools without gladness or much self-restraint...

Barbellion's outward demeanour gave no indication of the chaos he carried within him. After he had handed the typescript of the *Journal* to his brother Hal, he wrote to him, 'You don't know how anxious I have been these last few days lest the book nauseated you ... I knew it would pain you. Forgive me for that.' Hal confessed later that he had found it 'a disturbing revelation'.

John Middleton Murry described Barbellion as 'a man of scientific genius', who 'showed his genius most clearly in this, that, condemned to die, he set before himself the one scientific task he could achieve in the time allowed him. He presented the world with the fact of himself.' Wells described Barbellion, without implying criticism, as 'intensely egoistical'; Barbellion himself was appalled by the 'egotism business' in his *Journal*. If there were nothing more than this to his writing he would be merely pitiable. However, Barbellion is so enamoured of life, so omnivorous in his enthusiasms, that his own individuality repeatedly 'shrinks to a vanishing-point' in the contemplation of nature or the behaviour of his fellow men. His use of imagery, often drawn from nature, is always telling; he has the true critic's gift for apt quotation from whatever he is reading; his ear for dialogue is infallible; his comments on himself have an objectivity that makes them universally applicable. If this were not enough there is always that unfailing antidote to egotism – a sense of humour; Barbellion's is of the dry, ironic variety, it wears well in the most gruesome conditions. The charge (voiced by Pollard) that Barbellion paid scant attention to the war, is not borne out by a careful reading of either journal. The war was the yardstick by which Barbellion attempted to keep his own tragedy in proportion. He wrote to Hal in April 1918, 'The idea of my carefully guarded existence beside the thousands of young men being butchered in France is not a pleasant one. I feel like a guarded mummy.'

In an essay 'On Journal Writers', Barbellion wrote that the habit of keeping a journal 'is not infrequently fostered by uncongenial or unsympathetic surroundings or by incurable misfortune'. Living in a seedy boarding house in Kensington, with few friends, his health wretched, Barbellion fell back on his Journal 'just as some other poor devil takes to drink'. It provided an outlet for the 'irresistible overflow' of his inner life. It was also an appeal to something beyond himself – that ideal reader called Posterity. In a moment of black despair he once wrote, 'I am determined that some day some one shall know': the sentiment of the castaway as he flings the message in a bottle out to sea.

Of his spiritual pedigree Barbellion said, 'My father was Sir Thomas Browne and my mother Marie Bashkirtseff. See what a curious hybrid I am!' His name has frequently been coupled with that of Bashkirtseff, a talented Russian art student who died of consumption in Paris in 1884. She was the *egoiste par excellence*. Barbellion identified with her and worshipped her. It is possible that his expression 'self-portrait in the nude' is an echo of the opening of Mathilde Blind's introduction to the English translation of Bashkirtseff's *Journal:* 'An autobiography such as this Journal of Marie Bashkirtseff – a book in the nude, breathing and palpitating with life so to say – has never, to my knowledge, been given to the world.' Such a salvo would have acted like the song of the sirens on Barbellion.

Another journal writer sometimes linked with Barbellion is Denton Welch, who was invalided at the age of twenty in a road accident. But Welch was effete where Barbellion was virile. Welch came from a privileged background and achieved literary recognition in his lifetime; Barbellion's origins were humble and his literary career posthumous. Welch, acutely aware of contemporary detail, has dated: Barbellion remains refreshingly modern.

Wells lamented that in Barbellion 'biological science loses one of the most promising of its recent recruits.' From the evidence of his writing and the testimony of his brothers, it seems likely that even if Barbellion had survived, science would have lost him to literature. It is fruitless to speculate how he might have developed as a writer. After reading parts of James Joyce's *Ulysses*, he exclaimed, 'Damn! it's all my idea, the technique I projected.' The career of the naturalist W. H. Hudson suggests a more obvious direction. As early as 1914 Barbellion wrote, 'for a long time past my hope has simply been to last long enough to convince others of what I might have done, had I lived'. It is the supreme irony of his tragic existence that in recording his failure he produced an enduring literary masterpiece.

Deborah Singmaster, London 1983

INTRODUCTION

Your egoist, like the solitary beasts, lives only for himself; your altruist declares that he lives only for others; for either there may be success or failure, but for neither can there be tragedy. For even if the altruist meets nothing but ingratitude, what has he to complain of? His premises abolish his grounds of complaint. But both egoist and altruist are philosophical abstractions. The human being by nature and necessity is neither egoist nor altruist; he trims a difficult course between the two; for the most part we are, within the limits of our powers of expression, *egotists*, and our desire is to think and if possible talk and write about this marvellous experiment of ourselves, with all the world—or as much as we can conveniently assemble—for audience. There is variety in our styles. Some drape the central figure; some let it rather appear than call attention to it; some affect a needless frankness: '*I* am an egotist, mind you, and I pretend nothing else'; some by adopting a pose with accessories do at least develop so great and passionate an interest in the accessories as to generalise and escape more or less completely from self. An egotism like an eggshell is a thing from which to escape; the art of life is that escape. The fundamental art of life is to recover the sense of that great self-forgetful continuous life from which we have individually budded off. Many people have done this through religion, which begins with a tremendous clamour to some saviour god or other to recognise us and ends in our recognition of him; or through science, when your egotist begins with: 'Behold me! I, I your humble servant, am a scientific man, devoted to the clear statement of truth,' and ends with so passionate a statement of truth that self is forgotten altogether.

In this diary of an intensely egotistical young naturalist, tragically caught by the creeping approach of death, we have one of the most moving records of the youthful aspects of our universal struggle. We begin with one of those bright schoolboys that most of us like to fancy we once were, that many of us have come to love as sons or nephews or younger brothers, and this youngster is attracted by natural science, by the employments of the naturalist and by the thought of being himself some day a naturalist. From the very beginning we find in this diary the three qualities, from the narrowest to broadest 'Observe me,' he says to himself, 'I am observing nature.' There is the self-conscious, self-centred boy. But he also says 'I am observing nature !' And at moments comes the clear light. He forgets himself in the twilight cave with the bats or watching the starlings in the evening sky, he becomes just you and I and the mind of mankind gathering knowledge. And the diary, as the keen edge of untimely fate cuts down into the sensitive tissue shows us presently, after outcries and sorrow and darkness of spirit, the habits of the observer rising to the occasion. Not for him, he realises, are the long life, the honours of science, the Croonian lecture, the listening Royal Society, one's memory embalmed in specific or generic names, the sure place in the temple of fame, that once filled his boyish dreams. But here is something close at hand to go on observing manfully to the end, in which self may be forgotten, and that is his own tormented self, with desire still great and power and hope receding. 'I will go on with this diary,' I read between the lines. 'You shall have at least one specimen, carefully displayed and labelled Here is a recorded unhappiness. When you talk about life and the rewards of life and the justice of life and its penalties, what you say must square with this.'

INTRODUCTION

Such is what we have here. It will be going beyond the necessities of this preface to expatiate upon a certain thread of unpremeditated and exquisite beauty that runs through the story this diary tells. To all sensitive readers it will be plain enough, and those who cannot see it plain do not deserve to have it underlined for them, that, still unseeing, they may pretend to see. Nor need we dilate upon the development of the quality of this diary from the rather fussy egotism of the earlier half. But it may be well to add a few explanatory facts that the opening chapters rather take for granted. Barbellion began life at a material as well as a physical disadvantage; neither of his parents were sturdy people, his mother died at last of constitutional heart weakness, and his father belonged to that most unfortunate class, the poor educated, who live lives of worry in straitened circumstances. Barbellion's father was a newspaper reporter in a west country town, his income rarely exceeded a couple of hundred pounds a year; the educational facilities of the place were poor, and young Barbellion had to get such learning as he could as a day boy at a small private school, his father supplementing this meagre training and presently taking him on as an apprentice reporter. How the passion for natural science arose does not appear in this diary; we already find the naturalist formed in the first schoolboy entries. An uncle, a chemist, seems to have encouraged the tendency, and to have given him textbooks and other help. Somehow at any rate he acquired a considerable amount of knowledge; by the time he was eighteen he was already publishing quite excellent observations of his own in such periodicals as the *Zoologist*, and by the time he was twenty he could secure an appointment as assistant naturalist to the director of a well-known marine biological station. It was a success, as the reader will learn, gained only to be renounced. His father was ill and he had to stand by his family; our economical country cannot afford to make biologists out of

INTRODUCTION

men who can earn a living as hack reporters. Poverty and
science are sisters wherever the flag of Britain waves; for
how could the rich live if we wasted money on that sort of
thing ? But the dream was not altogether abandoned, and
in 1911 Barbellion got a post, one of the dozen or so of rare
and coveted opportunities to toil in a scientific atmosphere
that our Empire affords; he secured an assistantship at the
Natural History Museum, South Kensington, to which a
living wage was attached, a fair equivalent to a reporter's
earnings. The rest of the story needs no helping out. Let
me only add that since 1911 Barbellion, in spite of his steadily
diminishing strength, has published articles in both British
and American periodicals, that entirely justify the statement
that in him biological science loses one of the most promising
of its recent recruits. His scientific work is not only full and
exact but it has those literary qualities, the grace, the power
of handling, the breadth of reference, which have always distinguished the best English biological work, and which mark
off at once the true scientific man from the mere collector
and recorder of items. With this much introduction Barbellion may be left to tell the tragedy of his hopes and of the
dark, unforeseen, unforeseeable, and inexplicable fate that
has overtaken him.

H. G. WELLS.

PART 1

' I returned, and saw under the sun, that the
race is not to the swift, nor the battle to the
strong, neither yet bread to the wise, nor yet
riches to men of understanding, nor yet favour
to men of skill; but time and chance
happeneth to them all. For man
also knoweth not his time; as the
fishes that are taken in an evil
net, and as the birds that are
caught in the snare; so are
the sons of men snared in
an evil time, when it
falleth suddenly
upon them.'

The Journal begins when its author is a little over 13 years old. (The following are selected entries.)

1903

January 3.

Am writing an essay on the life-history of insects and have abandoned the idea of writing on 'How Cats Spend their Time.'

January 17.

Went with L—— out catapult shooting. While walking down the main road saw a Goldfinch, but very indistinctly —it might not have been one. Had some wonderful shots at a tree creeper in the hedge about a foot away from me. While near a stream, L—— spotted what he thought to be some Wild Duck and brought one down, hitting it right in the head. He is a splendid shot. We discovered on examining it that it was *not* a Wild Duck at all but an ordinary tame Wild Duck—a hen. We ran away, and to-night L—— tells me he saw the Farmer enter the poulterer's shop with the bird in his hand.

January 19.

Went to A—— Wood with S—— and L——. Saw a Barn Owl (*Strix flammea*) flying in broad daylight. At A—— Woods, be it known, there is a steep cliff where we were all out climbing to inspect and find all the likely places for birds to build in, next spring. S—— and I got along all right, but L——, being a bit too careless, let go his hold on a tree and fell headlong down. He turned over and over and seemed to us to pitch on the back of his neck. However, he got up as cheerfully as ever, saying, 'I don't like that—a bit of a nasty knock.'

February 8.

Joe became the mother of one kitten to-day. It was

1

born at 1.20. It is a tiny little thing. One would almost call it deformed. It is gray.

March 18.

Our Goldfinch roosts at 5.30. Joe's kitten is a very small one. 'Magpie' is its name.

March 28.

Went our usual ramble. But we were unfortunate from the very beginning. First, when we reached the 'Nightjar Field,' we found there were two men at the bottom of it cutting the hedge, so we decided not to venture on, as Gimbo and Bounce were with us, and it would look like poaching. Later on, we came to a splendid wood, but had to withdraw hastily from it, an old farmer giving us a severe chase. There were innumerable rabbits in the wood, so, of course, the dogs barked hard. I gave them a sound beating when we got back out of danger. The old farmer is known as 'Bale the Bell-hanger.'

April 2.

I was glad yesterday to see the egg season so well in. I shall have to get blow-pipes and egg drills. Spring has really arrived and even the grasshoppers are beginning to stridulate, yet Burke describes these little creatures as being 'loud and troublesome' and the chirp unpleasant. Like Samuel Johnson, he must have preferred brick walls to green hedges. Many people go for a walk and yet are unable to admire Nature simply because their power of observation is untrained. Of course some are not suited to the study at all and do not trouble themselves about it. In that case they should not talk of what they do not understand. . . . I might have noticed that I have used the term 'Study of Nature.' But it cannot be called a *study*. It is a pastime of sheer delight, with naught but beautiful dreams and lovely thoughts, where we are urged forward by the fact that we are in God's world which He made for us to be our comfort in time of trouble. . . . Language cannot express the joy and happy forget-

fulness during a ramble in the country. I do not mean
that all the ins and outs and exact knowledge of a naturalist
are necessary to produce such delight, but merely the
common objects—Sun, Thrush, Grasshopper, Primrose,
and Dew.

April 21.

S—— and I have made a little hut in the woods out of a
large natural hole in the ground by a big tree. We have
pulled down branches all around it and stuck in upright
sticks as a paling. We are training ivy to grow over the
sticks. We smoke 'Pioneer' cigarettes here and hide the
packets in a hole under the roots of the tree. It's like a sort
of cupboard.

August 6.

In the evening, S—— and I cycled to S——, and when it
was dark we went down on the rocks and lit a fire which
crackled and burnt in the dusk of the evening. . . .
Intend to do a bit to Beetles these hols. Rev. J. Wood
in the *B.O.P.* has incited me to take them up, and it is
really time, for at present I am as ignorant as I can hang
together of the Coleoptera.

December 24.

Went out with L—— to try to see the squirrels again. We
could not find one and were just wondering if we should
draw blank when L—— noticed one clinging to the bark of
a tree with a nut in its mouth. We gave it a good chase,
but it escaped into the thickest part of the fir tree, still
carrying the nut, and we gave up firing at it. Later on,
L—— got foolishly mischievous—owing, I suppose, to our
lack of sport—and unhinged a gate which he carried
two yards into a copse, and threw it on the ground. Just
then, he saw the Squirrel again and jumped over the
hedge into the copse, chasing it from tree to tree with his
catty. Having lost it, he climbed a fir tree into a Squirrel's
drey at the top and sat there on the tree top, and I, below,
was just going to lift the gate back when I looked up

and saw a farmer watching me, menacing and silent.
I promptly dropped the gate and fled. L—— from his
Squirrel's drey, not knowing what had happened, called
out to me about the nest—that there was nothing in it.
The man looked up and asked him who he was and who
I was. L—— would not say and would not come down.
The farmer said he would come up. L—— answered that
if he did he would 'gob' [*i.e.* spit] on him. Eventually
L—— climbed down and asked the farmer for a glass of
cider. The latter gave him his boot and L—— ran away.

1904

January 23.

Went to the meet of the Stag hounds. Saw a hind in
the stream at L—— with not a horse, hound, or man in sight.
It looked quite unconcerned and did not seem to have
been hunted. I tried to head it, but a confounded sheep-
dog got there before me and drove it off in the wrong
direction. I *was* mad, because if I had succeeded in heading
it and had there been a kill, I should have got a slot. Got
home at 6.30, after running and walking fifteen miles—
tired out.

April 5.

Just read *Stalky & Co.* Of Stalky, Beetle, and M'Turk,
I like Beetle best.

April 14.

Won the School Gymnasium championship (under
fifteen).

August 25.

Had quite an adventure to-day. D—— and I cycled to
the Lighthouse at ——. On the way, in crossing the
sands near the Hospital Ship we espied a lame Curlew
which could hardly fly. I gave chase, but it managed to
scramble over a gut full of water about two yards wide.
D—— took off his boots and stockings and carried me over

on his back, and we both raced across the sands to where
the Curlew lay in an exhausted state. I picked him up
and carried him off under my arm, like the boy with the
Goose that laid the golden eggs. All the time, the bird
screamed loudly, opening its enormously long bill and
struggling to escape. Arrived at the gut again, we found
that the incoming tide had made the gut wider and deeper
so that we were cut off from the mainland, and found it
necessary to wade across at once before it got deeper.
As I had to carry a pair of field-glasses as well as my
boots and stockings, I handed over the struggling bird to
D——. While wading across, I suddenly sank to my waist
in a sandpit. This frightened me, and I was glad to reach
the other side in safety. But on arrival I found D——, but
no Curlew. In wading across the current, he grew flurried
and let it go. The tide swept it upstream, and the poor
bird, I fear, perished by drowning. . . . Knocked up
my friend P——. who is skipper of the ship N——., and
asked him if he had a fire so that I could dry myself. He
replied that they had no fire but that his 'missus' would
look out a pair of pants for me. Before falling in with
this plan unconditionally, I thought it best to inspect the
garment. However, it was quite clean—a pair of blue
serge seaman's trousers, very baggy in the seat and far
too long. But I turned up the bottoms and hid the
baggy part underneath my overcoat. So, I got back
home !

September 8.

Wet all day. Toothache.

September 9.

Toothache.

September 10.

Toothache.

September 11.

Toothache.

Xmas Day.

Mother and Dad wanted to give me one of G. A. Henty's, but, fearing lest I did not want it, they did not put my name in it, so that if I wished I could change it. Intend doing this. Am reading the *Origin of Species*. It requires careful study, but I understand it so far and shall go on.

December 26.

I have caught nothing in my traps yet. A little while ago I set a springe and two horse-hair nooses in the reed bed for water rails. I have bought a book on practical trapping.

1905

January 15.

I am thinking that on the whole I am a most discontented mortal. I get fits of what I call 'What's the good of anything?' mania. I keep asking myself incessantly till the question wears me out: 'What's the good of going into the country *naturalising*? what's the good of studying so hard? where is it going to end? will it lead anywhere?'

February 17.

When I can get hold of any one interested in Natural History I talk away in the most garrulous manner and afterwards feel ashamed of myself for doing it.

May 15.

The Captain, in answer to my letter, advises me to join one of the ordinary professions and then follow up Nat. History as a recreation, or else join Science Classes at S. Kensington, or else by influence get a post in the Natural History Museum. But I shall see.

June 9.

During dinner hour, between morning and afternoon school, went out on the S—— B—— River Bank, and found another Sedge Warbler's nest. This is the fifth I have found this year. People who live opposite on the T—— V—— hear them sing at night and think they are Nightingales!

June 27.

On reviewing the past egg-season, I find in all I have discovered 232 nests belonging to forty-four species. I only hope I shall be as successful with the beetle-season.

August 15.

A hot, sultry afternoon, during most of which I was stretched out on the grass beside an upturned stone where a battle royal was fought between Yellow and Black Ants. The victory went to the hardy little Yellows. . . . By the way, I held a Newt by the tail to-day and it emitted a squeak! So that the Newt has a voice after all.

August 26.

In bed with a feverish cold. I am afraid I have very few Nat. His. observations to make. It is hard to observe anything at all when lying in bed in a dull bedroom with one small window. Gulls and Starlings pass, steam engines whistle, horses' feet clatter down the street, and sometimes the voice of a passer-by reaches me, and often the loud laugh that speaks the vacant mind. I can also hear my own cough echoing through my head, and, by the evening, the few pages of Lubbock's *Ants, Bees, and Wasps* which I struggled to get through during the day rattle through my brain till I am disgusted to find I have them by heart. The clock strikes midnight and I wait for the morning. Oh! what a weary world.

October 13.

Down with another cold. Feeling pretty useless. It's a wonder I don't develop melancholia.

November 6.

By 7 a.m. H—— and I were down on the mudflats of the River with field-glasses, watching Waders. Ringed Plover in great numbers.

1906

January 13.

I have always had one ambition to be a great naturalist. This is, I suppose, a child's fancy, and I can see my folly in hoping for such great things. Still, there is no reason why I should not become a *learned* naturalist if I study hard. I hope that whatever I do I shall do in the hope of increasing knowledge of truth and not for my own fame. This entry may suggest that I am horribly conceited. But really I am as humble as possible. I know I have advanced beyond many others, and I know I shall advance further, but why be conceited? . . . What a short life we have, and what heaps of glorious work to be done! Supper bell—so I am off. . . . This reads like Isaac Walton's funny mixtures of the sublime with the ridiculous. He discusses abstract happiness and the best salmon sauce all in one breath.

February 26.

Although it is a grand achievement to have added but one jot or tittle to the sum of human knowledge it is grander still to have added a thought. It is best for a man to try to be both poet and naturalist—not to be too much of a naturalist and so overlook the beauty of things, or too much of a poet and so fail to understand them or even perceive those hidden beauties only revealed by close observation.

March 17.

Woke up this morning covered with spots, chest inflamed, and bad cough. H—— carted me down from the Attic to the Lower Bedroom, and when the Dr came he confirmed the general opinion that I had measles. It is simply disgusting, I have somewhere near 10,000 spots on me.

April 27.

Went to A—— Woods, where, strange to say, I again saw Mary. But she had a tribe of friends with her, so did not speak, but watched her from a distance through my field-glasses.

May 8.

On interviewing my old friend Dr. H——, found I had chickenpox. This instead of being a Diary of a Naturalist's observations[1] will be one of infectious diseases.

May 28.

[Letter from Editor of *Countryside* to my brother saying that if the *Countryside* grew he might be able to offer me a billet. 'Meanwhile he will be able to get along with his pen . . . he will soon make a living and in time too a name.'] This is a bit of all right. I shall always be on the look-out for a job on a N. H. Journal.

December 7.

Went to F—— Duckponds. Flocks of Wigeon and Teal on the water. Taking advantage of a dip in the land managed to stalk them splendidly, and for quite a long time I lay among the long grass watching them through my field-glasses. But during the day Wild Duck are not particularly lively or interesting birds. They just rest serenely on the water like floating corks on a sheet of glass. Occasionally one will paddle around lazily. But for the most part they show a great ennui and seem so sleepy and tired that one would almost think to be able to approach and feed them out of the hand. But I moved one hand carelessly and the whole flock was up in a minute and whizzing across the river. Afterwards, at dusk, on returning to the ponds, they had come back; but now that the sun was down, those dozy, flapdoodle creatures of the afternoon were transformed into quacking, quarrelsome, blustering birds that squabbled and chivvied each other, every moment seizing the chance of a luxurious dip, flinging the ice-cold water off their backs with a shake of the tail that seemed to indicate the keenest-edged delight.

[1] Up to 1911, the Journal is mainly devoted to records of observations in general Natural History and latterly in Zoology alone.

It was now quite dark. A Snipe rose at my feet and disappeared into the darkness. Coots and Moorhens clekked, and a Little Grebe grew bold and began to dive and fish quite close to me, methodically working its way upstream and so quartering out its feeding area.

A happy half-hour! Alas! I enjoy these moments the more as they recede. Not often do I realise the living present. That is always difficult. It is the mere shades —the ghosts of the dead days—that are dearest to me.

Spent my last day at school. De Quincey says (or was it Johnson?) that whenever we do anything for the last time, provided we have done it regularly for years before, we are a little melancholy, even though it has been distasteful to us. . . . True.

December 14.

Signed my Death Warrant, *i.e.*, my articles apprenticing me to journalism for five years. By Jove! I shall work frantically during the next five years so as to be ready at the end of them to take up a Natural History appointment.

1907

March 1.

As long as he has good health, a man need never despair. Without good health, I *might* keep a long while in the race, yet as the goal of my ambition grew more and more unattainable I should surely remember the words of Keats and give up: 'There is no fiercer Hell than the failure of a great ambition.'

March 14.

Have been reading through the Chemistry Course in the Harmsworth *Self-Educator* and learning all the latest facts and ideas about radium. I would rather have a clear comprehension of the atom as a solar system than a private income of £100 a year. If only I had eyes to go on reading without a stop!

May 1.

Met an old gentleman in E——, a naturalist with a great contempt for the Book of Genesis. He wanted to know how the Kangaroo leapt from Australia to Palestine and how Noah fed the animals in the Ark. He rejects the Old T. theogony and advised me to read 'Darwin and J. G. Wood'! Silly old man!

May 22.

To Challacombe and then walked across Exmoor. This is the first time I have been on Exmoor. My first experience of the Moors came bursting in on me with a flood of ideas, impressions, and delights. I cannot write out the history of to-day. It would take too long and my mind is a palpitating tangle. I have so many things to record that I cannot record one of them. Perhaps the best thing to do would be to draw up an inventory of things seen and heard and trust to my memory to fill in the details when in the future I revert to this date. Too much joy, like too much pain, simply makes me prostrate. It wounds the organism. It is too much. I shall try to forget it all as quickly as possible so as to be able to return to egg-collecting and bird-watching the sooner as a calm and dispassionate observer. Yet these dear old hills. How I love them. I cannot leave them without one friendly word. I wish I were a shepherd!

At the 'Ring of Bells' had a long yarn with the landlord, who, as he told us the story of his life, was constantly interrupted but never disconcerted by the exuberant loyalty and devotion of his wife—a stout, florid, creamy woman, who capped every story with: ''Ees quite honest, sir; no 'arm at all in old Joshua.'

June 5.

A half-an-hour of to-day I spent in a punt under a copper beech out of the pouring rain listening to Lady ——'s gamekeeper at A—— talk about beasts and local politics—just after a visit of inspection to the Heronry in the firs on the island in the middle of the Lake. It was delightful to hear him describing a Heron killing an Eel with 'a dap on the niddick,' helping out the figure with a pat on the nape of his thick bull neck.

July 22.

Am reading Huxley's *Crayfish*. H—— brought me in that magnificent aculeate *Chrysis ignita*.

August 15.

Met *her* in the market with M——. I just lifted my hat and passed on. She has the most marvellous brown eyes I have ever seen. She is perfectly self-possessed. A bad sign this.

August 18.

When I feel ill, cinema pictures of the circumstances of my death flit across my mind's eye. I cannot prevent them. I consider the nature of the disease and all I said before I died—something heroic, of course!

August 31.

She is a ripping girl. Her eyes are magnificent. I have never seen any one better looking.

October 1.

In the afternoon dissected a Frog, following Milnes Marshall's Book. Am studying Chemistry and attending classes at the Evening School and reading Physiology (Foster's). Am also teaching myself German. I wish I had a microscope.

October 3.

What heaps of things to be done! How short the time to do them in! An appetite for knowledge is apt to rush one off one's feet, like any other appetite if not curbed. I often stand in the centre of the Library here and think despairingly how impossible it is ever to become possessed of all the wealth of facts and ideas contained in the books surrounding me on every hand. I pull out one volume from its place and feel as if I were no more than giving one dig with a pick in an enormous quarry. The Porter spends his days in the Library keeping strict vigil over this catacomb of books, passing along between the shelves and yet never paying heed to the almost audible susurrus of desire—the desire every book has to be taken down and read, to live, to come into being in somebody's mind. He even hands the volumes over the counter, seeks them out in their proper places or returns them there without once realising that a Book is a Person and not a Thing. It makes me shudder to think of Lamb's *Essays* being carted about as if they were fardels.

October 16.

Dissected an Eel. Cassell's *Natural History* says the Air-bladder is divided. This is not so in the one I opened. Found what I believe to be the lymphatic heart in the tail beneath the vent.

1908

March 10.

Am working frantically so as to keep up my own work with the daily business of reporting. Shorthand, type-writing, German, Chemistry classes, Electricity lectures, Zoology (including dissections) and field work. Am reading Mosenthal's *Muscle and Nerve*.

April 7.

Sectioned a leech. H—— has lent me a hand micro-tome and I have borrowed an old razor. My table in the Attic is now fitted up quite like a Laboratory. I get up every morning at 6 a.m. to dissect. Have worked at the Anatomy of *Dytiscus*, *Lumbricus*, another Leech, and *Petromyzon fluviatilis* all collected by myself. The 'branchial basket' of *Petromyzon* interested me vastly. But it's a brute to dissect.[1]

[1] There are numerous drawings of dissections scattered through the Journal about this period.

May 1.

Cycled to the Lighthouse at the mouth of the Estuary.
Underneath some telegraph wires, picked up a Landrail
in excellent condition.   The colour of the wings is a
beautiful warm chestnut.   While sweeping the sandhills
with my field-glasses in search of Ring Plover, which
nest there in the shingle beaches, I espied a Shelduck
(*Tadorna*) squatting on a piece of level ground.   On
walking up cautiously, found it was dead—a Drake in
splendid plumage and quite fresh and uninjured.   Put
him in my poacher's pocket, alongside of the Landrail.
My coat looked rather bulgy, for a Shelduck is nearly as
big as a Goose.   Heard a Grasshopper Warbler—a rare bird
in North ——.   Later, after much patient watching, saw
the bird in a bramble bush, creeping about like a mouse.

On the sea-shore picked up a number of Sea Mice
(*Aphrodite*) and bottled them in my jar of 70 per cent.,
as they will come in useful for dissection.   Also found
the cranium of a *Scyllium*, which I will describe later on.

Near the Lighthouse watched some fishermen bring in
a large Salmon in a seine net worked from the shore.   It
was most exciting.   Cycled down three miles of hard
sand with the wind behind me to the village where I had
tea and—as if nothing could stay to-day's good luck—
met Margaret ——.   I showed her one by one all my
treasures—Rail, Duck, Skull, Sea Mice, etc., and felt
like Thomas Edward, beloved of Samuel Smiles.   To her
I must have appeared a very ridiculous person.

'How do you know it's the skull of a dog-fish?' she
asked, incredulous.

'How do I know anything?' I said, a little piqued.

On arriving home found T—— awaiting me with the
news that he had discovered a Woodpecker's nest.   When
will the luck cease?   I have never had such a flawless
ten hours in *le grand air*.   These summer days eat into
my being.   The sea has been roaring into my ears and
the sun blazing down so that even the backs of my hands
are sunburnt.   And then: those coal-black eyes.   Ah!
me, she *is* pretty.

May 2.

Dissected the Sheldrake. Very entertained to discover the extraordinary asymmetry of the syrinx. . . .

May 3.

Dissected Corncrake, examining carefully the pessulus, bronchidesmus (incomplete), *tympani-form and semi-lunar* membranes of a very interesting syrinx. . . .

May 6.

Dissected one of the Sea Mice. It has a remarkable series of hepatic ducts running into the alimentary canal as in Nudibranchs. . . .

May 9.

Spring in the Woods

Among the Oak Saplings we seemed enveloped in a cloud of green. The tall green grasses threw up a green light against the young green of the Oaks, and the sun managed to trickle through only here and there. Bevies of swinging bluebells grew in patches among the grass. Overhead in the oaks I heard secret leaf whispers—those little noiseless noises. Birds and trees and flowers were secretive and mysterious like expectant motherhood. All the live things plotted together, having the same big business in hand. Out in the sunlit meadows, there was a different influence abroad. Here everything was gay, lively, irresponsible. The brook prattled like an inconsequential schoolgirl. The Marsh Marigolds in flamboyant yellow sunbonnets played ring-a-ring-a-roses.

An Oak Sapling should make an elderly man avuncular. There are so many tremendous possibilities about a well-behaved young oak that it is tempting to put a hand upon its shoulder and give some seasoned, timberly advice.

June 1.

A Small Red Viper

Went to L—— Sessions. After the Court rose, I transcribed my notes quickly and walked out to the famous Valley of Rocks which Southey described as the ribs of the old Earth poking through. At the bottom of one of the hills saw a snake, a Red Viper. Put my boot on him quickly so that he couldn't get away and then recognised him as a specimen of what I consider to be the fourth species of British Serpent—*Vipera rubra*. The difficulty was to know how to secure him. This species is more ferocious than the ordinary *V. bera*, and I did not like the idea of putting my hand down to seize him by the neck. I stood for some time with my foot so firmly pressed down on its back that my leg ached and I began to wonder if I had been bitten. I held on and presently hailed a baker's cart coming along the road. The man got out and ran across the grass to where I stood. I showed him what I had beneath my boot and he produced a piece of string which I fastened around the snake's tail and so gently hauled the little brute up. It already appeared moribund, but I squashed its head on the grass with my heel to make certain. After parting with the baker, to whom all thanks be given, I remember that Adders are tenacious of life and so I continue to carry him at string's length and occasionally wallop him against a stone. As he was lifeless I wrapped him in paper and put him in my pocket—though to make assurance doubly sure I left the string on and let its end hang out over my pocket. So home by a two hours' railway journey with the adder in the pocket of my overcoat and the overcoat on the rack over my head. Settled down to the reading of a book on Spinoza's *Ethics*. At home it proved to be quite alive, and, on being pulled out by the string, coiled up on the drawing-room floor and hissed in a fury, to my infinite surprise. Finished him off with the poker and so spoilt the skin.

July 18.

Have had toothache for a week. Too much of a coward to have it out. Started for P—— early in the morning to report Mr Duke, K.C. After a week's pain, felt a little dicky. All the way in the train kept hardening myself to the task in front of me by recollecting the example of Zola, who killed pain with work. So all day to-day I have endeavoured to act as if I had no pain—the worst of all pains—toothache. By the time I got home I was rather done up, but the pain was actually less. This gave me a furious joy, and, after days of morose silence, to-night at supper I made them all laugh by bursting out violently with, 'I don't know whether you know it but I've had a horrible day to-day.' I explained at length and received the healing ointment of much sympathy. Went to bed happy with tooth still aching. I fear it was scarcely playing the strict Zolaesque game to divulge the story of my sufferings. . . . No, I am not a martyr or a saint. Just an ordinary devil who's having a rough time.

August 17.

Prawning

Had a glorious time on the rocks at low tide prawning. Caught some Five-Bearded Rocklings and a large *Cottus bubalis*. The sun did not simply shine to-day—it came rushing down from the sky in a cataract and flooded the sands with light. Sitting on a rock, with prawning net over my knees I looked along three miles of flat hard and yellow sands. The sun poured down on them so heavily that it seemed to raise a luminous golden yellow dust for about three feet high.

On the rocks was a pretty flapper in a pink sunbonnet —also prawning in company of S——, the artist, who has sent her picture to the Royal Academy. They saw I was a naturalist, so my services were secured to pronounce my judgment on a 'fish' she had caught. It was a Squid, 'an odd little beast,' in truth, as she said.

'The same class of animal,' I volunteered, 'as the Cuttlefish and Octopus.'

'Does it sting?'

'Oh, no!'

'Well, it ought to with a face like that.' She laughed merrily, and the bearded but youthful artist laughed too.

'I don't know anything about these things,' he said hopelessly.

'Nor I,' said the naturalist modestly. 'I study fish.'

This was puzzling. 'Fish?' What was a Squid then? . . . The artist would stop now and then and raise his glasses at a passing ship, and Maud's face occasionally disappeared in the pink sunbonnet as she stooped over a pool to examine a seaweed or crab.

She's a dear—and she gave me the Squid. What a merry little cuss!

September 1.

Went with Uncle to see a Wesleyan minister whose fame as a microscopist, according to Uncle, made it worth my while to visit him. As I expected, he was just a silly old man, a diatomaniac fond of pretty-pretty slides and not a scientific man at all. He lectures Bands of Hope on the Butterfly's Life History and hates his next-door neighbour, who is also a microscopist and incidentally a scientific man, because he interests himself in 'parasites and those beastly things.'

I remarked that his friend next door had shown me an Amphioxus.

'Oh! I expect that's some beastly bacteria thing,' he said petulantly. 'I can't understand Wilkinson. He's a pervert.'

I told him what *Amphioxus* was and laughed up my sleeve. He likes to think of Zoology as a series of pretty pictures illustrating beautiful moral truths. The old fellow's saving grace was enthusiasm. . . . Having focused an object for us, he would stand by, breathless, while we squinted down his gas-tube, and gave vent to tremendous expletives of surprise such as 'Heavens,' or

'Jupiter.' His eyes would twinkle with delight and straightway another miracle is selected for us to view. 'They are all miracles,' he said.

'Those are the valves'—washing his hands with invisible soap—'no one has yet been able to solve the problem of the Diatom's valves. No one knows what they are—no, nor ever will know—why?—why can't we see behind the valves?—because God is behind the valves —that is why!' Amen.

October 1.

Telegraphed 1000 words of Lord ——'s speech at T——. Spent the night at a comfortable country inn and read Moore's lyrics. 'Row gently here, my Gondolier,' ran through my head continuously. The Inn is an old one with a long narrow passage that leads straight from front door to back with wainscoted smoke room and parlours on each side. China dogs, bran on the floor, and the picture of Derby Day with horses galloping incredibly, the drone of an old crony in the bar, and a pleasant barmy smell. Slept in a remarkable bedroom full of massive furniture, draped with cloth and covered with trinkets. The bed had a tremendous hood over it like a catafalque, and lying in it made me think I was an effigy. Read Moore till the small hours and then found I had left my handbag downstairs. Lit a candle and went on a voyage of discovery. Made a considerable noise, but roused no one. Entered drawing-room, kitchen, pantries, parlour, bar—everywhere looking for my bag and dropping candle grease everywhere! Slept in my day shirt. Tired out and slept like a top.

November 3.

Aristotle's Lantern

Dissected the Sea Urchin (*Echinus esculentus*). Very excited over my first view of Aristotle's Lantern. These complicated pieces of animal mechanism never smell of musty age—after æons of evolution. When I open a

Sea Urchin and see the Lantern, or dissect a Lamprey
and cast eyes on the branchial basket, such structures
strike me as being as finished and exquisite as if they
had just a moment before been tossed me fresh from the
hands of the Creator. They are fresh, young, they smell
new.

December 3.

Hard at work dissecting a Dogfish. Ruridecanal
Conference in the afternoon. I enjoy this double life I
lead. It amazes me to be laying bare the brain of a dogfish
in the morning and in the afternoon to be taking down
in shorthand what the Bishop says on Mission Work.

December 4.

Went to the Veterinary Surgeon and begged of him
the skull of a horse. Carried the trophy home under my
arm—bare to the public view. 'Why, Lor', 'tis an ole
'orse's jib,' M—— said when I got back.

                          1909
March 7.

My programme of work is: (1) Continue German.
(2) Sectioning embryo of (*a*) Fowl, (*b*) Newt. (3) Paper
on Arterial System of Newts. (4) Psychology of Newts.
(5) General Zoological Reading.

May 2.

To C—— Hill. Too much taken with the beauty of
the Woods to be able to do any nesting. Here are some
of the things I saw: the bark on several of the trees in
the mazzard orchards rubbed into a beautifully smooth,
polished surface by the Red Devon Cows when scratching
where it itched; I put my hand on the smooth almost
cherry-red patch of bark and felt delighted and grateful
that cows had fleas: the young shoots of the whortle-
berry plants on the hill were red tipped with the gold of
an almost horizontal sun. I caught a little lizard which

slipped across my path. . . . Afar off down in the valley
I had come through, in a convenient break in a holly bush,
I could just see a Cow sitting on her matronly haunches
in a field. She flicked her ears and two starlings settled
on her back. A Rabbit swept out of a sweet-brier bush
and a Magpie flew out of the hedge on my right.

In another direction I could see a field full of luscious,
tall, green grass. Every stalk was so full of sap that
had I cut one I am sure it would have bled great green
drops. In the field some lambs were sleeping; one woke
up and looked at me with the back of its head to the low
sun, which shone through its two small ears and gave
them a transparent pink appearance.

No sooner am I rebaptized in the sun than I have to
be turning home again. No sooner do 'the sudden lilies
push between the loosening fibres of the heart' than I
am whisked back into the old groove—the daily round.
If only I had more time!—more time in which to think,
to love, to observe, to frame my disposition, to direct
as far as in me lies the development and unfolding of my
character, if only I could direct all my energies to the
great and difficult profession of life, of being man instead
of trifling with one profession that bores me and dabbling
in another.

June 5.

On Lundy Island

Frankie is blowing Seagulls' eggs in the scullery. His
father, after a day's work at the farm, is at his supper
very hungry, yet immensely interested, and calls out
occasionally,—

"Ow you're getting on, Foreman?'

'All right, Capt.,' says Frankie affectionately, and the
unpleasant asthmatic, wheezy noise of the egg-blowing
goes on. . . . There are three dogs asleep under the
kitchen table; all three belong to different owners and
neither one to A——.

June 6.

Out egg-collecting with the Lighthouse Keepers. They walk about the cliffs as surefooted as cats, and feed their dogs on birds' eggs collected in a little bag at the end of a long pole. One dog ate three right off in as many minutes, putting his teeth through and cracking the shell, then lapping up the contents. Crab for tea.

June 7.

After a glorious day at the N. end of the Island with the Puffins, was forced to-night to take another walk, as the smell of Albert's tobacco, together with that of his stockinged feet and his boots removed, was asphyxi-ating.

June 9.

The governess is an awfully pretty girl. We have been talking together to-day and she asked me if I were a naturalist. I said 'Yes.' She said, 'Well, I found a funny little beetle yesterday and Mr S—— said I ought to have given it to you.' Later, I felt she was looking at me, so I looked at her, across the beach. Yes! it was true. When our eyes met she gave me one of the most provokingly pretty smiles, then turned and went up the cliff path and so out of my life—to my everlasting regret.

Return to-night in a cattle steamer.

June 18.

Dr ——, M.A., F.R.S., D.C.L., LL.D., called in the office to-day, and seeing Dad typing, said, 'Are you Mr Barbellion?' Dad replied in the affirmative, whereupon the Doctor handed him his card, and Dad said he thought it was his son he wanted to see. He is an old gentleman aged eighty or thereabouts, with elastic-sided boots, an umbrella, and a guardian nephew—a youngster of about sixty. But I paid him due reverence as a celebrated zoologist and at his invitation [and to my infinite pride] accompanied him on an excursion to the coast, where he wanted to see *Philoscia Couchii*, which I readily turned up for him.

I chanced to remark that I thought torsion in gastro-
pods one of the most fascinating and difficult problems
in Zoology. Why should a snail be twisted round?

'Humph,' said he, 'why do we stand upright?' I was
not such a fool as to argue with him, so pretended his
reply was a knock-out. But it enabled me to size him
up intellectually.

In the evening dined with him at his hotel. . . . He
knows Wallace and Haeckel personally, and I sat at his
feet with my tongue out listening to personal reminiscences
of these great men. However, he seemed never to have
heard of Gaskell's Theory on the Origin of Vertebrates.

June 27.

Walked to V——. As usual, Nature with clockwork
regularity had all her taps turned on—larks singing,
cherries ripening, and bees humming. It all bored me
a little. Why doesn't she vary it a little?

August 8.

A cold note from Dr —— saying that he cannot under-
take the responsibility of advising me to give up journalism for zoology.

A hellish cold in the head. Also a swingeing inflammation of the eyes. Just heard them singing in the Chapel
over the way : 'God shall wipe away all tears from their
eyes.' Hope so, I'm sure.

August 9.

A transformation. After a long series of drab experiences in Sheffield, etc., the last being the climax of yesterday, an anti-cyclone arrived this morning and I sailed
like an Eagle into cloudless, windless weather! *The
Academy* has published my article, my cold is suddenly
better, and going down by the sea this afternoon met
Mary —— !

August 20.

Had an amusing letter from my maiden-aunt, who does
not like ' the agnostic atmosphere ' in my *Academy* article.
Poor dear !   She is sorry if I really feel like that, and, if I do,
what a pity to put it into print.   Then a Bible reference
to the Epistle to the Romans.

Xmas Day.

Feeling ill—like a sloppy Tadpole.   My will is paralysed.
I visit the Doctor regularly to be stethoscoped, ramble
about the streets, idly scan magazines in the Library
and occasionally rink—with palpitation of the heart as
a consequence.   In view of the shortness, bitterness, and
uncertainty of life, all scientific labour for me seems
futile.

1910

January 10.

Better, but still very dicky : a pallid animal : a weevil
in a nut.   I have a weak heart, an enervated nervous
system; I suffer from lack of funds with which to carry
on my studies; I hate newspaper-reporting—particularly
some skinny-witted speaker like ——; and last, but not
least, there are women; all these worries fight over my
body like jackals over carrion.   Yet Zoology is all I want.
Why won't Life leave me alone?

January 15.

Reading Hardy's novels.   He is altogether delightful
in the subtlety with which he lets you perceive the first
tiny love presentiments between his heroes and heroines
—the casual touch of the hands, the peep of a foot or
ankle underneath the skirt—all these in Hardy signify
the cloud no bigger than a man's hand.   They are the
susurrus of the breeze before the storm, and you await
what is to follow with palpitating heart.

February 3.

For days past have been living in a state of mental ebullition. All kinds of pictures of Love, Life, and Death have been passing through my mind. Now I am too indolent and nerveless to set them down. Physically I am such a wreck that to carry out the least intention, such as putting on my boots, I have to flog my will like an Arab with a slave 'in a sand of Ayaman.' Three months ago when I got up before breakfast to dissect rabbits, dogfish, frogs, newts, etc., this would have seemed impossible.

February 6.

Still visit Dr ——'s surgery each week. I have two dull spots at the bottom of each lung. What a fine expressive word is *gloom*. Let me write it : GLOOM.... One evening coming home in the train from L—— County Sessions I noticed a horrible, wheezy sound whenever I breathed deep. I was scared out of my life, and at once thought of consumption. Went to the Doctor's next day, and he sounded me and reassured me. I was afraid to tell him of the little wheezy sound at the apex of each lung, and I believed he overlooked it. So next day, very harassed, I went back to him again and told him. He *hadn't* noticed it and looked glum. Have to keep out of doors as much as possible.

The intense internal life I lead, worrying about my health, reading (eternally reading), reflecting, observing, feeling, loving and hating—with no outlet for superfluous steam, cramped and confined on every side, without any friends or influence of any sort, without even any acquaintances excepting my colleagues in journalism (whom I contemn)—all this will turn me into the most self-conscious, conceited, mawkish, gauche creature in existence.

March 6.

The facts are undeniable : Life is pain. No sophistry can win me over to any other view. And yet years ago

I set out so hopefully and healthfully—what are birds'
eggs to me *now*? My ambition is enormous but vague.
I am too distributed in my abilities ever to achieve distinction.

March 22.

Had a letter from the Keeper of Zoology at the British
Museum, advising me of three vacancies in his Dept.,
and asking me if I would like to try, etc. . . . So that
Dr ——'s visit to me bore some fruit.[1] Spent the morning
day-dreaming. . . . Perhaps this is the flood tide at last !
I shall work like a drayhorse to pull through if I am
nominated. . . . I await developments in a frightfully
turbulent state of mind. I have a frantic desire to control
the factors which are going to affect my future so permanently. And this ferocious desire, of course, collides
with a crash all day long with the fact that however much
I desire there will still remain the unalterable logic of
events.

April 7.

. . . How delicious all this seemed ! To be alive—
thinking, seeing, enjoying, walking, eating — all quite
apart from the amount of money in your purse or the
prospects of a career. I revelled in the sensuous enjoyment of my animal existence.

June 2.

Up to now my life has been one of great internal strife
and struggle—the struggle with a great ambition and a
weak will—unequal to the task of coping with it. I have
planned on too big a scale, perhaps. I have put too great
a strain on my talents, I have whipped a flagging will,
I have been for ever cogitating, worrying, devising means
of escape. Meanwhile, the moments have gone by un-
heeded and unenjoyed.

---

[1] He had spoken about me to the Museum authorities, and it
was his influence which got me the nomination to sit for the
examination.

June 10.

Legginess is bad enough in a woman, but bandy legginess is impossible.

Solitude is good for the soul. After an hour of it, I feel as lofty and imperial as Marcus Aurelius.

The best girl in the best dress immediately looks disreputable if her stockings be downgyved.

Some old people on reaching a certain age go on living out of habit—a bad habit too.

How much I can learn of a stranger by his laugh.

Bees, Poppies, and Swallows!—and all they mean to him who really knows them! Or a White Gull on a piece of floating timber, or a troop of shiny Rooks close on the heels of a ploughman on a sunny autumn day.

June 30.

My egoism appals me. Likewise the extreme intensification of the consciousness of myself. Whenever I walk down the High Street on a market day, my self-consciousness magnifies my proportions to the size of a Gulliver—so that it is grievous to reflect that in spite of that the townsfolk see me only as an insignificant bourgeois youth who reports meetings in shorthand.

July 17.

We sang to-night in Church, 'But when I know Thee as Thou art, I'll praise Thee as I ought.' Exactly! Till then, farewell. We are a great little people, we humans. If there be no next world, still the Spirit of Man will have lived and uttered its protest.

July 22.

Our Simian Ancestry

How I hate the man who talks about the 'brute creation,' with an ugly emphasis on *brute*. Only Christians are capable of it. As for me, I am proud of my close kinship with other animals. I take a jealous pride in my Simian ancestry. I like to think that I was once a magnificent hairy fellow living in the trees and that my frame has come down through geological time *via* sea jelly and worms and Amphioxus, Fish, Dinosaurs, and Apes. Who would exchange these for the pallid couple in the Garden of Eden?

August 9.

I do not ever like going to bed. For me each day ends in a little sorrow. I hate the time when it comes to put my books away, to knock out my pipe and say 'Good-night,' exchanging the vivid pleasures of the day for the darkness of sleep and oblivion.

August 23.

Spent the afternoon and evening till ten in the woods with Mary ——. Had tea in the Haunted House, and after sat in the Green Arbor until dark, when I kissed her. 'Achilles was not the worse warrior for his probation in petticoats.'

September 1.

I hope to goodness she doesn't think I want to marry her. In the Park in the dark, kissing her. I was testing and experimenting with a new experience.

September 4.

Last evening, after much mellifluous cajolery, induced her to *kiss me*. My private opinion about this whole affair is that all the time I have been at least twenty degrees below real love heat. In any case I am constitutionally and emotionally unfaithful. I said things which I did not believe just because it was dark and she was charming.

September 5.

Read Thomas à Kempis in the train. It made me so angry I nearly flung it out of the window. 'Meddle not with things that be too deep for thee,' he says, 'but read such things as yield compunction to the heart rather than elevation to the head.' Forsooth! Can't you see me?

September 15.

A puzzling afternoon : weather perfect, the earth green and humming like a top, yet a web of dream overlaid the great hill, and at certain moments, which recurred in a kind of pulsation, accompanied by subjective feelings of vague strife and effort, I easily succeeded in letting all I saw—the field and the blackberry bush, the whole valley and the apple orchards—change into something unreal, flimsy, gauzelike, immaterial, and totally unexperienced. Suddenly when the impression was most vivid, the whole of this mysterious tapestry would vanish away and I was back where 2 and 2 make 4. Oh! Earth! how jealously you guard your secrets !

October 4.

Sat at the Civil Service Commission in Burlington House for the exam. for the vacancy in the B. M. No luck at all with the papers. The whole of my nine months' assiduous preparation helped me in only two questions. In fine, I have not succeeded, I shall not obtain the appointment, and in a few weeks I shall be back in the wilds of N—— again under the old régime, reporting platitudes from greasy guardians of the poor, and receiving condolences from people not altogether displeased at some one else's misfortune.

October 14.

Returned home from London. Felt horribly defeated in crossing the threshold. It was so obviously *returning* after an unsuccessful flight.

October 22.

Dissected a *Squilla* for which I paid 2s. 6d. to the Plymouth Marine Laboratory.

October 23.

Ambition

Am attempting to feel after some practical philosophy of living—something that will enable me to accept disappointment with equanimity and Town Council meetings with a broad and tolerant smile. At present, ambition consumes me. I was ambitious before I was breeched. I can remember wondering as a child if I were a young Macaulay or Ruskin and secretly deciding that I was. My infant mind even was bitter with those who insisted on regarding me as a normal child and not as a prodigy. Since then I have struggled with this canker for many a day, and as success fails to arrive it becomes more gnawing.

October 24.

In the morning a Town Council and in the afternoon a Rural Council. With this abominable trash in my notebook waiting to be written up and turned into 'copy,' and with the dream pictures of a quiet studious life in Cromwell Road not yet faded from my mind, where can I turn for consolation? That I have done my best? That's only a mother's saying to her child.

Perhaps after all it is a narrow life—this diving and delving among charming little secrets, plying diligently scalpel and microscope and then weaving the facts obtained into theoretic finespun. It is all vastly entertaining to the naturalist but it leaves the world unmoved. I sometimes envy the zealot with a definite mission in life. Life without one seems void. The monotonous pursuit of our daily vocations—the soldier, sailor, candlestick-maker—so they go on, never living but only working, never thinking but only hypnotising themselves by the routine and punctuality of their lives into just so many mechanical toys warranted to go for so long and then stop when Death takes them. . . . It amazes me that men must spend their precious days of existence for the most part in slaving for food and clothing and the bare necessaries of existence.

To sum up my despondency, what's the good of such a life? Where does it lead? Where am I going? Why should I work? What means this procession of nights and days wherein we are all seen moving along intent and stern as if we had some purpose or a goal? . . . Of

course to the man who believes in the next world and a
personal God, it is quite another matter. The Christian
is the Egoist *par excellence.* He does not mind annihilation
by arduous labour in this world if in the next he shall
have won eternal life. . . . He is reckless of to-day,
extravagant in the expenditure of his life. This intolerable fellow will be cheerful in a dungeon. For he flatters
himself that God Almighty up in Heaven is all the time
watching through the keyhole and marking him down
for eternal life.

October 26.

The nose-snuffling, cynical man who studies La Roche-
foucauld, and prides himself on a knowledge of human
motives, is pleased to point out that every action and
every motive is selfish, from the philanthropist who
advertises himself by his charities to the fanatic who lays
down his life for a cause. Even secret charities, for they
give pleasure to the doer. So your cynic thinks he has
thus, with one stroke of his psychological scalpel, laid
human nature bare in all its depravities. All he has done
really is to reclassify motives—instead of grouping them
as selfish and unselfish (which is more convenient) he
lumps them together as selfish, a method by which even
he is forced to recognise different grades of selfishness.
For example, the selfishness of a wife-beater is lower than
the selfishness of a man who gives up his life for another.

October 28.

The result arrived. As I thought, I have failed, being
fourth with only three vacancies.

November 7.

It is useless to bewail the course of fortune. It cannot
be much credit to possess—though we may covet—those
precious things, to possess which depends on circumstances
outside our control.

Novemoer 9.

Dined at the Devonshire Club in St James's Street,
W., with Dr H—— and Mr ——, the latter showing
the grave symptomatic phenomena of a monocle and
spats. A dinner of eight courses. Only made one mistake
—put my salad on my dish instead of on the side dish.
Horribly nervous and reticent. I was apparently expected to give an account of myself and my abilities—
and with that end in view, they gave me a few pokes in
my cranial ribs. But I am a peculiar animal, and, before
unbosoming myself, I would require a happier *mise en
scène* than a West End Club, and a more tactful method
of approach than ogling by two professors, who seemed
to think I was a simple penny-in-the-slot machine. I
froze from sheer nervousness and nothing resulted.

November 11.

Returned home and found a letter awaiting me from
Dr A—— offering me £60 a year for a temporary job
as assistant at the Plymouth Marine Laboratory.
    Left London horribly depressed. They evidently
intend to shuffle me off.
    Read Geo. Gissing's novel, *Born in Exile*. Godwin
Peak, with his intense pride of individuality, self-torturing
capacities, and sentimental languishment, reminds me
of myself.

November 20.

A purulent cold in the nose. My heart is weak. Palpitation after the least exertion. But I shall soon be
swinging my cudgels in the battle of life, so it won't do
to be hypochondriacal. . . . Let all the powers of the
world and the Devil attack me, yet I will win in the end
—though the conquest may very well be one which no
one but myself will view.
    Have accepted the Plymouth appointment.

November 30.

Struggling in the depths again within the past few
days with heart attacks. Am slowly getting better of
them and trying to forget as soon as may be visions of
sudden death, coffins, and obituary notices.

December 2.

Death

At first, when we are very young, Death arouses our
curiosity, as it did Cain in the beginning.[1] It is a strange
and very rare phenomenon which we cannot comprehend,
and every time we hear of some one's death, we try to
recall that person's appearance in life and are disappointed
if we can't. The endeavour is to discover what it is, this
Death, to compare two things, the idea of the person alive
and the idea of him dead. At last some one we know
well dies—and that is the first shock. . . . I shall never
forget when our Matron died at the D—— School. . . .
As the years roll on, we get used to the man with the
scythe and an acquaintance's death is only a bit of gossip.

Suppose the Hellfire of the orthodox really existed!
We have no assurance that it does not! It seems incredible, but many incredible things are true. We do
not *know* that God is not as cruel as a Spanish inquisitor.
Suppose, then, He is! If, after Death, we wicked ones
were shovelled into a furnace of fire—we should have to
burn. There would be no redress. It would simply be
the Divine Order of things. It is outrageous that we
should be so helpless and so dependent on any one—
even God.

December 9.

Sometimes I think I am going mad. I live for days
in the mystery and tears of things so that the commonest
object, the most familiar face—even my own—become
ghostly, unreal, enigmatic. I get into an attitude of
almost total scepticism, nescience, solipsism even, in a
world of dumb, sphinx-like things that cannot explain

[1] In Byron's poem.

themselves. The discovery of how I am situated—a
sentient being on a globe in space overshadows me. I
wish I were just nothing.

Later : While at a public meeting, the office-boy
approached me and immediately whispered without
hesitation,—

'Just had a telephone message to say that your father
is at the T—— Railway Station, lying senseless. He
has evidently had an apoplectic fit.'

(How those brutal words, 'lying senseless,' banged
and bullied and knocked me down. Mother was waiting
for me at the door in a dreadful state and expecting the
worst.)

Met the train with the Doctor, and took him home in
the cab—still alive, thank God, but helpless. He was
brave enough to smile and shake me by the hand—with
his left, though he was speechless and the right side of
his body helpless. A porter discovered him at the
railway terminus lying on the floor of a second-class
carriage.

December 10.

He is a trifle better. It is fifteen years since he had
the first paralytic stroke.

Am taking over all his work and have written at once
resigning the Plymouth appointment.

December 23.

It really did require an effort to go upstairs to-day to
his bedroom and say cheerfully I was not going to P.
after all, and that the matter was of no consequence to
me. I laughed gaily and Dad was relieved. A thundering
good joke. What annoys me is that other folk—the
brainless, heartless mob, as Schopenhauer remarks, still
continue to regard me as one of themselves. . . . I had
nearly escaped into a seaside laboratory, and now suddenly to be flung back into the dirt and sweat of the
newspaper world seems very hard, and it *is* very hard.

December 26.

Windy Ash

With the dog for a walk around Windy Ash. It was
a beautiful winter's morning—a low sun giving out a
pale light but no warmth—a luminant, not a fire—the
hedgerows bare and well trimmed, an Elm lopped close
showing white stumps which glistened liquidly in the
sun, a Curlew whistling overhead, a deeply cut lane washed
hard and clean by the winter rains, a gunshot from a
distant cover, a creeping Wren, silent and tame, in a
bramble bush, and over the five-barred gate the granite
roller with vacant shafts. I leaned on the gate and saw
the great whisps of cloud in the sky like comets' tails.
Everything cold, crystalline.

1911

January 2.

As a young man—a *very* young man—my purpose was
to plough up all obstacles, brook no delays, and without
let or hindrance win through to an almost immediate
success! But witness 1910! 'My career' so far has been
like the White Knight's, who fell off behind when the
horse started, in front when it stopped, and sideways
occasionally to vary the monotony.

January 30.

Feeling ill and suffering from attacks of faintness. My
ill health has produced a change in my attitude towards
work. As soon as I begin to feel the least bit down, I am
bound to stop at once as the idea of bending over a desk or
a dissecting dish, of reading or studying, nauseates me
when I think that perhaps to-morrow or next day or next
week, next month, next year I may be dead. What a
waste of life it seems to work! Zoology is repugnant
and philosophy superfluous beside the bliss of sheer living
—out in the cold polar air or indoors in a chair before
a roaring fire with hands clasped, watching the bustling,
soothing activity of the flames.

Then, as soon as I am well again, I forget all this, grow discontented with doing nothing and work like a Tiger.

February 11.

Walked in the country. Coming home, terrified by a really violent attack of palpitation. Almost every one I met I thought would be the unfortunate person who would have to pick me up. As each one in the street approached me, I weighed him in the balance and considered if he had presence of mind and how he would render first aid. After my friend, P. C.——, had passed, I felt sorry that the tragedy had not already happened, for he knows me and where I live. At length, after sundry leanings over the river wall, arrived at the Library, which I entered, and sat down, when the full force of the palpitation was immediately felt. My face burned with the hot blood, my hand holding the paper shook with the angry pulse, and my heart went bang! bang! bang! and I could feel its beat in the carotids of the neck and up along the Torcular Herophili and big vessels in the occipital region of the head. Drew in each breath very gently for fear of aggravating the fiend. Got home (don't know how) and had some sal volatile. Am better now but very demoralised.

February 13.

Feel like a piece of drawn threadwork, or an undeveloped negative, or a jelly fish on stilts, or a sloppy tadpole, or a weevil in a nut, or a spitchcocked eel. In other words and in short—ill.

February 16.

After some days with the vision of sudden death constantly before me, have come to the conclusion that it's a long way to go to die. Am coming back anyhow. Yet these are a few terrible pages in my history.

March 4.

. . . The Doctor's orders 'Cease Work' have brought on in an aggravated form my infatuation for zoological research. I lie in bed and manufacture rolling periods in praise of it, I get dithyrambic over the zoologists themselves—Huxley, Wallace, Brooks, Lankester. I chortle to reflect that in zoology there are no stock exchange ambitions, there is no mention of slum life, Tariff Reform is not included. In the repose of the spacious laboratory by the seaside or in the halls of some great Museum, life with its vulgar struggles, its hustle and obscenity, scarcely penetrates. Behind those doors, life flows slowly, deeply. I am ascetic and long for the monastic seclusion of a student's life.

March 5.

From One Maiden Lady to Another. (*Authentic*)

'My dear Sister,—You have been expecting to hear from me I know, I have had inflammation to my eyes twice in 3 weeks so I thought I had better let the Doctor see and he says it is catarrh of the eyes and windpipe. I am inhaling and taking lozenges and medicine. You will be sorry to learn Leonora Mims has been taken to a Sanatorium with Diptheria, we heard yesterday, she is better, poor Mrs Mims herself quite an invalid, she has to walk with a stick, I believe you know she has had to have her breast cut off, they keep a servant as she can't do anything, old Mrs Point is 87 I think it is so they too have a lot of trouble, Fred Mims has just got married. . . .

'Poor old Mrs Seemsoe is just the same, she doesn't know anybody but she talks, the nurse put a grape in her mouth but she didn't know what to do with it, I think it is very sad. She was taken about a fortnight before Easter. Will you tell me dear if this is right receipt for clothes ½ oz. carbolic in ½ pint of rose water. Harry Gammon's 2 little children have measles, poor Maisie has gone with her Aunt Susan, poor old Joe Gammon they say had very little to leave, we don't know where

Robert gets his money from. I dare say you saw that
Tom Sagg has married another of Ned Smith's daughters
and we hear these Smith girls are rare housekeepers and
this girl that has married Tom Sagg has made all her
own linen. Mrs Wilkins, the butcher's wife is going to
have a little one after 15 years, our Vicar has been laid
up with an abscess, he told us about his brother the other
day, he says as brothers they love each other very much.
We have 3 very sad cases of men ill in the village. We
had 4 but one man died of cancer.

'Yr loving Sister Amy.'

Voilà !

March 7.

If I die I should like to be buried in the cherry orchards
at V——.

How the beastly mob loves a tragedy ! The sudden
death of the Bank Manager is simply thrilling the town,
and the newspapers sell like hot cakes. Scarcely before
the body is cold the coincidence of his death on the anniversary of his birth is discussed in every household;
every one tells everybody else where they saw him last
—'he looked all right then.' The policeman and the
housemaid, the Mayor and the Town Clerk, the cabman
and the billposter, stand and discuss the deceased gentleman's last words or what the widow's left with. 'Ah !
well, it is very sad,' they remark to one another with no
emotion and continue on their way.

March 10.

On coming downstairs in the evening played Ludo
with H——. At one stage I laughed so much in conjunction with that harlequin H—— that I got cramp
in the abdominal muscles and the tears trickled down
my face.

March 13.

H—— and I play Ludo incessantly. We've developed
the gambling fever, and our pent-up excitement every

now and then explodes in fiendish cackles, and Mother
looks up over her spectacles and says, 'William, William,
they'll hear in the street presently.'

A Character

For this world's unfortunates, his is the ripe sympathy
of a well-developed nature, standing in strong contrast
with the rest of his personality, which is wholly self-
centred, a little ungenerous, and what strong men of
impeccable character call 'weak.' If you are ill he is
delightful, if you are robust or successful he can be very
objectionable. To an influenza victim he goes out of
his way to carry a book, but if you tell him with gusto
you have passed your exam. he says, 'Oh, but there's not
much behind it, is there?' 'Oh! no,' I answer, comforting
him, 'it is really a misfortune to be a success.' And so
only the bankrupts, dipsos (as he calls them), ne'er-do-
weels, and sudden deaths ever touch his heart or tap
his sympathy. He is a short, queery, dressy little fellow,
always spruce and clean. His joy consists in a glass of
beer, a full stomach, a good cigar, or a pretty girl to flirt
with. He frequents drinking saloons and billiard rooms,
goes to dances and likes to be thought a lady's man. 'Um,'
he will say, with the air of a connoisseur, 'a little too
broad in the beam,' as some attractive damsel walks down
the street. Any day about twelve you can see both of
us, 'the long and the short of it' (he is only half my height
and I call him .5), walking together in the Park, and
engaged in the most heated discussion over some entirely trivial matter, such as whether he would marry a
woman with sore eyes, etc., etc. More than once we
have caught cabmen idle on the cab-rank or policemen on point duty jerking their thumbs backward at
us and expressing some facetious remarks which we
longed to overhear. I usually walk in the gutter to bring
my height down a bit.

A good raconteur himself, he does not willingly suffer
a story from another. The varmint on occasion finishes

your joke off for you, which is his delicate way of intimating that he has heard it before. He is a first-class mimic, and sends every one into a thousand fits while he gives you in succession the Mayor and all the Corporation. He also delights me at times by mimicking me. His mind is receptive rather than creative : it picks up all sorts of gaudy ideas by the wayside like a magpie, and I some-times enjoy the exquisite sensation of hearing some of these petty pilferings (which he has filched from me) laid at my feet as if they were his own. The ideas which are his own are always unmistakable.

His favourite poems are Omar and the Ballad of Reading Jail, his favourite drinks Medoc or a Cherry Mixture. Me he describes as *serpentulous* with *Gibbon-like arms*, pinheaded, and so on. He amuses me. In fact I love him.

March 16.

No one will ever understand without personal experi-ence that an exceedingly self-conscious creature like myself driven in on himself to consume himself is the unhappiest of men. I have come to loathe myself : my finicking, hypersensitive, morbid nature, always think-ing, talking, writing about myself for all the world as if the world beyond did not exist ! I am rings within rings, circles concentric and intersecting, a maze, a tangle : watching myself behave or misbehave, always reflecting on what impression I am making on others or what they think of me. Introduce me to a stranger and I swell out as big as Alice. Self-consciousness makes me pneu-matic, and consequently so awkward and clumsy and swollen that I don't know how to converse—and God help the other fellow.

Later : Youth is an intoxication without wine, some one says. Life is an intoxication. The only sober man is the melancholiac, who, disenchanted, looks at life, sees it as it really is, and cuts his throat. If this be so, I want to be very drunk. The great thing is to live, to clutch at our existence and race away with it in some great and

enthralling pursuit. Above all, I must beware of all ultimate questions—they are too maddeningly unanswerable
—let me eschew philosophy and burn Omar.

In this week's *T. P.'s Weekly* a youth advertises :—

'Young thinkers interested in philosophy, religion,
social reform, the future of humanity, and all freethought,
please communicate with " Evolution," aged 21 ! ' All
right for 21.

Later : I have in mind some work on the vascular
system of larval newts. In the autumn I see a large piece of
work to be done in animal psychology—namely, fre-
quency of stimulus and its relation to habit formation.
Yet the doctor advises long rest and the office work
remains to be done. I must hack my way through somehow. I sit trying to disentangle these knots; then some
one plays a dreamy waltz and all my fine edifices of the
will vanish in mist. Is it worth while? Why not float
with the tide? But I soon throw off these temptations.
If I live, I shall play a fine game ! I am determined.
A lame-dog life is of no use.

April 17.

Railway Travel

A journey in a railway train makes me sentimental.
If I enter the compartment a robust-minded, cheerful
youth, fresh and whistling from a walk by the sea, yet,
as soon as I am settled down in one corner and the train
is rattling along past fields, woods, towns, and painted
stations, I find myself indulging in a saccharine sadness
—very toothsome and jolly. I pull a long face and gaze out
of the window wistfully and look sad. But I am really
happy—and incredibly sentimental.

The effect is produced, I suppose, by the quickly changing panoramic view of the country, and as I see everything
sliding swiftly by, and feel myself being hurtled forward
willy-nilly, I am sub-conscious of the flight of Time, of
the eternal flux, of the trajectory of my own life. . . .
Timid folk, of course, want some Rock of Ages, something

static. They want life a mill pond rather than the torrent which it is, a homely affair of teacups and tabby cats rather than a dangerous expedition.

April 22.

Who will rid me of the body of this death? My body is chained to me—a dead weight. It is my warder. I can do nothing without first consulting it and seeking its permission. I jeer at its grotesqueness. I chafe at the thongs it binds on me. On this bully I am dependent for everything the world can give me. How can I preserve my *amour propre* when I must needs be for ever wheedling and cajoling a despot with delicate meats and soft couches? —I who am proud, ambitious, and full of energy! In the end, too, I know it intends to carry me off. . . . I should like though to have the last kick and, copying De Quincey, arrange to hand it over for dissection to the medical men —out of revenge.

'Hope thou not much; fear thou not at all'—my motto of late.

April 30.

I can well imagine looking back on these entries later on and blushing at the pettiness of my soul herein revealed. . . . Only be charitable, kind reader. There are three Johns, and I am much mistaken if in these pages there will not be found something of the John known to himself, and an inkling, perhaps, of the man as he is known to his Creator. As a timid showman afraid that unless he emphasises the features of his exhibit, they will be overlooked, let me, hat in hand, point out that I know I am an ass, that I am still hoping (in spite of ill health) that I am an enthusiast.

May 2.

Maeterlinck's *Wisdom and Destiny* is distilled Marcus Aurelius. I am rather tired of these comfortable philosophers. If a man be harassed by Fate with a red rag and a picador let him turn and rend him—or try to, anyway.

May 8.

Staying by the Sea

.   .   .   .   .   .

I have been living out of doors a lot lately and am getting sunburnt. It gives me infinite pleasure to be sunburnt—to appear the man of the open air, the open road, and the wild life. The sun intoxicates me to-day. The sea is not big enough to hold me nor the sky for me to breathe in. I feel I should like to be swaying with all the passions, throbbing with life and a vast activity of heart and sinew—to live magnificently—with an unquenchable thirst to drink to the lees, to plumb the depth of every joy and every sorrow, to see my life flash in the heat. Ah! Youth! Youth! Youth!!! In these moments of ecstasy my happiness is torrential. I have the soul of the poppy flaming in me then. I am rather like the poppy in many ways. . . . It is peculiarly appropriate. It must be my flower! I am the poppy!!

May 9.

L—— was digging up the ground in his garden to-day and one shovelful came up thick and shapely. He laid the sod on its back gently without breaking it and said simply, 'Doesn't it come up nice?' His face was radiant! —Real happiness lies in the little things, in a bit of garden work, in the rattle of the teacups in the next room, in the last chapter of a book.

May 14.

Returned home. I hate living in this little town. If some one dies, he is sure to be some one you had a joke with the night before. A suicide—ten to one—implicates your bosom friend, or else the little man at the bookshop cut him down. There have been three deaths since I came home—I knew them all. It depresses me. The town seems a mortuary with all these dead bodies lying in it. Lucky for you, if you're a fat, rubicund, unimaginative physician.

May 16.

Two more people dead—one a school friend. Sat on
a seat on the river bank and read the *Journal of Animal
Behaviour*. It made me long to be at work. I foamed at
the mouth to be sitting there perforce in an overcoat on
a seat doing nothing like a pet dove. A weak heart
makes crossing a road an adventure and turns each day
into a dangerous expedition.

May 18.

A dirty ragamuffin on the river's bank held up a tin
can to me with the softly persuasive words,—
   "Ere, Mister, BAIT.'
   'What are you going to do with it?'
   'Fish.'
   'What for?'
   'Salmon.'
We have all tried to catch salmon with a bent pin.
No matter though if no salmon be caught. Richard
Jefferies said, 'If there be no immortality still we shall
have had the glory of that thought.'

May 19.

Old Diaries

Spent some happy time reading over old diaries. I
was grieved and surprised to find how much I had forgotten. To forget the past so easily seems scarcely loyal
to oneself. I am so selfishly absorbed in my present self
that I have grown not to care a damn about that ever
increasing collection of past selves—those dear, dead
gentlemen who one after the other have tenanted the
temple of this flesh and handed on the torch of my life
and personal identity before creeping away silently and
modestly to rest.

June 6.

Brilliantly fine and warm. Unable to resist the sun,
so I caught the ten train to S—— and walked across

the meadow (buttercups, forget-me-nots, ragged robins)
to the Dipper stream and the ivy bridge. Read ardently
in Geology till twelve. Then took off my boots and socks,
and waded underneath the right arch of the bridge in
deep water, and eventually sat on a dry stone at the
top of the masonry just where the water drops into the
green salmon pool in a solid bar. Next I waded upstream
to a big slab of rock tilted at a comfortable angle. I lay
flat on this with my nether extremities in water up to my
knees. The sun bathed my face and dragon flies chased
up and down intent on murder. But I cared not a tinker's
Demetrius about Nature red in tooth and claw. I was
quite satisfied with Nature under a June sun in the cool
atmosphere of a Dipper stream. I lay on the slab completely relaxed, and the cool water ran strongly between
my toes. Surely I was never again going to be miserable.
The voices of children playing in the wood made me
extra happy. As a rule I loathe children. I am too much
of a youth still. But not this morning. For these were
fairy voices ringing through enchanted woods.

June 8.

Brilliantly fine and warm. Went by train to C——
Woods. Took first-class return on account of the heat.
Crossed the meadow and up the hill to the mill leat, where
we bathed our feet and read. Ate a powerful lunch and
made several unsuccessful grabs at Caddie flies. I want
one to examine the mouth parts. After lunch we sat on
the foot-bridge over the stream, and I rested on it flat
in the face of the sun. The sun seemed to burn into my
very bones, purging away everything that may be dark
or threatening there. The physical sensation of the
blood flow beneath the skin was good to feel, and the
heat made every tissue glow with a radiant well-being.
When I got up and opened my eyes all the colours of the
landscape vanished under the silvery whiteness of the
intense sunlight.

We put on our boots and socks (our feet seemed to have
swollen to a very large size) and wandered downstream

to a little white house, a gamekeeper's cottage, where the old woman gave us cream and milk and home-made bread in her beautiful old kitchen with open hearth. China dogs, of course, and on the wall an old painting representing the person of a page boy (so she said) who was once employed up at the squire's. An unwholesome atmosphere of pigs pervaded the garden, but as this is not pretty I ought to leave it out. . . .

June 14.

Brilliantly fine. Went by the early train to S——. Walked to the ivy bridge and then waded upstream to the great slab of rock where I spread myself in the sun as before. The experiment was so delightful it is worth repeating a hundred times. In this position I read of the decline and fall of Trilobites, of the Stratigraphy of the Lias and so on. Geology is a very crushing science, yet I enjoyed my existence this morning with the other flies about that stream.

June 20.

Sat at Liverpool University for the practical exam. Zoology, Board of Education.

At the close the other students left but I went on working. Prof. Herdman asked me if I had finished. I said 'No,' so he gave me a little more time. Later he came up again, and again I said 'No,' but he replied that he was afraid I must stop. 'What could you do further?' he asked, picking up a dish of plankton. I pointed out a *Sagitta*, an *Oikopleura*, and a *Noctiluca*, and he replied, 'Of course I put in more than you were expected to identify in the time, so as to make a choice possible.' Then he complimented me on my written papers which were sent in some weeks ago, and looking at my practical work he added, 'And this, too, seems to be quite excellent.'

I thanked him from the bottom of a greedy and grateful heart, and he went on, 'I see you describe yourself in your papers as a journalist, but can you tell me exactly what has been your career in Zoology?'

I answered of course rather proudly that I had had *no* career in Zoology.

'But what school or college have you worked at?' he persisted.

'None,' I said a little doggedly. 'What I know I have taught myself.'

'So you've had no training in Zoology at all?'

'No, sir.'

'Well, if you've taught yourself all you know, you've done remarkably well.'

He still seemed a little incredulous, and when I explained how I got a great many of my marine animals for dissection and study at the Plymouth Marine Laboratory, he immediately asked me suspiciously if I had ever worked there. We shook hands, and he wished me all success in the future, to which I to myself devoutly said Amen.

Came home very elated at having impressed some one at last.

Now for Dublin.

June 30.

Oeconomic biology may be very useful but I am not interested in it. Give me the pure science. I don't want to be worrying my head over remedies for potato disease nor cures for fleas in fowls. Heaven preserve me from ever becoming a County Council lecturer or a Government Entomologist ! [1] . . . Give me the recluse life of a scholar or investigator, full of leisure, culture, and delicate skill. I would rather know Bergson than be able to stay at the Ritz Hotel. I would rather be able to dissect a starfish's water-vascular system than know the price of Consols. I should make a most industrious country gentleman with £5000 a year and a deer park. . . . My idea is to withdraw from the *mobile vulgus* and spend laborious days in the library or laboratory. The world is too much with us. I long for the monotony of monastic life ! Father Wasmann and the Abbé Spallanzani are

[1] See entry for October 8, 1913.

the type. Let me set my face towards them. Such lives afford poor material for novelists or dramatists, but so much the better. Hamlet makes fine reading, but I don't want to be Hamlet myself.

July 6.

In the afternoon went out dredging in fifteen fathoms off the pier at I——, but without much success.   . . Got a large number of interesting things, however, in the tow net, including some advanced eggs of *Loligo* and a *Tomopteris.* . . .

July 7.

Went to the trout stream again. After stretching a muslin net crosswise on the water for insects floating down, sat on the footbridge and read Geology for the Dublin Examination. Later, waded downstream to a hazel bush on the right bank beneath a shady oak. Squatted right down on the bush, which supported me like an arm-chair—and, with legs dangling in the cool water, opened a Meredith and enjoyed myself.

July 28.

Had to write backing out of the Dublin Examination for which I am nominated to sit. I am simply not fit for the racket of such a journey in my present state of health. My chances of success, too, are not such as to warrant my drawing on Dad for the money. He is still ill, and secretly agitated, I fear, because I am so bent on giving up his work. It looks, however, as if newspaper journalism is to be my fate. It was the refinement of torture having to write.

July 31.

Had a letter from Dr S—— enough to wring tears from a monument.

Sat like a valetudinarian in the Park all day getting fresh air—among the imbeciles, invalids, and children. Who cares? 'But, gentlemen, you *shall* hear.'

August 4.

Still another chance—quite unexpectedly received a second nomination this morning to sit for another exam. for two vacancies in the British Museum. Good luck this.

August 11.

Very hot, so went to S——, and bathed in the salmon pool. Stretched myself out in the water, delighted to find that I had at last got to the very heart of the country-side. I was not just watching from the outside—on the bank. I was in it, and plunging in it, too, up to my armpits. What did I care about the British Museum or Zoology then? All but the last enemy and object of conquest I had overcome — for the moment perhaps even Death himself was under heel—I was immortal—in that minute I was always prostrate in the stream—sunk deep in the bosom of old Mother Earth who cannot die !

August 14.

At 4 p.m. to the Salmon Pool for a bathe. 87.3 in the shade. The meadow was delicious in the sunshine. It made me want to hop, flirt my tail, sing. I felt ever such a bright-eyed wily bird !

August 17.

Caught the afternoon train to C——, but unfortunately forgot to take with me either watch or tubes (for insects). So I applied to the station-master, a youth of about eighteen, who is also signalman, porter, ticket-collector, and indeed very factotal—even to the extent of providing me with empty match boxes. I agreed with him to be called by three halloos from the viaduct just before the evening train came in. Then I went up to the leat, set up my muslin net in it for insects floating down, and then went across to the stream and bathed. Afterwards, went back and boxed the insects caught, and returned to the little station, with its creepers on the walls and over the roof, all as delightfully quiet as ever, and the station youth as delightfully silly. Then the little train came around the bend of the line—green puffing engine and red coaches, like a crawling caterpillar of gay colours.

August 20.

A trapper killed a specimen of *Tropidonotus natrix* and brought it to me. I gave him sixpence for it and am just going to dissect it.

August 21.

There are folk who notice nothing. (Witness Capt. M'Whirr in Conrad's *Typhoon.*) They live side by side with genius or tragedy as innocent as babies; there are heaps of people who live on a mountain, a volcano, even, without knowing it. If the stars of Heaven fell and the Moon were turned into blood some one would have to direct their attention to it. . . . Perhaps after all, the most obvious things are the most difficult to see. We all recognise Keats now, but suppose he was only 'the boy next door'—why should I read his verses?

August 27.

Preparing a Snake's Skull

Prepared the skull of grass snake. I fancy I scooped out the eyes with patent delight—I suppose symbolically, as though, on behalf of the rest of suffering humanity, I were wiping off the old score against the beast for its behaviour in the Garden of Eden.

September 5.

At 2.30 Dad had three separate 'strokes' of paralysis in as many minutes, the third leaving him helpless. They sent for me in the Library, where I was reading, and I hurried home. Just as I entered the bedroom where he and Mother were another attack came on, and it was with the utmost difficulty that with her help I managed to get him from the chair to the bed. He struggled with his left arm and leg and made inarticulate noises which

sounded as if they might be groans. I don't know if
he was in pain. Dear Mother.

September 14.

Dad cannot live long. Mother bears up wonderfully
well. Tried to do some examination work but failed
utterly. A—— is watching in the sick-room with Mother,
who will not leave.

8.30. The nurse says he will not live through the
night.

8.45. Telegraped for A—— to come.

11.0. A—— came downstairs and had a little supper.

12.0. Went to bed. H—— and the others lit a fire
and we have all sat around it silent, listening to its murmur.
Every one felt cold. Dad has been unconscious for over
an hour.

1.45 a.m. Heard a noise, then heard Mother coming
downstairs past my bedroom door with some one—
sobbing. I knew it must be all over. H—— was helping
her down. Waited in my bedroom in the dark for three
parts of an hour, when H—— came up, opened the door
slowly and said, 'He's gone, old man.' It was a tremendous relief to know that since he had to die his sufferings and cruel plight were over. Fell asleep from sheer
exhaustion and slept soundly.

September 18.

The funeral. *It is not death but the dreadful possibilities of
life which are so depressing.*[1]

September 21.

A Day in Autumn

A cool, breezy autumn day. The beach was covered
with patches of soapy foam that shook tremulously in
the wind—all the rocks and everything were drenched
with water, and the spray came off the breaking waves
like steam. A red sun went lower and lower and the

[1] Italics added 1917.

shadows cast by the rocks grew very long and grotesque.
Underneath the breaking waves, the hollows were green
and dark like sea caverns. Herring gulls played about
in the air balancing themselves as they faced the breeze,
then sweeping suddenly around and downwards with the
wind behind them. We all sat down on the rocks and
were very quiet, almost monosyllabic. We pointed out
a passing vessel to one another or chucked a bit of shingle
into the sea. You would have said we were bored. Yet
deep down in ourselves we were astir and all around us
we could hear the rumours of divine passage, soft and
mysterious as the flight of birds migrating in the dark.

The wind rose and tapped the line against the flag-
staff at the Coastguard Station. It roared through my
hair and past my ears for an hour on end till I felt quite
windswept and bleak. On the way home we saw the
wind darting hither and thither over the long grass like
a lunatic snake. The wind! Oh! the wind—I have an
enormous faith in the curative properties of the wind.
I feel better already.

October 17.

Staying in Surrey. Exam. over and I feel fairly con-
fident—after an agony for a few days before on account
of the development of a cold which threatened to snatch
the last chance out of my hands.

Justifiable Mendacity

Sitting on a gate on the N. Downs I saw a long way
below me in the valley a man standing in a chalk pit
and wielding a stick vigorously. For some reason or
another the idea came to me that it would be interesting
if he were in the act of killing a Snake—he so far away
below and I above and unnoticed quietly watching him.
At dinner to-night, this revised version of the story came
out quite pat and natural and obviously interested the
assembly. I added graphically that the man was too far
away for me to be able to say what *species* of Snake it was

he was killing. I possess the qualifications of an artistic liar. Yet I can't regard such a story as a lie—it was rather a justifiable emendation of an otherwise uninteresting incident.

October 24.

Un Caractère

. . . She is a tiny little old lady, very frail and very delicate, with a tiny voice like the noise of a fretsaw. She talks incessantly about things which do not interest you, until your face gets stiff with forcing a polite smile, and your voice cracked and your throat dry with saying, 'Yes,' and 'Really.'

To-night I attend the Zoological Society to read my first paper, so I am really in a fluster and want to be quiet. Therefore to prevent her from talking I write two letters which I represent as urgent. At 6.15 desperate, so went out for a walk in the dark London streets. Returned to supper and to Her. After the wife, the husband is intellectual pyrotechnics. Referring to the Museum,—

'Would you have there, I suppose, any insects, in a case like, what you might say to study to yourself when no one is by?' he inquired.

6.40. It is now one hour before I need leave for the meeting, and whether I sigh, cough, smoke, or read the paper, she goes on. She even refuses to allow me to scan the lines below photos in the *Illustrated London News*. I write this as the last sole resource to escape her devastating prattle and the ceaseless hum of her tiny gnat-like mind. She thinks (because I told her so) that I am preparing notes for the evening meeting.

Later : Spent an absolutely damnable day. Am sick tired, bored, frantic with her voice which I have been able to share with no one except the intellectual giant, her husband, at tea time. In order to break the flow of chatter, I would rudely interrupt and go on talking, by this means keeping my end up for as long as I could, and

enjoying a short respite from the fret-sawing voice. But
I tired of this and it was of no permanent value. When
I broke in, she still went on for a few sentences unable
to stop, and lo! here was the spectacle of two persons
alone together in a room both talking at the same time
and neither listening. I persisted though—and she had
to stop. Once started, I was afraid to stop—scared at
the certain fact of the voice beginning to saw again.
After a while the fountain of my artificial garrulity dried
up, and the Voice at once leaped into the breach, resuming
—amazing and incredible as it seems—at the precise
point where it had left off. At 7 I am quite exhausted
and sit on the opposite side of the hearth, staring with
glassy eyes, arms drooping at my sides and mouth druling.
At 7.5 her cough increases, and she has to stop to attend
to it. With a fiendish smile I push back my chair, and
quietly watch her cough. . . . She coughs continuously
now and can talk no longer. Thank God! 8 p.m., left
for the meeting, where I read my paper in a state of awful
nervousness. . . . I read out all I had to say and kept
them amused for about ten minutes. I was very excited
when Dr —— got up and praised the paper,[1] saying it
was interesting, and hoping I should continue the experiments. The chairman, Sir John Rose Bradford,
asked a question, I answered it and then sat down. After
the meeting we went upstairs to the library, had tea and
chatted with some of the big people. . . . Zoology is
certainly delightful, yet it seems to me the Zoologists are
much as other people. I like Zoology. I wish I could
do without Zoologists. . . .

October 30.

Home once more. The Natural History Museum impressed me enormously. It is a magnificent building—
too magnificent to work there—to follow one's profession
in a building like that seems an altogether too grandiose

[1] The paper was 'Distant Orientation in Batrachia'—detailing
experiments on the homing faculty in newts.

manner of life.   A pious zoologist might go up to pray
in it—but not to earn his daily bread there.

October 31.

I'm in, in, in ! ! ! ! ! ! ! ! ! being first with 141 marks
to spare. Old M——— [the servant] rushes up to my sister's
bedroom with the news just after 7 a.m., and she says,
'Fine, fine,' and comes down in her nightgown to my
bedroom, where we drink our morning cup of tea together
—and talk ! I'm delighted. What a magnificent obstacle
race it has been ! Still one ditch—the medical exam !
Wired to friends.

November 1.

This is the sort of letter which is balm to me :—

'My darling W———,—I need hardly tell you how
absolutely delighted we were at the grand news of this
morning. You must be feeling a huge glow of satisfaction
with the knowledge of your object attained through
untold difficulties. I don't wish to butter you up, or to
gush, but I must honestly say that I feel tip-top proud
of my old Beano. I admire your brains more than ever,
and also your indomitable pluck and grit, and your quiet
bravery in disappointment and difficulty. . . .'

November 14.

The three most fascinating books in Science that I
have so far read are (easily) :—1. Darwin's `*Expression
of the Emotions*. 2. Gaskell's *Origin of Vertebrates*. 3.
Bergson's *Le Rire*.

Went to the dentist in the afternoon. Evening chiefly
occupied in reading *Le Rire*. By my halidom, it is an
extraordinarily interesting book !

November 29.

. . . I am always looking out for new friends—assaying
for friendship. . . . There no more delightful adventure than an expedition into a rich, many-sided personality.
Gradually over a long probation—for deep minds are

naturally reticent—piece after piece is added to the geography of your friend's mind, and each piece pleases or entertains, while in return you let him steal away piece after piece of your own territory, perhaps saving a bit up here and there—such as an enthusiasm for Francis Thompson's poetry—and then letting it go unexpectedly. It's a delightful reciprocity.

I dream of 'the honeyed ease of the Civil Servant's working day' (Peacock). Yet the French say *Songes sont mensonges*.

December 13.

In the Park it was very dark and she said,—
'If I lose you I shan't be able to find my way home.'
'Oh! I'll look after you,' I said.
Both being of the same mind at the same time we sat down on a seat together when a fortunate thing happened. It began to rain. So I offered her part of my overcoat. She nestled in under my arm and I kissed her out of hand. *Voilà!* A very pretty little girl, 'pon my word.

December 20.

The thing is obsessing me. After an early supper called and found my lady ready to receive me. No one else at home. So walked into the oak-panelled room with the red-curtained windows, took off my coat and scarf. She followed and switched off the light. There was a roaring fire in the grate. She is very amorous and I am not Hippolytus, so we were soon closely engaged in the large chair before the fire. As we sailed thus, close hauled to the wind, with double entendres and she trembled in the storm (and I was at the helm) the garden gate slammed and both of us got up quickly. I next heard a key turn in the lock and a foot in the passage:
'Mr —— ' she said. . . .
She switched on the light, went out swiftly into the passage, and meeting him conducted him to her office, while I as swiftly put on overcoat and scarf, and slipped out through the open door, stumbling over his bicycle,

but of course not stopping to pick it up. Later she telephoned to say it was all right. Very relieved ! . . . She recalls Richepin's *La Glu*.

December 21.

She is a fine sedative. Her movements are a pleasant adagio, her voice piano to pianissimo, her conversation breaks off in thrilling aposiopeses.

An awful comedy this morning—for as soon as I was securely 'gagged' the dentist went out of the room. She approached, leered at me helpless, and said provokingly, 'Oh ! you do look funny.' Minx. On returning he said to her, 'Would you like to hold his hand?'

She : 'Oh ! not just now.'

And they grinned at one another and at me waiting to be tortured.

December 23.

. . . On the Station waited for an hour for the train. Gave her a box of sweets and the *Bystander*. We walked up the platform to extreme end in the dark and kissed ! But it was very windy and cold. (I noticed that !) So we entered an empty luggage guard's van on rail beside platform left there by shunters. Here we were out of the wind and far better off. But a shunter came along and turned us out. She gave me a silver match-box. But I believe for various reasons that it is one of her own and not a new one. Said 'Good-bye.'

December 28.

At R——. Played the negligent *flâneur*, reclining on the Chesterfield, leaning against the grand piano, or measuring my length on the mat before the fire.

December 31.

To-morrow I begin duties at the British Museum of Natural History. I cannot quite imagine myself a Museum assistant. Before I get there I know I shall be the strangest assistant on the staff. It will be singing my song in a strange land and weeping—I hope not too bitterly—down by the waters of a very queer Babylon.

Still, I have burnt my bridges like Cæsar—or burnt my ships like Cortez. So forward!

PART II—IN LONDON

1912

January 21.

Am at last beginning to get more content with the work at the Museum, so that I muse on Bernard Shaw's saying, 'Get what you like or you'll grow to like what you get.' I have a terrible suspicion that the security of tenure here is like the lion's den in the fable—*Nulla vestigia retrorsum.* Of course I am wonderfully proud of being at the Museum, although I am disappointed and write as if I were quite blasé.

January 25.

I should be disappointed if at the end of my career (if I live to see it through) I do not win the F.R.S. I should very much like it. . . . My nature is very mixed —ambitious above all things and yet soon giddy with the audacity of my aspirations. The B. M. and my colleagues make me feel most inferior in fact, but in theory—in the secrecy of my own bedchamber—I feel that there are few men there my equal.

April 26.

Down with influenza. A boarding-house with the 'flu !

May 8.

'Went home to recuperate, a beef jelly in one pocket and sal volatile in the other. On arrival, my blanched appearance frightened Mother and the others, so went to bed at once. 'Fate's a fiddler, life's a dance.'

May 12.

Weak enough to sit down before dressing-table while I shave and brush my hair. Dyspepsia appalling. The

Doctor in Kensington seemed to think me an awful wreck
and asked if I were concealing———.

Reading Baudelaire and Verlaine.

May 24.

Bathing

Sat on a seat overlooking the sand-hills with stick
between my legs like an old man, and watched a buxom
wench aet. 25 run down the path pursued by 'Rough'
and two little girls in blue. Later they emerged from a
striped bathing tent in the glory of blue bathing dresses.
It made me feel quite an old man to see the girl galloping
out over the hard level sands to the breakers, a child
clinging to each hand. Legs and arms twinkled in the
sun which shone with brilliance. If life were as level as
those sands and as beautiful as that trio of girls !

May 26.

Two Young Men Talking

With H—— in his garden. He is a great enthusiast.
'I disapprove entirely of your taste in gardening,' I
said. 'You object to the " ragged wilderness " style, I
like it. You like lawns laid out for croquet and your
privet hedges pruned into " God Save the King " or
" Dieu et mon droit." My dear boy, if you saw Mr
——'s wilderness at —— you'd be so shocked you'd cut
and run, and I imagine there'd be an affecting reunion
between you and your beloved geraniums. For my part,
I don't like geraniums : they're suburban, and all of a
piece with antimacassars and stuffed birds under glass
bells. The colour of your specimens, moreover,' I rapped
out, ' is vulgar — like the muddied petticoats of old
market women.'

H——, quite unmoved, replied slowly, 'Well, here are
some like the beautiful white cambric of a lady of fashion.
You've got no taste in flowers—you're just six feet of
grief and patience.' We roared with laughing.

'Do stop watering those damned plants,' I exclaimed

at last. But he went on. I exclaimed again and out of
sheer ridiculousness, in reply he proceeded to water the
cabbages, the gravel path, the oak tree—and me! While
I writhed with laughing.

May 27.

By the Sea

Sat upon a comfortable jetty of rock and watched the
waves without a glimmer of an idea in my mind about
anything—though to outward view I might have been
a philosopher in cerebral parturition with thoughts as
big as babies. Instead, little rustling dead leaves of
thoughts stirred and fluttered in the brain—the pimple
e.g. I recollected on my Aunt's nose, or the boyishness
of Dr ——'s handwriting, or Swinburne's lines : 'If the
golden-crested wren Were a nightingale — why, then
Something seen and heard of men Might be half as sweet
as when Laughs a child of seven.'
I continued in this pleasurable coma all the afternoon
and went home refreshed.

May 29.
Have returned to London and the B. M. My first
day at the M. Sat at my table in a state of awful apathy.
At least temporarily, I am quite disenchanted of Zoology.
I work—God save the mark—in the Insect Room !
On the way home, purchased :—
Peroxide of hydrogen (pyorrhœa threatened).   One
bottle of physic (for my appalling dyspepsia).
One flask of brandy for emergencies (as my heart is
intermittent again).
Prussic acid next.
Must have been near pneumonia at R——.   Auntie
was nervous, and came in during the night to see how I
was.

June 20.
It caused me anguish to see my article returned from
the *Fortnightly* and lying in a big envelope on the table

when I returned home this evening. I can't do any work because of it, and in desperation rushed off to the stately pleasure domes of the White City, and systematically went through all the thrills—from the Mountain Railway to the Wiggle Woggle and the 'Witching Waves.

June 21.

To-day I am easier. The cut worm forgives the plough. But how restless this disappointment has made me. . . . I have no plans for recuperation and cannot settle down to work.

July 6.

On my doctor's advice, went to see Dr P——, a lung specialist. M—— found a dull spot on one of my lungs, and, not feeling very sure, and without telling me the nature of his suspicion, he arranged for Dr P—— to see me, allowing me to suppose he was a stomach authority as my dyspepsia is bad.

Well : it is *not* consumption, but my lungs and physique are such that consumption might easily supervene. As soon as Dr P—— had gone, M—— appended the following lugubrious yarn :—

Whenever I catch cold, I must go and be treated at once, all my leisure must be spent out of doors, I must take cream and milk in prodigious quantities and get fat at all costs. There is even a question of my giving up work.

July 10.

A young but fat woman sitting in the sun and oozing moisture is as nasty as anything in Baudelaire.

July 14.

A 'Brilliant Career'

My old head master once prophesied for me 'a brilliant career.' That was when I was in the Third Form. Now I have more than a suspicion that I am one of those who, as he once pointed out, grow sometimes out of a brilliant boyhood into very commonplace men. This continuous ill health is having a very obvious effect on my work and activities. With what courage I possess I have to face the fact that to-day I am unable to think or express myself as well as when I was a boy in my teens—witness this Journal!

I intend to go on however. I have decided that my death shall be disputed all the way.

Oh! it is so humiliating to die! I writhe to think of being overcome by so unfair an enemy before I have demonstrated myself to maiden aunts who mistrust me, to colleagues who scorn me, and even to brothers and sisters who believe in me.

As an Egotist I hate death because I should cease to be I.

Most folk, when sick unto death, gain a little consolation over the notoriety gained by the fact of their decease. Criminals enjoy the pomp and circumstance of their execution. Voltaire said of Rousseau that he wouldn't mind being hanged if they'd stick his name on the gibbet. But my own death would be so mean and insignificant. Guy de Maupassant died in a grand manner—a man of intellect and splendid physique who became insane. Tusitala's death in the South Seas reads like a romance. Heine, after a life of sorrow, died with a sparkling witticism on his lips; Vespasian with a jest.

But I cannot for the life of me rake up any excitement over my own immediate decease—an unobtrusive passing away of a rancorous, disappointed, morbid, and self-assertive entomologist in a West Kensington Boarding House—what a mean little tragedy! It is hard not to be somebody even in death.

A sing-song to-night in the drawing-room; all the boarding-house present in full muster. There was a German, Schulz, who sat and leered at his inamorata— a sensual-looking, pasty-faced girl—while she gave us daggers-and-moonlight recitations with the most unwarranted self-assurance (she boasts of a walking-on part at one of the theatres); there was Miss M—— listening to her fiancé, Capt. O—— (home from India), singing Indian Love Songs at her; there was Miss T——, a sour old maid, who knitted and snorted, not fully conscious of this young blood coursing around her; Mrs Barclay Woods pursued her usual avocation of imposing on us all the great weight of her immense social superiority, clucking, in between, to her one chick—a fluffy girl of 18 or 19, who was sitting now in the draught, now too close to a 'common' musician of the Covent Garden Opera; finally our hostess, a divorcée, who hates all males, even Tom-cats. We were a pathetic little company—so motley, ill-assorted—who had come together not from love or regard but because man is a gregarious animal. In fact, we sat secretly criticising and contemning one another . . . yet outside there were so many millions of people unknown, and overhead the multitude of the stars was equally comfortless.

Later : . . . Zoology on occasion still fires my ambition ! Surely I cannot be dying yet.

Whatever misfortune befalls me I do hope I shall be able to meet it unflinchingly. I do not fear ill-health in itself, but I do fear its possible effect on my mind and character. . . . Already I am slowly altering, as the Lord liveth. Already for example my sympathy with myself is maudlin.

Whenever the blow shall fall, some sort of a reaction *must* be given. Heine flamed into song. Beethoven wrote the 5th Symphony. So what shall I do when my time comes ? I don't think I have any lyrics or symphonies to write, so I shall just have to grin and bear it— like a dumb animal. . . . As long as I have spirit and buoyancy I don't care what happens—for I know that for so long I cannot be accounted a failure. The only *real* failure is one in which the victim is left spiritless, dazed, dejected with blackness all around, and within, a knife slowly and unrelentingly cutting the strings of his heart.

My head whirls with conflicting emotions, struggling, desperate ideas, and a flood of impressions of all sorts of things that are never sufficiently sifted and arranged to be caught down on paper. I am brought into this world, hustled along it and then hustled out of it, with no time for anything. I want to be on a great hill and square up affairs.

August 28.

. . . After tea, we all three walked in Kensington Gardens and sat on a seat by the Round Pond. My umbrella fell to the ground, and I left it there with its nose poking up in a cynical manner, as She remarked.

' It's not cynical,' I said, ' only a little knowing. Won't you let yours fall down to keep it company ? Yours is a lady umbrella and a good-looking one—they might flirt together.'

' Mine doesn't want to flirt,' she answered stiffly.

September 13.

At C——, a tiny little village by the sea in N——.

Looking up from a rockpool, where I had been watching Gobies, I saw three children racing across the sands to bathe, I saw a man dive from a boat, and I saw a horseman gallop his mare down to the beach and plunge about in the line of breakers. The waters thundered, the mare whinnied, the children shouted to one another, and I turned my head down again to the rockpool with a great thumping heart of happiness: it was so lovely to be conscious of the fact that out there this beautiful picture was awaiting me whenever and as often as I chose to lift my head. I purposely kept my head down, for the picture was so beautiful I did not want to hurt it by breathing on it, and I kept my head down out of a playful self-cheating delight; I decided not to indulge myself.

September 16.

Out in the Bay dredging for Echinoderms with ' Carrots.'
Brilliantly fine. The haul was a failure, but, being out
in a boat on a waveless sea under a cloudless sky, I was
scarcely depressed at this ! We cruised along from one
little bay to another, past smugglers' caves and white
pebble beaches, the dredge all the while growling along the
sea bottom, and ' Carrots' and I lying listless in the bows.
I was *immensely happy*. My mercury was positively
ringing the bell.

Who, then, is ' Carrots ' ? He is a fine brawny boat-
man who jumps over the rocks like a Chamois, swims like
a Fish, pulls like an Ox, snorts like a Grampus—a sort
of compound zoological perfection, built eclectically.

September 18.

Early Boughies

Up the village, Mrs Beavan keeps a tiny little shop and
runs a very large garden. She showed us all about the
garden, and introduced us to her husband, whom we
discovered in an apple tree—an old man, aged 76, very
hard of hearing, and with an impediment in his speech.
He at once began to move his mouth, and I caught odd
jingles of sound that sounded like nothing at all—at first,
but which gradually resolved themselves on close attention to such familiar landmarks as ' Early Boughies,'
' Stubbits,' ' Ribstone Pippins ' into a discourse on Apples.

The following curious conversation took place between
me and the deaf gaffer, aged 76, standing in the apple
tree,—

' These be all appulls from Kent—I got 'em all from
Kent.'

' How long have you lived in C—— ?'

' Bunyard & Son—that's the firm—they live just outside
the town of Maidstone.'

' Do you keep Bees here ?'

' One of these yer appulls is called Bunyard after the
firm—a fine fruit too.'

' Your good wife must be of great assistance to you in
your work.'

' Little stalks maybe, but a large juishy appull for all
that.'

Just then I heard Mrs B—— saying to E——,—

' Aw yes, he's very active for 76. A little deaf, but he
manages the garden all 'eesulf, I bolsters 'un up wi' meat
and drink—little and often as they zay for children. . . .
Now there's a bootifull tree, me dear, that 'as almost
beared itself to death, as you may say.'

She picked an apple off it shouting to poor Tom still
aloft,—

' Tom what's the name of this one ?'

' You should come a bit earlier, zir,' replied T.   ' 'Tis
late a bit now doan't 'ee zee ?'

' No—what's its name I want,' shouted his spouse.

' Yes, yes, give the lady one to take home--there's
plenty for all,' he said.

' What is the NAME ?   THE NAME OF THIS YER
APPULL,' screamed Mrs B., and old Tom moving his
bones slowly down from the tree answered quite unmoved,—

' Aw the name ?   Why, 'tis a common kind of appull—
there's a nice tree of 'em up there.'

' Oh ! never mind, 'tis a Gladstone,' said Mrs B., turning
to us.

' A very fine Appull,' droned the old boy.

September 28.

Back in town again.   Wandered about in a somnambu-
listic way all the afternoon till I found myself taking tea
in Kew Gardens.   I enjoyed the wind in my face and hair.
Otherwise there is nothing to be said—a colourless day.

October 10.

Came across the following arresting sentence: ' Pale,
anæmic, cadaverous, bad teeth and disordered digestion
and a morbid egotism.'   Yes, but my teeth are *not* bad.

October 20.

On the N. Downs

Under the oak where I sat the ground was covered with
dead leaves. I kicked them, and I beat them with my
stick, because I was angry that they were dead. In the
coppice, leaves were quietly and majestically floating
earthwards in the pomp of death. It was very thrilling
to observe them.

It was a curious sensation to realise that since the last
time I sat under the old oak I had been right up to the
N. of England, then right down to the S.W., and back
once more to London town. I bragged about my kinetic
activity to the stationary oak and I scoffed at the old hill
for having to remain always in the same place.

It gave me a pleasing sense of infinite superiority to
come back and see everything the same as before, to sit
on the same old seat under the same old oak. Even that
same old hurdle was lying in the same position among the
bracken. How sorry I was for it! Poor wretch—unable
to move—to go to Whitby, to go to C——, to be totally
ignorant of the great country of London. . . .

Day dreamed. My own life as it unrolls day by day
is a source of constant amazement, delight, and pain.
I can think of no more interesting volume than a detailed,
intimate, psychological history of my own life. I want
a perfect comprehension at least of myself. . . .

We are all such egotists that a sorrow or hardship—
provided it is great enough—flatters our self-importance.
We feel that a calamity by overtaking us has distinguished
us above our fellows. A man likes not to be ignored even
by a railway accident. A man with a grievance is always
happy.

October 23.

Over to see E——. Came away disillusioned.

October 25.

Met her in Smith's book shop looking quite bewitching.
Hang it all, I thought I had finished. Went home with

her, watched her make a pudding in the kitchen, then we
sat by the firelight in the drawing-room and had supper.
Scrumptious (not the supper).

October 27.

Quarrelled with D——! The atmosphere is changed at
the flat—my character is ruined. D—— has told them
I'm a loose fellow. I've always contrived to give him
that impression—I liked to be cutting my throat—and
now it's cut!

November 1.

D—— came and carried me off to the flat, where they
asked why I hadn't been over—which, of course, pleased
me immensely.

November 6.

Doctor M—— is very gloomy about my health and talks
of S. Africa, Labrador, and so on. I'm not responding to
his treatment as I should.

November 11.

Met her this evening in Kensington Road. 'I timed
this well,' said she, ' I thought I should meet you.' Good
Heavens, I am getting embroiled. Returned to the flat
with her and after supper called her ' The Lady of Shalott.'
   ' I don't think you know what you're talking about '—
this stiffly.
   ' Perhaps not,' I answered. ' I leave it to you.'
   ' Oh! but it rests with you,' she said.
   Am I in love? God knows—but I don't suppose God
cares.

November 15.

On M——'s advice went to see a stomach specialist—
Dr Hawkins. As I got there a little too early walked up
the street—Portland Place—on the opposite side (from
shyness) past an interminable and nauseating series of
night bells and brass plates, then down again on the right

side till I got to No. 66 which made me flutter—for ten
doors ahead I mused is the house I must call at. It made
me shiver a little.

The specialist took copious notes of my evidence and
after examining me retired to consult with M——. What
a parade of ceremony ! On coming back, the jury returned
a verdict of ' Not proven.' I was told I ought to go out
and live on the prairies—and in two years I should be
a *giant!* But where are the prairies ? What 'bus ? If
I get worse, I must take several months' leave. I think
it will come to this.

November 16.

Arthur came down for the week end. He likes the
Lady of Shalott. She is ' not handsome, but arresting,
striking ' and ' capable of tragedy.' That I believe she
has achieved already. . . . If she were a bit more gloomy
and a bit more beautiful, she'd be irresistible.

November 22.

He: ' Have a cigarette ? I enjoy lighting your
cigarettes.'

She: ' I don't know how to smoke properly.'

He: ' You smoke only as *you* could.'

She: ' How's that ?'

H.: ' Gracefully, of course.'

S.: ' Do you think I like pretty things being said to
me ?'

H.: ' Why not, if they are true. Flattery is when you
tell an ugly woman she is beautiful. Have you so poor
an opinion of yourself to think all I say of you is flattery ?'

S.: ' Yes. I am only four bare walls,—with nothing
inside.'

H.: ' What a deliciously empty feeling that must be.
. . . But I don't think you're so simple as all that. You
bewilder me sometimes.'

S.: ' Why ?'

H.: ' I feel like Sindbad the Sailor.'

S.: ' Why ?'
H.: ' Because I'm not George Meredith.'
The title of ' husband ' frightens me.

December 9.

It's a fearful strain to go on endeavouring to live up
to time with a carefully laid-out time-table of future
achievements.   I am hurrying on with my study of Italian
in order to read the Life of Spallanzani in order to include
him in my book—to be finished by the end of next year;
I am also subsidising Jenkinson's embryological lectures
at University College with the more detailed account of
practical and experimental work in his text-book; I have
also started a lengthy research upon the Trichoptera—all
with a horrible sense of time fleeing swiftly and opportunities for work too few ever to be squandered, and, in
the background, behind all this feverish activity, the black
shadow that I might die suddenly with nothing done—
next year, next month, next week, to-morrow, now !

Then sometimes, as to-night, I have misgivings. Shall
I do these things so well now as I might once have done
them? Has not my ill-health seriously affected my
mental powers ? Surely the boy of 1908-10 was almost
a genius or—seen at this distance—a very remarkable
youth in the fanatical zeal with which he sought to
pursue, and succeeded in gaining, his own end of a
zoological education for himself.

It is a terrible suspicion to cross the mind of an ambitious youth that perhaps, after all, he is a very commonplace mortal—that his life, whether comedy or tragedy,
or both, or neither, is any way insignificant, of no account.

It is still more devastating for him to have to consider
whether the laurel wreath was not once within his grasp,
and. whether he must not ascribe his own incalculable loss
to his stomach simply.

December 15.

A very bad heart attack. As I write it intermits every
three or four beats. Who knows if I shall live thro'
to-night ?

December 16.

Here I am once more. A passable night. After break-fast the intermittency recommenced—it is better now, with a dropped beat only about once per half-hour, so that I am almost happy after yesterday, which was Hell. The world is too good to give up without remonstrance at the beck of a weak heart.

Before I went to sleep last night, my watch stopped—I at once observed the cessation of its tick and wondered if it were an omen. I was genuinely surprised to find myself still ticking when I awoke this morning. A moment ago a hearse passed down the street. . . . Yes, but I'm damned if I haven't a right to be morbid after yesterday. To be ill like this in a boarding house! I'd marry to-morrow if I had the chance.

December 22.

Sollas's ' Ancient Hunters '

Read Sollas's book *Ancient Hunters*—very thrilling—mind full of the Aurignacians, Mousterians, Magdalenians! I have been peering down such tremendous vistas of time and change that my own troubles have been eclipsed into ridiculous insignificance. It has been really a Pillar of Strength to me—a splendid tonic. Palæontology has its comfortable words too. I have revelled in my littleness and irresponsibility. It has relieved me of the harassing desire to live, I feel content to live dangerously, indifferent to my fate; I have discovered I am a fly, that we are all flies, that nothing matters. It's a great load off my life, for I don't mind being such a micro-organism—to me the honour is sufficient of belonging to the universe—such a great universe, so grand a scheme of things. Not even Death can rob me of that honour. For nothing can alter the fact that I *have* lived; *I have been I*, if for ever so short a time. And when I am dead, the matter which composes my body is indestructible—and eternal, so that come what may to my ' Soul,' my dust will always be going on, each separate atom of me playing its separate part—I shall

still have some sort of a finger in the Pie.   When I am
dead, you can boil me, burn me, drown me, scatter me—
but you cannot destroy me: my little atoms would merely
deride such heavy vengeance.   Death can do no more than
kill you.

December 27.

'It is a pleasure to note the success attending the career
of Mr W. N. P. Barbellion now engaged in scientific work
on the staff of the Natural History Museum . . .' etc.,
etc.

This is a cutting from the local paper—one of many
that from time to time I once delightedly pasted in the
pages of the Journal.   Not so now.

. . . .

. . . At 23, I am a different being.   Surrounded by all
the stimulating environment of scientific research, I am
cold and disdainful.   I keep up the old appearances but
underneath it is quite different.   I am a *hypocrite*.   I
have to wear the mask and cothornoi, finding the part
daily more difficult to bear.   I am living on my immense
initial momentum—while the machinery gradually slows
up.   My career !   Gadzooks.

1913

January 3.

From the drawing-room window I see pass almost daily
an old gentleman with white hair, a firm step, broad
shoulders, healthy pink skin, a sunny smile—always
singing to himself as he goes—a happy, rosy-cheeked old
fellow, with a rosy-cheeked mind. . . .   I should like to
throw mud at him.   By Jove, how I hate him.   He makes
me wince with my own pain.   It is heartless, indecently
so, for an *old* man to be so blithe.   Life has, I suppose,
never lain in wait for him.   The Great Anarchist has
spared him a bomb.

January 19.

My Aunt, aged 75, who has apparently concluded from my constant absences from Church that my spiritual life is in a parlous way, to-day read me her portion from a large book with a broad purple-tasseled bookmark. I looked up from ' *I Promessi Sposi* ' and said ' Very nice.' It was about someone whose soul was not saved and who would not answer the door when it was knocked. It is jolly to be regarded as a wicked, libidinous youth by an aged maiden Aunt.

January 22.

This Diary reads for all the world as if I were not living in mighty London. The truth is I live in a bigger, dirtier city—ill-health. Ill-health, when chronic, is like a permanent ligature around one's life. What a fine fellow I'd be if I were perfectly well. My energy for one thing would lift the roof off. . . .

We conversed around the text: ' To travel hopefully is better than to arrive and true success is to labour.' She is—well, so graceful. My God ! I love her, I love her, I love her ! ! !

February 3.

A Confession

H—— B—— invited me to tea to meet his fiancée. Rather pleased with the invitation—I don't know why, for my idea of myself is greater than my idea of him and probably greater than his idea of himself.

Yet I went and got shaved, and even thought of buying a new pair of gloves, but poverty proved greater than vanity, so I went with naked hands. On arriving at Turnham Green, I removed my spectacles (well knowing how much they damage my personal appearance). However, the beauty of the thing was that, tho' I waited as agreed, he never turned up, and so I returned home again, crestfallen—and, with my spectacles on again.

February 9.

. . . ' Now, W——, talk to me prettily,' she said as soon
as the door was closed on them.

' Oh! make him read a book ' whined her sister, but
we talked of marriage instead—-in all its aspects. Bless
their hearts, I found these two dear young things simply
sodden with the idea of it.

In the middle I did a knee-jerk which made them scream
with laughing—the patellar reflex was new to them, so I
seized a brush from the grate, crossed to Her and gently
tapped: out shot her foot, and —— cried: ' Oh, do do it
to me as well.'   It was rare fun.

> ' Oh! pretty knee, what do I see ?
> And he stooped and he tied up my garter for me.'

February 10.

News of Scott's great adventure! Scott dead a year
ago !! The news, when I saw it to-night in the *Pall Mall
Gazette*, gave me cold thrills. I could have wept. . . .
What splendid people we humans are! If there be no
loving God to watch us, it's a pity for His sake as much
as for our own.

February 15.

Tried to kiss her in a taxi-cab on the way home from
the Savoy—the taxi-cab danger is very present with us—
but she rejected me quietly, sombrely. I apologised on
the steps of the Flats and said I feared I had greatly
annoyed her. ' I'm not annoyed,' she said, ' only surprised '—in a thoughtful, chilly voice.

We had had supper in Soho, and I took some wine, and
she looked so bewitching it sent me in a fever, thrumming
my fingers on the seat of the cab while she sat beside me
impassive. Her shoulders are exquisitely modelled and a
beautiful head is carried poised on a tiny neck.

February 16.

Walking up the steps to her flat to-night made me pose
to H—— (who was with me) as Sydney Carton in the

picture in *A Tale of Two Cities* on the steps of the scaffold. He laughed boisterously, as he is delighted to know of my last evening's misadventure.

At supper, a story was told of a man who knocked at the door of his lady's heart four times and at last was admitted. I remarked that the last part of the romance was weak. She disagreed. H—— exclaimed, ' Oh ! but this man has no sentiment at all !'

' So much the worse for him,' chimed in the others.

' He was 66 years of age,' added Mrs ——.

' Too old,' said P. ' What do you think the best age for a man to marry ?'

H.: ' Thirty for a man, twenty-five for a woman.'

She: ' That's right: it still gives me a little time.'

P.: ' What do *you* think ?' (to me).

I replied sardonically,—

'A young man not yet and an old man not at all.

' That's right, old wet blanket,' chirruped P——.

' You know,' I continued, delighted to seize the opportunity to assume the rôle of youthful cynic, 'Cupid and Death once met at an Inn and exchanged arrows, since when young men have died and old men have doted.'

H—— was charming enough to opine that it was impossible to fix a time for love. Love simply came.

We warned him to be careful on the boat going out.

' Yes, I know,' said H—— (who is in love with P——). ' My brother had a dose of moonlight on board a boat when he sailed and he's been happy ever since.'

P.: ' How romantic !'

H.: ' A great passion !'

' The only difference,' I interjected in a sombre monotone, ' between a passion and a caprice is that the caprice lasts a little longer.'

' Sounds like a book,' She said in contempt.

It was—Oscar Wilde !

P—— insisted on my taking a biscuit. ' Don't mind me,' she said. ' Just think I'm a waitress and take no notice at all.'

H.: ' Humph !   I never see him taking no notice of a waitress.'

> (Sneers and Curtain.)

February 24.

H—— came home last night and told me that she said as he came away, ' Tell W—— I hate him.'   So it's all right.   I shall go over to-morrow again—Hurrah !   My absence has been felt then.

March 7.

Came home, lay on my bed, still dressed, and ruminated. . . .

First a suspicion then a conviction came to me that I was a cad—a callous, selfish, sensation-hunting cad. . . For the time being the bottom was knocked out of my smug self-satisfaction.   For several long half-hours I found myself drifting without compass or stars.   I was quite disorientated, temporarily thrown off the balance of my *amour propre*.   Then I got up, lit the gas and looking at myself in the mirror, found it was really true,—I was a mean creature, wholly absorbed in self.

As an act of contrition, I ought to have gone out into the garden and eaten worms.   But the mirror brought back my self-consciousness and I began to crawl back into my recently discarded skin—I began to be less loathesome to myself.   For as soon as I felt interested or amused or curious over the fact that I had been really loathesome to myself I began to regain my equilibrium.   *Now*, I and myself are on comparatively easy terms with one another. I am settled on the old swivel. . . .   I take a lot of knocking off it and if shot off soon return.

To-day, she was silent and melancholy but wonderfully fascinating.   One day I am desperate and the next cold and apathetic.   Am I in love ?   God knows !   She came to the door to say ' Good-night,' and I deliberately strangled my desire to say something.

March 9.

In bed till 12.30 reading Bergson and the O.T.

Over to the flat to supper. E—— was cold and silent. She spurned me. No wonder. I talked volubly and quite brilliantly with the definite purpose of showing up J——'s somnolence. I also pulled his leg. He hates me. No wonder. After supper, he went in to her studio and remained there alone with her while she worked. At 11 p.m. he was still there when I came away in a whirlwind of jealousy, regrets, and rage. G—— said he was going to stay on until he saw 'the blighter off the premises.' Neither of us would go in to turn him out.

I love her deeply and once my heart jumped when I thought I heard her coming into the room. But it was only P——. Did not see her again—even to say 'Goodnight.'

March 10

Work in the evening in our bedroom—two poor miserable bachelors—H—— reading Equity Law, a rug around his legs before an empty grate, while I am sitting at the table in top-coat, with collar up, and writing my *magnum opus*, which is to bring me fame, fortune and—E—— !

H—— says that this morning I was putting on my shoes when he pointed out a large hole in the heel of my sock.

'Damn! I shall have to wear boots,' I said—at least he says I said it, and I am quite ready to believe him. Such unconsciousness of self is rare with me.

March 15.

[At a public dinner at the Holborn Restaurant] J—— replied to the toast of the Ladies. Feeble! H—— and I stood and had a silent toast to E—— and N—— by just winking one eye at each other. He sat opposite me.

If I had been asked to reply to this toast I should have said with the greatest gusto, something as follows,—

[Here follows the imaginary speech in full, composed the same night before going to sleep]

Yet I am taken for a soft fool! My manner is soft, self-conscious, shy. What a lot of self-glorification I lose thereby! What a lot of self-torture I gain in its stead!

March 17.

To-day went to the B. M. but did very little work. Thought over the matter carefully and decided to ask E—— to marry me. Relief to be able to decide. I was happy too.

Yesterday P—— came in to us from E——'s studio and said,—

'E—— sends her love.'

'To whom?' H—— inquired.

'I don't know,' P—— replied, smiling at me.

March 18.

Had a long conversation with H—— last night. He says all E—— intended to convey was that the quarrel was over. . . . I felt relieved, because I have no money, but—a large ambition. Then I am selfish, and have not forgotten that I want to spend my holidays in the Jura, and next year three weeks at the Plymouth Laboratory.

March 19.

Went over to see E——. We had an awkward half-an-hour alone together. She was looking bewitching! I am plunging more and more into love. Had it on the tip of my tongue once. I am dreadfully fond of her.

'I have a most profound gloom over me,' I said.

'Why don't you try and get rid of it?' she asked.

'I can't until Zeus has pity and rolls away the clouds.'

April 21.

We are sitting up in our beds which are side by side in a room on the top story of a boarding house in —— Road. It is 11.30 p.m. and I am leaning over on one side lighting the oil lamp so as to boil the kettle to make Ovaltine before going to sleep.

'Whom have I seduced?' I screamed. 'You rotter, don't you know that a dead passion full of regrets is as terrible as a dead body full of worms? There, I talk literature, my boy, if you were only Boswell enough to take it down. . . . As for T—— I shall never invite him to dinner again. He comes to me and whines that nobody loves him, and so I say, "Oh! poor lad, never mind, if you're bored, why, come to my rooms of an evening and hear me talk—you'll have the time of your life." And now he's cheeky.'

H. (sipping his drink and very much preoccupied with it) replied abstractedly, 'When you die you'll go to Hell.' (I liked his Homeric simplicity.) 'You ought to be buried in a fireproof safe.'

Silence.

H. (returning to the attack), 'I hope she turns you down.'

'Thank you,' I said.

'As for P——,' he resumed, 'she's double-Dutch to me.'

'Go to the Berlitz School,' I suggested, 'and learn the language.'

'You bally fool. . . . All you do is to sit there and smile like a sanguinary cat. Nothing I say ever rouses you. I believe if I came to you and said, "Here, Professor, is a Beetle with 99 legs that has lived on granite in the middle of the Sahara for 40 days and 40 nights," you'd simply answer, "Yes, and that reminds me I've forgotten to blow my nose."'

The two pyjamaed figures shake with laughing, the light goes out and the sanguinary conversation continues on similar lines until we fall asleep.

April 26.

Two Months' Sick Leave

In a horrible panic—the last few days—I believe I am developing locomotor ataxy. One leg, one arm, and my speech are affected, *i.e.* the right side and my speech centre. M—— is serious. . . . I hope the disease, whatever it is, will be sufficiently lingering to enable me to complete my book.

R—— is a dear man. I shall not easily forget his kindness during this terrible week. . . . Can the Fates have the audacity ? . . . Who can say ?

April 27.

I believe there can be no doubt that I have had a slight partial paralysis of my right side (like Dad). I stutter a little in my speech when excited, I cannot write properly (look at this handwriting), and my right leg is rocky at the knee. My head swims.

It is too inconceivably horrible to be buried in the Earth in such splendid spring weather. Who can tell me what is in store for me ? . . . Life opens to me, I catch a glimpse of a vision, and the doors clang to again noiselessly. It is dark. That will be my history. Am developing a passionate belief in my book and a fever of haste to complete it before the *congé définitif*.

April 29.

Saw M—— again, who said my symptoms were alarming certainly, but he was sure no definite diagnosis could be made.

April 30.

Went with M—— to see a well-known nerve specialist —Dr H——. He could find no symptoms of a definite disease, tho' he asked me suspiciously if I had ever been with women.

Ordered two months' complete rest in the country. H—— chased me round his consulting room with a drumstick, tapping my nerves and cunningly working my reflexes. Then he tickled the soles of my feet and pricked me with a pin—all of which I stood like a man. He wears a soft black hat, looks like a Quaker, and reads the *Verhandlungen d. Gesellschaft d. Nervenarzten*.

M—— is religious and after I had disclosed my physique to him yesterday (for the 99th time) he remained on his

knees by the couch in his consulting room (after working
my reflexes) for a moment or two in the attitude of prayer.
When the Doctor prays for you—better call in the under-
taker. My epitaph ' He played Ludo well.' The game
anyhow requires moral stamina—ask H——.

May 5.

At R——. Mugged about all day. Put on a gramophone record—then crawled up into a corner of the large,
empty drawing room and ate my heart out. Heart has
a bitter taste—if it's your own.

May 6.

Sat in the ' morning room ' feeling ill. In the chair
opposite sat Aunt Fanny, aged 86, knitting. I listened
to the click of her needles, while out in the garden a thrush
sang, and there was a red sunset.

May 8.

Before I left R——, A—— [my brother] had written
to Uncle enclosing my doctor's letter. I don't know the
details except that Dr M—— emphasised the seriousness
and yet held out hope that two months' rest would allay
the symptoms.

May 11.

At Home

I made some offensive remark to H—— whom I met
in the street. This set him off.

' You blighter, I hope you marry a loose woman. May
your children be all bandy-legged and squint-eyed, may
your teeth drop out, and your toes have bunions,' and
so on in his usual lengthy commination.

I turned to the third man.

' Bob—this !—after all I've done for that young man !
I have even gone out of my way to cultivate in him a
taste for poetry—until he is now, in fact, quite wrapped
up in it—indeed, so much so, that for a time he was nothing
but a brown paper parcel labelled Poetry.'

H. (doggedly): ' When are you going to die ?'

'That, Master H——,' I answered menacingly, ' is on the knees of the Gods.'

H.: ' I shan't believe you're dead till I see your tomb-stone.   I shall then say to the Sexton, " Is he really dead, then ?" and the Sexton will say, " Well, 'ee's buried onny way." '

Bob was not quite in sympathy with our boisterous spirits.

May 15

Gardening

Sought out H—— as he was watering his petunias in the garden.   He informed me he was going to London on Monday.

H.: ' Mother is coming too.'

B.: ' Why ?'

H.: ' Oh! I'm buying my kit—shirts and things.   I sail at the beginning of July.'

B.: ' I suppose shirts are difficult to buy.   You wouldn't know what to do with one if you had one.   Your mother will lead you by the hand into a shop and say, " H——, dear, this is a shirt," and you'll reply with pathos, " Mother, what are the wild shirts saying ?" '

H.: ' You're a B.F.' (Goes on watering).

' I wonder what you'd do if you were let loose in a big garden,' I began.

H.: ' I should be as happy as a bird.   I should hop about, chirrup and lay eggs.   You should have seen my tomato plants last year—one was as tall as father.'

B.: ' Now tell me of the Gooseberry as big as Mother.'

Mutual execrations.   Then we grinned and cackled at each other, emitting weird and ferocious cachinnations. Several times a day in confidential, serious tones—after one of these explosions—we say, ' I really believe we're mad.'   You never heard such extraordinary caterwaulings. Our snappy conversations are interrupted with them every minute or so !

May 23.

Stagnancy

A stagnant day. Lay still in the Park all day with just
sufficient energy to observe. The Park was almost empty.
Every one but me at work. Nothing is more dreary than
a pleasure ground on work days. There was one man a
little way off throwing a ball to a clever dog. Behind me
on the path, some one came along wheeling a pram. I
listened in a kind of coma to the scrunching of the gravel
in the distance a long time after the pram was out of
sight. Far away—the tinkle of Church bells—in a village
across the river, and, in front, the man still throwing the
ball to his clever dog.

May 25.

Death

. . . I suppose the truth is I am at last broken in to
the idea of Death. Once it terrified me and once I hated
it. But now it only annoys me. Having lived with the
Bogey for so long, and broken bread with him so often,
I am used to his ugliness, tho' his persistent attentions
bore me. Why doesn't he do it and have done with me?
Why this deference, why does he pass me everything but
the poison? Why am I such an unconscionably long time
dying?

What embitters me is the humiliation of having to die,
to have to be pouring out the precious juices of my life
into the dull Earth, to be no longer conscious of what goes
on, no longer moving abroad upon the Earth creating
attraction and repulsions, pouring out one's ego in a
stream. To think that the women I have loved will be
marrying and forget, and that the men I have hated will
continue on their way and forget I ever hated them—the
ignominy of being dead! What voluble talker likes his
mouth to be stopped with earth, who relishes the idea of
the carrion worm mining in the seat of the intellect?

May 29.

Renunciation

Staying at the King's Hotel, ——. Giddiness very bad. Death seems unavoidable. A tumour on the brain ?

Coming down here in the train, sat in corner of the compartment, twined one leg around the other, rested my elbow on the window ledge, and gazed out helplessly at the exuberant green fields, green woods, and green hedgerows. The weather was perfect, the sun blazed down.

Certainly, I was rather sorry for myself at the thought of leaving it all. But I girded up my loins and wrapped around me for a while the mantle of a nobler sentiment; *i.e.* I felt sorry for the others as well—for the two brown carters in the road ambling along with a timber waggon, for the two old maids in the same compartment with me knitting bedsocks, for the beautiful Swallows darting over the stream, for the rabbit that lopped into the fern just as we passed—they too were all leaving it.

The extent of my benign compassion startled me—it was so unexpected. Perhaps for the first time in my life I forgot all about my own miserable ambitions—I forgave the successful, the time-servers, the self-satisfied, the overweening, the gracious and condescending—all, in fact, who hitherto have been thorns in my flesh and innocently enough have goaded me to still fiercer efforts to win thro'. 'Poor people,' I said. 'Leave them alone. Let them be happy if they can.' With a submissive heart, I was ready to sit down in the rows of this world's failures and never have thought one bitter word about success. To all those persons who in one way or another had foiled my purposes I extended a pardon with Olympian gravity, and, strangest of all, I could have melted such frosty moral rectitudes with a genuine interest in the careers of my struggling contemporaries. With perfect self-abnegation, I held out my hand to them and wished them all ' God Speed.'

It was a strange metempsychosis. Yet of a truth it is no use being niggardly over our lives. We are all of us 'shelling out.' And we can afford to be generous, for we shall all—some early, some late—be bankrupt in the end. For my part, I've had a short and boisterous voyage and shan't be sorry to get into port. I give up all my plans, all my hopes, all my loves and enthusiasms without remonstrance. I renounce all—I myself am already really dead.

May 30.

Last night the sea was as flat as a pavement, a pretty barque with all her sails out to catch the smallest puff of wind—the tiniest inspiration—was nevertheless without motion—a painted ship on a tapestry of violet. H—— Hill was an immense angular mass of indigo blue. Even rowing boats made little progress and the water came off the languid paddles in syrupy clots. Everything was utterly still, the air thick—like cottonwool to the touch and very stifling; vitality in living things leaked away under a sensuous lotus influence. Intermittently after the darkness had come, Bullpoint Lighthouse shone like the wink of a lascivious eye.

.   .   .   .

Pottering about all day on the Pier and Front, listening to other people's talk, catching snippets of conversation— not edifying. If there were seven wise men in the town, I would not save it. Damn the place!

May 31.

. . . I espied her first in the distance and turned my head away quickly and looked out to sea. A moment after, I began to turn my head round again slowly with the cautiousness and air of suspicion of a Tortoise poking its head out from underneath his shell. I was terrified to discover that in the meantime she had come and sat down on the seat immediately behind me with her back to mine. We sat like this back to back for some time and I enjoyed the novel experience and the tension. A few years ago, the bare sight of her gave me palpitation of the heart, and, on the first occasion that I had the courage to stop to speak, I felt livid and the skin on my face twitched uncontrollably.

Presently I got up and walked past—in the knowledge that she must now be conscious of my presence after a disappearance of three years. Later we met face to face and I broke the ice. She's a pretty girl. . . . So too is her sister.

    .   .   .   .

Few people, except my barber, know how amorous I am. He has to shave my sinuous lips.

June 3.

Spent many dreadful hours cogitating whether to accept their invitation to dinner. . . . I wanted to go for several reasons. I wanted to see her in a home-setting for the first time, and I wanted to spend the evening with three pretty girls. I also had the idea of displaying myself to the scrutinising gaze of the family as the hero of the old romance: and of showing Her how much I had progressed since last we met and what a treasure she had lost.

On the other hand, I was afraid that the invitation was only a casual one, I feared a snuffy reception, a frosty smile and a rigid hand. Could I go up and partake of meat at their board, among brothers and sisters taking me for an ogre of a jilt, and she herself perhaps opposite me making me blush perpetually to recall our one-time passionate kisses, our love letters and our execrable verses to each other! There seemed dreadful possibilities in such an adventure. Yet I badly wanted to experience the piquant situation.

At 7 p.m., half an hour before I was due, decided on strong measures. I entered a pub. and took a stiff whisky and soda, and then set off with a stout heart to take the icy family by storm—and if need be live down my evil reputation by my amiability and urbanity!

I went—and of course everything passed off in the most normal manner. She is a very pretty girl—like velvet. Before dinner, we walked in the garden—and talked only of flowers.

June 4.

On the Hill, this morning, felt the thrill of the news of my own Death: I mean I imagined I heard the words,—

' You've heard the news about B—— ?'

Second Voice: ' No, what ?'

' He's dead.'

Silence.

Won't all this seem piffle if I don't die after all! As an artist in life I *ought* to die; it is the only artistic ending —and I ought to die now or the Third Act will fizzle out in a long doctor's bill.

June 5.

A New Pile in the Pier

Watched some men put a new pile in the pier. There was all the usual paraphernalia of chains, pulleys, cranes, and ropes, with a massive wooden pile swinging over the water at the end of a long wire hawser. Everything was in the massive style—even the men—very powerful men, slow, ruminative, silent men.

Nothing very relevant could be gathered from casual remarks. The conversation was without exception mono-syllabic: ' Let go,' or ' Stand fast.' But by close attention to certain obscure movements of the man on the ladder near the water's edge, it gradually came thro' to my consciousness that all these powerful, silent men were up against some bitter difficulty. I cannot say what it was. The burly monsters were silent about the matter. . . . In fact they appeared almost indifferent—and tired, oh ! so very tired of the whole business. The attitude of the man nearest me was that for all he cared the pile could go on swinging in mid-air to the crack of Doom.

They continued slow, laborious efforts to overcome the secret difficulty. But these gradually slackened and finally ceased. One massive man after another abandoned his post in order to lean over the rails and gaze like a mystic into the depths of the sea. No one spoke. No one saw anything not even in the depths of the sea. One

spat, and with round, sad eyes contemplated the trajectory
of his brown bolus (he had been chewing) in its descent
into the water.

The foreman, an original thinker, lit a cigarette, which
relieved the tension. Then, slowly and with majesty, he
turned on his heel, and walked away. With the sudden
eclipse of the foreman's interest, the incident closed. I
should have been scarcely surprised to find him behind
the Harbour-master's Office playing ' Shove-ha'penny ' or
skittles with the pile still swinging in mid-air. . . . After
all it was only a bloody pile.

June 11.

Depression

Suffering from depression. . . . The melancholy fit
fell very suddenly. All the colour went out of my life,
the world was dirty gray. On the way back to my hotel
caught sight of H——, jumping into a cab, after a visit to
S—— Sands. But the sight of him aroused no desire in
me to shout or wave. I merely wondered how on earth
he could have spent a happy day at such a Sandy place.
On arriving at ——, sank deeper into my morass. It
suffocated me to find the old familiar landmarks coming
into view . . . the holiday-makers along the streets how
I hated them—the Peg Top Hill how desolate—all as
before—how dull. The very fact that they were all there
as before in the morning nauseated me. The sea-coast
here is magnificent, the town is pretty—I know that, of
course. But all looked dreary and cheerless—just the
sort of feeling one gets on entering an empty house with
no fire on a winter's day and nowhere to sit down. . . .
I felt as lonely and desolate as a man suddenly fallen from
the clouds into an unknown town on the Antarctic Continent built of ice and inhabited by Penguins. Who are
these people ? I asked myself irritably. There perhaps
on the other side of the street was my own brother.
But I was not even faintly interested and told the cabman
to drive on. The spray from the sea fogged my spectacles
and made me weary.

June 14.

The Restlessness of the Sea

The restlessness of the sea acts as a soporific on jangled nerves. You gaze at its incessant activities, unwillingly at first because they distract your attention from your own cherished worries and griefs,—but later you watch with complete self-abandon—it wrenches you out of yourself—and eventually with a kind of stupid hypnotic stare.

Dr Spurgeon

The day has been overcast, but to-night a soft breeze sprang up and swept the sky clear as softly as a mop. The sun coming out shone upon a white sail far out in the channel, scarcely another vessel hove in sight. The white sail glittered like a piece of silver paper whenever the mainsail swung round as the vessel tacked. Its solitariness and whiteness in a desert of marine blue attracted the attention and held it till at last I could look at nothing else. The sight of it—so clean and white and fair—set me yearning for all the rarest and most exquisite things my imagination could conjure up—a beautiful girl, with fair and sunburnt skin, brown eyes, dark eyebrows, and small pretty feet; a dewdrop in a violet's face; an orange-tip butterfly swinging on an umbel of a flower.

The sail went on twinkling and began to exert an almost moral influence over me. It drew out all the good in me. I longed to follow it on white wings—an angel I suppose—to quit this husk of a body ' as raiment put away,' and pursue Truth and Beauty across the sea to the horizon, and beyond the horizon up the sky itself to its last tenuous confines, no doubt with a still small voice summoning me and the rest of the elect to an Agapemone, with Dr Spurgeon at the door distributing tracts.

I can scoff like this now. But at the time my exaltation was very real. My soul strained in the leash. I was full of a desire for unattainable spiritual beauty. I wanted something. But I don't know what I want.

June 16.

My Sense of Touch

My sense of touch has always been morbidly acute. I
like to feel a cigarette locked in the extreme corner of my
mouth. When I remove it from my mouth then I hold
it probably up in the fork between two fingers. If I am
waiting for a meal I finger the cool knives and forks. If
I am in the country I plunge my hand with outspread
fingers into a mass of large-topped grasses, then close my
fingers, crush and decapitate the lot.

June 27.

Camping Out at S—— Sands

A brilliant summer day. Up early, breakfasted, and,
clad in sweater and trousers, walked up the sands to the
boathouse with bare feet.

Everything was wonderful ! I strode along over the
level sands infatuated with the sheer ability to put one
leg in front of the other and walk. I loved to feel the
muscles of my thighs working, and to swing my arms in
rhythm with the stride. The stiff breeze had blown the
sky clear, and was rushing through my long hair, and
bellowing into each ear. I strode as Alexander must have
done !

Then I stretched my whole length out along a flat plank
on the sands, which was as dry as a bone and warm. There
was not a soul on the sands. Everything was bare, clean,
windswept. My plank had been washed clean and white.
The sands—3 miles of it—were hard and purified, level.
My eye raced along in every direction—there was nothing
—not a bird or a man—to stop it. In that immense
windswept space nothing was present save me and the
wind and the sea—a flattering moment for the egotist.

. . . .

At the foot of the cliffs on the return journey met an
old man gathering sticks. As he ambled along dropping
sticks into a long sack he called out casually, ' Do you

believe in Jesus Christ ?' in the tone of voice in which one would say, ' I think we shall have some rain before night.' ' Aye, aye,' came the answer without hesitation from a boy lying on his back in the sands a few yards distant, ' and that He died to save me.'

Life is full of surprises like this. The only other sounds I have heard to-day were the Herring Gull's cackle. Your own gardener will one day look over his rake and give you the correct chemical formula for carbonic acid gas. I met a postman once reading Shelley as he walked his rounds.

June 28.

I am writing this by the lamp in the cabin among the sandhills waiting for H—— to arrive from town with provisions. I wear a pair of bags, a dirty sweater, and go without hat or shoes and stockings. There is a ' Deadwood Dick ' atmosphere here. I'm a sort of broncobreaker or rancher off duty writing home. In a minute I haven't the slightest doubt, H——. will gallop into the compound, tether his colt and come in ' raising Cain ' for a belly-full of red meat. . . . If I am going to live after all (touch wood) I shall go abroad and be in the open.

I eat greedily, am getting very sunburnt, am growing hairy (that means strength !), and utter portentous oaths. If I stayed here much longer I should grow a tail and climb trees.

After a supper of fried eggs and fried bread done to a nicety, turned in at ten, and both of us lay warm and comfortable in bed, smoking cigarettes and listening to Offenbach's Barcarolle on the gramophone. We put the lamp out, and it pleased us to watch the glow of each other's cigarettes in the dark. . . . Neither of us spoke. . . . Went to sleep at midnight. Awoke at sunrise to hear an Owl still hooting, a Lark singing, and several Jackdaws clattering on our tin roof with their claws as they walked.

July 1.

In London Again

Returned to London very depressed. Am not so well as I was three weeks ago. The sight of one eye is affected, and I am haunted by the possibility of blindness. Then I have a numb feeling on one side of my face, and my right arm is less mobile.

Left darling Mother in a very weak state in bed, with neuritis and a weak heart. She cried when I said ' Goodbye,' and asked me to go to Church as often as I could, and to read a portion of Scripture every day. I promised. Then she added, ' For Dad's sake;' just as if I would not do it for her. Poor dear, she suffers a deal of pain. She does not know how ill I am. I have not told her.

July 3.

Back at work. A terrible day. Thoughts of suicide—a pistol.

July 8.

I get thro' each day with the utmost difficulty. I have to wrestle with every minute. Each hour is a conquest. The three quarters of an hour at lunch comes as a Godsend. I look forward to it all the morning, I enter into it with joyful relief with no thought of the dreadful moment impending when I must return and re-enter my room. By being wise like this, I manage to husband my spirits and am relatively cheerful for one hour in the middle of each difficult day.

July 9.

Several times I have gone to bed and hoped I should never wake up. Life grows daily more impossible. To-day I put a slide underneath the microscope and looked at it. It was like looking at something thro' the wrong end of a telescope. I sat with eye glued to the ocular, so as to keep up a pretence of work in case some one came in My mind was occupied with quite different affairs. If one is pondering on Life and Death, it is a terrible task to have to study Mites.

July 10.

Am doing no work at all. . . . I sit mctionless in my chair and beat the devil's tatoo with my thumbs and think, think, think in the same horrible circle hour after hour. I am unable to work. I haven't the courage to. I've lost my nerve.

At five I return ' home ' to the Boarding-house and get more desperate.

Two old maids sat down to dinner to-night, one German youth (a lascivious, ranting, brainless creature), a lady typist (who takes drugs they say), a dipsomaniac (who has monthly bouts—H—— carried him upstairs and put him to bed the other night), two invertebrate violinists who play in the Covent Garden Orchestra, a colonial lady engaged in a bedroom intrigue with a man who sits at my table. What are these people to me ? I hate them all. They know it and are offended.

After dinner, put on my cap and rushed out anywhere to escape. Walked to the end of the street, not knowing where I was going or what doing. Stopped and stared with fixed eyes at the traffic in Kensington Road, undetermined what to do with myself and unable to make up my mind (volitional paralysis). Turned round, walked home, and went straight to bed 9 p.m., anxiously looking forward to to-morrow evening when I go to see her again, but at the same time wondering how on earth I am to get through to-morrow's round before the evening comes. . . . This is a hand-to-mouth existence. My own inner life is scorching up all outside interests. Zoology appears as a curious thing in a Bagdad bazaar. I sit in my room at the B. M. and play with it; I let it trickle thro' my fingers and roll away like a child playing with quicksilver.

July 11.

Over to the flat. She was looking beautiful in a black dress, with a white silk blouse, and a Byron collar, negli-

gently open in front as if a button had come out. She
said I varied: sometimes I went up in her estimation,
sometimes down; once I went down very low. I understood her to say I was now UP ! Alleluia !

July 14.

. . . It would take too long and I am too tired to write
out all the varying phases of this day's life—all its impressions and petty miseries chasing one another across
my consciousness or leap-frogging over my chest like
gleeful fiends.[1]

July 21.

Thoroughly enjoyed the journey up to town this morning.
I secretly gloated over the fact that the train was dashing
along over the rails to London bearing me and all the
rest of the train's company upon their pursuits—wealth,
fame, learning. I was inebriated with the speed, ferocity,
and dash of living. . . . If the train had charged into
the buffers I should have hung my head out of the window
and cheered. If a man had got in my way, I'd have
knocked him down. The wheels of the carriage were
singing a lusty song in which I joined.

July 30.

. . . We talked of men and women, and she said she
thought men were neither angels nor devils but just men.
I said I thought women were either angels or devils.
    ' I am afraid to ask you which you think me.'
    ' You needn't,' I said shortly.

August 9.

Horribly upset with news from home. Mother is really
ill. The Doctor fears serious nerve trouble and says she
will always be an invalid. This is awful, poor dear !
It's dreadful, and yet I have a tiny wish buried at the

---

[1] ' The life of the Soul is different; there is nothing more changing,
more varied, more restless . . . to describe the incidents of one
hour would require an eternity.'—*Journal of Eugénie de Guérin.*

bottom of my heart that she may be removed early from
us rather than linger in pain of body and mind. Especially
do I hope she may not live to hear any grievous news of
me. . . .   What irony that she should lose the use of her
right arm only two years after Dad's death from paralysis.
It is cruel for it reminds her of Dad's illness. . . .   What,
too, would she think if she could have heard M——'s first
words to me yesterday on one of my periodical visits to
his consulting room, ' Well, how's the *paralysis*?'

         .   .   .   .

In the evening went over to see her. She was wearing
a black silk gown and looked handsome. . . .   She is
always the same sombre, fascinating, lissom, soft-voiced
She ! She herself never changes. . . .   What am I to
do ? I cannot give her up and yet I do not altogether
wish to take her to my heart. It distresses me to know
how to proceed. I am a wily fish.

August 10.

Sat in the gardens with her. We sat facing the sun
for a while until she was afraid of developing freckles and
turned around, deliberately turning her back on good
King Sol. . . .   I said it was disrespectful.
  ' Oh! he doesn't mind,' she said. ' He's a dear. He
kissed me and said, " Turn round my dear if you like." '
  Isn't she tantalising ?
  I wanted to say sarcastically, ' I wonder you let him
kiss you,' but there was a danger of the remark reviving
the dead.

August 14.

I tried my best, I've sought every loophole of escape,
but I am quite unable to avoid the melancholy fact that
her thumbs are—lamentable. I am genuinely upset
about it for I like her. No one more than I would be more
delighted if they were otherwise. . . .   Poor dear ! how
I love her ! That's why I'm so concerned about her
thumbs.

August 21.

A wire from A—— came at 11.50 saying, 'Darling Mother passed peacefully away yesterday afternoon.' . . . Yesterday afternoon I was writing Zoology and all last night I slept soundly. . . . It was quite sudden. Caught the first train home.

August 23.

The funeral.

August 31.

Staying at the Hotel du Guesclin at Cancale near St Malo with my dear A——.

This flood of new experiences has knocked my diary habit out of gear. To be candid, I've forgotten all about myself. I've been too engrossed in living to stand the strain of setting down and in cold blood writing out all the things seen and heard. If I once began I should blow thro' these pages like a whirlwind. . . . But what a waste of time with M. le batelier waiting outside with his bisque to take us mackerel fishing ! . . .

September 8.

Returned to Southampton yesterday. Have spent the night at Okehampton in Devonshire *en route* for T—— Rectory. This morning we hatched the ridiculous idea of hiring two little Dartmoor ponies and riding out from the town. A—— rides fairly well tho' he has not been astride a beast for years. As for me, I cannot ride at all ! Yet I had the idea that I could easily manage a pretty little pony with brown eyes and a long tail. On going out into the Inn yard, was horrified—two horses saddled—one a large traction beast. . . . I climbed on to the smaller one, walked him out of the yard and down the road in good style without accident. Once in the country, however, my animal, the fresher of the two, insisted on a smart trot which shook me up a good deal so that I hardly kept my seat. This eventually so annoyed the animal that it began to fidget and zigzag across the road—no doubt preparing to break away at a stretch gallop when once it had rid itself of the incomprehensible pair of legs across its back.

I got off quickly and swopped horses with A——. Walked him most of the way, while A—— cantered forward and back to cheer me on. Ultimately however this beast, too, got sick of walking and began to trot. For a time I stood this well and began to rise in my saddle quite nicely. After two miles, horrible soreness supervened, and I had to get off—very carefully, with a funny feeling in my legs—even looked down at them to assure myself they were not bandy ! In doing so, the horse—this traction monster—stepped on my toe and I swore.

On nearing the village, L—— arrived, riding A——'s animal and holding his sides for laughing at me as I crawled along holding the carthorse by the bridle. Got on again and rode into the Rectory grounds in fine style like a dashing cavalier, every one jeering at me from the lawn.

September 28.

Having lived on this planet now for the space of 24 years, I can claim with some cogency that I am qualified to express some sort of opinion about it. I therefore hereby record that I find myself in an absorbingly interesting place where I live, move and have my being, dominated by one monstrous feature above all others—the mystery of it all ! Everything is so astonishing, my own existence so incredible !

Nothing explains itself. Every one is dumb. It is like walking about at a masqued Ball. . . . Even I myself am a mystery to me. How wonderful and frightening that is—to feel yourself—your innermost and most substantial possession to be a mystery, incomprehensible. I look at myself in the mirror and mock at myself. On some days I am to myself as strange and unfamiliar as a Pterodactyl. There is a certain grim humour in finding myself here possessed of a perfectly arbitrary arrangement of lineaments when I never asked to be here and never selected my own attributes. To the dignity of a human being it seems like a coarse practical joke. . . . My own freakish physique is certainly a joke.

October 4.

In London Again

K—— comes in from her dancing class, nods to me, hugs her sister around the neck and says,—

' Oh ! you dear thing, you've got a cold.'

' I shouldn't do that,' I remark, green-eyed, ' she's in an awful wax to-night.'

She: ' Oh ! I don't mind K—— !'

(Laughter !)

October 8.

Heard a knock at the door last night, and, thinking it was R——, I unbolted it and let in a tramp who at once asked God to bless me and crown all my sorrow with joy. An amiable fellow to be sure—so I gave him some coppers and he at once repeated with wonderful fervour, ' God bless you, sir.'

' I wish He would,' I answered, ' I have a horrible cold.'

' Ah, I know, I gets it myself and the hinfluenza—have you had that, sir ?'

In ten minutes I should have told him all my personal history. But he was thirsting for a drink and went off quickly and left me with my heart unburthened. London is a lonely place.

. . . .

To-day journeyed to —— where I gave evidence as an *expert* in Economic Entomology at the County Court in a case concerning damage to furniture by mites for which I am paid £8 8s. fee and expenses and travelled first class. What irony ! (See June 30, 1911.)

October 11.

I may be a weak, maundering, vacillating fool but I cannot help loving her on one day, being indifferent the next and on some occasions even disliking her. . . . To-day she was charming, with a certain warm glossy perfection on her face and hair. . . . And she loves me— I could swear it. ' And when a woman woos . . .' etc. How difficult for a vain and lonely man to resist her. She tells me many times in many dainty ways that she loves me without so much as stopping her work to talk.

I wish I were permanently and irresistibly enamoured. I want a *bouleversement.* . . .

October 13.

Went to see a Harley Street oculist about the sight of one eye, which has caused a lot of trouble and worry of late and continuously haunted me with the possibility of blindness. At times, I see men as trees walking and print becomes hopelessly blurred.

The Specialist however is reassuring. The eye is healthy —no neuritis—but the adjustment muscles have been thrown out of gear by the nervous troubles of last spring.

.   .   .   .

Was ever man more sorely tempted ? Here am I lonely and uncomfortable in diggings with a heart like nascent oxygen. . . . Shall I ? Yes, but. . . . And I have neither health nor wealth.

October 22.

The British Museum Reading Room

I saw it for the first time to-day ! Gadzooks ! ! This is the only fit ejaculation to express my amazement ! It's a pagan temple with the Gods in the middle and all around, various obscure dark figures prostrating themselves in worship.

October 29.

For any one who is not simply a Sheep or Cow or whose nervous organisation is a degree more sensitive than the village blacksmith's, it is a besetting peril to his peace of mind to be constantly moving about an independent being, with loves and hates, and a separate identity among other separate identities, who prowl and prowl around like the hosts of Midian—ready to snarl, fight, seize you, bore you, exasperate you, to arouse all your passions, call up all the worst from the depths where they have lain hidden. . . . A day spent among my fellows goads me to a frenzy by the evening. I am no longer fit for human companionship. People string me up to concert pitch. I develop suspicions of one that he is prying, of another that he patronises. Others make me horribly anxious to stand well in their eyes and horribly curious to know what they think of me. Others I hate and loathe—for no particular reason. There is a man I am acquainted with concerning whom I know nothing at all. He may be Jew, Gentile, Socinian, Pre-adamite, Anabaptist, Rosicrucian—I don't know, and I don't care, for I hate him. I should like to smash his face in. I don't know why. . . . In the whole course of our tenuous acquaintance we have spoken scarce a dozen words to each other. Yet I should like to blow up his face with dynamite. If I had £200 a year private income I should be in wait for him to-morrow round a corner and land him one—just to indicate my economic independence. He would call for the police and the policeman—discerning creature—on arrival, would surely say, ' With a face like that, I'm not surprised.'

.   .   .   .

R—— said to me this morning, ' Well, have you heard ?' with an exuberance of curiosity that made my blood boil— he was referring to my Essay still at the bar of the opinion of the Editor of the *English Review*. ' You beast,' I snapped and walked off.

R—— shouted with laughter for he realises my anger with him is only semi-serious: it is meant and not meant:

meant, for it is justified by the facts ; not meant, for I can't be too serious over anything *au fond.*

.   .   .   .

Of all the grim and ridiculous odds and ends of chance that Fortune has rolled up to my feet, my friendship with a man like B—— is the grimmest and most ridiculous. He is a bachelor of sixty, rather good-looking, of powerful physique and a faultless constitution. . . . His ignorance is colossal and he once asked whether Australia, for example, tho' surrounded by water, is not connected up with other land underneath the sea. Being himself a child in intelligence (tho' commercially cunning), he has a great respect for my brains. Being himself a strong man, he views my ill-health with much contempt. His private opinion is that I am in consumption. When asked once by a lady if I were not going to be ' a great man ' one day, he replied, ' Yes—if he lives.' I ought to walk six miles a day, drink a bottle of stout with my dinner, and eat plenty of *onions.* His belief in the curative properties of onions is strong as death. . . .

His system of prophylaxis may be quickly summarised,—

    (1) Hot whisky *ad lib.* and off to bed.

    (2) A woman.

These two sterling preventives he has often urged upon me at the same time tipping out a quantity of anathemas on doctors and physic. . . .

He is a cynic. He scoffs at the medical profession, the Law, the Church, the Press. Every man is guilty until he is proved innocent. The Premier is an unscrupulous character, the Bishop a salacious humbug. No doctor will cure, for it pays him to keep you ill. Every clergyman puts the Sunday-school teacher in the family way. His mouth is permanently distorted by cynicism.

He is vain and believes all women are in love with him. When playing the Gallant, he turns on a special voice, wears white spats, and looks like a Newmarket ' Crook.'

'I lost my 'bus,' a girl says to him. 'Lost your bust,' he answers, in broad Scotch. 'I can't see that you've done that.' . . . His sexual career has been a remarkable one, he claiming to have brought many women to bed, and actually to have lain with women of almost all European nationalities, for he has been a great traveller. . . .

This man is my devoted friend! . . . And truth to tell I get on with him better than I do with most people. I like his gamey flavour, his utter absence of self-consciousness, and his doggy loyalty to myself—his weaker brother. He may be depraved in his habits, coarse in his language, boorish in his manners, ludicrous in the wrongness of all his views. But I like him just because he is so hopeless. I get on with him because it is so impossible to reclaim him—my missionary spirit is not intrigued. If he only dabbled in vice (for an experiment), if he had pale, watery ideas about current literature—if—to use his own favourite epithet—he were *genteel*, I should quarrel.

October 30.

Have developed a passion for a piece of sculpture by R. Boeltzig called the Reifenwerferin—the most beautiful figure of a woman. I am already devoted to Rodin's 'Kiss' and have a photo of it framed in my bedroom. Have written to Bruciani's.

I suspect that my growing appreciation of the plastic art is with me only distilled sensuality. I enjoy my morning bath for the same reason. My bath is a daily baptism. I revel in the pleasure of the pain of the cold water. I whistle gleefully because I am clean and cool and nude early in the morning with the sun still low, before the day has been stained by clothes, dirt, pain, exasperation, death. . . . How I love myself as I rub myself down!—the cool, pink skin—I could eat it! I want to be all day in a cold bath to enjoy the pain of mortifying the flesh—it is so beautiful, so soft, so inscrutable—if I cut out chunks of it, it would only bleed.

November 8.

The other morning R—— said hyperbolically that he hadn't slept all night for fear that, before he had time to put an arresting hand on my shoulder and say ' Don't,' I might have gone and become ' Entangled.' . . .

. . . No, I'm as firm as a rock, my dear. But in imagination the affair was continued as follows,—

She: ' I am fond of you, you know.'

He: ' I wish you wouldn't say these things to me— they're quite embarrassing.'

She: ' Oh ! my dear, I'm not serious, you know—you're such a vain young man.'

He: ' Well, it's equally embarrassing any way.'

She: ' Then I *am* serious.'

Tears.

I say: ' I wish you would take me only for what I am— a blackguard with no good intentions, yet no very evil ones—but still a blackguard, whom you seem to find has engaging manners.'

I breathe freely hoping to have escaped this terrible temptation and turn to go. But she, looking up smiling thro' a curtain of wet eyelashes, asks,—

' Won't the blackguard stop a little longer ?' In a moment my earthworks, redoubts, and bastions fall down, I rush forward impetuously into her arms shouting, ' I *will*, I *will*, I will as long as for eternity.'

(Curtain.)

I dramatised this little picture and much more last night before going to sleep when I was in a fever. I should succumb at once to the first really skilful coquette.

November 9.

Ludo

We played Ludo together this evening and she won 2s. 6d. Handsomely gowned in black and wearing black ornaments, she sat with me in the lamplight on the sofa in the Morris Room, with the Ludo board between us placed on a large green cushion. Her face was white as parchment and her hair seemed an ebony black. I lolled in the opposite corner, a thin, elongated youth, with fair hair all stivvered up, dressed in a light-brown lounge suit with a good trouser crease, a soft linen collar and—a red tie! Between us, on its green cushion the Ludo board with its brilliantly coloured squares:—all of it set before a background formed by the straight-backed, rectangular, settle-like sofa, with a charming covering which went with the rest of the scheme.

'Rather decorative,' —— remarked in an audible voice, turning her head on one side and quizzing. I can well believe it was. *She* looked wholly admirable.

November 21.

My Nightmare

Can't get rid of my cough. I have so many things to do—I am living in a fever of haste to get them done. Yet this cough hinders me. There is always something which drags me back from the achievement of my desires. It's like a nightmare; I see myself struggling violently to escape from a monster which draws continuously nearer, until his shadow falls across my path, when I begin to run and find my legs tied, etc. The only difference is that mine is a nightmare from which I never wake up. The haven of successful accomplishment remains as far off as ever. Oh! make haste.

November 29.

The *English Review* has returned my Essay!—This is a keen disappointment to me. 'I wish I could use this, but I am really too full,' the Editor writes. To be faintly encouraged and delicately rejected—why I prefer the printed form.

December 1.

More Irony

Renewed my cold—I do nothing all day but blow my nose, cough, and curse Austin Harrison.

M—— thinks the lungs are all right. 'There is nothing there, I think,' said he, this morning. Alleluia! I've

had visions of consumption for weeks past and M——
himself has been expecting it.   I always just escape: I
always almost get something, do something, go somewhere,
I have dabbled in a variety of diseases, but never got one
downright[1]—but only enough to make me feel horribly
unfit and very miserable without the consolation of being
able to regard myself as the heroic victim of some incurable disorder.   Instead of being Stevenson with tuber-
culosis, I've only been Jones with dyspepsia.   So, too, in
other directions, big events have always just missed me:
by Herculean efforts I succeeded in giving up newspaper
journalism and breaking thro' that steel environment—
but only to become an Entomologist !   I once achieved
success in an Essay in the *Academy*, which attracted
attention—a début, however, that never developed.   I
had not quite arrived.   It is always *not quite*.

Yesterday, I received a state visit from the Editor of the
Furniture Record seeking advice on how to eradicate mites
from upholstering !   I received him ironically—but little
did he understand.

I shot up like a ball on a bagatelle board all steamy
into zoology (my once beloved science) but at once rolled
dead into the very low hole of Economic Entomology !
Curse. . . .   Why can't I either have a first-rate disease
or be a first-rate zoologist ?

Now just think what a much better figure I should
have cut, from the artistic view point, had I remained a
newspaper reporter who had taught himself prodigious
embryology out of F. M. Balfour's Textbook, who had
cut sections of fowls' eggs and newt embryos with a hand
microtome, who had passionately dissected out the hidden,
internal anatomy of a great variety of animals, who could
recite Wiedersheim's *Comparative Anatomy of Vertebrates*
and patter off the difference between a nephridium and a
cœlomic duct without turning a hair—or the phylogenetic
history (how absorbing !) of the kidney—pronephros,
mesonephros and metanephros and all the ducts ! . . .
All this, over now and wasted.   My hardly-won knowledge

[1] See entry for November 27, 1915.

wrenched away is never brought into use—it lies piled up in my brain rotting.   I could have become a first-rate comparative anatomist.

December 3.

Cold better.   So back at work—gauging ale at Dunfermline as R—— puts it.

December 9.

In the evening found it quite impossible to stay in the house any longer: some vague fear drove me out.   I was alarmed to be alone or to be still.   It is my cough, I think.

Had two glasses of port at the Kensington Hotel, conversed with the barmaid, and then came home.

December 10.

' Don't be an old fossil,' she said to me to-night, irrelevantly.

' *A propos* of what ?' I inquired.

' Mother, here's W—— proposing to E——!   Do come,' cried ——, with intent to confuse.   I laughed heartlessly.

Dear, dear, where will it all end ?   It's a sad business when you fall in love with a girl you don't like.

December 26.

Spent a romping day at the Flat.   Kissed her sister twice under the mistletoe, and in the evening went to a cinema.   After supper made a mock heroic speech and left hilarious.

1914

February 4.

. . . Finally and in conclusion I have fallen ill again, have again resumed my periodical visits to the Doctor, and am swallowing his rat-poison in a blind faith as aforetime.   In fact, I am in London, leading the same solitary life, seeing no one, talking to no one, and daily struggling with this demon of ill-health.   Can no one exorcise him? The sight of *both* my eyes is affected now.   Blindness ?

B—— continues whoring, drinking, sneering.   R—— as

usual, devoid of emotion, cold, passionless, Shavian, and
self-absorbed, still titillates his mind with etching, sociology,
music, etc., and I have at last ceased to bore him with
what he probably calls the febrile utterances of an over-
wrought mind.

Such is my world! Oh! I forgot—on the floor below
me is a corpse—that of an old gentleman who passed
away suddenly in the night. In the small hours, the landlady went for the Doctor over the way, but he refused to
come, saying the old man was too aged. So the poor
gentleman died alone—in this rat hole of a place.

February 7.

Intending to buy my usual 3d. packet of Goldflakes,
entered a tobacconist's in Piccadilly, but once inside
surprised to find myself in a classy west-end establishment,
which frightened my flabby nature into buying De Reszke's
instead. I hadn't the courage to face the aristocrat behind
the counter with a request for Goldflakes—probably not
stocked. What would he think of me? Besides, I shrank
from letting him see I was not perfectly well-to-do.

February 14.

I wonder what this year has in store for me? The
first twenty-four years of my life have hunted me up and
down the keyboard—I have been right to the top and
also to the bottom—very happy and very miserable. Yet
I prefer the life that is a hunt and an adventure. I don't
really mind being chased like this. I almost thrive on the
excitement. If I knew always where to look with any
degree of certainty for my next day's life I should yawn!
'What if to-day be sweet,' I say, and never look ahead.
To me, next week is next century.

The danger and uncertainty of my life make me cherish
and hug closely to my heart various little projects that
otherwise would seem unworthy. I work at them quickly,
frantically, sometimes, afraid to whisper to a living soul
what expectations I dare to harbour in my heart. What
if *now* the end be near? Not a word! Let me go onward.

February 16.

To-day I have reviewed the situation carefully, exhaustively. I have peered into every aspect of my life and achievements and everything I have seen nauseates me. I can find no ray of comfort in anything I have done or in anything I might do. My life seems to have been a wilderness of futile endeavour. I started wrong from the very beginning. At the moment of my birth I was coming into the world in the wrong place and under wrong conditions. Why seek to overcome such colossal initial disadvantages? In this mood I found fault with my parentage, my inheritance, all my mental and physical disabilities. . . .

This must be a form of incipient insanity. Even as a boy, I can remember being preternaturally absorbed in myself and preternaturally discontented. I was accustomed to exhaust my mind by the most harassing cross-examinations—no Counsel at the Bar ever treated a witness more mercilessly. After a day of this sort of thing, when silently and morbidly in every spare moment, at meals, in school, or on a walk, I would incessantly ply the questions, ' What is the ultimate value of your work, *cui bono* ?" etc. I went to bed in the evening with a feeling of hopelessness and dissatisfaction—haggard with considerations and reconsiderations of my outlook, my talent, my character, my future. In bed, I tossed from side to side, mentally exhausted with my efforts to obtain some satisfying conclusion—always hopeful, determined to the last to be able to square up my little affairs before going to sleep. But out of this mazy, vertiginous mass of thinking no satisfaction ever came. *Now*, I thought— or the *next moment*—or as soon as I review and revise myself in this or in that aspect, I shall be content. And so I went on, tearing down and reforming, revising and reviewing, till finally from sheer exhaustion and very unhappy I fell asleep.

Next morning I was all right.

February 20.

Am feeling very unwell. My ill-health, my isolation, baulked ambitions, and daily breadwinning all conspire to bring me down. The idea of a pistol and the end of it grows on me day by day.

February 21.

After four days of the most profound depression of spirits, bitterness, self-distrust, despair, I emerged from the cloud to-day quite suddenly (probably the arsenic and strychnine begins to take effect) and walked up Exhibition Road with the intention of visiting the Science Museum Library so as to refer to Schäfer's *Essentials of Histology* (I have to watch myself carefully so that I may act *at once* as soon as the balance of mind is restored). In the lobby was a woman screaming as if in pain, with a passer-by at her side saying sternly, ' What is the matter with you ?' as if she were making herself ridiculous by suffering pain in public.

I passed by quickly, pretending not to notice lest—after all—I should be done out of my *Essentials of Histology*. Even in the Library I very nearly let the opportunity slide by picking up a book on squaring the circle, the preface and introduction of which I was forced to read.

March 4.

The Entomological Society

There were a great many Scarabees present who exhibited to one another poor little pinned insects in collecting-boxes. . . . It was really a one-man show, Prof. Poulton, a man of very considerable scientific attainments, being present, and shouting with a raucous voice in a way that must have scared some of the timid, unassuming collectors of our country's butterflies and moths. Like a great powerful sheep-dog, he got up and barked, ' Mendelian characters,' or ' Germ plasm,' what time the obedient flock ran together and bleated a pitiful applause. I suppose, having frequently heard these and similar phrases fall from the lips of the great man at these reunions, they have come to regard them as symbols of a ritual which they think it pious to accept without any question. So every time the Professor says, ' Allelomorph,' or some such phrase, they cross themselves and never venture to ask him what the hell it is all about.

March 7.   •
A Scots Fir

Have been feeling very ' down ' of late, but yesterday I saw a fine Scots Fir by the roadside—tall, erect, as straight as a Parthenon pillar. The sight of it restored my courage. It had a tonic effect. Quite unconsciously I pulled my shoulders back and walked ahead with renewed vows never to flinch again. It is a noble tree. It has strength as a giant, and a giant's height, and yet kindly withal, the branches drooping down graciously towards you—like a kind giant extending its hands to a child.

March 22.
A Stagnant Day

Went to bed late last night so I slept on soundly till 9 a.m. Went down to the bath-room, but found the door was shut, so went back to my bedroom again, lay down and dosed a while, thinking of nothing in particular. Went down again—door still locked—swore—returned once more to my room and reclined on the bed, with door open, so that I could hear as soon as the bath-room door opened. . . . Rang the bell, and Miss —— brought up a jug of hot water to shave with, and a tumbler of hot water to drink (for my dyspepsia). She, on being interrogated, said there was some one in the bath-room. I said I wanted a bath too, so as she passed on her way down she shouted, ' Hurry up, Mr Barbellion wants a bath as well.' Her footsteps then died away as she descended lower into the basement, where the family lives, sleeps, and cooks our food.

At length, hearing the door open, I ejaculated, ' the

Lord be praised,' rushed down, entered the bath-room and secured it from further intruders. I observed that Miss —— senior had been bathing her members, and that the bath, tho' empty, was covered inside with patches of soap—unutterably black! Oh! Miss —— !

Dressed leisurely and breakfasted. When the table was cleared wrote a portion of my essay on *Spallanzani*. . . . Then, being giddy and tired,•rang for dinner. Miss —— laid the table. She looked very clean. I said, ' Good-morning,' and she suitably replied, and I went on reading, the *Winning Post*. Felt too slack to be amiable. Next time she came in, I said as pleasantly as I could, ' Is it all ready ?' and being informed proceeded to eat forthwith.

In the afternoon, took a 'bus to Richmond. No room outside, so had to go inside—curse—and sit opposite a row—curse again—of fat, ugly, elderly women, all off to visit their married daughters, the usual Sunday jaunt. At Hammersmith got on the outside, and at Turnham Green was caught in a hail storm. Very cold all of a sudden, so got off and took shelter in the doorway of a shop, which was of course closed, the day being Sunday. Rain, wind, and hail continued for some while, as I gazed at the wet, almost empty street, thinking, re-thinking and thinking over again the same thought, viz., that the 'bus ride along this route was exceptionally cheap—probably because of competition with the trams.

The next 'bus took me to Richmond. Two young girls sat in front, and kept looking back to know if I was ' game.' I looked *through* them. Walked in the Park just conscious of the singing of Larks and the chatter of Jays, but harassed mentally by the question, ' To whom shall I send my essay, when finished ?' To shelter from the rain sat under an oak where four youths joined me and said, ' Worse luck,' and ' Not half,' and smoked cigarettes. They gossiped and giggled like girls, put their arms around each other's necks. At the dinner last night, they said, they had Duck and Tomato Soup and Beeswax (' Beesley, you know, the chap that goes about with Smith a lot ') wore a fancy waistcoat with a dinner

jacket. When I got up to move on, they became con-
vulsed with laughter. I scowled.

Had tea in the Pagoda tea-rooms, dry toast and brown
bread and butter. Two young men opposite me were
quietly playing the fool.

' Hold my hand,' one said audibly enough for two lovers
to hear, comfortably settled up in a corner. Even at a
side view I could see them kissing each other in between
mouthfuls of bread and butter and jam.

On rising to go, one of the two hilarious youths removed
my cap and playfully placed it on top of the bowler which
his friend was wearing.

' My cap, I think,' I said sharply, and the young man
apologised with a splutter. I glared like a kill-joy of
sixty.

On the 'bus, coming home, thro' streets full of motor
traffic and all available space plastered with advertisements that screamed at you, I espied in front three pretty
girls, who gave me the ' Glad Eye.' One had a deep,
musical voice, and kept on using it, one of the others a
pretty ankle and kept on showing it.

At Kew, two Italians came aboard, one of whom went
out of his way to sit among the girls. He sat level with
them, and kept turning his head around, giving them a
sweeping glance as he did so, to shout remarks in Italian
to his friend behind. He thought the girls were prostitutes,
I think, and he may have been right. I was on the seat
behind this man and for want of anything better to do,
studied his face minutely. In short, it was fat, round, and
greasy. He wore black moustachios with curly ends, his
eyes were dark, shining, bulgy, and around his neck was
wrapped a scarf inside a dirty linen collar, as if he had
a sore throat. I sat behind him and hated him steadily,
perseveringly.

At Hammersmith the three girls got off, and the bulgy-
eyed Italian watched them go with lascivious eyes, looking
over the rail and down at them on the pavement—still
interested. I looked down too. They crossed the road
in front of us and disappeared.

Came home and here I am writing this. This is the content of to-day's consciousness. This is about all I have thought, said, or done, or felt. A stagnant day!

March 26.

Home with a bad influenza cold. In a deplorable condition. The best I could do was to sit by the fire and read newspapers one by one from the first page to the last till the reading became mechanical. I found myself reading an account of the Lincoln Handicap and a column article on Kleptomania, while advertisements of new books were devoured with relish as delicacies. My mind became a morass of current Divorce Court News, Society Gossip— 'if Sir A. goes Romeward, if Miss B. sings true'—and advertisements. I went on reading because I was afraid to be alone with myself.

B—— arrived at tea and after saying he felt very 'pin-eyed' swallowed a glass of Bols gin—the Gin of Antony Bols—and recovered sufficiently to inform me delightedly that he had just won £50. He told me all the story; meanwhile, I, tired of wiping and blowing my nose, sat in the dirty armchair hunched up with elbows on knees and let it drip on to the dirty carpet. B——, of course noticed nothing, which was fortunate.

Some kinds of damned fool would have been kindly and sympathetic. I must say I like old B——. I like him for his simpleness and utter absence of self-conscious-ness, which make him as charming as a child. Moreover, he often makes me a present of invaluable turf tips. Of course, he is a liar, but his lies are harmless and on his mouth like milk on an infant's. My own lies are much more dangerous. And when you are ill, to be treated as tho' you were well is good for hypochondriacs.

April 15.

H——'s wedding. Five minutes before time, I am told I made a dramatic entry into the church clad in an audaci-ously light pair of Cashmere trousers, lemon-coloured gloves, with top hat and cane. The latter upset the respectability frightfully—it is not *comme il faut*.

April 16.

. . . If I am to admit the facts they are that I eagerly anticipate love, look everywhere for it, long for it, am unhappy without it. She fascinates me—admitted. I could, if I would, surrender myself. Her affection makes me long to do it. I am sick of living by myself. I am frightened of myself. My life is miserable alone, and sometimes desperately miserable when I long for a little sympathy to be close at hand.

I have often tried to persuade R—— to share a flat with me, because I don't really wish to marry. I struggle against the idea, I am egotist enough to wish to shirk the responsibilities.

But then I am a ridiculously romantic creature with a wonderful ideal of a woman I shall never meet or if I do she won't want me—' that (wholly) impossible She.' R—— in a flat with me would partly solve my difficulties. I don't love her enough for marriage. Mine must be a grand passion, a *bouleversement*—for I am capable of it.

April 17.

A Humble Confession

The Hon. ——, son and heir of Lord ——, to-day invited me to lunch with him in —— Square. He is a handsome youth of twenty-five, with fair hair and blue eyes . . . and O ! such an aristocrat. Good Lord.

But to continue: the receipt of so unexpected an invitation from so glorious a young gentleman at first gave me palpitation of the heart. I was so surprised that I scarcely had enough presence of mind to listen to the rest of his remarks and later, it was only with the greatest difficulty that I could recall the place where we arranged to meet. His remarks, too, are not easy to follow, as he talks in a stenographic, Alfred-Jingle-like manner, jerking out disjected members of sentences, and leaving you to make the best of them or else to Hell with you—by the Lord, I speak English, don't I? If I said, 'I beg your pardon,' he jerked again, and left me often equally unenlightened.

On arriving at his home, the first thing he did was to shout down the stairs to the basement: 'Elsie, Elsie,' while I gazed with awe at a parcel on the hall table addressed to 'Lord ——.' Before lunch we sat in his little room and talked about ——, but I was still quite unable to regain my self-composure. I couldn't for the life of me forget that here was I lunching with Lord ——'s son, on equal terms, with mutual interests, that his sisters perhaps would come in directly or even the noble Lord himself. I felt like a scared hare. How should I address a peer of the realm? I kept trying to remember and every now and then for some unaccountable reason my mind travelled into ——shire and I saw Auntie C—— serving out tea and sugar over the counter of the baker's shop in the little village. I luxuriated in the contrast, tho' I am not at all inclined to be a snob.

He next offered me a cigarette, which I took and lit. It was a Turkish cigarette with one end plugged up with cotton-wool—to absorb the nicotine—a thing I've never seen before. I was so flurried at the time that I did not notice this and lit the wrong end. With perfect ease and self-possession, the Honourable One pointed out my error to me and told me to throw the cigarette away and have another.

By this time I had completely lost my nerve. My pride, chagrin, excessive self-consciousness were entangling all my movements in the meshes of a net. Failing to tumble to the situation, I inquired, 'Why the *wrong* end? Is there a right and a wrong end?' Lord ——'s son and heir pointed out the cotton-wool end, now blackened by my match.

'That didn't burn very well, did it?'

I was bound to confess that it did not, and threw the smoke away under the impression that these wonderful cigarettes with right and wrong ends must be some special brand sold only to aristocrats, and at a great price, and

possessing some secret virtue. Once again, handsome
Mr —— drew out his silver cigarette-case, selected a
second cigarette for me, and held it towards me between
his long delicate fingers, at the same time pointing out
the plug at one end and making a few staccato remarks
which I could not catch.

I was still too scared to be in full possession of my
faculties, and he apparently was too tired to be explicit
to a member of the bourgeoisie, stumbling about his
drawing-room. The cotton-wool plug only suggested to
me some sort of a plot on the part of a dissolute scion of
a noble house to lure me into one of his bad habits, such
as smoking opium or taking veronal. I again prepared to
light the cigarette at the wrong end.

' Try the other end,' repeated the young man, smiling
blandly. I blushed, and immediately recovered my
balance, and even related my knowledge of pipes fitted
to carry similar plugs. . . .

During lunch (at which we sat alone) after sundry visits
to the top of the stairs to shout down to the kitchen, he
announced that he thought it wasn't last night's affair
after all which was annoying the Cook (he got home late
without a latch-key)—it was because he called her ' Cook '
instead of Mrs Austin. He smiled serenely and decided
to indulge Mrs A., his indulgent attitude betraying an
objectionable satisfaction with the security of his own
unassailable social status. There was a trace of gratifica-
tion at the little compliment secreted in the Cook's annoyance. She wanted Mr Charles to call her Mrs Austin,
forsooth. Very well! and he smiled down on the little
weakness *de haute en bas.*

·   ·   ·   ·   ·   ·   ·

I enjoyed this little experience. Turning it over in my
mind (as the housemaid says when she decides to stay on)
I have come to the conclusion that the social parvenu
is not such a vulgar fellow after all. He may be a bore—
particularly if he sits with his finger tips apposed over a
spherical paunch, festooned with a gold chain, and keeps

on relating *in extenso* how once he gummed labels on
blacking bottles. Often enough he is a smug fellow, yet,
truth to tell, we all feel a little interested in him. He is
a traveller from an antique land, and we sometimes like to
listen to his tales of adventure and all he has come through.
He has traversed large territories of human experience, he
has met strange folk and lodged in strange caravanserai.
Similarly with the man who has come down in the world
—the fool, the drunkard, the embezzler—he may bore us
with his maudlin sympathy with himself yet his stories
hold us. It must be a fine experience within the limits
of a single life to traverse the whole keyboard of our social
status, whether up or down. I should like to be a peer
who grinds a barrel organ or (better still) a one-time organ-
grinder who now lives in Park Lane. It must be very
dull to remain stationary—once a peer always a peer.

April 20.

Miss —— heard me sigh to-day and asked what it might
mean. 'Only the sparks flying upward,' I answered
lugubriously.

A blackguard is often unconscious of a good deal of his
wickedness. Charge him with wickedness and he will
deny it quite honestly—honest then, perhaps, for the first
time in his life.

An Entomologist is a large hairy man with eyebrows
like antennæ.

Chronic constipation has gained for me an unrivalled
knowledge of all laxatives, aperients, purgatives and
cathartic compounds. At present I arrange two gun-
powder plots a week. It's abominable. Best literature
for the latrine: picture puzzles.

April 23.

A Foolish Bird

With a menacing politeness, B—— to-day inquired of
a fat curate who was occupying more than his fair share
of a seat on top of a 'bus,—

'Are you going to get up or stay where ye are, sir ?'

The foolish bird was sitting nearly on top of B——, mistaking a bomb for an egg.

' I beg your pardon,' replied the fat curate.

B—— repeated his inquiry with more emphasis in the hideous Scotch brogue.

' I suppose I shall stay here till I get down presently.'

' I don't think you will,' said B——.

' What do you mean ?' asked the fat one in falsetto indignation.

' This,' B—— grunted, and shunted sideways so that the poor fellow almost slid on to the floor.

. . . .

A posse of police walking along in single file always makes me laugh. A single constable is a Policeman, but several in single file are ' Coppers.' I imagine every one laughs at them and I have a shrewd suspicion it is one of W. S. Gilbert's legacies—the *Pirates of Penzance* having become part of the national Consciousness.

On Lighting Chloe's Cigarette

R—— remarked to-day that he intended writing a lyric on lighting Chloe's cigarette.

' Ah !' I said at once appreciative, ' now tell me, do you balance your hand—by gently (ever so gently) resting the extreme tip of your little finger upon her chin, and ' (I was warming up) ' do you hold the match vertically or horizontally, and do you light it in the dark or in the light ? If you have finesse, you won't need to be told that the thing is to get a steady flame and the maximum of illumination upon her face to last over a period for as long as possible.'

' Chloe,' replied R——, ' is wearing now a charming blouse with a charming V-shaped opening in front. Her Aunt asked my Mother last night tentatively, " How do you like Chloe's blouse ? Is it too low ?" My Mother scrutinised the dear little furry, lop-eared thing and answered doubtfully, " No, Maria, I don't think so." '

' How ridiculous ! Why, the V is a positive signpost !

My dear fellow,' I said to R——, ' I should refuse to be
bluffed by those old women.   Tell them you *know*.'

.   .   .   .

Carlyle called Lamb a despicable abortion.   What a
crime !

May 2.

Developed a savage fit.   Up to a certain point, perhaps,
but beyond that anxiety changes into recklessness—you
simply don't care.   The aperients are causing dyspepsia
and intermittent action of the heart, which frightens me.
After a terrifying week, during which at crises I have felt
like dropping suddenly in the street, in the gardens, anywhere, from syncope, I rebelled against this humiliating
fear.   I pulled my shoulders back and walked briskly
ahead along the street with a dropped beat every two or
three steps.   I laughed bitterly at it and felt it could stop
or go on—I was at last indifferent.   In a photographer's
shop was the picture of a very beautiful woman and I
stopped to look at her.   I glowered in thro' the glass
angrily and reflected how she was gazing out with that
same expression even at the butcher's boy or the lamp-
lighter.   It embittered me to think of having to leave
her to some other man.   To me she represented all the
joy of life which at any moment I might have had to quit
for ever.   Such impotence enraged me and I walked off
up the street with a whirling heart and the thought, ' I
shall drop, I suppose, when I get up as far as that.'   Yet
don't think I was alarmed.   Oh ! no.   The iron had
entered me, and I went on with cynical indifference waiting
to be struck down.

   . . . She is a very great deal to me.   Perhaps I love
her very much after all.

May 3.

Bad heart attack all day.   Intermittency is very refined
torture to one who wants to live very badly.   Your pump
goes a ' dot and carry one,' or say ' misses a stitch,' what

time you breathe deep, begin to shake your friend's hand
and make a farewell speech.   Then it goes on again and
you order another pint of beer.

It is a fractious animal within the cage of my thorax,
and I never know when it is going to escape and make
off with my precious life between its teeth.   I humour
and coax and soothe it, but, God wot, I haven't much
confidence in the little beast.   My thorax it appears is an
intolerable kennel.

May 10.

In a very cheerful mood.   Pleased with myself and
everybody till a seagull soared overhead in Kensington
Gardens and aroused my vast capacities for envy—I wish
I could fly.

May 24.

In L—— with my brother, A——.   The great man is
in great form and very happy in his love for N——.   He
is a most delightful creature and I love him more than
any one else in the wide world.   There is an almost
feminine tenderness in my love.

We spent a delightful day, talking and arguing and
insulting one another. . . .   At these séances we take
delight in anæsthetising our hearts for the purposes of
argument, and a third person would be bound to suppose
we were in the throes of a bitter quarrel.   We pile up
one vindictive remark on another, ingeniously seeking out
—and with malice—weak points in each other's armour,
which previous exchange of confidences makes it easy to
find.   Neither of us hesitates to make use of such private
confessions, yet our love is so strong that we can afford
to take any liberty.   There is, in fact, a fearful joy in
testing the strength of our affection by searching for
cutting rejoinders—to see the effect.   We rig up one
another's cherished ideals like Aunt Sallies and then knock
them down, we wax sarcastic, satirical, contemptuous in
turn, we wave our hands animatedly (hand-waving is a

great trick with both of us), get flushed, point with our
fingers and thump the table to clinch some bit of repartee.
Yet it's all smoke. Our love is unassailable—it's like the
law of gravitation, you cannot dispute it, it underlies our
existence, it is the air we breathe.

N—— is charming, and thought we were quarrelling,
and therefore intervened on his side !

May 31.

R—— outlined an impression he had in Naples one
day during a sirocco of the imminence of his own death.
It was evidently an isolated experience and bored me a
little as I could have said a lot myself about that. When
he finished I drew from my pocket an envelope with my
name and three addresses scribbled on it to help the
police in case of syncope as I explained. I have carried
this with me for several years and at one time a flask of
brandy.

June 3.

Went to see the Irish Players in *The Playboy*. Sitting
in front of me was a charming little Irish girl accompanied
by a male clod with red-rimmed eyes like a Bull-terrier's,
a sandy, bristly moustache like a housemaid's broom, and
a face like a gluteal mass, and a horrid voice that crepitated
rather than spoke.

She was dark, with shining blue eyes, and a delightful
little nose of the utmost import to every male who should
gaze upon her. Between the acts, the clod hearkened to
her vivacious conversation—like an enchanted bullock.
Her vivacity was such that the tip of her nose moved up
and down for emphasis and by the end of the Third Act
I was captured entirely. Lucky dog, that clod !

After the play this little Irish maiden caught my eye
and it became a physical impossibility for me to check a
smile—and oh ! Heavens !—she gave me a smile in return.
Precisely five seconds later, she looked again to see if I
was still smiling—1 was—and we then smiled broadly and
openly on one another—her smile being the timorous

ingénue's not the glad eye of a *femme de joie*.   Later, on
the railway platform whither I followed her, I caught her
eye again (was ever so lucky a fellow ?), and we got into
the same carriage.   But so did the clod—ah ! dear, was
ever so unlucky a fellow ?   Forced to occupy a seat some
way off, but she caught me trying to see her thro' a midnight forest of opera hats, lace ruffles, projecting ears and
fat noses.

Curse !   Left her at High Street Station and probably
will never see her again.   This is a second great opportunity.   The first was the girl on Lundy Island.   These
two women I shall always regret.   There must be so many
delightful and interesting persons in London if only I could
get at them.

June 4.

Rushed off to tell R—— about my little Irish girl.   Her
face has been ' shadowing ' me all day.

June 6.

A violent argument with R—— *re* marriage.   He says
Love means appropriation, and is taking the most elaborate
precautions to forfend passion—just as if it were a militant
suffragette.   Every woman he meets he first puts into
a long quarantine, lest perchance she carries the germ of
the infectious disease.   He quotes Hippolytus and talks
like a mediæval ascetic.   Himself, I imagine, he regards
as a valuable but brittle piece of Dresden china which must
be saved from rough handling and left unmolested to
pursue its high and dusty destiny—an old crock as I
warned him.   By refusing to plunge into life he will live
long and be a well preserved man, but scarcely a living
man—a mummy rather.   I told him so amid much
laughter.

' You're a reactionary,' says he.

' Yes, but why should a reactionary be a naughty
boy ?'

June 7.

My ironical fate lured me this evening into another discussion on marriage in which I had to take up a position exactly opposite to the one I defended yesterday against R——. In fact, I actually subverted to my own pressing requirements some of R——'s own arguments! The argument, of course, was with Her.

Marriage, I urged, was an economic trap for guileless young men, and for my part (to give myself some necessary stiffening) I did not intend to enter upon any such hazardous course, even if I had the chance. Miss —— said I was a funk—to me who the day before had been hammering into R—— my principle of ' Plunge and damn the consequences.' I was informed I was an old woman afraid to go out without an umbrella, an old tabby cat afraid to leave the kitchen fire, etc., etc.

' Yes, I *am* afraid to go out without an umbrella,' I argued formally, ' when it's raining cats and dogs. As long as I am dry, I shall keep dry. As soon as I find myself caught in the rain or victimised by a passion, I shan't be afraid of falling in love or getting wet. It would be a misadventure, but I am not going in search of one.'

All the same the discussion was very galling, for I was acting a part.

. . . The truth is I have philandered abominably with her. I know it. And now I am jibbing at the idea of marriage. . . . I am such an egotist, I want, I believe, a Princess of the Blood Royal.

June 9.

Some days ago sent a personal advertisement to the newspaper to try to find my little Irish girl who lives at Notting Hill Gate. To-day they return me the money and advert., no doubt mistaking me for a White Slave trafficker. And by this time, I'm thinking, my little Irish girl can go to blazes. Shall spend the P.O. on sweets or monkey nuts.

June 10.

Lupus

It is raining heavily. I have just finished dinner. In the street an itinerant musician is singing dolefully ' O Rest in the Lord.' In my dirty little sitting room I begin to feel very restless, so put on my hat and cloak and walk down towards the Station for a paper to read. It is all very dark and dismal, and I gaze with hungry eyes in thro' some of the windows disclosing happy comfortable interiors. At intervals thunder growls and lightning brightens up the deserted dirtiness of the Station Waiting Room. A few bits of desolate paper lie about on the floor, and up in one corner on a form a crossing-sweeper, motionless and abject, driven in from his pitch by the rain. His hands are deep in his trousers' pockets, and the poor devil lies with legs sprawling out and eyes closed: over the lower part of his face he wears a black mask to hide the ravages of lupus. . . . He seemed the last man on earth—after every one else had died of the plague. Not a soul in the station. Not a train. And this is June !

June 15.

Measuring Lice

Spent the day measuring the legs and antennæ of lice to two places of decimals !

To the lay mind how fantastic this must seem   Indeed, I hope it is fantastic. I do not mind being thought odd. It seems almost fitting that an incurable dilettante like myself should earn his livelihood by measuring the legs of lice. I like to believe that such a bizarre manner of life suits my incurable frivolousness.

I am a Magpie in a Bagdad bazaar, hopping about, useless, inquisitive, fascinated by a lot of astonishing things: *e.g.*, a book on the quadrature of the circle, the *gubbertushed fustilugs* passage in Burton's *Anatomy of Melancholy*, names like Mr Portwine or Mr Hogsflesh, Tweezer's Alley or Pickle Herring Street, the excellent,

conceitful sonnets of Henry Constable or Petticoat Lane
on a Sunday morning.

Colossal things such as Art, Science, etc., frighten me.
I am afraid I should develop a thirst that would make
me wish to drink the sea dry. My mind is a disordered
miscellany. The world is too distracting. I cannot apply
myself for long. London bewilders me. At times it is a
phantasmagoria, an opium dream out of De Quincey.

June 17.

Prof. Geo. Saintsbury's book on Elizabethan literature
amuses me. *George,* there can be no doubt, is a very
refined, cultivated fellow. I bet he don't eat periwinkles
with a pin or bite his nails—and you should hear him
refer to folk who can't read Homer in the original or who
haven't been to Oxford—to Merton above all. He also
says *non so che* for *je ne sais quoi.*

June 26.

. . . I placed the volume on the mantelpiece as if it
were a bottle of physic straight from my Dispensary, and
I began to expostulate and expound, as if she were a sick
person and I the doctor. . . . She seemed a little nettled
at my proselytising demeanour and gave herself out to be
very preoccupied—or at any rate quite uninterested in
my physic. I read the book last night at one sitting and
was boiling over with it.

' I fear I have come at an inconvenient time,' I said,
with a sardonic smile and strummed on the piano. . . .
' I must really be off. Please read it (which sounded like
" three times a day after meals ") and tell me how you
like it. (Facetiously) Of course don't give up your
present manual for it, that would be foolish and unnecessary.' . . . I rambled on—disposed to be very
playful.

At last calmly and horribly, in a thoughtful voice she
answered,—

' I think you are very rude: you play the piano after I

asked you to stop and walk about just as if it were your own home.'

I remained outwardly calm but inwardly was very surprised and full of tremors.   I said after a pause,—

' Very well, if you think so. . . .   Good-bye.'

No answer; and I was too proud to apologise.

' Good-bye,' I repeated.

She went on reading her novel in silence while I got as far as the door—very upset.

' *Au revoir.*'

No answer.

' Oh,' said I, and went out of the room leaving my lady for good and all and I'm not sorry.

In the passage met Miss ——.   ' What ?' she said, ' going already ?'

' Farewell,' I said sepulchrally.   ' A very tragic farewell,' which left her wondering.

June 29.

At the Albert Hall

Went with R—— to the Albert Hall to the *Empress of Ireland* Memorial Concert with massed bands.   We heard the Symphonie Pathétique, Chopin's Funeral March, Trauermarsch from Götterdammerung, the Ride of the Valkyries and a solemn melody from Bach.

This afternoon I regard as a mountain peak in my existence.   For two solid hours I sat like an Eagle on a rock gazing into infinity—a very fine sensation for a London Sparrow. . . .

I have an idea that if it were possible to assemble the sick and suffering day by day in the Albert Hall and keep the Orchestra going all the time, then the constant exposure of sick parts to such heavenly air vibrations would ultimately restore to them the lost rhythm of health. Surely, even a single exposure to—say Beethoven's Fifth Symphony—must result in some permanent reconstitution of ourselves body and soul.   No one can be quite the same after a Beethoven Symphony has streamed thro' him.

If one could *develop* a human soul like a negative the effect
I should say could be seen. . . . I'll tell you what I
wish they'd do—seriously: divide up the arena into a
series of cubicles where, unobserved and in perfect privacy,
a man could execute all the various movements of his
body and limbs which the music prompts. It would be
such a delicious self-indulgence and it's torture to be
jammed into a seat where you can't even tap one foot or
wave an arm.

The concert restored my moral health. I came away
in love with people I was hating before and full of compassion for others I usually contemn. A feeling of im-
measurable well being—a jolly bonhomie enveloped me
like incandescent light. At the close when we stood up to
sing the National Anthem we all felt a genuine spirit of
camaraderie. Just as when Kings die, we were silent
musing upon the common fate, and when the time came
to separate we were loath to go our several ways, for we
were comrades who together had come thro' a great
experience. For my part I wanted to shake hands all
round—happy travellers, now alas! at the journey's end
and never perhaps to meet again—never.

.   .   .   .

R—— and I walked up thro' Kensington Gardens like
two young Gods!

'I even like that bloody thing,' I said, pointing to the
Albert Memorial.

We pointed out pretty girls to one another, watched the
children play ring-a-ring-a-roses on the grass. We laughed
exultingly at the thought of our dismal colleagues . . .
tho' I said (as before!) I loved 'em all—God bless 'em—
even old ——. R—— said it was nothing short of insolence on their part to have neglected the opportunity of
coming to the Concert.

Later on, an old gaffer up from the country stopped us
to ask the way to Rotten Row—I overwhelmed him with
directions and happy descriptive details. I felt like
walking with him and showing him what a wonderful
place the world is.

After separating from R—— very reluctantly—it was horrible to be left alone in such high spirits, walked up towards the Round Pond, and caught myself avoiding the shadows of the trees—so as to be every moment out in the blazing sun. I scoffed inwardly at the timorousness of pale, anæmic folk whom I passed hiding in the shadows of the elms.

At the Round Pond, came across a Bulldog who was biting out great chunks of water and in luxuriant waste-fulness letting it drool out again from each corner of his mouth. I watched this old fellow greedily (it was very hot), as well pleased with him and his liquid ' chops ' as with anything I saw, unless it were a girl and a man lying full length along the grass and kissing beneath a sunshade. I smiled; she saw me, and smiled, too, in return, and then fell to kissing again.

June 30.

Dinosaurs

There are books which are Dinosaurs—Sir Walter Ralegh's *History of the World*, Gibbon's *Decline and Fall of the Roman Empire*. There are men who are Dinosaurs—Balzac completing his Human Comedy, Napoleon, Roosevelt. I like them all. I like express trains and motor lorries. I enjoy watching an iron girder swinging in the air or great cubes of ice caught up between iron pincers. I must always stop and watch these things. I like everything that is swift or immense: London, lightning, Popocatapetl. I enjoy the smell of tar, of coal, of fried fish, or a brass band playing a Liszt Rhapsody. And why should those foolish Mænads shout Women's Rights just because they burn down a church ? All bonfires are delectable. Civilisation and top hats bore me. My own life is like a tame rabbit's. If only I had a long tail to lash it in feline rage ! I would return to Nature—I could almost return to Chaos. There are times when I feel so dour I would wreck the universe if I could.[1]

[1] ' I could eat all the elephants of Hindustan and pick my teeth with the Spire of Strassburg Cathedral.'

(1917: I think after three years of Armageddon I feel quite ready to go back to top hats and civilisation.)

July 8.

Sunset in Kensington Gardens

The instinct for worship occurs rhythmically—at morning and evening. This is natural, for twice a day at sunrise and sunset—however work-sodden we may be, however hypnotised by daily routine—our natural impulse is (provided we are awake) to look to the horizon at the sun and stand a moment with mute lips. During the course of the day or night, we are too occupied or asleep—but sunrise is the great hour of the departure and sunset is the arrival at the end. Everything puts on a mysterious appearance—to-night the tops of the elms seemed supernaturally high and, pushing up into the sky, had secret communion with the clouds; the clouds seemed waiting for a ceremony, a way had been prepared by the tapissier, a moment of suspense while one cloud stretched to another like courtiers in whispered conversation; a rumour of the approach; then slowly the news came thro' that the sun had arrived for immediate departure.

July 14.

Have finished my essay. But am written out—obviously. To-night I struggled with another, and spent two hours sucking the end of my pen. But after painfully mountainous parturition, all I brought forth were the two ridiculous mice of one meretricious trope and one grammatical solecism. I can sometimes sit before a sheet of paper, pen in hand, unable to produce a word.

July 19.

For a walk with R—— in the country, calling for tea at his Uncle's house at ——. Played clock golf and made the acquaintance of Miss ——, a tall, statuesque lady, with golden hair, as graceful as an antelope and very comely, her two dear little feet clad in white shoes peeping out (as R—— said) like two white mice one after the other as she moved across the lawn.

Coming home I said to R—— histrionically, ' Some golden-haired little boy will some day rest his head upon her bosom, beautiful in line and depth, all unconscious of his luck or of his part in a beautiful picture—would that I were the father to make that group a *fait accompli*.' R——, with meticulous accuracy, always refers to her as ' that elegant virgin.'

July 25.

While sketching under Hammersmith Bridge yesterday, R—— heard a whistle, and, looking up, saw a charming ' young thing ' leaning over the Bridge parapet smiling like the blessed Damozel out of Heaven.

' Come down,' he cried.

She did, and they discussed pictures while he painted. Later he walked with her to the Broadway, saw her into a 'bus and said ' Good-bye,' without so much as an exchange of names.

' Even if she *were* a whore,' I said, ' it's a pity your curiosity was so sluggish. You should have seen her home, even if you did not go home with her. Young man, you preferred to let go of authentic life at Hammersmith Broadway, so as to return at once to your precious water-colour painting.'

' Perhaps,' replied he enigmatically.

' Whatever you do, if ever you meet her again,' I rejoined, ' don't introduce her to that abominable ——. He is abominably handsome, and I hate him for it. To all his other distinctions he is welcome—parentage, money, success, but I can never forgive him his good looks and the inevitable marriage to some beautiful fair-skinned woman.'

R. (reflectively): ' Up to now, I was inclined to think that envy as a *passion* did not exist.'

' Have you none ?'

' Not much,' he answered, and I believe it.

'Smug wretch, then. All I can say is, I may have
instincts and passions but I am not a pale water-colour
artist. . . . What's the matter with you,' I foamed,
' is that you like pictures. If I showed you a real woman,
you would exclaim contemplatively, " How lovely;" then
putting out one hand to touch her, unsuspectingly, you'd
scream aghast, "Oh ! it's alive, I hear it ticking." "Yes,
my boy," I'd answer severely with a flourish, "*That* is
a woman's heart." '

R—— exploded with laughter and then said, 'A truce
to your desire for more life, for actual men and women.
. . . I know this that last night I would not have exchanged
the quiet armchair reading the last chapter of Dostoievsky's
The Possessed for a Balaclava Charge.'

'A matter of temperament, I suppose,' I reflected, in
cold detachment. 'You see, I belong to the raw meat
school. *You* prefer life cooked for you in a book. You
prefer the confectioner's shop to cutting down the wheat
with your own scythe.'

July 26.

The B. M. is a ghastly hole. They will give me none of
the apparatus I require. If you ask the Trustees for a
thousand pounds for the propagation of the Gospel in
foreign parts they say, 'Yes.' If you ask for twenty
pounds for a new microscope they say, 'No, but we'll cut
off your nose with a big pair of scissors.'

July 27.

To a pedantic prosy little old maid who was working in
my room this morning, I exclaimed,—
'I'd sooner make a good dissection than go to a Lord
Mayor's Banquet. Turtle Soup ain't in it.'
She was uninspired, and said, 'Oom,' and went on
pinning insects. Then more brightly, and with great
punctilio in the pronunciation of her words, having cleared
her throat and drawn herself up with great deliberation
to deliver herself of a remark, she volunteered,—

" I whish I had nevah taken up such a brittle grooop as the Stones (Stoneflies).   One dare not loook at a Stone.'

Poor dear little old maid.   This was my turn to say ' Oom.'

' Pretty dismal work,' I added ambiguously.   Then with malice aforethought I whistled a Harry Lauder tune, asked her if she had ever heard Willie Solar sing, ' You made me love you,' and then absent-mindedly and in succession inquired,—

' What's become of all the gold ?'

' What's become of Waring ?'

' What shall I sing when all is sung ?'

To which several categorical interrogations she ventured no reply, but presently in the usual voice,—

' I have placed an Agrionine in this drawer for security and, now I want it, cannot find it.'

' Life is like that,' I said.   ' I never can find my Agrionines !'

August 1.

All Europe is mobilising.

August 2.   •

Will England join in ?

August 12.

We all await the result of a battle between two millions of men.   The tension makes me feel physically sick.

August 21—August 24.

In bed with a fever.   I never visit the flat now, but her mother kindly came over to see me.

September 25.

[Living now in rooms alone.]

I have—since my return from Cornwall—placed all my journals in a specially made cabinet.   R—— came to dinner and after a glass or so of Beaune and a cigarette,

I open my 'coffin'[1] (it is a long box with a brass handle
at each end), and with some show of deliberation select
a volume to read to him, drawing it from its division with
lavish punctiliousness, and inquiring with an oily voice,
'A little of 1912?' as if we were trying wines. R——
grins at the little farce and so encourages me.

September 26.

Doctor's Consulting Rooms—my life has been spent in
them ! Medical specialists—Harley Street men—I have
seen four and all to no purpose. M—— wrote me the
other day,—

'Come along and see me on Tuesday; some day I dare
say we shall find something we can patch.'

He regards me with the most obvious commiseration
and always when I come away after a visit he shakes me
warmly by the hand and says, 'Good-bye, old man, and
good luck.' More luck than the pharmacopœia.

My life has always been a continuous struggle with ill-
health and ambition, and I have mastered neither. I try
to reassure myself that this accursed ill-health will not
affect my career. I keep flogging my will in the hope of
winning thro' in the end. Yet at the back of my mind
there is the great improbability that I shall ever live long
enough to realise myself. For a long time past my hope
has simply been to last long enough to convince others
of what I might have done—had I lived. That will be
something. But even to do that I will not allow that I
have overmuch time. I have never at any time lived
with any sense of security. I have never felt permanently
settled in this life—nothing more than a shadowy *locum
tenens*, a wraith, a festoon of mist likely to disappear any
moment.

At times, when I am vividly conscious of the insecurity
of my tenure here, my desires enter on a mad race to
obtain fulfilment before it is too late . . . and as fulfilment recedes ambition obsesses me the more. I am

[1] See January 2nd, 1915.

daily occupied in calculating with my ill-health: trying to circumvent it, to carry on in spite of all. I conquer each day. Every week is a victory. I am always surprised that my health or will has not collapsed, that, by Jove! I am still working and still living.

One day it looks like appendicitis, another stoppage, another threatened blindness, or I develop a cough and am menaced with consumption. So I go on in a hurricane of bad dreams. I struggle like Laocoon with the serpents—the serpents of nervous depression that press around the heart tighter than I care to admit. I must use every kind of blandishment to convince myself that my life and my work are worth while. Frequently I must smother and kill (and it calls for prompt action) the shrill voice that cries from the tiniest corner of my heart, ' Are you quite sure you are such an important fellow as you imagine ?' Or I fret over the condition of my brain, finding that I forget what I read, I lose in acuteness of my perceptions. My brain is a tumefaction. But I won't give in. I go on trying to recollect what I have forgotten, I harry my brain all day to recall a word or name, I attack other folk importunately. I write things down so as to look them up in reference books—I am always looking up the things I remember I have forgotten. . . .

There is another struggle, too, that often engrosses all my energies. . . . It is a horrible thing that with so large an ambition, so great a love of life, I should nevertheless court disaster like this. Truly Sir Thomas Browne you say, ' Every man is his own Atropos.'

In short, I lead an unfathomably miserable existence in this dark, gray street, in these drab, dirty rooms—miserable in its emptiness of home, love, human society. Now that I never visit the flat, I visit about two houses in London—the Doctor's and R——'s Hotel. I walk along the streets and stare in the windows of private houses, hungry for a little society. It creates in me a gnawing, rancorous discontent to be seeing people everywhere in London—millions of them—and then to realise my own ridiculously circumscribed knowledge of them. I am passionately eager to have acquaintances, to possess at least a few friends. If I die to-morrow, how many persons shall I have talked to? or how many men and women shall I have known? A few maiden aunts and one or two old fossils. I am burning to meet real live men, I have masses of mental stuff I am anxious to unload. But I am ignorant of people as of countries and live in celestial isolation.

This, I fear, reads like a wail of self-commiseration. But I am trying to give myself the pleasure of describing myself at this period truthfully, to make a bid at least for some posthumous sympathy. Therefore it shall be told that I who am capable of passionate love am sexually starved, and endure the pangs of a fiendish solitude in rooms, with an ugly landlady's face when . . . I despair of ever finding a woman to *love*. I never meet women of my own class, and am unprepossessing in appearance and yet I fancy that once my reserve is melted I am not without attractions. 'He grows on you,' a girl said of me once. But I am hypercritical and hyperfastidious. I want too much. . . . I search daily in the streets with a starved and hungry look. What a horrible and powerful and hateful thing this love instinct is! I hate it, hate it, hate it. It will not let me rest. I wish I were a eunuch.

'There's a beautiful young thing,' R——— and I say to one another sardonically, hoping thereby to conceal the canker within.

I could gnash my teeth and weep in anger—baulked, frustrated as I am at almost every turn of life—in my profession, in my literary efforts, and in my love of man and woman kind. I would utter a whole commination service in my present state of mind.

October 7.

To me woman is *the* wonderful fact of existence. If there be any next world and it be as I hope it is, a jolly gossiping place, with people standing around the mantelpiece and discussing their earthly experiences, I shall thump my fist on the table as my friends turn to me on entering and exclaim in a loud voice, ' WOMAN.'

October 11.

Since I grew up I have wept three times. The first time they were tears of exasperation. Dad and I were sitting down side by side after a wordy combat in which he had remained adamant and I was forced both by conscience and argument to give in, to relinquish my dissections, and go off to some inquest on a drowning fatality. The second time was when Mother died, and the third was *to-day*. But I am calm now. To-day they were tears of remorse. . . .

On occasion bald confession in this Journal is sweet for the soul and strengthens it. It gives me a kind of false backbone to communicate my secrets: for I am determined that some day some one shall know. If God really intervenes in our affairs, here is an opportunity. Let Him save me. I challenge Him to save me from perishing in this ditch. . . . It is not often I am cornered into praying but I did this morning, for I feel defeated this day, and almost inarticulate in my misery.

Nietzsche in a newspaper I read to-day: ' For myself I have felt exceptionally blest having Hell's phantoms inside me to thrust at in the dark, internal enemies to dominate till I felt myself an ecstatic victor, wrenching at last good triumphant joys thro' the bars of my own sickness and weakness—joys with which your notions of happiness, poor sleek smug creatures, cannot compare ! You must carry a chaos inside you to give birth to a dancing star.'

But Nietzsche is no consolation to a man who has once been weak enough to be brought to his knees. There I am and there I think I have prayed a little somehow to-day. But it's all in desperation, not in faith. Internal chaos I have, but no dancing star. Dancing stars are the consolation of genius.

October 12.

Am better to-day. My better self is convinced that it is silly and small-minded to think so much about my own puny destiny—especially at times like these when—God love us all—there is a column of casualties each day. The great thing to be thankful for is that I am *alive* and alive *now*, that I was alive *yesterday*, and even may be to-morrow. Surely that is thrilling enough. What, then, have I to complain of ? I'm a lucky dog to be alive at all. My plight is bad, but there are others in a worse one. I'm going to be brave and fight on the side of Nietzsche. Who knows but that one day the dancing star may yet be born !

October 13.

Spent the evening in my lodgings struggling with my will. Too flabby to work, disinclined to read, a dreadful vague unrest possessing me. I couldn't sit still in my chair, so walked around the table continuously like a squirrel in a cage. I wanted to be going out somewhere, talking to some one, to be among human beings.

Many an evening during the past few months, I have got up and gone down the road to look across at the windows of the flat, to see if there were a red light behind the curtains, and, if so, wonder if she were there, and how she was. My pride would never allow me to visit there again on my own initiative. K—— has managed to bring about a rapprochement but I go very seldom. Pride again.

I wanted to do so to-night. I thought I would just go down the road to look up at the windows. That seemed to be some comfort. Why do I wish to do this ? I do not know. From a mere inspection one would say that I am in love. But remember I am also ill. Three times to-night I nearly put on my boots and went down to have a look up ! What ridiculous weakness ! Yet this room can be a frightful prison. Shall I ? I cannot decide. I see her figure constantly before me—gentle, graceful, calm, stretching forth both hands and to me. . . .

Seized a pack of cards and played Patience and went on playing Patience because I was afraid to stop. Given a weak constitution, a great ambition, an amorous nature, and at the same time a very fastidious one, I might have known I was in for trouble.

October 14.

Marie Bashkirtseff

Some time ago I noticed a quotation from one, Marie Bashkirtseff in a book on Strindberg, and was struck with the likeness to a sentiment of my own. Who *are* you? I wondered.

This evening went to the Library and read about her in Mathilde Blind's introductory essay to her Journal. I am simply astounded. It would be difficult in all the world's history to discover any two persons with temperaments so alike. She is the 'very spit of me'! I devoured Mathilde Blind's pages more and more astonished. We are identical! Oh, Marie Bashkirtseff! how we should have hated one another! She feels as I feel. We have the same self-absorption, the same vanity and corroding ambition. She is impressionable, volatile, passionate— ill! So am I. Her journal is my journal. All mine is stale reading now. She has written down all my thoughts and forestalled me! Already I have found some heart-rending parallels. To think I am only a replica: how humiliating for a human being to find himself merely a duplicate of another. Is there anything in the trans-migration of souls? She died in 1886. I was born in 1889.

October 15.

A man is always looking at himself in the mirror if for no other reason than to tie his tie and brush his hair. What does he think of his face? He must have private opinions. But it is usually considered a little out of taste to entertain opinions about one's personal appearance.

As for myself, some mirrors do me down pretty well,

others depress me ! I am bound to confess I am biassed
in favour of the friendly mirror. I am not handsome,
but I look interesting—I hope distinguished. My eyes
are deep-set . . . but my worst moments are when the
barber combs my hair right down over my forehead, or
when I see a really handsome man in Hyde Park. Such
occasions direct my gaze reflexly, and doubt like a thief
in the night forces the back door !

.   .   .   .

To-day, M—— sent me dancing mad by suggesting that
I copied R—— in my manner of speech and opinions.
Now R—— has a damned pervasive way of conducting
himself—for all the world as if he were a high official of
the Foreign Office. I, on the contrary, am shy, self-
conscious, easily overlooked, and this makes me writhe.
As we are inseparable friends—everybody assumes that I
am his tacky-lacky, a kind of appoggiatura to his big note.
He, they suppose, is my guide, philosopher, and Great
Mæcenas—Oxford befriending the proletariat. The thought
of it makes me sick—that any one should believe I imbibe
his ideas, echo his conceits, and even ape his gestures and
manner of voice.

' Lost yourself ?' inquired a despicable creature the
other morning as I came out of R——'s room after finding
him out. I could have shot him dead ! . . . As for ——
more than one person thinks that he alone is the brilliant
author until at last he himself has got into the way of
thinking it.

' It makes me hate you like mad,' I said to him to-day.
' How can I confront these people with the naked truth ?'

R—— chuckled complacently.

' If I deny your alleged supremacy, as I did this morning,
or if suddenly, in a fit of spleen, I'm induced to declare
that I loathe you (as I sometimes do) '—(more chuckles)
—' that your breath stinks, your eyes bulge, that you
have swollen jugulars and a platter face: they will think
I am either jealous or insincere. . . . To be your Echo
tho' !—my God !' I spat. We then grinned at one

another, and I, being bored, went to the lavatory and
read the newspaper secure from interruption.

Resignation

In the Tube, a young widow came in and sat in front
of me—pale-faced, grief-stricken, demure—a sort of ' Thy
Will be Done ' look. The adaptability of human beings
has something in it that seems horrible. It is dreadful to
think how we have all accommodated ourselves to this
War. Christian resignation is a feeble thing. Why won't
this demure widow with a loud voice blaspheme against
this iniquitous world that permits this iniquitous war ?

October 21.

I myself (licking a stamp): ' The taste of gum is really
very nice.'
R.: ' I hate it.'
I: ' My dear fellow ' (surprised and entreating), ' en-
velope gum is simply delicious.'
R.: ' I never lick stamps—it's dangerous—microbes.'
I: ' I always do: I shall buy a bookful and go away to
the seaside with them.'
R.: ' Yes, you'll need to.'
(Laughter.)
Thus gaily and jauntily we went on to discuss wines,
whiskies, and Worthington's, and I rounded it up in a
typical cock-eyed manner,—
' Ah ! yes, it's only when the day is over that the day
really begins—what ?'

October 23.

I expressed to R—— to-day my admiration for the
exploit of the brave and successful Submarine Commander
Max Kennedy Horton. (Name for you !) R—— was
rather cold. ' His exploits,' said this bloody fool, ' in-
volve loss of life and scarcely make me deliriously
eulogistic.'
I cleared my throat and began,—

'Your precious sociology again—it will be the ruin of
your career as an artist. It is so interwoven into the
fibre of your brain that you never see anything except in
relation to its State value. You are afraid to approve of
a lying, thieving rogue, however delightful a rascal he
may be, for fear of what Karl Marx might say. . . . You'll
soon be drawing landscapes with taxpayers in the fore-
ground, or we shall get a picture of Ben Nevis with Keir
Hardie on the summit.' And so on to our own infinite
mutual amusement.

.   .   .   .

The *English Review* returns my Essay. I am getting
simply furious with an ambition I am unable to satisfy,
among beautiful London women I cannot get to know,
and in ill-health that I cannot cure. Shall I ever find
any one ? Shall I ever be really well ? My one solace is
that I do not submit, it infuriates me, I resent it; I will
never be resigned and milky. I will keep my claws sharp
and fight to the end.

October 24.

Went to Mark Lane by train, then walked over the
Tower Bridge, and back along Lower Thames Street to
London Bridge, up to Whitechapel, St Paul's, Fleet Street,
and Charing Cross, and so home.

Near Reilly's Tavern, I saw a pavement artist who had
drawn a loaf with the inscription in both French and
English: 'This is easy to draw but hard to earn.' A
baby's funeral trotted briskly over the Tower Bridge
among Pink's jam waggons, carts carrying any goods
from lead pencils and matches to bales of cotton and chests
of tea.

In the St Catherine's Way there is one part like a deep
railway cutting, the whole of one side for a long way,
consisting of the brickwall of a very tall warehouse with
no windows in it and beautifully curved and producing
a wonderful effect. Walked past great blocks of ware-
houses and business establishments—a wonderful sight;

and everywhere bacon factors, coffee roasters, merchants.
On London Bridge, paused to feed the sea-gulls and looked
down at the stevedores. Outside Billingsgate Market was
a blackboard on an easel—for market prices—but instead
some one had drawn an enormously enlarged chalk picture
of a cat's rear and tail with anatomical details.

In Aldgate, stopped to inspect a street stall containing
popular literature—one brochure entitled *Suspended for
Life* to indicate the terrible punishment meted out to ——,
a League footballer. The frontispiece enough to make
a lump come in the juveniles' throats ! Another stall
held domestic utensils with an intimation, ' Anything on
this stall *lent* for 1d.' A newsvendor I heard exclaim to
a fellow-tradesman in the same line of business,—

' They come and look at your bloody plakaard and then
parsse on.'

Loitered at a dirty little Fleet Street bookshop where
Paul de Kock's *The Lady with the Three Pairs of Stays*
was displayed prominently beside a picture of Oscar Wilde.

In Fleet Street, you exchange the Whitechapel sausage
restaurants for Taverns with ' snacks at the bar,' and the
chestnut roasters, with their buckets of red-hot coals, for
Grub Street camp followers, selling *L'Indépendance Belge*
or pamphlets entitled, *Why We Went to War*.

In the Strand you may buy war maps, buttonhole flags,
etc., etc. I bought a penny stud. One shop was turned
into a shooting gallery at three shots a penny where the
Inner Temple Barristers in between the case for the defence
and the case for the prosecution could come and keep their
eye in against the time the Germans come.

Outside Charing Cross Station I saw a good-looking,
well-dressed woman in mourning clothes, grinding a barrel
organ. . . .

Returned to the Library and read the *Dublin Review*
(article on Samuel Butler), *North American Review* (one
on Henry James) and dined at seven. After dinner, read:
Evening Standard, Saturday Westminster, and the *New
Statesman*. Smoked six cigarettes and went to bed.
To-morrow Fifth Symphony of Beethoven.

October 25.

Too Late

Yesterday's ramble has left me very sore in spirit. London was spread out before me, a vast campagne. But I felt too physically tired to explore. I could just amble along—a spectator merely—and automatically register impressions. Think of the misery of that! I want to see the Docks and Dockland, to enter East End public-houses and opium-dens, to speak to Chinamen and Lascars: I want a first-rate, first-hand knowledge of London, of London men, London women. I was tingling with antici-pation yesterday and then I grew tired and fretful and morose, crawled back like a weevil into my nut. By 6.30 I was in a Library reading the *Dublin Review!*

What a young fool I was to neglect those priceless opportunities of studying and tasting life and character in North ——, at Borough Council meetings, Boards of Guardians, and electioneering campaigns—not to mention inquests, police courts, and country fairs. Instead of appraising all these precious and genuine pieces of ex-perience at their true value, my diary and my mind were occupied only with—Zoology, if you please. I ignored my exquisite chances, I ramped around, fuming and fretting, full of contempt for my circumscribed existence, and impatient as only a youth can be. What I shall never forgive myself is my present inability to recall that life, so that instead of being able now to push my chair back and entertain myself and others with descriptions of some of those antique and incredible happenings, my memory is rigid and formal: I remember only a few names and one or two isolated events. All that time is just as if it had never been. My recollections form only an indefinite smudge—odd Town Clerks, Town Criers (at least five of them in wonderful garb), policemen (I poached with one), ploughing match dinners (platters of roast beef and boiled potatoes and I, bespectacled student of Zoology, sitting uncomfortably among valiant trenchermen after their day's ploughing), election meetings in remote Exmoor

villages (and those wonderful Inns where I had to spend
the night !)—all are gone—too remote to bear recital—
yet just sufficiently clear to harass the mind in my constant endeavours to raise them all again from the dead in
my consciousness. I hate to think it is lost; that my
youth is buried—a cemetery without even headstones. To
an inquest on a drowned sailor—disclosing some thrilling
story of the wild seas off the coast—with a pitiful myopia
—I preferred Wiedersheim's *Comparative Anatomy of
Vertebrates*. I used to carry Dr Smith Woodward's
Palæontology with me to a Board of Guardians meeting,
mingling *Pariasaurus* and Holoptychians with tenders for
repairs and reports from the Master. Now I take Keats
or Tchehov to the Museum !

London certainly lies before me. Certainly I am alive
at last. Yet now my energy is gone. It is too late. I
am ill and tired. It costs me infinite discomfort to write
this entry, all the skin of my right hand is permanently
' pins and needles ' and in the finger tips I have lost all
sense of touch. The sight of my right eye is also very
bad and sometimes I can scarcely read print with it, etc.,
etc. But why should I go on ?

A trance-like condition supervenes in a semi-invalid
forced to live in almost complete social isolation in a great
whirling city like London. Days of routine follow each
other as swiftly as the weaver's shuttle and numb the
spirit and turn palpitating life into a silent picture show.
Everywhere always in the street people—millions of them
—whom I do not know, moving swiftly along. I look
and look and yawn and then one day as to-day I wake
up and race about beside myself—a swollen bag ready to
burst with hope, love, misery, joy, desperation.

Apologia pro vita mea

How may I excuse myself for continuing to talk about
my affairs and for continuing to write zoological memoirs
during the greatest War of all time ?

Well, here are some precedents:—

Goethe sat down to study the geography of China, while his fatherland agonised at Leipsig.

Hegel wrote the last lines of the *Phenomenology of Spirit* within sound of the guns of Jena.

While England was being rent in twain by civil war, Sir Thomas Browne ensconced in old Norwich, reflected on Cambyses and Pharaoh and on the song the Sirens sang.

Lacépède composed his *Histoire des Poissons* during the French Revolution.

Then there were Diogenes and Archimedes.

This defence of course implicates me in an unbounded opinion of the importance of my own work. ' He is quite the little poet,' some one said of Keats. ' It is just as if a man remarked of Buonaparte,' said Keats, in a pet, ' that he's quite the little general.'

A Woman and a Child

On the way to the Albert Hall came upon the most beautiful picture of young maternity that ever I saw in my life. She was a delightfully girlish young creature— a perfect phœnix of health and beauty. As she stood with her little son at the kerb waiting for a 'bus, smiling and chatting to him, a luminous radiance of happy, satisfied maternal love, maternal pride, womanliness streamed from her and enveloped me.

We got on the same 'bus. The little boy, with his long hair and dressed in velvet like little Lord Fauntleroy, said something to her—she smiled delightedly, caught him up on her knees and kissed him. Two such pretty people never touched lips before—I'm certain of it. It was impossible to believe that this virginal creature was a mother—childbirth left no trace. She must have just budded off the baby boy like a plant. Once, in her glance, she took me in her purview, and I knew she knew I was watching her. In travelling backwards from Kensington Gardens to the boy again, her gaze rested on me a moment and I, of course, rendered the homage that was due. As

a matter of fact there was no direct evidence that she
was the mother at all.

The Albert Hall Hag

While waiting outside the Albert Hall, an extraordinarily
weird contrast thrust itself before me— she was the most
pathetic piece of human jetsam that ever I saw drifting
about in this sea of London faces. Tall, gaunt, cadaverous,
the skin of her face drawn tightly over her cheekbones
and over a thin, pointed, hook-shaped nose, on her feet
brown sandshoes, dressed in a long draggle-tailed skirt,
a broken-brimmed straw hat, beneath which some scanty
hair was scraped back and tied behind in a knot—this
wretched soul of some thirty summers (and what summers !)
stood in the road beside the waiting queue and weakly
passed the bow across her violin which emitted a slight
scraping sound. She could not play a tune and the fingers
of her left hand never touched the strings—they merely
held the handle.

A policeman passed and, with an eye on the queue,
muttered audibly, ' Not 'arf,' but no one laughed.   Then
she began to rummage in her skirt, holding the violin by
the neck in her right hand just as she must hold her brat
by the arm when at home. Simultaneously sounds issued
from her mouth in a high falsetto key; they were unearthly
sounds, the tiny voice of an articulating corpse underneath
the coffin lid.   For a moment no one realised that she was
reciting. For she continued to rummage in her skirt as
she squeaked, ' Break, break, break, on thy cold gray
stones, O sea,' etc. The words were scarcely audible
tho' she stood but two yards off. But she repeated the
verse and I then made out what it was. She seemed
ashamed of herself and of her plight, almost without the
courage to foist this mockery of violin-playing on us—one
would say she was frightened by her own ugliness and her
own pathos.

After conscientiously carrying out her programme but
with the distracted, uncomfortable air of some one scurrying over a painful task—like a tired child gabbling its

prayers before getting into bed—she at length produced
from her skirt pocket a small canvas money bag which
she started to hand around. This was the climax to this
harrowing incident—for each time she held out the bag,
she smiled, which stretched the skin still more tightly down
over her malar prominence and said something—an
inarticulate noise in a very high pitch. 'A woman,' I
whispered to R——, 'she claims to be a woman.' If any
one hesitated a moment or struggled with a purse she
would wait patiently with bag outstretched and head
turned away, the smile vanishing at once as if the pinched
face were but too glad of the opportunity of a rest from
smiling. She stood there, gazing absently—two lifeless
eyes at the bottom of deep socket holes in a head
which was almost a bare skull. She was perfunctorily
carrying out an objectionable task because she could not
kill the will to live.

As she looked away and waited for you to produce the
copper, she thought, 'Why trouble? Why should I wait
for this man's aid?' The clink of the penny recalled her
to herself, and she passed on, renewing her terrible grimacing
smile.

Why didn't I do something? Why? Because I was
bent on hearing Beethoven's Fifth Symphony, if you
please. . . . And she may have been a well-to-do vagrant
—well got up for the occasion—a clever simulator? . . .

October 28.

Rigor Bordis

Rigor bordis!—I write like this as if it were a light
matter. But to-night I was *in extremis*. . . . First I
read the paper; then I finished the book I was reading—
'*Thus Spake Zarathustra.*' Not knowing quite what next
to do, I took my boots off and poured out another cup
of coffee. But these manœuvres were only the feeble
attempts of a cowardly wretch to evade the main issue
which was:—

How to occupy myself and keep myself sane during the
hour and a half before bedtime.

Before now I have tried going off to bed. But that does not work—I don't sleep. Moreover, I have been in the grip of a horrible mental unrest. To sit still in my chair, much less to lie in bed doing nothing seemed ghastly. I experienced all the cravings of a dissolute neurotic for a stimulus, but what stimulus I wanted I did not know. Had I known I should have gone and got it. The dipsomaniac was a man to be envied.

Some mechanical means were necessary for sustaining life till bedtime. I sat down and played a game of Patience —no one knows how I loathe playing Patience and how much I despise the people who play it. Tiring of that, sat back in my chair, yawned, and thought of a word I wanted to look up in the Dictionary. This quest, forgotten until then, came like a beam of bright light into a dark room. So looked the word up leisurely, took out my watch, noted the time, and then stood up with elbows on the mantelpiece and stared at myself in the glass. . . . I was at bay at last. There was simply nothing I could do. I would have given worlds to have some one to talk to. Pride kept me from ringing for the landlady. I must stand motionless, back to the wall, and wait for the hour of my release. I had but one idea, viz., that I was surely beaten in this game of life. I was very miserable indeed. But being so miserable that I couldn't feel more so, I began to recover after a while. I began to visualise my lamentable situation, and rose above it as I did so. I staged it before my mind's eye and observed myself as hero of the plot. I saw myself sitting in a dirty armchair in a dirty house in a dirty London street, with the landlady's dirty daughter below-stairs singing, ' Little Grey Home in the West,' my head obscured in a cloud of depression, and in my mind the thought that if life be a test of endurance I must hang on grimly to the arms of the chair and sit tight till bedtime.

This attitude proved a useful means of self-defence. When I had dramatised my misery, I enjoyed it, and acute mental pain turned into merely æsthetic malaise.

November 4.

A lurid day. Suffering from the most horrible physical languor. Wrote the Doctor saying I was rapidly sliding down a steep place into the sea (like the swine I am). Could I see him?

.   .   .   .

Endured an hour's torture of indecision to-night asking myself whether I should go over to ask her to be my wife or should I go to the Fabian Society and hear Bernard Shaw. Kept putting off the decision even till after dinner. If I went to the flat, I must shave; to shave required hot water—the landlady had already cleared the table and was rapidly retreating. Something must be done and at once. I called the old thing back impulsively and ordered shaving water, consoling myself with the reflection that it was still unnecessary to decide; the hot water could be at hand in case the worst happened. If I decided on matrimony I could shave forthwith. Should I? (After dark I always shave in the sitting-room because of the better gaslight.)

Drank some coffee and next found myself slowly, mournfully putting on hat and coat. You can't shave in hat and coat so I concluded I had decided on Shaw. Slowly undid the front door latch and went off.

Shaw bored me. He is mid-Victorian. Sat beside a bulgy-eyed youth reading the *Freethinker*.

November 9.

In the evening asked her to be my wife. She refused. Once perhaps . . . but now . . .

I don't think I have any moral right to propose to any woman seeing the state of my health and I did not actually intend or wish to. . . . It was just to get it off my mind —a plain statement. . . . If I don't really and truly love her it was a perfectly heartless comedy. But I have good reason to believe I do. With me, moments of headstrong passion alternate with moods of perfectly immobile self-introspection. It is a relief to have spoken.

November 10.

Very miserable.   Asked R—— three times to come and
have dinner with me.   Each time he refused.   My nerves
are completely jangled.   *Tu l'as voulu, George Dandin*—
that's the rub.

November 11.

She observed me carefully—I'm looking a perfect wreck
—*tu l'as voulu, George Dandin*—but it's mainly ill-health
and not on her account.

I said,—

' Some things are too funny to laugh at.'

' Is that why you are so solemn ?'

' No,' I answered, ' I'm not solemn, I am laughing—
some things are too solemn to be serious about.'

She saw me off at the door and smiled quietly—an
amused faraway smile of feline satisfaction. . . .

November 12.

Horrible nervous depression.   Thinking of suicide with
a pistol—a Browning.   Or of 10 days' mysterious disappearance, when I will go and live in a good Hotel, spend
all my money, and live among human beings with eyes and
noses and legs.   This isolation.   Am I going mad ?   If I
disappeared, it would be interesting to see if any one
missed me.

November 13.

Still thinking of suicide.   It seems the only way out.
This morning my Essay was returned by the Editor of ——.
One by one I have been divested of all my most cherished
illusions.   Once my ambitions gave me the fuel with
which to keep myself alive.   One after another they have
been foiled, and now I've nothing to burn.   I am daily
facing the fact that my ambitions have overtaxed my
abilities and health.   For years, my whole existence has
rested on a false estimate of my own value, and my life
been revolving around a foolish self-deception.   But I

know myself as I am at last—and am not at all enamoured.
The future has nothing for me. I am wearied of my life
already. What is there for any of us to do but die ?

November 14.

Before going over to-night bought *London Opinion*
deliberately in order to find a joke or better still some
cynicism about women to fire off at her. Rehearsed one
joke, one witticism from Oscar Wilde, and one personal
anecdote (the latter for the most part false), none of which
came off, tho' I succeeded in carrying off a nonchalant
or even jaunty bearing.

'Don't you ever swear ?' I asked. 'It's a good thing,
you know, swearing is like pimples, better to come out,
cleanses the moral system. The person who controls
himself must have lots of terrible oaths circulating in his
blood.'

'Swearing is not the only remedy.'

'I suppose you prefer the gilded pill of a curate's sermon:
I prefer pimples to pills.'

Is it a wonder she does not love me ?

.   .   .   .

I wonder why I paint myself in such horrid colours—
why have I this morbid pleasure in pretending to those I
love that I am a beast and a cynic? I suffer, I suppose,
from a lacerated self-esteem, from a painful loneliness,
from the consciousness of how ridiculous I have made
myself, and that most people if they knew would regard
me with loathing and disgust.

I am very unhappy. I am unhappy because she does
not care for me, and I am chiefly unhappy because I do
not care for her. Instead of a passion, only a dragging
heavy chain of attraction . . . some inflexible law makes
me gravitate to her, seizes me by the neck and suspends
me over her, I cannot look away. . . .

In the early days when I did my best to strangle my
love—as one would a bastard child—I took courage in
the fact that for a man like me the murder was necessary.

There were books to write and to read, and name and fame perhaps. To these everything must be sacrificed. . . . That is all gone now. No man could have withstood for ever that concentrated essence of womanhood that flowed from her. . . .

Still the declaration has made amends. She is pleased about it—it is a scalp.

Yet how can I forgive her for saying she supposed it was a natural instinct for a girl not to feel drawn to an invalid like me? That was cruel tho' true.

November 19.

I might be Captain Scott writing his last words amid Antarctic cold and desolation. It is very cold. I am sitting hunched up by the fire in my lodgings after a meal of tough meat and cold apple-tart. I am full of self-commiseration—my only pleasure now. It is very cold and I cannot get warm—try as I will.

My various nervous derangements take different forms. This time my peripheral circulation is affected, and the hand, arm, and shoulder are permanently cold. My right hand is blue—tho' I've shut up the window and piled up a roaring fire. It's Antarctic cold and desolation. London in November from the inside of a dingy lodging-house can be very terrible indeed. This celestial isolation will send me out of my mind. I marvel how God can stick it—lonely, damp, and cold in the clouds. That is how I live too—but then I am not God.

I fall back on this Journal just as some other poor devil takes to drink. I, too, have toyed with the idea of drinking hard. I have frequented bars and billiard saloons and in fits of depression done my best to forget myself. But I am not sufficiently fond of alcohol (and it would take a lot to make *me* forget myself). So I plunge into these literary excesses and drown my sorrows in Stephens' Blue-black Ink. It gives me a sulky pleasure to think that some day somebody will know . . .

It is humiliating to feel ill as I do. If I had consumption, the disease would act as a stimulus—I could strike an attitude feverishly and be histrionic. But to be merely 'below par'—to feel like a Bunny rabbit perennially 'poorly,' saps my character and mental vigour. I want to crawl away and die like a rat in a hole. A bronzed healthy man makes me wince. Healthy people regard a chronic sickly man as a leper. They suspect him, something fishy.

November 20.

Still at home ill.

If anything, R—— is more of a précieux than I am myself. At the present moment he is tickling himself with the idea that he's in love with a certain golden-haired damsel from the States. He reports to me fragments of his conversations with her, how he snatches a fearful joy by skirting dangerous conversational territory, or he takes a pencil and deftly outlines her profile or the rondeur of her bosom. Or he discourses at length on her nose or eye. I can well imagine him driving a woman crazy and then collecting her tears in a bottle as mementoes. Then whenever he requires a little heart stimulus he could take the phial from his waistcoat pocket and watch the tears condensing.

'Why don't you marry her out of hand and be done with all this dalliance ? I can tell you what's the matter with you,' I growled, 'you're a landscape artist. . . . You'll grow to resemble that mean, Jewy, secretive, petty creature, J. M. W. Turner, and allow no human being to interfere with your art. A fine artist perhaps—but what a man ! You'll finish up with a Mrs Danby.'

'Yes,' he answered, quoting Tennyson with great aptness, 'and " lose my salvation for a sketch," like Romney deserting his wife. If I were not married I should have no wife to desert.'

It is useless to argue with him. His cosmogony is wrongly centred in Art not life. Life interests him—he can't altogether resign himself to the cowl and the tonsured head, but he will not plunge. He insists on being a spectator, watching the maelstrom from the bank and

remarking exquisitely, ' Ah ! there is a very fine sorrow,'
or, ' What an exquisite sensation.' The other day after
one of our furious conversational bouts around this subject,
I drew an insect, cut it out, and pinned the slip in a collecting box. Then suddenly producing the box, and opening
it with a facetious grin, I said,—

' Here is a jolly little sorrow I caught this morning.'
The joke pleased him and we roared, bellowed.

' That terrible forefinger of yours,' he smiled.

' Like Cardinal Richelieu's eyes—piercing ?' I suggested with appreciation. (It is because I tap him on his
shirt front in the space between waistcoat and tie aggres-
sively for emphasis in conversation.)

" You must regard my passion for painting,' he began
once more, ' as a sort of dipsomania—I really can't help
myself.'

I jumped on him vehemently,—

' Exactly, my pernickety friend; it's something abnormal and unnatural. When, for purposes of self-culture,
I see a man deliberately lop off great branches of himself
so as to divert his strength into one limb, I know that if
he is successful he'll be something as vulgar as a fat woman
at a country fair; and if he is unsuccessful he'll be just a
pathetic mutilation. . . . You are trying to pervert a
natural instinct. You want to paint, I believe. Quite so.
But when a boy reaches the age of puberty he does not
grow a palette on his chin but hair. . . . Still, now you
recognise it as a bad habit, why need I say more ?' (' Why
indeed ?') ' It's a vice, and I'm very sorry for you, old
boy. I'll do all I can—come and have some dinner with
me to-night.'

' Oh ! thank you very much,' says my gentleman, ' but
I'm not at all sorry for myself.'

' I thought as much. So that we are not so very much
agreed after all. We're not shaking hands after the boxing
contest, but scowling at each other from the ropes and
shaping for another round.'

' Your pulpit orations, my dear Barbellion, in full canon-
icals,' he reflected, ' are worthy of a larger audience. . . .

To find *you* of all people preaching. I thought you were philosopher enough to see the angle of every one's vision and broadminded so as to see every point of view. Besides, you are as afraid of marriage as I am, and for the same reasons.'

' I confess, when in the philosophic citadel of my own armchair,' I began, ' I *do* see every one's point of view. You sit on the other side of the rug and put out the suggestion tentatively that murder may be a moral act. I examine your argument and am disposed to accept it. But when you slit up my brother's abdomen before my eyes, I am sufficiently weak and human to punch you on the nose. . . . You are too cold and Olympian, up above the snowline with a box of paints.'

' It is very beautiful among the snows.'

' I suppose so.'

(Exit.)

November 23.

Great physical languor, especially in the morning. It is Calvary to get out of bed and shoulder the day's burden.

' What's been the matter ?' they ask.

' Oh ! senile decay—general histolysis of the tissues,' I say, fencing.

To-night, I looked at myself accidentally in the glass and noticed at once the alarming extent of my dejection. Quite unconsciously I turned my head away and shook it, making the noise with my teeth and tongue which means, ' Dear, dear.' M—— tells me these waves of ill-health are quite unaccountable unless I were ' leading a dissolute life, which you do not appear to be doing.' Damn his eyes.

Reading Nietzsche

Reading Nietzsche. What splendid physic he is to Pomeranian puppies like myself ! I am a hopeless coward. Thunderstorms always frighten me. The smallest cut alarms for fear of blood poisoning, and I always dab on antiseptics at once. But Nietzsche makes me feel a perfect mastiff.

The Test for True Love

The test for true love is whether you can endure the thought of cutting your sweetheart's toe-nails—the onychiotomic test. Or whether you find your Julia's sweat as sweet as otto of roses. I told her this to-night. Probably she thinks I only 'saw it in a book.'

Chopin

On Sunday, went to the Albert Hall, and warmed myself at the Orchestra. It is a wonderful sight to watch an orchestra playing from the gallery. It spurts and flickers like a flame. Its incessant activity arrests the attention and holds it just as a fire does—even a deaf man would be fascinated. Heard Chopin's Funeral March and other things. It would be a rich experience to be able to be in your coffin at rest and listen to Chopin's Funeral March being played above you by a string orchestra with Sir Henry Wood conducting.

Sir Henry like a melanic Messiah was crucified as usual, the Hungarian Rhapsody No. 2 causing him the most awful agony. . .

November 28.

Rodin

More than once lately have been to see and admire Rodin's recent gifts to the nation exhibited at the Victoria and Albert Museum. The 'Prodigal Son' is Beethoven's Fifth Symphony done in stone. It was only on my second visit that I noticed the small pebble in each hand—a superb touch!—what a frenzy of remorse!

The 'Fallen Angel' I loved most. The legs of the woman droop lifelessly backwards in an intoxicating curve. The eye caresses it—down the thighs and over the calves to the tips of the toes—like the hind limbs of some beautiful dead gazelle. He has brought off exactly the same effect in the woman in the group called 'Eternal Spring,' which I have only seen in a photograph.

This morning at 9 a.m. lay in bed on my back, warm and comfortable, and, for the first time for many weeks, with no pain or discomfort of any kind. The mattress curved up around my body and legs and held me in a soft warm embrace. . . . I shut my eyes and whistled the saccharine melody for solo violin in Chopin's Funeral March. I wanted the moment prolonged for hours. Ill-health chases the soul out of a man. He becomes a body, purely physical.

November 29.

This evening she promised to be my wife after a long silent ramble together thro' dark London squares and streets ! I am beside myself !

.   .   .   .

December 6.

I know now—I love her with passion. Health and ambition and sanity are returning. Projects in view:—

(1) To make her happy and myself worthy.

(2) To get married.

(3) To prepare and publish a volume of this Journal.

(4) To write two essays for *Cornhill* which shall surely induce the Editor to publish and not write me merely long complimentary and encouraging letters as heretofore.

Wired to A——, ' The brave little pennon has been hauled down.'

December 7.

Have so many projects in view and so little time in which to get them done ! Moreover I am always haunted by the fear that I may never finish them thro' physical or temperamental disabilities—a breakdown in health or in purpose. I am one of those who are apt to die unexpectedly and no one would be surprised. An inquest would probably be unnecessary. I badly want to live say another twelve months. Hey ! nonny-no ! a man's a fool that wants to die.

December 9.

. . . I shook her angrily by the shoulders to-night and said, ' Why do I love you ?—Tell me,' but she only smiled gently and said, ' I cannot tell. . . .' I ought not to love her, I know—every omen is against it. . . . Then I am full of self-love: an intellectual Malvolio proud of his brains and air of distinction. . . .

Then I am fickle, passionate, polygamous . . . I am haunted by the memory of how I have sloughed off one enthusiasm after another. I used to dissect snails in a pie-dish in the kitchen while Mother baked the cakes—the unravelling of the internal economy of a *Helix* caused as great an emotional storm as to-day the Unfinished Symphony does ! I look for the first parasol in Kensington Gardens with the same interest as once I sought out the first snowdrop or listened for the first Cuckoo. I am as anxious to identify an instrument in Sir Henry's Orchestra as once to identify the song of a new bird in the woods. Nothing is further from my intention or desire to continue my old habit of nature study. I never read nature books —my old favourites—Waterton's *Wanderings*, Gilbert White, *The Zoologist*, etc.—have no interest for me—in fact they give me slight mental nausea even to glance at. Wiedersheim (good old Wiedersheim) is now deposed by a text book on Harmony. My main desire just now is to hear the best music. In the country I wore blinkers and saw only zoology. Now in London, I've taken the bit into my mouth—and it's a mouth of iron—wanting a run for all my troubles before Death strikes me down.

All this evidence of my temperamental instability alarms and distresses me on reflection and makes the soul weary. I wish I loved more steadily. I am always sidetracking myself. The title of ' husband ' scares me.

December 12.

Sir Henry Wood conducting

Went to the Queen's Hall, sat in the Orchestra and watched Sir Henry's statuesque figure conducting thro' a forest of bows, ' which pleased me mightily.' He would

be worth watching if you were stone deaf. If you
could not hear a sound, the animation and excitement
of an orchestra in full swing, with the conductor cutting
and slashing at invisible foes, make a magnificent
spectacle.

The face of Sir Henry Wood strikes me as very much like
the traditional pictures of Jesus Christ, tho' Sir Henry is
dark—the melanic Messiah I call him (very much to my
own delight). Rodin ought to do him in stone—Chesterfield's ideal of a man—a Corinthian edifice on Tuscan
foundations. In Sir Henry's case there can be no dis-
puting the Tuscan foundations. However swift and
elegant the movements of his arms, his splendid lower
extremities remain as firm as stone columns. While the
music is calm and serene his right hand and bâton execute
in concert with the left, perfect geometric curves around
his head. Then as it gathers in force and volume, when
the bows begin to dart swiftly across the fiddles and the
trumpets and trombones blaze away in a conflagration,
we are all expectant—and even a little fearful, to observe
his sabre-like cuts. The tension grows . . . I hold my
breath. . . . Sir Henry snatches a second to throw back
a lock of his hair that has fallen limply across his forehead,
then goes on in unrelenting pursuit, cutting and slashing
at hordes of invisible fiends that leap howling out towards
him. There is a great turmoil of combat, but the Conductor struggles on till the great explosion happens. But
in spite of that, you see him still standing thro' a cloud of
great chords, quite undaunted. His sword zigzags up and
down the scale—suddenly the closed fist of his left hand
shoots up straight and points to the zenith—like the arm of a
heathen priest appealing to Baal to bring down fire from
Heaven. . . . But the appeal avails nought and it looks
as tho' it were all up for poor Sir Henry. The music is
just as infuriated—his body writhes with it—the melanic
Messiah crucified by the inappeasable desire to express by
visible gestures all that he feels in his heart. He surrenders
—so you think—he opens out both arms wide and baring
his breast, dares them all to do their worst—like the

picture of Moffat the missionary among the savages of the Dark Continent !

And yet he wins after all.   At the very last moment he seems to summon all his remaining strength and in one final and devastating sweep mows down the orchestra rank by rank. . . .   You awake from the nightmare to discover the victor acknowledging the applause in a series of his inimitable bows.

One ought to pack one's ears up with cotton wool at a concert where Sir Henry conducts.   Otherwise, the music is apt to distract one's attention.   R.L.S. wanted to be at the head of a cavalry charge—sword over head—but I'd rather fight an orchestra with a bâton.

Beethoven's Fifth Symphony

This symphony always works me up into an ecstasy; in ecstatic sympathy with its dreadfulness I could stand up in the balcony and fling myself down passionately into the arena below.   Yet there were women sitting alongside me to-day—knitting !   It so annoyed and irritated me that at the end of the first movement I got up and sat elsewhere. They would have sat knitting at the foot of the Cross, I suppose.

At the end of the second movement, two or three other women got up and went home to tea !   It would have surprised me no more to have seen a cork extract itself from its bottle and promenade.

Tschaikovsky

Just lately I've heard a lot of music including Tschai-kovsky's Pathétique and Fifth Symphonies, some Debussy, and odd pieces by Dnkas, Glinka, Smetana, Mozart.   I am chock-full of impressions of all this precious stuff and scarcely know what to write.   As usual, the third move-ment of the Pathétique produced a frenzy of exhilaration; I seemed to put on several inches around my chest and wished to shout in a voice of thunder.   The conventions of a public concert hall are dreadfully oppressive at such times. I could have eaten ' all the elephants of Hindustan and picked my teeth with the spire of Strassburg Cathedral.'

In the last movement of the Fifth Symphony of that splendid fellow Tschaikovsky, the orchestra seemed to gallop away leaving poor Landon Ronald to wave his whip in a ridiculously ineffective way. They went on crashing down chords, and just before the end I had the awful presentiment that the orchestra simply could not stop. I sat still straining every nerve in the expectancy that this chord or the next or the next was the end. But it went on pounding down—each one seemed the last but every time another followed as passionate and emphatic as the one before, until finally, whatever this inhuman orchestra was attempting to crush and destroy must have been reduced to shapeless pulp. I wanted to board the platform and plead with them, elderly gentlemen turned their heads nervously, everyone was breathless, we all wanted to call ' For God's sake, stop '—to do anything to still this awful lust for annihilation. . . . The end came quickly in four drum beats in quick succession. I have never seen such hate, such passionate intensity of the will to destroy. . . . And Tschaikovsky was a Russian!

Debussy was a welcome change. ' L'Apres-midi d'un Faun ' is a musical setting to an oscitatory exercise. It is an orchestral yawn. Oh! so tired !

Came away thoroughly delighted. Wanted to say to every one ' Bally good, ain't it ?' and then we would all shake hands and go home whistling.

December 14.

My rooms are littered with old concert programmes and the Doctor's prescriptions (in the yellow envelopes of the dispenser) for my various ailments and diseases, and books, books, books.

Among the latter those lying on my table at this moment are—

Plays of M. Brieux.

Joseph Vance.

A Sequel to Pragmatism: The Meaning of Truth, by William James.

Beyond Good and Evil.

Dostoievsky's *The Possessed.*

Marie Bashkirtseff's *Journal.*

I have found time to read only the first chapter of this last and am almost afraid to go on.   It would be so humiliating to find I was only her duplicate.

On my mantelpiece stands a photograph of Huxley—the hero of my youth—which old B—— has always taken to be that of my grandpapa! A plaster-cast mask of Voltaire when first hung up made him chuckle with indecent laughter.   'A regular all-nighter.   Who is it?' he said.

December 15.

Petticoat Lane

This morning, being Sunday, went to Petticoat Lane and enjoyed myself.

On turning the corner to go into Middlesex Street, as it is now called, the first thing I saw was a little girl—a Jewess—being tackled for selling Belgian button-hole flags by two policemen who ultimately marched her off to the police station.

In the Lane, first of all, was a 'Royal Ascot Jockey Scales' made of brass and upholstered in gaudy red velvet—a penny a time. A very fat man was being weighed and looked a little distressed on being given his ticket.

'Another stone,' he told the crowd mournfully.

'You'll have to eat less pork,' some one volunteered and we all laughed.

Next door to the Scales was a man selling gyroscopes. 'Something scientific, amusing as well as instructive, illustrating the principles of gravity and stability. What I show you is what I sell—price one shilling.   Who?'

I stopped next at a stall containing nothing but caps—

' any size, any colour any pattern, a shilling apiece—now
then!' This show was being run by two men—a Jew in
a fur cap on one side of the stall and a very powerful-
looking sort of Captain Cuttle on the other—a seafaring
man, almost as broad as he was long, with a game leg and
the voice of a skipper in a hurricane. Both these men
were selling caps at a prodigious pace, and with the in-
souciance of tradesmen sure of their custom.   The skipper
would seize a cap, chuck it across to a timid prospective
purchaser, and, if he dropped it, chuck him over another,
crying, with a ' yo-heave-ho ' boisterousness, ' Oh! what
a game, what a bees' nest.'

Upon the small head of another customer, he would
squash down his largest sized cap saying at once,—

' There, you look the finest gentleman—oh! ah! a little
too large.'

At which we all laughed, the customer looked silly, but
took no offence.

' Try this,' yells the skipper above the storm, and takes
off his own cap. ' Oh! ye needn't be afraid—I washed
my hair last—year.' (Laughter.)

Then to. his partner, the Jew on the other side of the
stall, ' Oh! what a face you've got.   Here! 6d. for any one
who can tell me what it is.   Why not take it to the trenches
and get it smashed in ?'

The Jew wore spectacles and had a soft ingratiating
voice and brown doe-like eyes—a Jew in every respect.
' Oh!' says he, in the oleaginous Semitic way, and accurately
taking up his cue (for all this was rehearsed patter), ' my
wife says " my face is my fortune." '

' No wonder you're so hard up and 'ave got to take in
lodgers.   What's yer name?'

' John Jones,' in a demure wheedling voice.

' Hoo—that's not your name in your own bloody country
—I expect it's Hullabullinsky.'

' Do you know what my name really is ?'

' No.'

' It's Assenheimopoplocatdwizlinsky Kovorod.'

(Loud laughter.)

' I shall call you " ass " for short.'

I was laughing loudly at these two clowns and the skipper observing as much, shouted out to me,—

' Parlez-vous Français, M'sieur ?'

' Oui, oui,' said I.

' Ah! lah, you're one of us—oh! what a game! what a bees' nest,' and all the time he went on selling caps and chucking them at the purchasers.

Perhaps one of the most extraordinary things I saw was a stream of young men who, one after another, came up to a stall, paid a penny and swallowed a glass of 'nerve tonic'—a green liquid syphoned out of a large jar— warranted a safe cure for

' Inward weakness, slightest flurry or body oppressed.'

Another man was pulling teeth and selling tooth powder. Some of the little urchins' teeth, after he had cleaned them as a demonstration, were much whiter than their faces or his. This was ' the original Chas. Assenheim.'

Mrs Meyers, ' not connected with any one else of the same name in the Lane ' was selling eels at 2d., 3d. and 6d. and doing a brisk trade too.

But I should go on for hours if I were to tell everything seen in this remarkable lane during an hour and a half on a Sunday morning. Each stall-holder sells only one kind of article—caps or clocks or songs, braces, shawls, indecent literature, concertinas, gramophones, coats, pants, reach-me-downs, epergnes. The thoroughfare was crowded with people (I saw two Lascars in red fez caps) inspecting the goods displayed and attentively observed by numerous policemen. The alarm clocks were all going off, each gramophone was working a record (a different one !) and every tradesman shouting his wares—a perfect pandemo-nium.

December 31.

A Conversation

' There is that easily calculable element in your nature, dear boy,' I said, ' by which you forego the dignity of a free-willed human being and come under an inflexible natural law. I can anticipate your movements, intentions, and opinions long beforehand. For example. I know quite well that every Saturday morning will see you with *The New Statesman* under your arm; I know that the words " Wagner " or " Shaw " uttered slowly and deliberately in your ear will produce a perfectly definite reaction.'

' I bet you can't predict what I am going to buy now,' R—— replied gaily, advancing to the newspaper stall. He bought the *Pink 'Un* and I laughed. . . .

' And so you read *Pragmatism*,' he mused, ' while the fate of the Empire stands in the balance.'

' Yes,' said I, ' and the Paris Academy of Sciences were discussing the functions of θ and the Polymorphism of Antarctic diatoms last September when the Germans stood almost at the gates of Paris.'

This was a lucky stroke for me, for he knew he was rubbing me on the raw. We are, of course, great friends. but sometimes we get on one another's nerves.

' I am polychromatic,' I declaimed, ' rhetorical, bass. You—besides being a bally fool—are of a pretty gray colour, a baritone and you paint in water-colours.'

' Whereas you, of course, would paint in blood ?' he answered facetiously.

His Oxford education has a firm hold on him. He says for example ' e converso ' instead of ' on the other hand ' and ' entre nous ' for ' between ourselves.' He labels his paragraphs a, β, γ, instead of a, b, c, and quotes Juvenal, knows Paris and Naples, visits the Alps for the winter sports, all in the approved manner of dons.

Not infrequently he visits the East End to study ' how the poor live,' he lectures at Toynbee Hall, and calls the proletariat ' the prolly.' In fact, he does everything according to the regulations, being a socialist and an agnostic, a follower of Shaw and a devotee of Bunyan. ' Erotic ' he is careful to pronounce *eròtic* to show he knows Greek, and the ' Duma,' the *Dumà*. tho' he doesn't know Russian. Like any don, he is always ready to discuss and give an opinion on any sub- supra- or circum-lunary subject from bimetallism to the Symphony as an art-form.

' That's a dominant fifth,' I said to him the other day;
no answer.

' You ignorant devil,' I said, ' you don't know what a
dominant fifth is !'

We made grimaces at one another.

' Who's the Master of the Mint ?' I asked him.   ' That
is an easy one.'

' The Chancellor of the Exchequer,' was the prompt reply.

' Oh! that's right,' I said sarcastic and crestfallen.
' Now tell me the shortest verse in the Bible and the date
of Rameses II.'

We laughed. R—— is a very clever man and the most
extraordinarily versatile man I know. He is bound to
make his mark. His danger is—too many irons in the
fire. Here are some of his occupations and acquirements:
Art (etching, drypoint, water-colours), music (a charming
voice), classics, French, German, Italian (both speaking
and reading knowledge), biology, etc., etc. He is for ever
titillating his mind with some new thing. ' For God's
sake, do leave it alone—you simply rag your mind to
death. Put it out to grass—go thro' an annual season of
complete abstinence from knowledge—an intellectual
Lent.'

No one more than he enjoys my ragging him like this
—and I do it rather well.

1915

January 1.

I have grown so ridiculously hypercritical and fastidious
that I will refuse a man's invitation to dinner because he
has watery blue eyes, or hate him for a mannerism or an
impediment or affectation in his speech. Some poor devil
who has not heard of Turner or Debussy or Dostoievsky
I gird at with the arrogance of a knowledgeable youth of 17.
Some oddity who should afford a sane mind endless amusement, I write off as a *lusus naturæ* and dismiss with a
flourish of contempt. My intellectual arrogance—excepting at such times as I become conscious of it and pull

myself up—is incredible. It is incredible because I have
no personal courage and all this pride boils up behind a
timid exterior. I quail often before stupid but overbearing
persons who consequently never realise my contempt of
them. Then afterwards, I writhe to think I never stood
up to this fool; never uttered an appropriate word to interfere with another's nauseating self-love. It exasperates
me to be unable to give a Roland for an Oliver—even
servants and underlings 'tick me off'—to fail always in
sufficient presence of mind to make the satisfying rejoinder or riposte. I suffer from such a savage *amour
propre* that I fear to enter the lists with a man I dislike
on account of the mental anguish I should suffer if he
worsted me. I am therefore bottled up tight—both my
hates and loves. For a coward is not only afraid to tell
a man he hates him, but is nervous too of letting go of his
feeling of affection or regard lest it be rejected or not
returned. I shudder to think of such remarks as (referring to me), 'He's one of my admirers, you know'
(sardonically), or, 'I simply can't get rid of him.'

If however my cork *does* come out, there is an explosion,
and placid people occasionally marvel to hear violent
language streaming from my lips and nasty acid and
facetious remarks.

Of course, to intimate friends (only about three persons
in the wide, wide world), I can always give free vent to
my feelings, and I do so in privacy with that violence
in which a weak character usually finds some compensation
for his intolerable self-imposed reserve and restraint in
public. I can never marvel enough at the ineradicable
turpitude of my existence, at my *double-facedness*, and the
remarkable contrast between the face I turn to the outside
world and the face my friends know. It's like leading a
double existence or artificially constructing a puppet to
dangle before the crowd while I fulminate behind the
scenes. If only I had the moral courage to play my part
in life—to take the stage and be myself, to enjoy the
delightful sensation of making my presence felt, instead
of this vapourish mumming—then this Journal would be

quite unnecessary. For to me self-expression is a necessity of life, and what cannot be expressed one way must
be expressed in another. When colossal egotism is driven
underground, whether by a steely surface environment or
an unworkable temperament or as in my case by both,
you get a truly remarkable result, and the victim a truly
remarkable pain—the pain one might say of continuously
unsuccessful attempts at parturition.

It is perhaps not the whole explanation to say that my
milky affability before, say bores or clods, is sheer personal
cowardice. . . . It is partly real affability. I am so
glad to have opposite me some one who is making himself
pleasant and affable and sympathetic that I forget for
the moment that he is an unconscionable time-server, a
sycophant, lick-spittle, toady, etc. My first impulse is
always to credit folk with being nicer, cleverer, more
honest and amiable than they are. Then, on reflection, I
discover unpleasing characteristics, I detect their little
motives, and hate myself for not speaking. The fellow is
intolerable, why did I not tell him so ? Bitter recrimina-
tions from my critical self upon my flabby amiable half.

On the whole, then, I lead a pretty disgraceful inner
life—excepting when I pull myself together and smile
benignly on all things with a philosophical smugness, such
as is by no means my mood at this present moment. I
am so envious that a reprint of one of Romney's Ramus
girls sends me into a dry tearless anger—for the moment
till I turn over the next page. . . . Inwardly I was exa-
cerbated this morning when R—— recited, ' Come and
have a tiddle at the old Brown Bear,' and explained how
a charming ' young person ' sang this at breakfast the other
morning. It was simply *too* charming for him to hear.

To-night as I brushed my hair, I decided I was quite
good-looking, and *I believe* I mused that E—— was really
a lucky girl. . . . All that is the matter with me is a
colossal conceit and a colossal discontent, qualities exaggerated where a man finds himself in an environment
which . . .

.　　　.　　　.　　.　　　.　　　.　　.

You observant people will notice that this explanation is something of a self-defence whereby the virtue goes out of my confession. I plead guilty, but great and unprecedented provocation as well. Intense pride of individuality forbids that I should ever be other than, shall I say, amiably disposed towards myself *au fond*, however displeased I may be with my environment. It is indeed impossible without sending him to a lunatic asylum ever to knock a man off the balance of his self-esteem. . . . A man's loyalty to himself is the most pig-headed thing imaginable.

January 2.

The Fire Bogey

'This Box contains Manuscripts. One guinea will be paid to any one who in case of danger from fire saves it from damage or loss.'

Signed: W. N. P. BARBELLION.

I have had this printed in large black characters on a card, framed and nailed to my 'coffin' of Journals. I told the printer first to say *Two Guineas*, but he suggested that One Guinea was quite enough. I agreed but wondered how the devil *he* knew what the Journals were worth—nobody knows.

Next month, I expect I shall have a 'hand' painted on the wall and pointing towards the box. And the month after that I shall hire a fireman to be on duty night and day standing outside No. 101 in a brass helmet and his hatchet up at the salute.

These precious Journals! Supposing I lost them! I cannot imagine the anguish it would cause me. It would be the death of my real self and as I should take no pleasure in the perpetuation of my flabby, flaccid, anæmic, amiable puppet-self, I should probably commit suicide.

August 7.

Harvey who discovered the circulation of the blood also conducted a great many investigations into the Anatomy and development of insects. But all his MSS. and drawings disappeared in the fortunes of war, and one half of his life work thus disappeared. This makes me feverish, living as I do in Armageddon !

Again, all Malpighi's pictures, furniture, books and MSS. were destroyed in a lamentable fire at his house in Bononia, occasioned it is said by the negligence of his old wife.

About 1618, Ben Jonson suffered a similar calamity thro' a fire breaking out in his study. Many unpublished MSS. perished.

A more modern and more tragic example I found recently in the person of an Australian naturalist Dr Walter Stimpson, who lost all his MSS., drawings, and collections in the great fire of Chicago, and was so excoriated by this irreparable misfortune that he never recovered from the shock, and died the following year a broken man and unknown.

Of course the housemaid who lit the fire with the *French Revolution* is known to all, as well as Newton's ' Fido, Fido, you little know what you have done.'

There are many dangers in preserving the labours of years in MS. form. Samuel Butler (of *Erewhon*) advised writing in copying ink and then pressing off a second copy to be kept in another and separate locality. My own precautions for these Journals are more elaborate. Those who know about it think I am mad. I wonder. . . . But I dare say I am a pathetic fool—an incredible self-deceiver !

Anyhow—the ' coffin ' of raw material I sent down to T—— while I retain the two current volumes. This is to avoid Zeppelins. R—— took the ' coffin ' down for me on her way home from school, and at Taunton, inquisitive porters mistaking it, I suppose, for an infant's coffin carried it reverently outside the station and laid it down. She caught them looking at it just in time before her train left. Under her instructions they seized it by the brass handles and carried it back again. I sit now and with a good deal of curiosity fondle the idea of porters carrying about my Journals of confession. It's like being tickled in the palm of the hand. . . . Two volumes of abstracted entries I keep here, and, as soon as I am married, I intend to make a second copy of these. . . . Then all in God's good time I intend getting a volume ready for publication.

January 30.

Hearing Beethoven

To the Queen's Hall and heard Beethoven's Fifth and Seventh Symphonies.

Before the concert began I was in a fever. I kept on saying to myself, ' I am going to hear the Fifth and Seventh Symphonies.' I regarded myself with the most ridiculous self-adulation—I smoothed and purred over myself—a great contented Tabby cat—and all because I was so splendidly fortunate as to be about to hear Beethoven's Fifth and Seventh Symphonies.

It certainly upset me a little to find there were so many other people who were singularly fortunate as well, and it upset me still more to find some of them knitting and some reading newspapers as if they waited for sausage and mashed.

How I gloried in the Seventh ! I can't believe there was any one present who gloried in it as I did ! To be processing majestically up the steps of a great, an unimaginable palace (in the ' Staircase ' introduction), led by Sir Henry, is to have had at least a crowded ten minutes of glorious life—a suspicion crossed the mind at one time ' Good Heavens, they're going to knight me.' I cannot say if that were their intentions. But I escaped however . . .

I love the way in which a beautiful melody flits around the Orchestra and its various components like a beautiful bird.

January 19.

An Average Day

After a morning of very mixed emotions and more than one annoyance . . . at last sat down to lunch and a little peace and quiet with R——. We began by quoting

verse at one another in open competition. Of course
neither of us listened to the other's verses. We merely
enjoyed the pleasure of recollecting and repeating our own.
I began with Tom Moore's ' Row gently here, my Gondolier.' R—— guessed the author rightly at once and
fidgeted until he burst out with, ' The Breaths of kissing
night and day '—to me an easy one.   I gave, ' The Moon
more indolently sleeps to-night' (Baudelaire), and in
reply he did a great stroke by reciting some of the old
French of François Villon which entirely flummuxed me.

I don't believe we really love each other, but we cling
to each other out of ennui and discover in each other a
certain cold intellectual sympathy.

At the pay desk (Lyons' is our rendezvous) we joked with
the cashier—a cheerful, fat little girl, who said to R——
(indicating me),—

' He's a funny boy, isn't he ?'

' Dangerous,' chirped R——, and we laughed.   In the
street we met an aged, decrepit newsvendor—very dirty
and ragged—but his voice was unexpectedly fruity.

' British Success,' he called, and we stopped for the
sake of the voice.

' I'm not interested,' I said—as an appetiser.

' What ! Not . . . Just one, sir: I haven't sold a
single copy yet and I've a wife and four children.'

' That's nothing to me—I've three wives and forty
children,' I remarked.

' What !' in affected surprise, turning to R——, ' he's
Brigham Young from Salt Lake City. Yes I know it—
I've been there myself and been dry ever since. Give us
a drink, sir—just one.'

In consideration of his voice we gave him 2d. and passed
on. . . .

After giving a light to a Belgian soldier whose cigarette
had gone out, farther along we entered a queer old music
shop where they sell flageolets, serpents, clavichords, and
harps. We had previously made an appointment with the
man to have Schubert's Unfinished Symphony played to
us, so as to recall one or two of the melodies which we

can't recall and it drives us crazy. 'What is that one in
the second movement which goes like this?' and R——
whistled a fragment. 'I don't know,' I said, 'but let's
go in here and ask.' In the shop, a youth was kind enough
to say that if we cared to call next day, Madame A——,
the harp player would be home and would be ready to
play us the symphony.

So this morning, before Madame's appearance, this kind
and obliging youth put a gramophone record of it on, to
which we listened like two intelligent parrots with heads
sideways. Presently, the fat lady harpist appeared and
asked us just what we wanted to find out—a rather awkward question for us, as we did not want to 'find out'
anything excepting how the tunes went.

I therefore explained that as neither of us had sisters
or wives, and we both wanted, etc. . . . so would she
. . . ? In response, she smiled pleasantly and played us
the second movement on a shop piano. Meanwhile, Henry
the boy, hid himself behind the instruments at the rear of
the shop and as we signed to her she would say,—

'What's that, Henry?'

And Henry would duly answer from his obscurity,
'Wood wind,' or 'Solo oboe,' or whatever it was, and the
lad really spoke with authority. In this way, I began to
find out something about the work. Before I left, I presented her with a copy of the score, which she did not
possess and because she would not accept any sort of
remuneration.

'Won't you put your name on it?' she inquired.

I pointed gaily to the words 'Ecce homo,' which I had
scribbled across Schubert's name and said, 'There you are.'
Madame smiled incredulously and we said, 'Good-bye.'

It was a beautifully clement almost springlike day, and
at the street corner, in a burst of joyousness, we each
bought a bunch of violets off an old woman, stuck them
on the ends of our walking-sticks, and marched off with
them in triumphant protest to the B. M. Carried over our
shoulders, our flowers amused the police and ——, who
scarcely realised the significance of the ritual. 'This is

my protest,' said R——, 'against the war. It's like Oscar Wilde's Sunflower.'

On the way, we were both bitterly disappointed at a dramatic meeting between a man and woman of the artizan class which instead of beginning with a stormy, ' Robert, where's the rent, may I ask?' fizzled out into, ' Hullo, Charlie, why you *are* a stranger.'

At tea in the A.B.C. shop, we had a violent discussion on Socialism, and on the station platform, going home, I said that before marriage I intended saving up against the possibility of divorce—a domestic divorce fund.

' Very dreadful,' said R—— with mock gravity, ' to hear a recently affianced young man talk like that.'

. . . What should I do then? Marry? I suppose so. Shadows of the prison-house. At first I said I ought not to marry for two years. Then when I am wildly excited with her I say ' next week.' We could. There are no arrangements to be made. All her furniture—flat, etc. But I feel we ought to wait until the War is over.

At dinner-time to-night I was feverish to do three things at once: write out my day's Journal, eat my food, and read the *Journal* of Marie Bashkirtseff. Did all three—but unfortunately not at once, so that when I was occupied with one I would surreptitiously cast a glance sideways at the other—and repined.

After dinner, paid a visit to the —— and found Mrs —— playing Patience. I told her that 12,000 lives had been lost in the great Italian earthquake. Still going on dealing out the cards, she said in her gentle voice that that was dreadful and still absorbed in her cards inquired if earthquakes had aught to do with the weather.

' An earthquake must be a dreadful thing,' she gently piped, as she abstractedly dealt out the cards for a new game in a pretty Morris-papered room in Kensington.

January 20.

At a Public Dinner

. . . The timorous man presently took out his cigarette-case and was going to take out a cigarette, when he recollected that he ought first to offer one to the millionaire on his right. Fortunately the cigarette case was silver and the cigarettes appeared—from my side of the dinner-table—to be fat Egyptians. Yet the timorous and un-assuming bug-hunter hesitated palpably. Ought he to offer his cigarettes? He thought of his own balance at the bank and then of the millionaire's and trembled. The case after all was only silver and the cigarettes were not much more than a halfpenny each. Was it not im-pertinent? He sat a moment studying the open case which he held in both hands like a hymn book, while the millionaire ordered not wines—but a bass! At last courage came, and he inoffensively pushed the cigarettes towards his friend.

'No, thanks!' smiled the millionaire, 'I don't smoke.'

And so, 'twas a unicorn dilemma after all.

February 15.

Spent Xmas week at work in her studio, transcribing my Journals while she made drawings. All unbeknown to her I was copying out entries of days gone by—how scanda-lised she would be if . . . !

February 22.

What an amazing Masque is Rotten Row on a Sunday morning! I sat on a seat there this morning and watched awhile.

It was most exasperating to be in this kaleidoscope of human life without the slightest idea as to who they all were. One man in particular, I noticed—a first-class 'swell'—whom I wanted to touch gently on the arm, slip a half-a-crown into his hand and whisper, 'There, tell me all about yourself.'

Such 'swells' there were that out in the fairway, my little cockle-shell boat was wellnigh swamped. To be in the wake of a really magnificent Duchess simply rocks a small boat in an alarming fashion. I leaned over my paddles and gazed up. They steamed past unheeding, but I kept my nerve all right and pulled in and out quizzing and observing.

It is nothing less than scandalous that here I am aged 25 with no means of acquainting myself with contemporary men and women even of my own rank and station. The worst of it is, too, that I have no time to lose—in my state of health. This accursed ill-health cuts me off from everything. I make pitiful attempts to see the world around me by an occasional visit (wind, weather, and health permitting) to Petticoat Lane, the Docks, Rotten Row, Leicester Square, or the Ethical Church. To-morrow I purpose going to the Christian Scientists'. Meanwhile, the others participate in Armageddon.

February 23.

Looking for Lice at the Zoo

The other day went to the Zoological Gardens, and, by permission of the Secretary, went round with the keepers and searched the animals for ectoparasites.

Some time this year I have to make a scientific Report to the Zoological Society upon all the Lice which from time to time have been collected on animals dying in the gardens and sent me for study and determination.

We entered the cages, caught and examined several Tinamous, *Rhinochetus, Eurypygia,* and many more, to the tune of ' The Policeman's Holiday ' whistled by a Mynah!   It was great fun.

Then we went into the Ostrich House and thoroughly searched two Kiwis. These, being nocturnal birds, were roosting underneath a heap of straw. When we had finished investigating their feathers, they ran back to their straw at once, the keeper giving them a friendly tap on the rear to hurry them up a bit. They are just like little old women bundling along.

The Penguins, of course, were the most amusing, and, after operating fruitlessly for some time on a troublesome Adèle, I was amused to find, on turning around, all the other Adèles clustered close around my feet in an attitude of mute supplication.

The Armadillo required all the strength of two keepers to hold still while I went over his carcase with lens and forceps. I was also allowed to handle and examine the Society's two specimens of that amazing creature the *Echidna*.

Balæniceps rex like other royalty had to be approached decorously. He was a big, ill-tempered fellow, and quite unmanageable except by one keeper for whom he showed a preference. While we other conspirators hid ourselves outside, this man entered the house quietly and approached the bird with a gentle cooing sound. Then suddenly he grabbed the bill and held on. We entered at the same moment and secured the wings, and I began the search—without any luck. We must have made an amusing picture—three men holding on for dear life to a tall, grotesque bird with an imperial eye, while a fourth searched the feathers for parasites !

February 28.

What a boon is Sunday ! I can get out of bed just when the spirit moves me, dress and bath leisurely, even with punctilio. How nice to dawdle in the bath with a cigarette, to hear the holiday sound of Church bells ! Then comes that supreme moment when, shaven, clean, warm and hungry for breakfast and coffee, I stand a moment before the looking-glass and comb out my towzled hair with a parting as straight as a line in Euclid. That gives the finishing touch of self-satisfaction, and I go down to breakfast ready for the day's pleasure. I hate this weekday strain of having to be always each day at a set time in a certain place.

March 3.

I often sit in my room at the B. M. and look out at the traffic with a glassy, mesmerised face—a fainéant. How different from that extremely busy youth who came to London in 1912. Say—could that lad be I ? How many hours do I waste day-dreaming. This morning I dreamed and dreamed and could not stop dreaming—I had not the will to shake myself down to my task. . . . My memories simply trooped the colour.

It surprised me to find how many of them had gone out of my present consciousness and with what poignancy of feeling I recognised them again! How selfishly for the most part we all live in our present selves or in the selves that are to be.

Then I raced thro' all sorts of future possibilities—oh! when and how is it all going to end? How do you expect me to settle down to scientific research with all this internal unrest! The scientific man above all should possess the ' quiet mind in all changes of fortune '—Sir Henry Wotton's *How happy is he born and taught.*

The truth is I am a hybrid: a mixture of two very distinct temperaments and they are often at war. To keep two different natures and two different mental habits simultaneously at work is next to impossible. Consequently plenty of waste and fever and—as I might have discovered earlier for myself—success almost out of the question. If only I were pure-bred science or pure-bred art!

March 4.

Life is a dream and we are all somnambuloes. We know that for a fact at all times when we are most intensely alive—at crises of unprecedented change, in sorrow or catastrophe, or in any unusual incident brought swiftly to a close like a vision!

.   .   .   .   .   .

I sit here writing this—a mirage! Who am I? No one can say. What am I? ' A soap-bubble hanging from a reed.'

Every man is an inexhaustible treasury of human personality. He can go on burrowing in it for an eternity if he have the desire—and a taste for introspection. I like to keep myself well within the field of the microscope, and, with as much detachment as I can muster, to watch myself live, to report my observations of what I say, feel, think.

In default of others, I am myself my own spectator and self-appreciator—critical, discerning, vigilant, fond !—my own stupid Boswell, shrewd if silly. This spectator of mine, it seems to me, must be a very moral gentleman and eminently superior. His incessant attentions, while I go on my way misconducting myself, goad me at times into a surly, ill-tempered outbreak, like Dr. Johnson. I hate being shadowed and reported like this. Yet on the whole —like old Samuel again—I am rather pleased to be Boswelled. It flatters me to know that at least one person takes an unremitting interest in all my ways.

And, mind you, there are people who have seen most things but have never seen themselves walking across the stage of life. If someone shows them glimpses of themselves they will not recognise the likeness. How do you walk ? Do you know your own idiosyncrasies of gait, manner of speech, etc. ?

I never cease to interest myself in the Gothic architecture of my own fantastic soul.[1]

March 6.
The Punch and Judy Show.

Spent a most delightful half-an-hour to-day reading an account in the *Encyclopædia Britannica* (one of my favourite books—it's so ' gey disconnekkit ') the history of the Punch and Judy Show. It's a delightful bit of antiquarian lore and delighted me the more because it had never occurred to me before that it had an ancient history. I am thoroughly proud of this recent acquisition of knowledge and as if it were a valuable freehold I have been showing it off saying, ' Rejoice with me—see what I have got here.' I fired it off first in detail at ——; and H—— and D—— will probably be my victims to-morrow. After all, it is a charming little cameo of history: compact, with plenty of scope for conjecture, theory, research, and just that combination of all three which would suit my taste and capacity if I had time for a Monograph.

[1] 1917. I am now editing my own Journal—bowdlerising my own book!

March 22.

I waste much time gaping and wondering. During a walk or in a book or in the middle of an embrace, suddenly I awake to a stark amazement at everything. The bare fact of existence paralyses me—holds my mind in mortmain. To be alive is so incredible that all I do is to lie still and merely breathe—like an infant on its back in a cot. It is impossible to be interested in anything in particular while overhead the sun shines or underneath my feet grows a single blade of grass. ' The things immediate to be done,' says Thoreau, ' I could give them all up to hear this locust sing.' All my energies become immobilised, even my self-expression frustrated. I could not exactly master and describe how I feel during such moments.

March 23.   *Johnson v. Yves Delage.*

I expect we have all of us at one time or another heard ourselves addressing to annoying, objectionable acquaintances some such stinging castigation as Hazlitt's letter to Gifford, or Burke's letter to a Noble Lord, or Johnson's letter to Lord Chesterfield, or Rousseau's letter to the Archbishop of Paris. If only I could indulge myself ! At this moment I could glut my rancours on six different persons at least !

What a raging discontent I have suffered to-day ! What cynicism, what bitterness of spirit, what envy, hate, exasperation, childish petulance, what pusillanimous feelings and desires, what crude efforts to flout simple, ingenuous folk with my own thwarted, repressed self-assertiveness !

A solemn fellow told me he had heard from Johnson who said he had already had much success from collecting in moss.[1] With an icy politeness I asked who Johnson was. Who the Hell is Johnson ? As a *quid pro quo* I began to talk of Yves Delage, which left him as much in the dark as he left me. Our Gods differ, we have a different hierarchy.

[1] A method of collecting insects in winter by shaking moss over white paper.

' Well, how's your soul?' said R——, bursting in with
a sardonic smile.

I gave him a despairing look and said:

' Oh! a pink one with blue spots,' and he left me to my
fate.

Had tea with the —— and was amazed to find on the
music tray in the drawing-room of these inoffensive artists
a copy of ——'s Memoir on *Synapta*. Within his hearing,
I said, ' Did you and Mrs —— find this exciting reading?'
And I held it up with a sneer. I felt I had laid bare a
nerve and forthwith proceeded to make it twinge. ——,
of course, was glib with an explanation, yet the question
remains incalculable—just how pleased that young man
is with himself.

After tea went out into the Studio and watched these
two enthusiasts paint. I must have glowered at them.
I—the energetic, ambitious, pushing youth—of necessity
sitting down doing nought, as unconsidered as a child
playing on the floor. I recollected my early days in my
attic laboratory and sighed. Where is my energy now?

Mrs —— plays Chopin divinely well. How I envied
this man—to have a wife play you Chopin!

March 24.

It is fortunate I am ill in one way for I need not make
my mind up about this War. I am not interested in it
—this filth and lunacy. I have not yet made up my mind
about myself. I am so steeped in myself—in my moods,
vapours, idiosyncrasies, so self-sodden, that I am unable
to stand clear of the data, to marshal and classify the
multitude of facts and thence draw the deduction what
manner of man I am. I should like to know—if only as
a matter of curiosity. So what in God's name am I?
A fool, of course, to start with—but the rest of the diagnosis?

One feature is my incredible levity about serious
matters. Nothing matters, provided the tongue is not
furred. I have coquetted with death for so long now, and
endured such prodigious ill-health that my main idea when

in a fair state of repair is to seize the passing moment and squeeze it dry. The thing that counts is to be drunken; as Baudelaire says, ' One must be for ever drunken; that is the sole question of importance. If you would not feel the horrible burden of time that bruises your shoulders and bends you to the earth, you must be drunken without cease.'

Another feature is my insatiable curiosity. My purpose is to move about in this ramshackle, old curiosity shop of a world sampling existence. I would try everything, meddle lightly with everything. Religions and philosophies I devour with a relish, Pragmatism and Bishop Berkeley and Bergson have been my favourite bagatelles in turn. My consciousness is a ragbag of things: all quips, quirks, and quillets, all excellent passes of pate, all the ' obsolete curiosities of an antiquated cabinet ' take my eye for a moment ere I pass on. In Sir Thomas Browne's *Pseudodoxia*, I am interested to find ' why Jews do not stink, what is the superstition of sneezing after saluting, wherefore negroes are black,' and so forth. There is a poetic appropriateness that in A.D. 1915 I should be occupied mainly in the study of Lice. I like the insolence of it.

They tell me that if the Germans won it would put back the clock of civilisation for a century. But what is a meagre 100 years ? Consider the date of the first Egyptian dynasty ! We are now only in A.D. 1915—surely we could afford to chuck away a century or two ? Why not evacuate the whole globe and give the ball to the Boches to play with—just as an experiment to see what they can make of it. After all there is no desperate hurry. Have we a train to catch ? Before I could be serious enough to fight, I should want God first to dictate to me his programme of the future of mankind.

March 25.

Often in the middle of a quite vivid ten seconds of life, I find I have switched myself off from myself to make room for the person of a disinterested and usually

vulgar spectator. Even in the thrill of a devotional
kiss I have overheard myself saying, 'Hot stuff, this
witch.' Or in a room full of agreeable and pleasant people,
while I am being as agreeable as I know how, comes the
whisper in a cynical tone, 'These damned women.' I am
apparently a triple personality:

(1) The respectable youth.
(2) The foul-mouthed commentator and critic.
(3) The real but unknown I.

Curious that these three should live together amiably
in the same tenement !

In a Crowd

A crowd makes egotists of us all. Most men find it
repugnant to them to submerge themselves in a sea of
their fellows. A silent, listening crowd is potentially full
of commotion. Some poor devils suffocating and unable
any longer to bear the strain will shout, 'Bravo,' or 'Hear,
hear,' at every opportunity. At the feeblest joke we all
laugh loudly, welcoming this means of self-survival.
Hence the success of the Salvation Army. To be preached
at and prayed for in the mass for long on end is what
human nature can't endure in silence and a good deal of
self can be smuggled by an experienced Salvationist into
'Alleluia' or 'The Lord be praised.'

Naming Cockroaches

I had to determine the names of some exotic cock-
roaches to-day and finding it very difficult and dull raised
a weak smile in two enthusiasts who know them as
'Blattids' by rechristening them with great frivolity,
'Fat 'eds.'

'These bloody insects,' I said to an Australian entomologist of rare quality.

'A good round oath,' he answered quietly.

'If it was a square one it wouldn't roll properly,' I said.
It is nice to find an entomologist with whom I can swear
and talk bawdy.

March 26.
A Test of Happiness

The true test of happiness is whether you know what day of the week it is. A miserable man is aware of this even in his sleep. To be as cheerful and rosy-cheeked on Monday as on Saturday, and at breakfast as at dinner is to—well, make an ideal husband.

. . . .

. . . It is a strange metempsychosis, this transformation of an enthusiast—tense, excitable, and active, into a sceptic, nerveless, ironical, and idle. That's what ill-health can do for a man. To be among enthusiasts— zoologists, geologists, entomologists—as I frequently am, makes me feel a very old man, regarding them as children, and provokes painful retrospection and sugary sentimentality over my past flame now burnt out.

I do wonder where I shall end up; what shall I be twenty years hence? It alarms me to find I am capable of such remarkable changes in character. I am fluid and can be poured into any mould. I have moments when I see in myself the most staggering possibilities. I could become a wife-beater, and a drug-taker (especially the last). My curiosity is often such a ridiculous weakness that I have found myself playing Peeping Tom and even spying into private documents. In a railway carriage I will twist my neck and risk any rudeness to see the title of the book my neighbour is reading or how the letter she is reading begins.

April 10.

'Why,' asks Samuel Butler, 'should not chicken be born and clergymen be laid and hatched? Or why, at any rate, should not the clergyman be born full grown and in Holy Orders, not to say already beneficed? The present arrangement is not convenient . . . it is not only not perfect but so much the reverse that we could hardly find words to express our sense of its awkwardness if we could look upon it with new eyes. . . .

As soon as we are born, if we could but get up, bath

dress, shave, breakfast once for all, if we could ' cut '
these monotonous cycles of routine. If once the sun rose
it would stay up, or once we were alive we were immortal!
—how much forrader we should all get—always at the
heart of things, working without let or hindrance in a
straight line for the millennium! Now we waltz along
instead. Even planets die off and new ones come in their
place. How infinitely wearisome it seems. When an old
man dies what a waste, and when a baby is born what a
redundancy of labour in front!

Two People I hate in particular

The man walking along the pavement in front of me
giving me no room to pass under the satisfactory impression that he is the only being on the pavement or in the
street, city, country, world, universe: and it all belongs
to him even the moon and sun and stars.

The woman on the 'bus the other night—pouring out an
interminable flow of poisonous chatter into the ear of her
man—poor, exhausted devil who kept answering dreamily
' Oom ' and ' Yes ' and ' Oom '—how I hated her for his
sake!

April 11.

Beethoven's Fifth Symphony

If music moves me, it always generates images—a procession of apparently disconnected images in my mind.
In the Fifth Symphony, for example, as soon as the first
four notes are sounded and repeated, this magic population springs spontaneously into being. A nude, terror-
stricken figure in headlong flight with hands pressed to
the ears and arms bent at the elbows—a staring, bulgy-
eyed mad-woman such as one sees in Raemaeker's cartoons
of the Belgian atrocities. A man in the first onset of
mental agony on hearing sentence of death passed upon him.
A wounded bird, fluttering and flopping in the grass. It
is the struggle of a man with a steam-hammer—Fate. As
tho' thro' the walls of a closed room—some mysterious
room, a fearful spot—I crouch and listen and am conscious

that inside some brutal punishment is being meted out
—there are short intervals, then unrelenting pursuit, then
hammerlike blows—melodramatic thuds, terrible silences
(I crouch and wonder what has happened), and the pursuit begins again. I see clasped hands and appealing eyes
and feel very helpless and mystified outside. An epileptic
vision or an opium dream—*Dostoievsky* or De Quincey
set to music.

In the Second Movement the man is broken, an un-
recognisable vomit. I see a pale youth sitting with arms
hanging limply between the knees, hands folded, and with
sad, impenetrable eyes that have gazed on unspeakable
horrors. I see the brave, tearful smile, the changed life
after personal catastrophe, the Cross held before closing
eyes, sudden absences of mind, reveries, poignant retro-
spects, the rustle of a dead leaf of thought at the bottom
of the heart, the tortuous pursuit of past incidents down
into the silence of yesterday, the droning of comfortable
words, the painful collection of the wreckage of a life with
intent to ' carry on ' for a while in duty bound, for the
widow consolation in the child; a greyhound's cold wet
nose nozzling into a listless hand, and outside a Thrush
singing after the storm, etc., etc.

In the Third Movement comes the crash by which I
know something final and dreadful has happened. Then
the resurrection with commotion in Heaven: tempests and
human faces, scurryings to and fro, brazen portcullises
clanging to, never to open more, the distant roll of drums
and the sound of horses' hoofs. From behind the inmost
veil of Heaven I faintly catch the huzzas of a great multitude. Then comes a great healing wind, then a few ghost-
like tappings on the window pane till gradually the Avenue
of Arches into Heaven comes into view with a solemn
cortège advancing slowly along.

Above the great groundswell of woe, Hope is restored and
the Unknown Hero enters with all pomp into his Kingdom, etc., etc.

I am not surprised to learn that Beethoven was once on
the verge of suicide.

April 15.

There is an absurd fellow . . . who insists on taking
my pirouettes seriously. I say irresponsibly, ' All men
are liars,' and he replies with the jejuneness and exactitude of a pronouncing dictionary, ' A liar is one who makes
a false statement with intent to deceive.' What can I do
with him ? ' Did I ever meet a lady,' he asked, ' who
wasn't afraid of mice ?' ' I don't know,' I told him, ' I
never experiment with ladies in that way.'

He hates me.

May 11.

This mysterious world makes me chilly. It is chilly to
be alive among ghosts in a nightmare of calamity. This
Titanic war reduces me to the size and importance of a
debilitated housefly. So what is a poor egotist to do ?
To be a common soldier is to become a pawn in the game
between ambitious dynasts and their ambitious marshals.
You lose all individuality, you become a ' bayonet ' or a
' machine gun,' or ' cannon fodder,' or ' fighting material.'

May 22.

Generosity may be only weakness, philanthropy (beautiful word), self-advertisement, and praise of others sheer
egotism. One can almost hear a eulogist winding himself
up to strike his eulogy that comes out sententious, pom-
pous, and full of self.

May 23.

The following is a description of Lermontov by Maurice
Baring :

' He had except for a few intimate friends an impossible
temperament; he was proud, over-bearing, exasperated
and exasperating, filled with a savage *amour-propre* and
he took a childish delight in annoying; he cultivated " le
plaisir aristocratique de déplaire." . . . He could not
bear not to make himself felt and if he felt he was unsuccessful in this by fair means he resorted to unpleasant ones.

Yet he was warm-hearted, thirsting for love and kindness and capable of giving himself up to love if he chose. . . . At the bottom of all this lay no doubt a deep-seated disgust with himself and with the world in general, and a complete indifference to life resulting from large aspirations which could not find an outlet and recoiled upon himself.'

This is an accurate description of Me.

May 26.

The time will come—it's a great way off—when a joke about sex will be not so much objectionable as unintelligible. Thanks to Christian teaching, a nude body is now an obscenity, of the congress of the sexes it is indecent to speak and our birth is a corruption. Hence come a legion of evils: reticence, therefore ignorance and therefore venereal disease; prurience especially in adolescence, poisonous literature, and dirty jokes. The mind is contaminated from early youth; even the healthiest-minded girl will blush at the mention of *the wonder of creation*. Yet to the perfectly enfranchised mind it should be as impossible to joke about sex as about mind or digestion or physiology. The perfectly enfranchised poet—and Walt Whitman in 'The Song of Myself' came near being it—should be as ready to sing of the incredible raptures of the sexual act between 'twin souls' as of the clouds or sunshine. Every man or woman who has loved has a heart full of beautiful things to say but no man dare—for fear of the police, for fear of the coarse jests of others and even of a breakdown in his own highmindedness. I wonder just how much wonderful lyric poetry has thus been lost to the world !

May 27.
The Pool: A Retrospect

From above, the pool looked like any little innocent sheet of water. But down in the hollow itself it grew sinister. The villagers used to say and to believe that it had no bottom and certainly a very great depth in it could be *felt* if not accurately gauged as one stood at the water's edge. A long time ago, it was a great limestone quarry, but to-day the large mounds of rubble on one side of it are covered with grass and planted with mazzard trees, grown to quite a large girth. On the other side one is confronted by a tall sheet of black, carboniferous rock, rising sheer out of the inky water—a bare sombre surface on which no mosses even—'tender creatures of pity,' Ruskin calls them—have taken compassion by softening the jagged edges of the strata or nestling in the scars. It is an excellent example of ' Contortion ' as Geologists say, for the beds are bent into a quite regular geometrical pattern —syncline and anticline in waves—by deep-seated plutonic force that makes the mind quake in the effort to imagine it.

On the top of this rock and overhanging the water—a gaunt, haggard-looking Fir tree impends, as it seems in a perilous balance, while down below, the pool, sleek and shiny, quietly waits with a catlike patience.

In summer time, successive rows of Foxgloves one behind the other in barbaric splendour are ranged around the grassy rubble slopes like spectators in an amphitheatre awaiting the spectacle. Fire-bellied Efts slip here and there lazily thro' the water. Occasionally a Grass-snake would swim across the pool and once I caught one and on opening his stomach found a large fire-bellied Eft inside. The sun beats fiercely into this deep hollow and makes the water tepid. On the surface grows a glairy Alga, which was once all green but now festers in yellow patches and causes a horrible stench. Everything is absolutely still, air and water are stagnant. A large *Dytiscus* beetle rises to the surface to breathe and every now and then large bubbles of marsh gas come sailing majestically up from the depth and explode quietly into the fetid air. The *horrificness* of this place impressed me even when I was intent only on fishing there for bugs and efts. Now, seen in retrospect, it haunts me.

May 28.

It is only by accident that certain of our bodily functions are distasteful. Many birds eat the fæces of their young. The vomits of some Owls are formed into shapely pellets, often of beautiful appearance, when composed of the glittering multi-coloured elytra of Beetles, etc. The common Eland is known to micturate on the tuft of hair on the crown of its head, and it does this habitually, when lying down, by bending its head around and down—apparently because of the aroma, perhaps of sexual importance during mating time, as it is a habit of the male alone.

At lunch time, had an unpleasant intermittency period in my heart's action and this rather eclipsed my anxiety over a probable Zeppelin Raid. Went home to my rooms by 'bus, and before setting off to catch my train for West Wycombe to stay for the week-end at a Farm with E——swallowed two teaspoonfuls of neat brandy, filled my flask, and took a taxi to Paddington. At 3.50 started to walk to C—— H—— Farm from W. Wycombe Station, where E—— has been lodging for some weeks taking a rest cure after a serious nervous breakdown thro' overwork. As soon as I stepped out of the train, I sniffed the fresh air and soon made off down the road, happy to have left London and the winter and the war far behind. The first man of whom I inquired the way happened to have been working at the Farm only a few weeks ago, so I relied implicitly on his directions, and as it was but a mile and a half decided that my wobbly heart could stand the strain. I set out with a good deal of pleasurable anticipation. I was genuinely looking forward to seeing E——, altho' in the past few weeks our relations had become a little strained, at least on my part, mainly because of her little scrappy notes to me scribbled in pencil, undated, and dull! Yet I could do with a volume of ·Sonnets from the Portuguese.' These letters chilled me. In reply, I wrote with cold steel short, lifeless formal notes, for I felt genuinely aggrieved that she should care so little how she wrote to me or how she expressed her love. I

became ironical with myself over the prospect of marrying
a girl who appeared so little to appreciate my education
and mental habits. [What a popinjay!—1917.]   My
petty spirit grew disenchanted, out of love.   I was false
to her in a hundred inconsiderable little ways and even
deliberately planned the breaking off of the engagement
some months hence when she should be restored to
normal health.

But once in the country and, as I thought, nearing my
love at every step and at every bend in the road, even
anticipating her arms around me with real pleasure (for
she promised to meet me half way), I on a sudden grew
eager for her again and was assured of a happy week-end
with her.   Then the road grew puzzling and I became con-
fused, uncertain of the way.   I began to murmur she
should have given me instructions.   Every now and then
I had to stop and rest as my heart was beating so furiously.
Espying a farm on the left I made sure I had arrived at my
destination and walked across a field to it and entered the
yard where I heard some one milking a cow in a shed.   I
shouted over the five-barred gate into empty space, ' Is
this C—— H—— Farm ?' A labourer came out of the shed
and redirected me.   It was now ten to five.   I was tired
and out of sorts, and carried a troublesome little handbag.
I swore and cursed and found fault with E—— and
the Universe.

I trudged on, asking people, as I went, the way, finally
emerging from the cover of a beautiful wood thro' a wicket
gate almost at the entrance to the Farm I sought.   At the
front door we embraced affectionately and we entered at
once, I putting a quite good face upon my afternoon's
exertions—when I consider my unbridled fury of a short
time before.   E——, as brown as a berry, conducted me
to my bedroom and I nearly forgot to take this obvious
opportunity of kissing her again.

' How are you ?' I asked.
' All right,' she said, fencing.
' But really ?'
' All right.'

(A little nettled): ' My dear, that isn't going to satisfy me. You will have to tell me exactly how you are.'

After tea, I recovered myself and we went for a walk together. The beauty of the country warmed me up, and in the wood we kissed—I for my part happy and quite content with the present state of our relations, *i.e.*, affectionate but not perfervid.

May 29.

Got up early and walked around the Farm before breakfast. Everything promises to be delightful—young calves, broods of ducklings, and turkeys, fowls, cats and dogs. In the yard are two large Cathedral barns, with enormous pent roofs sloping down to within about two feet of the ground and entered by way of great double doors that open with the slowness and solemnity of a Castle's portal studded with iron knobs. It thrilled me to the marrow on first putting my head outside to be greeted with the grunt of an invisible pig that I found scraping his back on the other side of the garden wall.

In the afternoon, E—— and I sat together in the Beech Wood: E—— on a deck chair and I on a rug on the ground. In spite of our beautiful surroundings we did not progress very well, but I attributed her slight aloofness to the state of her nerves. She is still far from recovered. These wonderful Beech Woods are quite new to me. The forest beech is a very different plant from the solitary tree. In the struggle to reach the light the Forest Beech grows lean and tall and gives an extraordinary suggestion of wiry powerful strength. On the margins of the wood, Bluebells were mobilised in serried ranks. Great Tits whistled— in the language of our allies—' Bijou, Bijou ' and I agreed with every one of them.

Some folk don't like to walk over Bluebells or Buttercups or other flowers growing on the ground. But it is foolish to try to pamper Nature as if she were a sickly child. She is strong and can stand it. You can stamp on and crush a thousand flowers—they will all come up again next year.

By some labyrinthine way which I cannot now recall, the conversation worked round to a leading question by E.—if in times like these we ought not to cease being in love ? She was quite calm and serious. I said ' No, of course not, silly.' My immediate apprehension was that she had perceived the coldness in my letters and I was quite satisfied that she was so well able to read the signs in the sky. ' But you don't wish to go on ?' she persisted. I persisted that I did, that I had no misgivings, no second thoughts, that I was not merely taking pity on her, etc. The wild temptation to seize this opportunity for a break I smothered in reflecting how ill she was and how necessary to wait first till she was well again. These thoughts passed swiftly, vaguely like wraiths thro' my mind: I was barely conscious of them. Then I recalled the sonnet about coming in the rearward of a conquered woe and mused thereon. But I took no action. [Fortunately—for me. 1916.]

Presently with cunning I said that there was no cloud on my horizon whatever—only her ' letters disappointed me a little—they were so cold,' but ' as soon as I saw you again darling, those feelings disappeared.'

As soon as they were spoken I knew they were not as they might seem, the words of a liar and hypocrite. They *became* true. E—— looked very sweet and helpless and I loved her again as much as ever.

' It's funny,' she said, ' but I thought your letters were cold. Letters are so horrid.'

The incident shews how impossible is intellectual honesty between lovers. Truth is at times a hound which must to kennel.

' Write as you would speak,' said I. ' You know I'm not one to carp about a spelling mistake ! '

The latter remark astonished me. Was it indeed I who was speaking ? All the week I had been fuming over this. Yet I was honest: the Sun and E.'s presence were dispelling my ill-humours and crochets. We sealed our conversation with a kiss and swore never to doubt each other again. E.'s spell was beginning to act. It is always the same. I cannot resist

the actual presence of this woman. Out of her sight,
I can in cold blood plan a brutal rupture. I can pay her
a visit when the first kiss is a duty and the embrace a
formality. But after 5 minutes I am as passionate and
devoted as before. It is always thus. After leaving her,
I am angry to think that once more I have succumbed.

In the evening we went out into a field and sat together
in the grass. It is beautiful. We lay flat on our backs
and gazed up at the sky.

.   .   .   .

S. H. has died of enteric at Malta. In writing to Mrs
H., instead of dwelling on what a splendid fellow he was
I belaboured the fact that I still remembered our boyish
friendship in every detail and still kept his photo on my
mantelpiece and altho' ' in later years ' I didn't suppose
we ' had a great deal in common I discovered that a
friendship even between two small boys cannot wholly
disappear into the void.' Discussing myself when I ought
to have been praising him! Ugh! She will think what
a conceited, puff-breasted Jackanapes. These phrases
have rankled in my mind ever since I dropped the letter
into the letter-box. ' Your Stanley, Mrs H., was of course
a very inferior sort of person and naturally, you could
hardly expect me to remain friendly with him but rest
assured I hadn't forgotten him,' etc.

The Luxury of Lunacy

Yesterday, I read a paper at the Zoological Society about
lice. There was a goodly baldness of sconce and some
considerable length of beard present that listened or
appeared to listen to my innocent remarks with great
solemnity and sapience. . . . I badly wanted to tell
them some horrid stories about human lice but I had not
the courage. I wanted to jolt these middle-aged gentlemen by performing a few tricks but I am too timid for
such adventures. But before going to sleep I imagined a
pandemonium in which with a perfectly glacial manner I

produced lice alive from my pockets, conjured them down from the roof in a rain, with skilful sleight of hand drew them out of the chairman's beard, made the ladies scream as I approached, dared to say they were all lousy and unclean and finished up with an eloquent apostrophe after the manner of Thomas de Quincey (and of Sir Walter Raleigh before him) beginning:

'O just, subtle and eloquent avenger, pierce the hides of these abominable old fogies, speckle their polished calvaria with the scarlet blood drops. . . .'

But I hadn't the courage. Shelley in a crowded omnibus suddenly burst out: 'O let us sit upon the ground and tell sad stories of the deaths of Kings, etc.' I've always wanted to do something like that and when I have £5 to spare I hope to pull the communication cord of an express train—my hands tingle as often as I look at it. Dr. Johnson's courage in tapping the lamp-posts is really everyone's envy tho' we laugh at him for it and say, green-eyed, that he was mad. In walking along the pavement, I sometimes indulge myself in the unutterable, deeply rooted satisfaction of stepping on a separate flagstone where this is possible with every stride. And if this is impossible or not easy, there arises in me a vague mental uneasiness, some subconscious suspicion that the world is not properly geometrical and that the whole universe perhaps is working out of truth. I am also rather proud of my courageous self-surrender to the dæmon of laughter, especially in those early days when H. and I used to sit opposite one another and howl like hyenas. After the most cacophonous cachinnations as soon as we had recovered ourselves he or I would regularly remark in serious and confidential tones, 'I say—we *really* are going mad.' But what a delightful luxury to be thus mad amid the great, spacious, architectural solemnity with gargoyles and effigies of a scientific meeting ! Some people never do more than chuckle or smile—and they are often very humorous happy people, ignorant nevertheless of the joy of riding themselves on the snaffle and losing all control.

While boating on —— last summer, we saw two persons,

a man and a girl sitting together on the beach reading a
book with heads almost touching.

'I wonder what they're reading?' I said, and I was
dying to know. We made a few facetious guesses.

'Shall I ask?'

'Yes, do,' said Mrs ——.

The truth is we all wanted to know. We were suddenly
mad with curiosity as we watched the happy pair turning
over leaf after leaf.

While R—— leaned on his oars, I stood up in the boat
and threatened to shout out a polite enquiry—just to prove
that the will is free. But seeing my intention the boat-
load grew nervous and said seriously, 'No,' which unnerved
me at the last moment so I sat down again. Why was I
so afraid of being thought a lunatic by two persons in the
distance whom I had never seen and probably would
never see again? Besides I *was* a lunatic—we all were.

In our post-prandial perambulations about S. Kensington
G—— and I often pass the window of a photographer's
shop containing always a profusion of bare arms, chests,
necks, bosoms belonging to actresses, aristocrats and
harlots—some very beautiful indeed. Yet on the whole
the window annoys us, especially one picture of a young
thing with an arum lily (ghastly plant!) laid exquisitely
across her breast.

'Why do we suffer this?' I asked G——, tapping the
window ledge as we stood.

'I don't know,' he answered lamely—morose. (Pause
while the two embittered young men continue to look in
and the beautiful young women continue to look out.)

Thoroughly disgruntled I said at last: 'If only we had
the courage of our innate madness, the courage of children,
lunatics and men of genius, we should get some stamp
paper, and stick a square beneath each photograph with
our comments.'

Baudelaire describes how he dismissed a glass vendor
because he had no coloured glasses—'glasses of rose and
crimson, magical glasses, glasses of Paradise'—and, stepping out on to his balcony, threw a flowerpot down on the

tray of glasses as soon as the man issued into the street below, shouting down furiously, 'The Life Beautiful! The Life Beautiful.'

Bergson's theory is that laughter is a 'social gesture' so that when a man in a top hat treads on a banana skin and slips down we laugh at him for his lack 'of living pliableness.' At this rate we ought to be profoundly solemn at Baudelaire's action and moreover a 'social gesture' is more likely to be an expression of society's will to conformity in all its members rather than any dangerous 'living pliableness.' Society hates living pliableness and prefers drill, routine, orthodoxy, conformity. It hated the living pliableness of Turner, of Keats, of Samuel Butler and a hundred others.

But to return to lunacy: the truth is we are all mad fundamentally and are merely schooled into sanity by education. Pascal wrote: 'Men are so necessarily mad that not to be mad would amount to another form of madness.' And, in fact, the man who has succeeded in extirpating this intoxication of life is usually said to be 'temporarily insane.' In those melancholy interludes of sanity when the mind becomes rationalised we all know how much we have been deceived and gulled, what an extraordinary spectacle humanity presents rushing on in noise and tumult no one knows why or whither. Look at that tailor in his shop—why does he do it? Some day in the future he thinks he will. . . . But the day never comes and he is nevertheless content.

May 30.

A brilliantly sunny day. This funny old farm-house where we are staying quite delights me. It is pleasant, too, to dawdle over dressing, to put away shaving tackle for a day or so, to jump out of bed in the morning and thrust my head out of the window into the fresh and stock-scented air of the garden, listen to the bird chorus or watch a 'scrap' in the poultry-run. Then all unashamed, I dress myself before a dear old lady in a flowery print gown concealing 4 thin legs and over the top of the mirror a piece

of lace just like a bonnet, caught up in front by a piece
of pink ribbon. On the walls Pear's Soap Annuals, on
a side table *Swiss Family Robinson* and *Children of the
New Forest*. Then there are rats under the floors, two
wooden staircases which wind up out of sight, two white
dairies, iron hapses on all the doors and a privy at the top
of the orchard. (Tell me—how do you explain the psy-
chosis of a being who on a day must have seized hammer
and nail and an almanac picture of a woman in the snow
with a basket of goodies—'An Errand of Mercy'—carried
all three to the top of the orchard and nailed the picture
up on the dirty wall in the semi-darkness of an earth-
closet ?)

Got up quite early before breakfast and went birds'-
nesting. . . . It would take too long and be too sentimental for me to record my feelings on looking into the
first nest I found—a Chaffinch's, the first wild bird's eggs
I have seen for many years. As I stood with an egg between thumb and forefinger, my memories flocked down
like white birds and surrounded me. I remained still, fed
them with my thoughts and let them perch upon my person
—a second St. Francis of Assisi. Then I shoo'ed them all
away and prepared for the more palpitating enjoyment of
to-day.

After breakfast we sat in the Buttercup field—my love
and I—and 'plucked up kisses by the roots that grew
upon our lips.' The sun was streaming down and the
field thickly peopled with Buttercups. From where we
sat we could see the whole of the valley below and Farmer
Whaley—a speck in the distance—working a machine in
a field. We watched him idly. The gamekeeper's gun
went off in one of the covers. It was jolly to put our heads
together right down deep in the Buttercups and luxuriously
follow the pelting activities of the tiny insects crawling
here and there in the forest of grass, clambering over a
broken blade athwart another like a wrecked tree or busily
enquiring into some low scrub at the roots. A chicken
came our way and he seemed an enormous bird from the
grass-blade's point of view. How nice to be a chicken in

a field of Buttercups and see them as big as Sunflowers!
or to be a Gulliver in the Beech Woods! to be so small
as to be able to climb a Buttercup, tumble into the corolla
and be dusted yellow or to be so big as to be able to pull
up a Beech-tree with finger and thumb! If only a man
were a magician, could play fast and loose with rigid
Nature? what a multitude of rich experiences he could
discover for himself!

I looked long and steadily this morning at the magnificent torso of a high forest Beech and tried to project myself
into its lithe tiger-like form, to feel its electric sap vitalising
all my frame out to the tip of every tingling leaf, to possess
its splendid erectness in my own bones. I could have
flung my arms around its fascinating body but the aus-
terity of the great creature forbad it. Then a Hawk fired
my ambition!—to be a Hawk, or a Falcon, to have a
Falcon's soul, a Falcon's heart—that splendid muscle in
the cage of the thorax—and the Falcon's pride and saga-
cious eye![1]

.   .   .   \ .   .   .   .

When the sun grew too hot we went into the wood where
waves of Bluebells dashed up around the foot of the Oak
in front of us. . . . I never knew before, the delight of
offering oneself up—an oblation of one's whole being; I
even longed for some self-sacrifice, to have to give up
something for her sake. It intoxicated me to think I was
making another happy. . . .

After a lunch of scrambled eggs and rhubarb and cream
went up into the Beech Wood again and sat on a rug at
the foot of a tree. The sun filtered in thro' the greenery
casting a 'dim, religious light.'

'It's like a cathedral,' I chattered away, 'stained glass
windows, pillars, aisles—all complete.'

[1] 1917. Cf. Sainte-Beuve's Essay on Maurice de Guérin: 'Il
aimait à se répandre et presque à se ramifier dans la Nature. Il
a exprimé en mainte occasion cette sensation diffuse, errante; il
y avait des jours ou, dans son amour ou calme, il enviait la vie
forte et muette qui règne sous l'écorce des chênes; il rêvait à je
ne sais quelle métamorphose en arbre. . . .'

' It would be nice to be married in a Cathedral like this,'
she said.   ' At C—— Hall Cathedral, by the Rev. Canon
Beech . . .'

' Sir Henry Wood was the organist.'

' Yes,' she said, ' and the Rev. Blackbird the precentor.'
We laughed over our silliness!

Shrew-mice pattered over the dead leaves and one came
boldly into view under a bramble bush—she had never
seen one before.   Overhead, a ribald fellow of a Blackbird
whistled a jaunty tune.   E—— laughed.   ' I am sure that
Blackbird is laughing at us,' she said.   ' It makes me feel
quite hot.'

. . . .

This evening we sat on the slope of a big field where by
lowering our eyes we could see the sun setting behind the
grass blades—a very pretty sight which I do not remember
ever to have noted before.   A large blue *Carabus* beetle
was stumbling about, Culvers cooed in the woods near by.
It was delightful to be up 600 feet on a grassy field under
the shadow of a large wood at sunset with my darling.

May 31.

Sitting at tea in the farm house to-day E—— cried
suddenly, pointing to a sandy cat in the garden:

' There,—he's the father of the little kittens in the barn
and I'll tell you how we know.   P—— noticed the kittens
had big feet and later on saw that old Tom stalking across
the garden with big feet of exactly the same kind.'

' So you impute the paternity of the kittens to the gentleman under the laurel bushes ?'

I looked at the kittens to-night and found they had
extra toes.   ' Mr Sixtoes,' as E—— calls him also pos-
sesses six toes, so the circumstantial evidence looks black
against him.

June 1.

In the Beech Wood all the morning.   Heigh-ho! it's
grand to lie out as straight as a line on your back, gaze upwards into the tree above, and with a caressing eye follow

its branches out into their multitudinous ramifications
forward and back—luxurious travel for the tired eye.
. . . Then I would shut my eyes and try to guess where
her next kiss would descend. Then I opened my eyes and
watched her face in the most extravagant detail, I counted
the little filaments on her precious mole and saw the sun
thro' the golden down of her throat. . . .

Sunlight and a fresh wind. A day of tiny cameos, little
coups d'oeil, fleeting impressions snapshotted on the mind:
the glint on the keeper's gun as he crossed a field a mile
away below us, sunlight all along a silken hawser which
some Spider engineer had spun between the tops of two
tall trees spanning the whole width of a bridle path, the
constant patter of Shrew-mice over dead leaves, the pen-
dulum of a Bumble-bee in a flower, and the just perceptible
oscillation of the tree tops in the wind. While we are at
meals the perfume of Lilac and Stocks pours in thro' the
window and when we go to bed it is still pouring in bv
the open lattice.

June 2.

Each day I drop a specially selected Buttercup in past
the little ' Peeler,' at the apex of the ' V ' to lie among the
blue ribbons of her camisoles—those dainty white leaves
that wrap around her bosom like the petals around the
heart of a Rose. Then at night when she undresses, it falls
out and she preserves it.

In the woods, hearing an extra loud patter on the leaves,
we turned our heads and saw a Frog hopping our way. I
caught him and gave an elementary lesson in Anatomy.
I described to her the brain, the pineal organ in Anguis,
Sphenodon's pineal eye, etc. Then we fell to kissing
again. . . . Every now and then she raises her head and
listens (like a Thrush on the lawn) thinking she hears
someone approach. We neither of us speak much . . .
and at the end of the day, the nerve endings on my lips
are tingling.

Farmer Whaley is a funny old man with a soft pious voice. When he feeds the Fowls, he sucks in a gentle, caressing noise between his lips for all the world as if he fed them because he loved them, and not because he wants to fatten them up for killing. His daughter Lucy, aged 22, loves all the animals of the farm and they all love her; the Cows stand monumentally still while she strokes them down the blaze or affectionately waggles their dewlaps. This morning, she walked up to a little Calf in the farm-yard scarce a fortnight old which started to 'back' in a funny way, spraddling out its legs and lowering its head. Miss Lucy laughed merrily and cried 'Ah! you funny little thing,' and went off on her way to feed the Fowls who all raced to the gate as soon as they heard her footsteps. She brought in two double-yolked Ducks' eggs for us to see and marvel at. In the breakfast room stands a stuffed Collie dog in a glass case. I'd as soon embalm my grand-mother and keep her on the sideboard.

I asked young George, the farm-boy, what bird went like this: I whistled it. He looked abashed and said a Chaffinch. I told Miss Lucy, who said George was a silly boy, and Miss Lucy told Farmer Whaley, who said George ought to know better—it was a Mistle-Thrush.

The letters are brought us each morning by a tramp with a game leg who secretes his Majesty's Mails in a shabby bowler hat, the small packages and parcels going to the roomy tail pocket of a dirty morning coat. A de-cayed gentleman of much interest to us.

June 3.

We have made a little nest in the wood and I lead her into it by the hand over the briars and undergrowth as if conducting her to the grand piano on a concert platform. I kissed her. . . .

Then in a second we switch back to ordinary conversa-tion. In an ordinary conversational voice I ask the trees, the birds, the sky.

' What's become of all the gold ?'

' What's become of Waring ?'
' What is Love ?   'Tis not hereafter.'
' Where are the snows of yesteryear ?'
' Who killed Cock Robin ?'
' Who's who ?'
And so on thro' all the great interrogatives that I could
think of till she stopped my mouth with a kiss and we
both laughed.

' Miss Penderkins,' I say. ' Miss Penderlet, Miss
Pender-au-lait, Miss Pender-filings.'

' What do I mean ?' she cries.   ' What's the point of the
names ?   Why take my name in vain ?   Why ?   What ?
How ?'

She does not know that clever young men sometimes
trade on their reputation among simpler folk by pretending that meaningless remarks conceal some subtlety or
cynicism, some little Attic snap.

.   .   .   .

I have been teaching her to distinguish the songs of
different birds and often we sit a long while in the Cathedral Wood while I say, ' What's that ?' and ' What's that ?'
and she tells me.   It is delightful to watch her dear serious
face as she listens. . . .   This evening I gave a *viva voce*
examination as per below:

' What does the Yellow Hammer say ?'
' What colour are the Hedge Sparrow's eggs ?
' Describe the Nightjar's voice.'
' How many eggs does it lay ?'

' Oh! you never told me about the Nightjar,' she cried
outraged.

' No: it's a difficult question put in for candidates taking
honours.'

Then we rambled on into Tomfoolery.   ' Describe the
call-note of a motor omnibus.'   ' Why does the chicken
cross the road ?' and ' What's that ?'—when a railway
engine whistled in the distance.

Measure by this our happiness !

June 4.

At a quarter past eight, this morning, the horse and trap were awaiting me outside, and bidding her ' Goodbye ' I got in and drove off—she riding on the step down so far as the gate. Then we waved till we were out of sight. Back in London by 10 a.m. She makes slow progress, poor dear—her nerves are still very much of a jangle. But I am better, my heart is less wobbly.

June 5.

R—— cannot make me out. He says one day I complain bitterly at not receiving a Portuguese sonnet once a week, and the next all is well and Love reigneth. ' Verily a Sphinx.'

June 7.

Spent the afternoon at the Royal Army Medical College in consultation with the Professor of Hygiene. Amid all the paraphernalia of research, even when discussing a serious problem with a serious Major, I could not take myself seriously. I am incurably trivial and always feel myself an irresponsible youth, wondering and futile, among owlish grown-ups.

At 4 p.m. departed and went down on Vauxhall Bridge and watched a flour-barge being unloaded before returning to the Museum. I could readily hang on behind a cart, stare at an accident, pull a face at a policeman and then run away.

June 20.

. . . It annoys me to find the *laissez-faire* attitude of our relatives. Not one with a remonstrance for us and yet all the omens are against our marriage. In the state of my nervous system and in the state of hers—we have both had serious nervous break-downs—how impossible it seems ! Yet they say all the old conventional things to us, about our happiness and so on ! . . .

. . . Am I a moral monster ? Surely a man who can

combine such calculating callousness with really generous impulses of the heart is—what ?

The truth is I think I am in love with her: but I am also mightily in love with myself. One or the other has to give.

June 25.

If sometimes you saw me in my room by myself, you would say I was a ridiculous coxcomb. For I walk about, look out of the window then at the mirror—turning my head sideways perhaps so as to see it in profile. Or I gaze down into my eyes—my eyes always impress me—and wonder what effect I produce on others. This, I believe, is not so much vanity as curiosity. I know I am not prepossessing in appearance—my nose is crooked and my skin is blotched. Yet my physique—because it is mine—interests me. I like to see myself walking and talking. I should like to hold myself in my hand in front of me like a Punchinello and carefully examine myself at my leisure.

June 28.

Saw my brother A—— off at Waterloo en route for Armageddon. Darling fellow. He shook hands with P—— and H——, and P—— wished him ' Goodbye, and good luck.' Then he held my hand a moment, said ' Goodbye, old man,' and for a second gave me a queer little nervous look. I could only say ' Goodbye,' but we understand each other perfectly. . . . It is horrible. I love him tenderly.

June 29.

Sleep

Sleep means unconsciousness: unconsciousness is a solemn state—you get it for example from a blow on the head with a mallet. It always weightily impresses me to see someone asleep—especially someone I love as to-day, stretched out as still as a log—who perhaps a few minutes ago was alive, even animated. And there is nothing so welcome, unless it be the sunrise, as the first faint gleam of recognition in the half-opened eye when consciousness like a mighty river begins to flow in and restore our love to us again.

When I go to bed myself, I sometimes jealously guard my faculties from being filched away by sleep. I almost fear sleep: it makes me apprehensive—this wonderful and unknowable Thing which is going to happen to me for which I must lay myself out on a bed and wait, with an elaborate preparedness. Unlike Sir Thomas Browne, I am not always so content to take my leave of the sun and sleep, if need be, into the resurrection. And I sometimes lie awake and wonder when the mysterious Visitor will come to me and call me away from this thrilling world, and how He does it, to which end I try to remain conscious of the gradual process and to understand it: an impossibility of course involving a contradiction in terms. So I shall never know, nor will anybody else.

July 2.

I've had such a successful evening—you've no idea ! The pen simply flew along, automatically easy, page after page in perfect sequence. My style trilled and bickered and rolled and ululated in an infinite variety; you will find in it all the subtlest modulations, inflections and suavities. My afflatus came down from Heaven in a bar of light like the Shekinah—straight from God, very God of very God. I worked in a golden halo of light and electric sparks came off my pen nib as I scratched the paper.

July 3.

The Clever Young Man

Argued with R—— this morning. He is a type specimen of the clever young man. We both are. Our flowers of speech are often forced hot-house plants, paradoxes and cynicisms fly as thick as driving rain and Shaw is our great exemplar. I could write out an exhaustive analysis of the clever young man and being one myself can speak from ' inspired sources ' as the newspapers say.

A common habit is to underline and memorise short, sharp, witty remarks he sees in books and then on future occasions dish them up for his own self-glorification. If the author be famous he begins, ' As —— says, etc.' If unknown the quotation is quietly purloined. He is always very self-conscious and at the same time very self-possessed and very conceited. You tell me with tonic candour that I am insufferably conceited. In return, I smile, making a sardonic avowal of my good opinion of myself, my theory being that as conceit is, as a rule, implicit and, as a rule, blushingly denied, you will mistake my impudent confession for bluff and conclude there is really something far more substantial and honest beneath my apparent conceit. If, on the other hand, I am conceited, why I have admitted it—I agree with you—but tho' there is no virtue in the confession being quite detached and unashamed—still you haven't caught me by the tail. It is very difficult to circumvent a clever young man. He is as agile as a monkey.

His principal concern of course is to arouse and maintain a reputation for profundity and wit. This is done by the simple mechanical formula of antithesis : if you like winkles he proves that cockles are inveterately better; if you admire Ruskin he tears him to ribbons. If you want to learn to swim—as it is safer, he shows it is more dangerous to know how to swim and so on. I know his whole box of tricks. I myself am now playing the clever young man by writing out this analysis just as if I were not one myself.

You doubt my cleverness ? Well, some years ago in R——'s presence I called —— ' the Rev. Fastidious Brisk,'—the nickname be it recalled which Henley gave to Stevenson (without the addition of ' Rev.'). At the time I had no intention of appropriating the witticism as I quite imagined R—— was acquainted with it. His unexpected explosion of mirth, however, made me uncomfortably uncertain of this, yet for the life of me I couldn't muster the honesty to assure him that my feather was a borrowed one. A few weeks later he referred to it again

as ' certainly one of my better ones '—but still I remained
dumb and the time for explanations went for once and all.
Now see what a pretty pickle I am in: the name ' Brisk ' or
' F. B.' is in constant use by us for this particular person
—he goes by no other name, meanwhile I sit and wonder
how long it will be before R—— finds me out. . There are
all sorts of ways in which he might find out: he might
read about it for himself, someone might tell him or—
worst of all—one day when we are dining out somewhere
he will announce to the whole company my brilliant
appellation as a little after-dinner diversion: I shall at once
observe that the person opposite me *knows* and is about
to air his knowledge; then I shall look sternly at him and
try to hold him: he will hesitate and I shall land him with
a left and right: ' I suppose you've read Henley's verses
on Stevenson ?' I remark easily and in a moment or so
later the conversation has moved on.

August 1.

Am getting married at —— Register Office on September 15th. It is impossible to set down here all the
labyrinthine ambages of my will and feelings in regard to
this event. Such incredible vacillations, doubts, fears.
I have been living at a great rate below surface recently.
' If you enjoy only twelve months' happiness,' the Doctor
said to me, ' it is worth while.' But he makes a recom-
mendation. . . . At his suggestion E—— went to see
him and from his own mouth learnt all the truth about the
state of my health, to prevent possible mutual recrimina-
tions in the future.[1] To marry an introspective dyspeptic
—what a prospect for her ! . . . I exercise my micro-
scopic analysis on her now as well as on myself. . . . This
power in me is growing daily more automatic and more
repugnant. It is a nasty morbid unhealthy growth that
I want to hide if I cannot destroy. It amounts to being
able at will to switch myself in and out of all my most
cherished emotions ; it is like the case in Sir Michael Foster's

[1] Cf. 1916, November 6.

Physiology of a man who, by pressing a tumour in his neck could stop or at any rate control the action of his heart.

August 2.

House pride in newly-wed folk, for example, H. and D. to-day at Golder's Green or the Teignmouth folk, is very trying to the bachelor visitor. They will carry a chair across the room as tenderly as tho' it were a child and until its safe transit is assured, all conversation goes by the board. Or the wife suddenly makes a remark to the husband *sotto voce*, both thereupon start up simultaneously (leaving the fate of Warsaw undecided) while you, silenced by this un-expected manœuvre, wilt away in your chair, the preg-nant phrase still-born on your lips. Presently they re-enter the room with the kitten that was heard in the scullery or with a big stick used to flourish at a little Tomtit on the rose tree. *She* apologises and both settle down again, recompose their countenances into a listening aspect and with a devastating politeness, pick up the poor, little, frayed-out thread of the conversation where it left off with: ' Europe? you were saying . . .' I mobilise my scattered units of ideas but it is all a little chilly for the lady of the house if she listens with her face and speaks with her lips—her heart is far from me: she fixes a glassy eye on the tip of my cigarette, waiting to see if the ash will fall on her carpet.

August 6.

The most intimate and extensive journal can only give each day a relatively small sifting of the almost infinite number of things that flow thro' the consciousness. How-ever vigilant and artful a diarist may be, plenty of things escape him and in any event re-collection is not re-creation. . . .

To keep a journal is to have a secret liaison of a very sentimental kind. A *journal intime* is a super-confidante to whom everything is told and confessed. For an en-gaged or married man to have a secret super-confidante who

knows things which are concealed from his lady seems to
me to be deliberate infidelity.   I am as it were engaged
to two women and one of them is being deceived.   The
word ' Deceit ' comes up against me in this double life I
lead, and insists I shall name a plain thing bluntly.   There
is something very like sheer moral obliquity in these entries behind her back. . . .   Is this journal habit slowly
corrupting my character ?   Can an engaged or married
man conscientiously continue to write his *journal
intime?*

This question of giving up my faithful friend after
September I must consider.

Of course most men have something to conceal from
someone.   Most married men are furtive creatures, and
married women too.   But I have a Gregers Werle-like
passion for life to be lived on a foundation of truth in every
intercourse.   I would have my wife know all about me
and if I cannot be loved for what I surely am, I do not
want to be loved for what I am not.   If I continue to write
therefore she shall read what I have written. . . .

My Journal keeps open house to every kind of happening
in my soul.   Provided it is a veritable autochthon—I don't
care how much of a tatterdemalion or how ugly or repulsive
—I take him in and—I fear sponge him down with excuses
to make him more creditable in other's eyes.   You may
say why trouble whether you do or whether you don't tell
us all the beastly little subterranean atrocities that go on
in your mind.   Any eminently ' right-minded ' *Times* or
Spectator reader will ask: ' Who in Faith's name is interested in your introspective muck-rakings—in fact, who
the Devil are you ?'   To myself, a person of vast importance and vast interest, I reply,—as are other men if I
could but understand them as well.   And in the firm
belief that whatever is inexorably true however unpleasant
and discreditable (in fact true things can never lack a
certain dignity), I would have you know Mr *Times*- and
Mr *Spectator*-reader that actual crimes have many a time
been enacted in the secrecy of my own heart and the only
difference between me and an habitual criminal is that

the habitual criminal has the courage and the nerve and I
have not. What, then, may these crimes be? Nothing
much—only murders, theft, rape, etc. None of them
thank God! fructify in action—or at all events only the
lesser ones. My outward and visible life if I examine it
is merely a series of commonplace, colourless and thoroughly
average events. But if I analyse myself, my inner life,
I find I am both incredibly worse and incredibly better
than I appear. I am Christ and the Devil at the same
time—or as my sister once called me—a child, a wise man,
and the Devil all in one. Just as no one knows my crimes
so no one knows of my good actions. A generous impulse
seizes me round the heart and I am suddenly moved to
give a poor devil a £5 note. But no one knows this because
by the time I come to the point I find myself handing him
a sixpenny-bit and am quite powerless to intervene.
Similarly my murders end merely in a little phlegm.

August 7.

Two Adventures

On a 'bus the other day a woman with a baby sat opposite, the baby bawled, and the woman at once began to
unlace herself, exposing a large, red udder, which she
swung into the baby's face. The infant, however, continued to cry and the woman said,—

'Come on, there's a good boy—if you don't, I shall give
it to the gentleman opposite.'

Do I look ill-nourished?

.   .   .   .

'"Arma virumque cano,"' a beggar said to me this
morning in the High Street, 'or as the boy said, "Arms
and the man with a dog," mistaking the verb for the noun.
Oh! yes, sir, I remember my Latin. Of course, I feel it's
rather invidious my coming to you like this, but everything
is absolutely "non est" with me,' and so on.

'My dear sir,' I answered expansively, 'I am as poor as
you are. You at least have seen better days you say—
but I never have.'

He changed in a minute his cringeing manner and rejoined:

'No I shouldn't think you had,' eyeing me critically and slinking off.

Am I *so* shabby ?

August 8.

By Jove ! I hope I live ! . . . Why does an old crock like myself go on living ? It causes me genuine amazement. I feel almost ashamed of myself because I am not yet dead seeing that so many of my full-blooded contemporaries have perished in this War.   I am so grateful for being allowed to live so long that nothing that happens to me except death could upset me much.   I should be happy in a coal mine.

August 12.

Suffering from indigestion.   The symptoms include:
Excessive pandiculation,
Excessive oscitation,
Excessive eructation,
Dyspnœa,
Sphygmic flutters,
Abnormal porrigo,
A desiccated epidermis.

August 16.

Lice or ' Creeping Ferlies '[1]

I probably know more about Lice than was ever before stored together within the compass of a single human mind ! I know the Greek for Louse, the Latin, the French, the German, the Italian.   I can reel off all the best remedies for Pediculosis: I am acquainted with the measures adopted for dealing with the nuisance in the field by the German Imperial Board of Health, by the British R.A.M.C., by the armies of the Russians, the French, the Austrians, the Italians.   I know its life history and structure, how

---

[1] Cf. Burns's poem ' On a Louse.'

many eggs it lays and how often, the anatomy of its brain and stomach and the physiology of all its little parts. I have even pursued the Louse into ancient literature and have read old medical treatises about it, as, for example, the *De Phthiriasi* of Gilbert de Frankenau. Mucius the lawgiver died of this disease, so also did the Dictator Scylla, Antiochus Epiphanes, the Emperor Maximilian, the philosopher Pherecydes, Philip II. of Spain, the fugitive Ennius, Callisthenes, Alcman and many other distinguished people including the Emperor Arnauld in 899. In 955, the Bishop of Noyon had to be sewn up in a leather sack before he could be buried. (See *Des Insectes reputés venimeux*, par M. Amoureux Fils, Doctor of Medicine in the University of Montpellier, Paris, 1789.) In Mexico and Peru, a poll-tax of Lice was exacted and bags of these treasures were found in the Palace of Montezuma (see Bingley, *Animal Biog.*, first edition, iii.). In the *United Service Magazine* for 1842 (clix., 169) is an account of the wreck of the *Wager*, a vessel found adrift, the crew in dire straits and Captain Cheap lying on the deck—'like an ant-hill.'

So that as an ancient writer puts it, ' you must own that for the quelling of human pride and to pull down the high conceits of mortal man, this most loathesome of all maladies (Pediculosis) has been the inheritance of the rich, the wise, the noble and the mighty—poets, philosophers, prelates, princes, Kings and Emperors.'

In his well-known *Bridgewater Treatise*, the Rev. Dr Kirby, the Father of English Entomology, asked: ' Can we believe that man in his pristine state of glory and beauty and dignity could be the receptacle of prey so loathesome as these unclean and disgusting creatures?' (Vol. I., p. 13). He therefore dated their creation *after* the Fall.

The other day a member of the staff of the Lister Institute called to see me on a lousy matter, and presently drew some live Lice from his waistcoat pocket for me to see. They were contained in pill boxes with little bits of muslin stretched across the open end thro' which the Lice

could thrust their little hypodermic needles when placed
near the skin.   He feeds them by putting these boxes into
a specially constructed belt and at night ties the belt
around his waist and all night sleeps in Elysium.   He is not
married.

In this fashion, he has bred hundreds from the egg
upwards and even hybridised the two different species !

In the enfranchised mind of the scientific naturalist,
the usual feelings of repugnance simply do not exist.
Curiosity conquers prejudice.

August 27.

Am spending my summer holidays in the Lakes at
Coniston with G—— and R——. . . .   I am simply con-
sumed with pride at being among the mountains at last !
It is an enormous personal success to have arrived at
Coniston !

August 29.

Climbed a windy eminence on the other side of the Lake
and had a splendid view of Helvellyn—like a great hog's
back.   It is fine to walk over the elastic turf with the wind
bellowing into each ear and swirling all around me in a
mighty sea of air until I was as clean-blown and resonant
as a sea-shell.   I moved along as easily as a disembodied
spirit and felt free, almost transparent.   The old earth
seemed to have soaked me up into itself, I became dissolved
into it, my separate body was melted away from me, and
Nature received me into her deepest communion—until,
UNTIL I got on the lee side of a hedge where the calm
brought me back my gaol of clay.

September 1.

Fourteen days hence I shall be a married man.   But I
feel most dejected about it.   When I fell down the other
day, I believe I slightly concussed my spinal column, with
the result that my 1913 trouble has returned, but this time
on the *left* side ! paralysis and horrible vertigo and presentiments of sudden collapse as I walk.

September 2.

I fear I have been overdoing it in this tempting mountain region. Walking too far, etc. So I am slacking It was fortunate I did not get concussion of the brain—I came within an inch of it: the hair of my head brushed the ground !

A Buxom Rogue in Earthenware

I knocked at the door of Sunbeam Cottage the other morning to know if they had a boat for hire. The door was promptly opened by a plump, charming little wench of about 17, and I caught a glimpse of the kitchen with its gunrack holding two fowling pieces, a grandfather clock in one corner and a dresser full of blueish china.

'We don't let our boat out for hire,' she answered with a smile so honest and natural and spontaneous that I was already saying to myself I had never met with anything like it at all when she stretched up her bare, dairy-maid arm—strong, creamy and soft, just reached a big key strung to a wooden block and lying on the top shelf of the dresser and at once handed it to me with:

'But you are quite welcome to use it and here is the key to the boathouse.'

I now felt certain that she was one in a million and thanked her most awfully. I have never met such swiftly-moving generosity.

'It's very nice on the Lake just now,' she said. 'I like to lie in the boat with a book and let her drift.'

I asked her if she would not come too, but this tight little fairy was too busy in the house. She is Clara Middleton done in earthenware.

Subsequently R—— and I often visited the cottage and we became great friends, her mother showing us some letters she received as a girl from John Ruskin—a great friend of hers. The gamekeeper himself said that for his part he could never read Ruskin's books—it was like driving a springless cart over a rocky road. We all laughed and I said he was prejudiced in view of the letters which began: 'My darling,' and finished up 'Yr loving J. R.'

But Mrs —— said he had never read them, and Madge
(ah! that name!) said her father had never shewn the least
interest in them at which we laughed again, and the gamekeeper laughed too.   He is such a jolly man—they all are
delightfully simple, charming folk and we talked of Beasts
and Birds that live on the mountains.

September 4.

Bathed in the Lake from the boat.   It was brilliantly
fine.   R—— dipped her paddles in occasionally just to
keep the boat from grounding.   Then I clambered over
the bows and stood up to dry myself in the sun like one
of Mr. Tuke's young men.

September 7.

My 26th birthday.   In London again.   Went straight
to the Doctor and reported myself.   I quite expected him
to forbid the marriage as I could scarcely hobble to his
house.   To my amazement, he apparently made light of
my paralysis, said it was a common accident to bruise the
os coccyx, etc.

September 8.

Am staying at —— for a few days to rest and try to be
better by that fateful 11th, when I am married.

Later : My first experience of a Zeppelin raid.   Bombs
dropped only a quarter of a mile away and shrapnel from
the guns fell on our roof.   We got very panicky and
went into a neighbour's house, where we cowered down
in our dressing-gowns in absolute darkness while bombs
exploded and the dogs barked.

I was scared out of my life and had a fit of uncontrollable
trembling.   Later we rang up —— and ——, and thank
Heavens both are safe.   A great fire is burning in London,
judging by the red glare.   At midnight sat and drank
sherry and smoked a cigar with Mr ——, my braces de-
pending from my trousers like a tail and shewing in spite
of dressing-gown.   Then went home and had some neat

brandy to steady my heart. H—— arrived soon after midnight. A motor-omnibus in Whitechapel was blown to bits. Great scenes in the city.

September 9.

Very nervy to-day. Hobbled down the road to see the damage done by the bombs.

September 10.

A swingeing cold in the head thro' running about on the night of the raid. Too feeble to walk far, so Mrs —— went into the town for me and purchased my wedding-ring, which cost £2 5s. 0d.

PART III—MARRIAGE

This evening we walked thro' the Churchyard reading tombstone inscriptions. What a lot of men have had wives !

I can't make out what has come over folk recently: the wit, wisdom and irony on the old tombstones have given place to maudlin sentiment and pious Bible references. Then on the anniversary of the death the custom among poorer classes is to publish such pathetic doggerel as the following—cuttings I have taken from time to time from the local newspaper in ——:

' Her wish:

' " Farewell dear brother, Mother, sisters,
My life was passed in love for thee.
Mourn not for me nor sorrow take
But love my husband for my sake
Until the call comes home to thee,
Live thou in peace and harmony." '

Again:

' A day of remembrance sad to recall
But still in my heart he is loved best of all
No matter how I think of him—his name I oft recall;
There is nothing left to answer me but his photo on the wall.'

Or:

' One year has passed since that sad day,
When one we loved was called away.
God took her home; it was His will,
Forget her ?—No, we never will.'

These piteous screeds fill me with lovingkindness and with contempt alternately in a pendulum-like rhythm. What is the truth about them ?   Is the grief of these people as mean and ridiculous as their rhymes ?   Or is it a pitiful inarticulateness ?   Or is it merely vulgar advertisement of their sorrow ?   Or does it signify a passionate intention

219

never to forget?—or a fear of forgetting, the rhymes being
used as a fillip to the memory? Or—most miserable of all
—is it just a custom, and one followed in order to appear
respectable in others' eyes? Are they poor souls? or
contemptible fools?

September 14.

There is a ridiculous Cocker spaniel at the house where
we are staying. He must have had a love affair and been
jilted, or else he's a sort of village idiot. The landlady
says he's not so silly as he looks—but he looks very silly:
he languishes sentimentally, and when we laugh at him he
looks ' hurt.' To-day we took him up on the Down and
it seemed to brighten him up. Really, he is sane enough,
with plenty of commonsense and good manners. But he
is kept at home in the garden so much, lolling about all
day, that as E—— said, having nothing to do, he falls in love.

.   .   .   .

The *Saturday Review* writes: The effect of the ' Brides
and the Bath ' Case on people with any trace of *nice feeling*
is perhaps not particularly mischievous, tho' the thing is
repulsive and hateful to them. . . . To gloat over the
details of repulsive horrors, simply *from motives of curiosity*
—this is bad and degrading.

What a lot of repulsive things the nice refined people
who read the *Saturday Review* must find in the world just
now. For example the War. ' Simply from motives of
curiosity.' Why certainly, no other than these, concerning one of the most remarkable murders in the annals of
crime. And murders anyhow are damned interesting—
which the *Saturday Review* isn't.

Chibbles

I was surprised to discover the other day that when I
talked of Chibbles no one understood what I meant! It
proves to be a dialect word familiar to all residents in
Devonshire and designating spring onions. Anyway you

won't find it in Murray's Dictionary; yet etymologically
it is an extremely interesting word and a thoroughly good
word with a splendid pedigree.   To wit:

Italian: Cipollo.

Spanish: Cebolla.

French: Ciboule.

Latin: Cæpulla, dim. of cæpa (*cf.* cive, civot).

Now how did this pretty little alien manage to settle
down among simple Devon folk ?   What has been the
relation between Italy and—say Appledore, or Plymouth ?[1]

October 6.

In London once more, living at her flat and using her
furniture.

The Chalcidoidea

The Chalcidoidea are minute winged insects that para-
sitise other insects, and in the *Memoirs of the Queensland
Museum* (Vol. I., 1912) you shall find an enormous catalogue
of them by a person named Girault who writes the following
dedication:

' I respectfully dedicate this little portion of work to
science, common sense or true knowledge.   I am convinced
that human welfare is so dependent upon science that
civilisation would not endure without it, and that what is
meant by progress would be impossible.   Also I am convinced that the great majority of mankind are too ignorant,
that education is too archaic and impractical as looked at
from the standpoint of intrinsic knowledge.   There is too
little known of the essential unity of the Universe and of
things included, for instance, man himself.   Opinions and
prejudices rule in the place of what is true. . . .'

Part II. is dedicated to:

' The genius of mankind, especially to that form of it

[1] The English Dialect Dictionary derives the word from Old
French *chiboule*, and gives a reference to Piers Plowman.   Why
hasn't such an old and useful word become a part of the English
language like others also brought over at the time of the Norman
Conquest ?

expressed in monistic philosophy, whose conceived perception is the highest attainment reached by man.'

I can only echo Whistler's remark one day as he stood before an execrably bad drawing: 'God bless my soul' —uttered slowly and thoughtfully and then repeated.

The beauty of it is that the Editor adds a serious footnote, dissociating himself, and a Scarabee to whom I showed the Work, read it with a clouded brow and then said: 'I think it rather out of place in a paper of this sort.' (Tableau.)

October 12.

Down with influenza.

October 13.

A Zeppelin raid last night. I am down with a temperature, but our little household remained quite calm, thank God. We heard guns going off, and I had a fit of trembling as I lay in bed. Many dead of heart failure owing to the excitement.

October 14.

Still in bed. No raid last night. There were two raids on Wednesday, one at 9.30, and another at midnight. The first time the caretaker of the flats came up very alarmed to say 'Zeppelins about,' so we put out the lights. Then at midnight when everyone else was asleep I heard a big voice shout up from the street: 'Lights out there. They're about again.' Lay still in bed and waited. Distant gunfire.

October 17.

Bad heart attack.

October 18.

Heart intermits. Every three or four minutes. M—— said that I ought to be getting used to it by now! Phew!! Very nervy and pusillanimous. Taking strychnine in

strong doses. I hope dear E—— does not catch the 'flu.
She swallows quinine with large hopes.

October 19.

Staying at R——. Had a ghastly journey down,
changing trains twice, at Clapham Junction and at Croydon,
heart intermitting all the time in every position. Poor
E—— with me. To-day surprised to find myself still alive.

October 20.

Better to-day. After much persuasion, I have got
E—— to let the flat so that we can get away into the
country outside the Zeppelin zone.

October 24.

Back in London again. Am better, bolstered up with
arsenic and strychnine. Too nervously excited to do any
work.

October 25.

The letting of our flat is now in the hands of an agent,
and E——, poor dear, is quite resigned to abandoning all
her precious wallpapers, etc.

November 7.

The flat is let and we are now living in rooms at ——,
20 miles out of London, to the Westward.

November 8.

It is a great relief to be down in the country. Zeppelins
terrify me. Have just had a delightful experience in
reading Conrad's new book, *Victory*—a welcome relief
from all the tension of the past two months. To outward
view, I have been merely a youth getting married, catching
the 'flu and giving up a London flat.

Inwardly, I have been whizzing around like a Catherine
Wheel. Consider the items:

Concussion of the spine.

Resulting paralysis of left leg ten days before marriage.

Zeppelin raid (heard a cannon go off for the first time).

Severe cold in the head day before marriage (and therefore wild anxiety).

Successful marriage with abatement of cold.

Return to our home.

Ten days later, down with influenza.

A second Zeppelin raid.

Bad heart attack.

Then flat sub-let and London evacuated.

The record nauseates me. I am nauseated with myself and my self-centredness. . . . Suppose I have been 'whizzing' as I call it—what then? They are but subjective trifles—meanwhile other men are seeing great adventures in Gallipoli and elsewhere. 'The *Triumph* is gone,' exclaimed the Admiral who in a little group of naval officers on board the flagship had been watching H.M.S. *Triumph* sink in the Ægean. He shuts his telescope with a click and returns in great dudgeon to his own quarters. How I envy all these men who are participating in this War—soldiers, sailors, war correspondents—all who live and throb and are not afraid. I am a timid youth, anæmic, wear spectacles, and am frightened by a Zep raid! How humiliating! I hate myself for a white-livered craven: I am suffocated for want of more life and courage. My damnable body is slowly killing off all my spirit and buoyancy. Even my mind is becoming blurred. My memory is like an old man's exactly. (Ask ——.)

* * * * * *

Yet thro' all my nausea, here I remain happy to discuss myself and my little mishaps. I'm damned sick of myself and all my neurotic whimperings, and so I hereby and now intend to lead a new life and throw this Journal to the Devil. I want to mangle it, tear it to shreds. You smug, hypocritical readers! you'll get no more of me. All you say I know is true before you say it and I know *now* all the criticism you are going to launch. So please spare yourselves the trouble. You cannot enlighten me upon myself. I *know*. I disgust myself—and you, and as for you, you can go to the Devil with this Journal.

Finis

November 27.

To-day, armed with a certificate from my Doctor in a sealed envelope and addressed ' to the Medical Officer examining Mr W. N. P. Barbellion,' I got leave to attend the recruiting office and offer my services to my King and Country. At the time, the fact that the envelope was sealed caused no suspicion and I had been comfortably carrying the document about in my pocket for days past.

Of course I attended merely as a matter of form under pressure of the authorities, as I knew I was totally unfit—but not quite *how* unfit. After receiving this precious certificate, I learnt that K—— was recruiting Doctor at W——, and he offered to ' put me thro' in five minutes,' as he knows the state of my health. So at a time agreed upon, I went to-day and was immediately rejected as soon as he had stethoscoped my heart. The certificate therefore was not needed, and coming home in the train I opened it out of curiosity. . . .

I was quite casual and thought it would be merely interesting to see what M—— said.

It was.

' Some 18 months ago,' it ran, ' Mr Barbellion shewed the just visible symptoms of —— —— '—and altho' this fact was at once communicated to my relatives it was withheld from me and M—— therefore asked the M.O. to respect this confidence and to reject me without stating on what grounds. He went on to refer to my patellar and plantar reflexes, by which time I had had enough, tore the paper up and flung it out of the railway carriage window.

I then returned to the Museum intending to find out what —— —— was in Clifford Allbutt's System of Medicine. I wondered whether it was brain or heart; and the very thought gave me palpitation. I hope

it is heart—something short and sharp rather than lingering. But I believe it must be —— of the brain, the
opposite process of softening occurring in old age. I recall
M——'s words to me before getting married: that I had
this ' nerve weakness,' but I was more likely to succumb to
pneumonia than to any nervous trouble, and that only
12 months' happiness would be worth while.

·   ·   ·   ·   ·   ·   ·

On the whole I am amazed at the calm way in which I
take this news. I was a fool never to have suspected
serious nerve trouble before. Does dear E—— know ?
What did M—— tell her when he saw her before our
marriage ?

November 28.

As soon as I woke up in this clear, country air this
morning, I thought : —— ——. I have decided never
to find out what it is. I shall find out in good time by
the course of events.

A few years ago, the news would have scared me. But
not so now. It only interests me. I have been happy,
merry, and quite high-spirited to-day.

December 5.

I believe it's creeping paralysis. My left leg goes lame
after a short walk. Fortunately E—— does not take
alarm.

December 17.

Spent the last two days, both of us, in a state of unre-
lieved gloom. The clouds never lifted for a moment—
it's awful. I scarcely have spoken a word. . . . And
eugenically, what kind of an infant would even a Mark
Tapley expect of a father with a medical history like mine,
and a mother with a nervous system like hers ? . . .
Could anything be more unfortunate ? And the War ?
What may not have happened by this time next year ?
My health is grotesque.

December 20.

I wonder if she knows. I believe she does but I am afraid to broach the matter in case she doesn't. I think she must know something otherwise she would show more alarm over my leg, and when I went to the Recruiting Office she seemed to show no fear whatever lest they took me. Several times a day in the middle of a talk, or a meal, or a kiss, this problem flashes thro' my mind. I look at her but find no solution. However—for the present—the matter is not urgent.

1916

February 1.

Since I last wrote—a month ago—I have recovered my buoyancy after a blow which kept me under water so long I thought I should never come up and be happy again. . . . I was reciting my woes to R——, and gaining much relief thereby, when we espied another crony on the other side of the street, crossed over at once, bandied words with him and then walked on, picking up the thread of my lugubrious story just where I had left off—secretly staggered at my emotional agility. I've got to this now,— I simply don't care.

February 2.

' And she draiglet all her petticoatie, Coming thro' the rye.' These words have a ridiculous fascination for me; I cannot resist their saccharine, affectionate, nay amorous jingle and keep repeating them aloud all over the house— as Lamb once kept reciting ' Rose Aylmer.'

February 16.

We took possession of our country cottage to-day: very charming and overlooking a beautiful Park.

.   .   .   .

Have just discovered the Journal of the De Goncourts and been reading it greedily. Life has really been a commodity. I am boiling over with vitality, chattering amiably to everyone about nothing—argumentative, sanguine, serious, ridiculous. I called old R—— a Rapscallion, a Curmudgeon, and a Scaramouche, and E—— a trull, a drab, a trollop, a callet. ' You certainly are a unique husband,' said that sweet little lady, and I . . .

With me, one of the symptoms of delirium is always a melodramatic truculence ! I shake my fist in R——'s face and make him explode with laughing. . . . The sun to-day, and the great, whopping white clouds all bellied out, made me feel inside quite a bright young dog wriggling its body in ecstatic delight let loose upon the green sward.

' You must come down for a week end,' I said to R—— at lunch. ' Come down as soon as you can. You will find every comfort. It is an enormous house—I have not succeeded in finding my way about it and—it's dangerous to lose yourself—makes you late for dinner. When you arrive our gilded janitor will say: " I believe Mr Barbellion is in the library." '

' Black eunuchs wait on you at dinner, I suppose,' R—— rejoined.

' Oh ! yes and golden chandeliers and a marble staircase—all in barbaric splendour. '

' Yes, I shall certainly be glad to come down,' said R——, phlegmatically.

And so on and so on. Words, idle words all day in a continuous rush. And I am sure that the match which fired the gun-powder was the discovery of the De Goncourts' Journal ! It's extraordinary how I have been going on from week to week quite calmly for all the world as if I had read all the books and seen all the places and done everything according to the heart's desire. This book has really jolted me out of my complacency: to think that all this time, I have been dead to so much ! Why I might have died unconscious that the De Goncourts had ever lived and written their colossal book and now I am aware of it, I am all in a fever to read it and take it up into my brain: I might die now before I have finished it—a thought that makes me wild with desire just as I once endured most awful pangs when I felt my health going, and believed that I might die before having ever been in love—to die and never to have been in love ! —for an instant at a time this possibility used to make me writhe.

March 22.

R—— has an unpleasant habit of making some scarifying announcement drawing forth an explosive query from me and then lapsing at once into an eleusinian silence : he appears to take a sensuous pleasure in the pause that keeps you expectant. I could forgive a man who keeps you on tenterhooks for two puffs in order to keep his pipe alight, but R—— shuts up out of sheer self-indulgence and goes on gazing at the horizon with the eyes of a seer (he thinks) trying to cod me he sees a portent there only revealed to God's elect.

I told him this in the middle of one of his luxurious silences. ' I will tell you,' he said deliberately, ' when we reach the Oratory.' (We were in Brompton Road.)

' Which side of it ?' I enquired anxiously. ' This or that ?'

' That,' said he, ' will depend on how you behave in the meantime.'

April 3.

We met a remarkable Bulldog to-day in the street, humbly following behind a tiny boy to whom it was attached by a piece of string. At the time we were follow-ing in the wake of three magnificent Serbian Officers, and I was particularly interesting myself in the curious cut of their top boots. But the Bulldog was the Red Herring in our path.

' Is that a Dog ?' I asked the little boy.

He assured me that it was, and so it turned out to be, tho' Bull-frog would have been a better name for it, the forelegs being more bandied, the back broader and the mouth wider than in any Bulldog I have ever seen. It was a super-Bulldog.

We turned and walked on. 'There,' said R——, 'now we have lost our Serbian Officers.'

April 4.

'May I use your microscope?' he asked.

'By all means,' I said with a gesture of elaborate politeness.

He sat down at my table, in my chair, and used my instrument—becoming at once absorbed and oblivious to my banter as per below:

'As Scotchmen,' I said, 'are monuments rather than men, this latest raid on Edinboro's worthy inhabitants must be called vandalism rather than murder.'

No answer. I continued to stand by my chair.

'How pleased Swift, Johnson, Lamb, and other anti-Caledonians would be. . . .'

'Hope you don't mind my occupying your chair a little longer,' the Scotchman said, 'but this is a larva, has curious maxillæ . . .' and his voice faded away in abstraction.

'Oh! no—go on,' I said, 'I fear it is a grievous absence of hospitality on my part in not providing you with a glass of whiskey. Can I offer you water, Sir?'

No answer.

Another enthusiast ushered himself in, was greeted with delight by the first and invited to sit down. I pulled out a chair for him and said:

'Shave, sir, or hair cut?'

'If you follow along to the top of the galea,' No. 1 droned on imperturbably, 'you will . . .' etc.

I got tired of standing and talking to an empty house but at last they got up, apologising and making for the door.

I entreated them not to mention the matter—my fee should be nominal—I did it out of sheer love, etc.

They thanked me again and would have said more but I added blandly:

'You know your way out?' They assured me they did (having worked in the place for 30 years and more)—I thanked God—and sat down to my table once more.

(These reports of conversations are rather fatuous: yet they give an idea of the sort of person I have to deal with, and also the sort of person I am among this sort of person.)

April 6.

The Housefly Problem—1916

For weeks past we have all been in a terrible flutter scarcely paralleled by the outbreak of Armageddon in August, 1914. The spark which fired almost the whole building was a letter to the *Times* written by Dr ——, making public an ignominious confession of ignorance on the part of Entomologists as to how the Housefly passed the winter. In reply, many correspondents wrote to say they hibernated, and one man was even so temerarious as to quote to us Entomologists the exact Latin name of the Housefly: viz., *Musca domestica*. We asked for specimens and enormous numbers of flies at once began to arrive at the Museum, alive and dead—and not a Housefly among them! So there was a terrible howdedo.

One of the correspondents was named 'Masefield.' 'Not Masefield the poet?' an excited dipterist asked. I reassured him.

'I've a good mind,' said Dr ——, 'to reply to this chap who's so emphatic and give him a wigging—only he's climbing down a bit in this second letter in to-day's issue.' I strongly advocated clemency.

But still the affair goes on. Every morning sees more letters and more flies sent by all sorts of persons—we seem to have set the whole world searching for Houseflies— Duchesses, signalmen, farmers, footmen. Every morning each fresh batch of flies is mounted on pins by experts in the Setting Room, and an Assistant's whole time is devoted to identifying, arranging, listing and reporting upon the new arrivals. At the last meeting of the Trustees a sample collection was displayed to show indubitably that the

insects which hibernate in houses are not *Musca domestica*
but *Pollenia rudis*. I understand the Trustees were
appreciative.

An observant eye can now discover state visits to our
dipterists from interested persons carrying their flies with
them, animated discussions in the corridor, knots of
excited enthusiasts in the Lavatory, in the Library, everywhere—and everywhere the subject discussed is the same:
How does the Housefly pass the winter ? As one passes
one catches : ' In Bakehouses certainly they are to be
found but . . .' or a wistful voice, ' I wish I had caught
that one in my bathroom three winters ago—I am certain
it was a Housefly.' The Doctor himself—a gallant Captain—wanders from room to room stimulating his lieu-
tenants to make suggestions, and examining every answer
to the great interrogative on its merits, no matter how
humble or insignificant the person who makes it. Then
of an afternoon he will entirely disappear, and word goes
round that he has set forth to examine a rubbish heap in
Soho or Pimlico. As the afternoon draws to its close
someone enquires if he has come back yet ; next morning
a second asks if I had seen him, then a third announces
mournfully that he has just been holding conversation with
him, but that nothing at all was found in the rubbish heap.

The great sensation of all occurred last week when
somebody ran along the corridor crying that Mr —— had
just found a Housefly in his room. We were all soon agog
with the news, and the excited Captain was presently
espied setting out for the scene of operations with a killing
bottle and net. The insect was promptly impounded and
identified as a veritable *Musca domestica*. A consultation
being held to sit on the body, a lady finally laid information
that two ' forced Houseflies ' hatched the day before had
escaped from her possession. She suggested Mr ——'s
specimen was one of them.

' How would it get from your room to Mr ——'s ?' she
was immediately asked. And breathless, we all heard her
answer deliberately and quite audibly that the fugitive
may have gone out of her window, up the garden and in

by Mr ——'s window, *or* it may have gone out of her door, up the corridor and in by his door. I wanted to know why it should have entered Mr ——'s room as he is not a dipterist but a microlepidopterist. They looked at me sternly and we slowly dispersed.

This morning, the Dr. came to me with a newspaper cutting in his hand, saying, '*The Times* is behindhand.' He handed me the slip. It was a clipping from to-day's *Times* about a sackful of flies which had been taken from Wandsworth Clock Tower in a state of hibernation.

'Behindhand?' I asked timidly, for I felt that all the story was not in front of me.

'Why, yes. Don't you know?'

I knew nothing, but was prepared for anything.

'*The Star, two days ago*,' he informed me, ' had a paragraph about this—headed "Tempus fugit"'—this last in a resentful tone as tho' the frivolous reporter were attempting to discredit our mystery.

There was a long pause. Neither of us spoke. Then he slowly said:

'I wonder why *The Times* is so behindhand. This is two days late.'

May 5.

Hulloa, old friend: how are you? I mean my Diary. I haven't written to you for ever so long, and my silence as usual indicates happiness. I have been passing thro' an unbroken succession of calm happy days, walking in the woods with my darling, or doing a little gentle gardening on coming home in the evening—and the War has been centuries away. Later on towards bedtime, E—— reads Richard Jefferies, I play Patience and Mrs —— makes garments for Priscilla.

The only troubles have been a chimney which smokes and a neighbour's dog which barks at night. So to be sure, I have made port after storm at last—and none too soon. To-day my cheerfulness had been rising in a crescendo till to-night it broke in such a handsome crest of pure delight that I cannot think of going to bed without recording it.

Pachmann

After sitting on the wall around the fountain in the middle of Trafalgar Square, eating my sandwiches and feeding the Pigeons with the crumbs, I listened for a moment to the roar of the traffic around three sides of the Square as I stood in the centre quite alone, what time one fat old pigeon, all unconcerned, was treading another. It was an extraordinary experience: motor horns tooted incessantly and it seemed purposelessly, so that one had the fancy that all London was out for a joy-ride—it was a great British Victory perhaps, or Peace Day.

Then walked down Whitehall to Westminster Bridge in time to see the 2 o'clock boat start upstream for Kew. I loitered by the old fellow with the telescope who keeps his pitch by Boadicea: I saw a piper of the Scots Guards standing near gazing across the river but at nothing in particular—just idling as I was. I saw another man sitting on the stone steps and reading a dirty fragment of newspaper. I saw the genial, red-faced sea-faring man in charge of the landing stage strolling up and down his small domain,—chatting, jesting, spitting, and making fast a rope or so. Everything was *alive* to the finger tips, vividly shining, pulsating.

Arrived at Queen's Hall in time for Pachmann's Recital at 3.15. . . . As usual he kept us waiting for 10 minutes. Then a short, fat, middle-aged man strolled casually on to the platform and everyone clapped violently—so it was Pachmann: a dirty greasy looking fellow with long hair of dirty grey colour, reaching down to his shoulders and an ugly face. He beamed on us and then shrugged his shoulders and went on shrugging them until his eye caught the music stool, which seemed to fill him with amazement. He stalked it carefully, held out one hand to it caressingly, and finding all was well, went two steps backwards, clasping his hands before him and always gazing at the little stool in mute admiration, his eyes sparkling with pleasure, like Mr. Pickwick's on the discovery of the archæological treasure. He approached once more, bent down and ever so gently moved it about ⅝ths of an inch nearer the piano. He then gave it a final pat with his right hand and sat down.

He played Nocturne No. 2, Prelude No. 20, a Mazurka and two Études of Chopin and Schubert's Impromptu No. 4.

At the close we all crowded around the platform and gave the queer, old-world gentleman an ovation, one man thrusting up his hand which Pachmann generously shook as desired.

As an encore he gave us a Valse—' Valse, Valse,' he exclaimed ecstatically, jumping up and down in his seat in time to the music. It was a truly remarkable sight: on his right the clamorous crowd around the platform; on his left the seat holders of the Orchestra Stalls, while at the piano bobbed this grubby little fat man playing divine Chopin divinely well, at the same time rising and falling in his seat, turning a beaming countenance first to the right and then to the left, and crying, ' Valse, Valse.' He is as entertaining as a tumbler at a variety hall.

As soon as he had finished, we clapped and rattled for more, Pachmann meanwhile standing surrounded by his idolaters in affected despair at ever being able to satisfy us. Presently he walked off and a scuffle was half visible behind the scenes between him and his agent who sent him in once more.

The applause was wonderful. As soon as he began again it ceased on the instant, and as soon as he left off it started again immediately—nothing boisterous or rapturous but a steady, determined thunder of applause that came regularly and evenly like the roar from some machine.

May 20.

Spent a quiet day. Sat at my escritoire in the Studio this morning writing an Essay, with a large 4-fold window on my left, looking on to woods and fields, with Linnets, Greenfinches, Cuckoos calling. This afternoon while E——rested awhile I sat on the veranda in the sun and read *Antony and Cleopatra* . . . Yes, I'm in harbour at last. I'd be the last to deny it but I cannot believe it will last.

It's too good to last and it's all too good to be even true.
E—— is too good to be true, the home is too good to be
true, and this quiet restful existence is too wonderful to
last in the middle of a great war. It's just a little deceitful
April sunshine, that's all. . . .[1]

Had tea at the ——. A brilliant summer's evening.
Afterwards, we wandered into the garden and shrubbery
and sat about on the turf of the lawn, chatting and smoking.
Mr —— played with a rogue of a white Tomcat called
Chatham, and E—— talked about our neighbour, ' Shamble
legs,' about garden topics, etc. Then I strolled into the
drawing-room where Cynthia was playing Chopin on a
grand piano. Is it not all perfectly lovely ?

How delicious to be silent, lolling on the Chesterfield,
gazing abstractedly thro' the lattice window and listening
to the lulling charities of Nocturne No. 2, Op. 37 ! The
melody in the latter part of this nocturne took me back
at once to a cloudless day in an open boat in the Bay of
Combemartin, with oars up and the water quietly and
regularly lapping the gunwales as we rose and fell. A
state of the most profound calm and happiness took
possession of me.

June 2.

From the local paper:
' A comrade in the Gloucesters writing to a friend at
—— mentions that Pte. J—— has been fatally shot in
action. J—— was well known here for years as an
especially smart young newsvendor.'

June 3.

What a bitter disappointment it is to realise that people
the most intimately in love with one another are really
separated by such a distance. A woman is calmly knitting
socks or playing Patience while her husband or sweetheart
lies dead in Flanders. However strong the tie that binds
them together yet they are insufficiently *en rapport* for

[1] So it proved. See September 26 *et seq.*

her to sense even a catastrophe—and she must wait till
the War Office forsooth sends her word. How humiliating that the War Office must do what Love cannot. Human
love seems then such a superficial thing. Every person is
a distinct egocentric being. Each for himself and the
Devil take the hindmost. 'Ah! but she didn't know.'
'Yes, but she *ought* to have known.' Mental telepathy
and clairvoyance should be common at least to all lovers.

.   .   .   .

This morning in bed I heard a man with a milkcart say
in the road to a villager at about 6.30 a.m., '. . . battle
. . . and we lost six cruisers.' This was the first I knew
of the Battle of Jutland. At 8 a.m. I read in the *Daily
News* that the British Navy had been defeated, and thought
it was the end of all things. The news took away our
appetites. At the railway station, the *Morning Post* was
more cheerful, even reassuring, and now at 6.30 p.m. the
Battle has turned into a merely regrettable indecisive
action. We breathe once more.

June 4.

It has now become a victory.

June 11.

Old systems of Classification : Rafinesc's Theory of
Fives, Swainson's Theory of Sevens, Edward Newman's
book called *Sphinx Vespiformis* tracing fives throughout
the animal world, Sir Thomas Browne's Quincunx, chasing
fives throughout the whole of nature—in the words of
Coleridge, ' quincunxes in Heaven above, quincunxes in
the Earth below, quincunxes in the mind of man, in optic
nerves, in roots of trees, in leaves, in everything !'

.   .   .   .

Old false trails:
The Philosopher's Stone (Balthazar Clæs).[1]

[1] In ' La Récherche de l'Absolu ' (Balzac).

A universal catholicon (Bishop Berkeley's tar-water).
Mystical numbers (as per above).

.   .   .   .

My father was Sir Thomas Browne and my mother
Marie Bashkirtseff.   See what a curious hybrid I am !

.   .   .   .

I toss these pages in the faces of timid, furtive, respectable people and say: ' There ! that's me !   You may like
it or lump it, but it's true.   And I challenge you to follow
suit, to flash the searchlight of your self-consciousness into
every remotest corner of your life and invite everybody's
inspection.   Be candid, be honest, break down the parti-
tions of your cubicle, come out of your burrow, little
worm.'   As we are all such worms we should at least be
honest worms.

.   .   .   .

My gratitude to E—— for plucking me out of the hideous
miseries of my life in London is greater than I can express.
If I were the cheap hero of a ladies' novel I should immo-
late my journals as a token, and you would have a pretty
picture of a pale young man watching his days go up in
smoke by the drawing-room fire.   But I have more confidence in her sterling good sense, and if I cannot be loved
for what I am, I do not wish to be loved for what I am not.

.   .   .   .

Since the fateful Nov. 27th, my life has become entirely
posthumous.   I live now in the grave and am busy fur-
nishing it with posthumous joys.   I accept my fate with
great content, my one-time restless ambition lies asleep
now, my one-time, furious self-assertiveness is anæsthetised by this great War; the War and the discovery about
my health together have plucked out of me that canker of
self-obsession.   I sit at home here in this country cottage
in perfect isolation—flattened out by a steam hammer
(tho' it took Armageddon to do it !), yet as cheerful and

busy as a Dormouse laying up store for the winter.   For I
am almost resigned to the issue in the knowledge that some
day, someone will know, perhaps somebody will understand and—immortal powers!—even sympathise, 'the
quick heart quickening from the heart that's still.'

July 19.

Omniscience

An omniscient Caledonian asked me to-day:
'Where are the Celebes?   Are they E. or N.E. of the
Sandwich Group?'
I marked him down at once as my legitimate prey.
Sitting back in my chair, I replied slowly in my most
offensive manner:
'The Island of Celebes is of enormous size and curious
shape situated in the Malay Archipelago.'
The Caledonian made no sign.   Instead of grinning at
his error and confessing to a 'floater,' he endeavoured to
carry on by remarking, 'That of course would be N. of
Papua,' just for all the world as if his error was a minor
one of latitude and longitude.
Ignoring his comment, I continued:
'From the Zoogeographical point of view, Celebes is
unequalled in importance, having the strangest fauna
almost of any island on the face of the globe.   Then there's
"Wallace's Line,"' I said, being purposely obscure.
The Caledonian said nought but 'looked hurt.'   It was
so obvious that he didn't know, and it was so obvious that
I knew that he didn't know, that after my farcical truculence I expected the tension to dissolve in laughter.   Yet
it is hard for a Caledonian to say 'God be merciful to me,
ignorant devil that I am.'   So I pursued him with more
information about 'Wallace's Line,' with an insouciant
air, as much as to say, 'Wallace's Line of course you heard
discussed before you were breeched.'
'Some do say, you know, that the Line is "all my eye
and Betty Martin," *e.g.*, R——.'
This gave him his first opportunity of finding his feet in

this perilously deep water. So he said promptly, eager to
seem knowledgeable with an intelligent rejoinder:

'Ah! yes, R—— is an authority on Fishes.'

I assented. 'At the last meeting of the British Ass. he
tore the idea to shreds.'

The drowning Caledonian seized at any straw:

'Fishes, however, are not of paramount importance in
cases of geographical distribution, are they?'

I knew he was thinking of *marine* fishes, but I did not
illumine him, and merely said:

'Oh! yes, of very great importance,' at which he looked
still more 'hurt,' decamped in silence and left me conqueror
of the field but without the spoils of victory: it was impossible to bring him to say 'I do not know'—four mono-
syllables was all I wanted from the man who for months
past has been lecturing me on all things from Music and
the Drama to Philosophy, Painting and—Insects.

July 20.

The cradle came a few days ago but I had not seen it
until this morning when I unlocked the cupboard door,
looked in and shuddered.

'That's the skeleton in our cupboard,' I said on coming
down to breakfast. She laughed, but I really meant it.

E—— keeps a blue bowl replenished with flaming
Poppies in our room. The cottage is plagued with Ear-
wigs which fly in at night and get among the clothes and
bedlinen. This morning, dressing, she held up her chemise
to the light saying: 'I always do this—you can see their
little heathen bodies then against the light. . . .' Isn't
she charming?

July 30.

The other day R—— and I were sitting on a stile on the
uplands in perfect summer weather and talking of happy
days before the War—he was in khaki and I was resting
my 'gammy' leg. . . . As we talked, we let our eyes
roam, resting luxuriously wherever we pleased and occasionally interrupting the conversation with 'Look at that

cow scratching herself against the Oak,' or ' Do you see
the oats waving ?' In the distance we saw a man and a
boy walking up towards us along the path thro' the corn,
but the eye having momentarily scrutinised them wandered
away and the conversation never paused. When next I
looked, they were much nearer—crossing the furrows in
the potato field in fact, and we both stopped talking to
watch—idly. The boy seemed to be about 10 years old,
and it amused us to see his great difficulty in stepping
across the furrows.

' Poor little chap,' R—— said, and we laughed.

Then the boy stumbled badly and all at once the man
lifted his walking-stick and beat him, saying ill-naturedly,
' Step between the furrows,' and again, ' Step between the
furrows.' Our enchanting little picture was transfigured
in an instant. The ' charming little boy ' was a natural
idiot—a gross, hefty creature perhaps 30 years of age,
very short and very thick, dressed in a little sailor suit.
I said, ' Heavens,' and R—— looked positively scared.
We stood aside for them to get over the stile, the ' boy '
still suffering from his over exertion, breathing stertorously
like a horse pulling uphill and still evidently fearful of the
big stick behind. He scrambled over the stile as best he
could, rolling a wild eye at us as he did so—a large, bulgy
eye with the lower lid swollen and sore, like the eye of a
terrified ox on the way to the slaughter house. So much
then for our little picture of charming childhood ! The
man followed close at his heels and looked at me with
stern defiant eyes. ' Yes, that is my son,' his eyes declaimed, ' and I'll thank you to avert your gaze or by the
Lord I'll beat you too.'

A Yellow Cat

Last week, I saw a yellow cat perched up quite high
on a window ledge at the S—— Underground Station in
celestial detachment from the crowd of serious, black-
coated gentlemen hustling along to and from the trains.
He had his back turned to us, but as I swept past in the

stream, I was forced to look back a moment, and caught the outline of his whiskers—it made me smile intensely to myself and secretly I gave the palm to the cat for wisdom.

July 31.

This War is so great and terrible that hyperbole is impossible. And yet my gorge rises at those fatuous journalists continually prating about this 'Greatest War of all time,' this 'Great Drama,' this 'world catastrophe unparalleled in human history,' because it is easy to see that they are really more thrilled than shocked by the immensity of the War. They indulge in a vulgar Yankee admiration for the Big Thing. Why call this shameful Filth by high sounding phrases—as if it were a tragedy from Euripides? We ought to hush it up, not brag about it, to mention it with a blush instead of spurting it out brazen-faced.

Mr Garvin, for example, positively gloats over the War each week in the *Observer*: 'Last week was one of those pivotal occasions on which destiny seems to swing'—and so on every week, you can hear him, historical glutton smacking his lips with an offensive relish.

For my part, I never seem to be in the same mind about the War twice following. Sometimes I am wonderstruck and make out a list of all the amazing events I have lived to see since August 1914, and sometimes more often I am swollen with contempt for its colossal imbecility. And sometimes I am swept away with admiration for all the heroism of the War, or by some particularly noble self-sacrifice, and think it is really all worth while. Then—and more frequently—I remember that this War has let loose on the world not only barbarities, butcheries and crimes, but lies, lies, lies—hypocrisies, deceits, ignoble desires for self-aggrandizement, self-preservation such as no one before ever dreamed existed in embryo in the heart of human beings.

The War rings the changes on all the emotions. It twangs all my strings in turn and occasionally all at once, so that I scarcely know how to react or what to think. You see, here am I, a compulsory spectator, and all I can do is to reflect.   A Zeppelin brought down in flames that lit up all London—now that makes me want to write like Mr Garvin.   But a Foreign Correspondent's eager discussion of ' Italy's aspirations in the Trentino,' how Russia insists on a large slice of Turkey, and so forth, makes me splutter.   How insufferably childish to be slicing up the earth's surface !   How immeasureably ' above the battle ' I am at times.   What a prig you will say I am when I sneer at such contemptible little devilries as the Boches' trick of sending over a little note, ' Warsaw is fallen,' into our trenches, or as ours in reply : ' Gorizia !'

' There is no difference in principle between the case of a man who loses a limb in the service of his country and that of the man who loses his reason ; both have an obvious claim to the grateful recognition of the State.'—A morning paper.

A jejune comment like this makes me grin like a gargoyle !   Hark to the fellow—this leader-writer over his cup of tea.   But it is a lesson to show how easily and quickly we have all adapted ourselves to the War.   The War is everything ; it is noble, filthy, great, petty, degrading, inspiring, ridiculous, glorious, mad, bad, hopeless yet full of hope.   I don't know what to think about it.

August 13.

I hate elderly women who mention their legs.   It makes me shudder.

.   .   .   .

I had two amusing conversations this morning, one with a jealous old man of 70 summers who, in spite of his age, is jealous—1 can find no other term—of me in spite of mine, and the other with a social climber.   I always tell the first of any of my little successes and regularly hand him all my memoirs as they appear, to which he as regularly protests that he reads very little now.

' Oh! never mind,' I always answer gaily, ' you take it and read it going down in the train—it will amuse you.' He submits but is always silent next time I see him—a little, admonitory silence. Or, I mention I am giving an address at ——, and he says ' Oom,' and at once begins his reminiscences, which I have heard many times before, and am sometimes tempted to correct him when, his memory failing, he leaves out an essential portion of his story. Thus do crabbed age and boastful youth tantalise one another.

To the social climber I said slyly:

' You seem to move in a very distinguished entourage during your week ends.'

He smiled a little self-consciously, hesitated a moment and then said:

' Oh! I have a few nice friends, you know.'

Now I am sorry, but though I scrutinised this lick-spittle and arch belly-truck rider very closely, I am quite unable to say whether that smile and unwonted diffidence meant simple pleasure at the now certain knowledge that I was duly impressed, or whether it was genuine confusion at the thought that he had perhaps been overdoing it.

Curiously enough, all bores of whatever kind make a dead set at me. I am always a ready listener and my thrusts are always gentle. Hence the pyramids ! I constantly act as phlebotomist to the vanity of the young and to the anecdotage of the senile and senescent.

August 13.

. . . I stood by his chair and looked down at him, and surveyed carefully the top of his head, neck, and collar, and with admirable restraint and calm, considered my most reasonable contempt of him. In perfect silence, we remained thus, while I looked down at a sore spot in the centre of his calvarium which he scratches occasionally, and toyed with the fine flower of my scorn. . . .   But it is a dangerous license to take. One never knows. . . .

Equilibrium Restored

To clear away the cobwebs and to purge my soul of evil thoughts and bitter feelings, went for a walk this evening over the uplands.   Among the stubble, I sat down for a while with my back against the corn pook and listened to the Partridges calling.   Then wandered around the edge of this upland field with the wind in my face and a shower of delicious, fresh rain pattering down on the leaves and dry earth.   Then into a wood among tall forest Beeches and a few giant Larches where I rested again and heard a Woodpecker tapping out its message aloft.

This ramble in beautiful B——shire country restored my mental and spiritual poise.   I came home serene and perfectly balanced—my equilibrium was something like the just perceptible oscillation of tall Larch-tree tops on the heights of a cliff and the sea below with a just perceptible swell on a calm and perfect June day.   I felt exquisite —superb.   I could have walked all the way home on a tight rope.

September 2.

Just recently, I have been going fairly strong.   I get frequent colds and sometimes show unpleasant nerve symptoms, but I take a course of arsenic and strychnine every month or so in tabloid form, and this helps me over bad patches.

Under the beatific influence of more comfortable health, the rare flower of my ambition has raised its head once more: my brain has bubbled with projects.   To wit:

(1) An investigation of the Balancers in Larval Urodeles.

(2) The Present Parlous State of Systematic Zoology (for ' Science Progress ').

(3) The Anatomy of the Psocidæ.

Etc.

The strength of my ambition at any given moment is the measure of my state of health.   It must really be an extraordinarily tenacious thing to have hung on thro' all my recent experiences. Considerately enough this great Crab lets go of my big toe when I am sunk low in health, yet pinches devilishly hard as now when I am well.[1]

A Bad Listener

When I begin to speak, T—— will sometimes interrupt with his loud, rasping voice. I usually submit to this from sheer lack of lung power or I may have a sore throat. But occasionally after the fifth or sixth interruption I lose my equanimity and refuse to give him ground. I keep straight on with what I intended to say, only in a louder voice; he assumes a voice louder still, but not to be denied, I pile Pelion on Ossa and finally overwhelm him in a thunder of sound. For example:

' The other day '—I begin quietly collecting my thoughts to tell the story in detail, ' I went to the——'

' Ah ! you must come and see my pictures——' he breaks in; but I go on and he goes on and as I talk, I catch phrases: ' St. Peter's ' or ' Michael Angelo ' or ' Botticelli ' in wondrous antiphon with my own ' British Museum ' and ' I saw there,' ' two Syracusan,' ' tetradrachms,' until very likely I reach the end of my sentence before he does his, or perhaps his rasp drives my remarks out of my head. But that makes no difference, for rather than give in I go on improvising in a louder and louder voice when suddenly, at length made aware of the fact that I am talking too, he stops ! leaving me bellowing nonsense at the top of my voice, thus: ' and I much admired these Syracusan tetradrachms, very charming indeed, I like them, the Syracusan tetradrachms I mean you know, and it will be good to go again and see them (louder) if possible and the weather keeps dry (louder) and the moon and the stars keep in their courses, if the slugs on the thorn (loudest)——' he stops, hears the last few words of my remarks, pretends to be appreciative but wonders what in Heaven's name I can have been talking about.

---

[1] See September 3 (next entry). ' A Jolt,' and September 24 (infra).

September 3.

This is the sort of remark I like to make: Someone says to me: ' You *are* a pessimist.'

' Ah well,' I say, looking infernally deep, ' pessimism is a good policy; it's like having your cake and eating it at the same time.'

Chorus: ' Why ?'

' Because if the future turns out badly you can say, ' I told you so,' to your own satisfaction, and if all is well, why you share everyone else's satisfaction.'

Or I say: ' No I can't swim; and I don't want to !'

Chorus: ' Why ?'

' Because it is so dangerous.'

Chorus: ' Why ?'

The Infernally Wise Youth: ' For several reasons. If you are a swimmer you are likely to be oftener near water and oftener in danger than a non-swimmer. Further, as soon as you can swim even only a little, then as an honourable man, it behoves you to plunge in at once to save a drowning person, whereas, if you couldn't swim it would be merely tempting Providence.'

Isn't it sickening ?

A Jolt

Yesterday the wind was taken out of my sails. Racing along with spinnaker and jib, feeling pretty fit and quite excited over some interesting ectoparasites just collected on some Tinamous, I suddenly shot into a menacing dead calm: that stiflingly still atmosphere which precedes a Typhoon. That is to say, my eye caught the title of an enormous quarto memoir in the *Trans. Roy. Soc.*, Edinburgh: The Histology of —— ——.

I was browsing in the library at the time when this hit me like a carelessly handled gaff straight in the face. I almost ran away to my room.

.   .   .   .

My Pink Form just received amazes me ! To be a soldier ? C'est incroyable, ma foi ! The possibility even is distracting! To send me a notice requesting me to prepare myself for killing men! Why I should feel no more astonished to receive a War Office injunction under dire penalties to perform miracles, to move mountains, to raise from the dead: My reply would be: 'I cannot.' I should sit still and watch the whole universe pass to its destruction rather than raise a hand to knife a fellow. This may be poor, anæmic; but there it is, a positive fact.

. . . . . .

There are moments when I have awful misgivings: Is this blessed Journal worth while? I really don't know, and that's the harassing fact of the matter. If only I were sure of myself, if only I were capable of an impartial view! But I am too fond of myself to be able to see myself objectively. I wish I knew for certain what I am and how much I am worth. There are such possibilities about the situation: it may turn out tremendously, or else explode in a soap bubble. It is the torture of Tantalus to be so uncertain. I should be relieved to know even the worst. I would almost gladly burn my MSS. in the pleasure of having my curiosity satisfied. I go from the nadir of disappointment to the zenith of hope and back several times a week, and all the time I am additionally harassed by the perfect consciousness that it is all petty and pusillanimous to desire to be known and appreciated, that my ambition is a morbid diathesis of the mind. I am not such a fool either as not to see that there is but little satisfaction in posthumous fame, and I am not such a fool as not to realise that all fame is fleeting, and that the whole world itself is passing away.

. . . . . .

I smile with sardonic amusement when I reflect how the War has changed my status. Before the War I was an interesting invalid. Now I am a lucky dog. Then, I was a star turn in tragedy; now I am drowned and ignored in an overcrowded chorus. No valetudinarian was ever more unpleasantly jostled out of his self-compassion. It is difficult to accustom myself to the new rôle all at once: I had begun to lose the faculty for sympathising in others' griefs. It is hard to have to realise that in all this slaughter, my own superfluous life has become negligible and scarcely anyone's concern but my own. In this colossal *sauve qui peut* which is developing, who can stay to consider a useless mouth? Am I not a comfortable parasite? And, God forgive me, an Egotist to boot?

The War is searching out everyone, concentrating a beam of inquisitive light upon everyone's mind and character and publishing it for all the world to see. And the consequence to many honest folk has been a keen personal disappointment. We ignoble persons had thought we were better than we really are. We scarcely anticipated that the War was going to discover for us our emotions so despicably small by comparison, or our hearts so riddled with selfish motives. In the wild race for security during these dangerous times, men and women have all been sailing so closehauled to the wind that their eyes have been glued to their own forepeaks with never a thought for others: fathers have vied with one another in procuring safe jobs for their sons, wives have been bitter and re-criminating at the security of other wives' husbands. The men themselves plot constantly for staff appointments, and everyone is pulling strings who can. Bereavement has brought bitterness and immunity indifference.

And how pathetically some of us cling still to fragments of the old régime that has already passed—like ship-wrecked mariners to floating wreckage, to the manner of the con-servatoire amid the thunder of all Europe being broken up; to our newspaper gossip and parish teas, to our cherished aims—wealth, fame, success—in spite of all, *ruat coelum!* Mr A. C. Benson and his trickling, comfortable Essays, Mr Shaw and his Scintillations—they are all there as before, revolving like haggard windmills in a devastated landscape! A little while ago, I read in the local newspaper which I get up from the country two columns concerning the acci-dental death of an old woman, while two lines were used to record the death of a townsman at the front from an

aerial dart.   Behold this poor rag ! staggering along under
the burden of the War in a passionate endeavour to preserve the old-time interest in an old woman's decease.
Yet more or less we are all in the same case: I still write my
Journal and play Patience of an evening, and an old lady
I know still reads as before the short items of gossip in the
papers, neglecting articles and leaders. . . .   We are like
a nest of frightened ants when someone lifts the stone.
That is the world just now.

September 5.

. . . I was so ashamed of having to fall back upon such
ignominious publications for my literary efforts that on
presenting him with two copies, I told the following lie to
save my face:
' They were two essays of mine left over at the beginning
of the War, you know.   My usual channel became blocked
so I had to have recourse to these.'
' Where do you publish as a rule ?' he innocently asked.
' Oh ! several in the *Manchester Guardian*,' I told him out
of vanity.   ' But of course every respectable journal now
has closed down to extra-war topics.'
I lie out of vanity.   And then I confess to lying—out of
vanity too.   So that one way or another I am determined
to make kudos out of myself.   Even this last reflection is
written down with an excessive appreciation of its wit and
the intention that it shall raise a smile.

September 9.

Still nothing to report.   The anxiety is telling on us all.
The nurse has another case on the 22nd.

.   .   .   .

I looked at myself in the mirror this morning—nude, a
most revolting picture.   An emaciated human being is the
most unlovely thing in creation.   Some time ago a smart
errand boy called out ' Bovril ' after me in the street.
On my way to the Station met two robust, brawny curates
on the way to the daily weekday service—which is attended

only by two decrepit old women in black, each with her prayer-book caught up to her breast as if she were afraid it might gallop off. That means a parson apiece—and in war time too.

September 10.

My sympathy with myself is so unfailing that I don't deserve anybody else's. In many respects, however, this Journal I believe gives the impression that I behave myself in the public gaze much worse than I actually do. You must remember that herein I let myself go at a stretch gallop: in life I rein in, I am almost another person. Would you believe it, E—— says I am full of quick sympathy with others and extraordinarily cheerful, nay gay. Verily I lead a curious double existence: among most people, I pass for a complaisant, amiable, mealy-mouthed, furry if conceited creature. Here I stand revealed as a contemptuous, arrogant malcontent. My life has embittered me *au fond*, I have the crabbed temper of the disappointed man insufficiently developed yet to be very plainly visible beneath my innate affable, unassuming, humble, diffident, cheerful characteristics. With fools on every hand I am becoming insolent, aggressive, self-declamatory. Last evening came home and got down Robert Buchanan's sonnet, ' When He returns and finds the world so drear,' and felt constrained to read it out to E——. I poured out its acid sentiment with the base revenge of a vitriol thrower, and then became quiescent.

It is a helpless feeling, sitting still and watching circumstances pounding away at my malleable character and moulding it wrongly.

September 14.
An American Neighbour

We have a delightful American neighbour here whose life revolves like the fly-wheel of an engine. Even when not in eruption his volcanic energy is always rumbling and can be heard. Seeing he is a globe trotter, I was sur-

prised to observe his most elaborate precautions for catching
the train and getting a seat when he takes his wife and
family to town.   He first of all plants himself and all his
property down at a certain carefully selected point along
the platform as if he were in the wild west lying in wait
for a Buffalo.   Then as the train comes in, his eye fixes on
an empty compartment as it passes and he dashes off after
it in furious pursuit up the platform, shouting to his family
to follow him.   Having lassooed the compartment, squaw
and piccaninnies are hustled in as if there was not a moment
to lose, what time the black-coated, suburban Englishmen
look on in pain and silence, and then slowly with offensive
deliberation enter their respective carriages.

The Stockbroker

Another neighbour who interests me is mainly notable
for his extraordinary gait.   He is a man with a large,
round head, a large round, dissolute looking face and fairly
broad shoulders, below which everything tapers away to a
pair of tiny feet neatly booted.   These two little feet are
excessively sensitive to road surface—one would say he
had special sense organs on his toes, to judge by the manner
in which he picks out his path along the country road in
short, quick, fussy steps: his feet seem to dissect out the
road as if boning a herring.   A big bunion is as good as a
sense organ, but his feet are too small and elegant.

September 24.

The second nurse arrived to-day.   Great air raid last
night of which we heard nothing, thank God !

My nerves are giving way under the strain. . . . One
leg (the left) drags abominably. . . . We shall want a
bath-chair as well as a perambulator.

Crawled up thro' the path-fields to the uplands and sat
in a field in the sun with my back against a haystack.   I
was so immobile in my dejection that Flies and Grasshoppers came and perched about me.   This made me
furious.   'I am not dead yet,' I said, 'get away,' and I

would suddenly drive them off. . . . In horrible dejection. . . .

Even my mental powers are disintegrating—that's the rub.
Some quite recent incidents I cannot remember even when
reminded of them: they seem to have passed clean out of
my mind—a remarkable sensation this.

My sensibility is dulled too.   It chagrins me to find that
my present plight by no means overwhelms me with
anguish as it would have done once.   It only worries me.
I am just a worried ox.

September 26.

The numbness in my right hand is getting very trying.
. . . The Baby puts the lid on it all.   Can't you see the
sordid picture ?   I can, and it haunts me.   To be paralysed with a wife and child and no money—ugh !

Retribution proceeds with an almost mathematical
accuracy of measure.   It would necessitate a vernier rather
than a chain.   There is no mercy in Cause and Effect.   It is
inhuman clockwork.   Every single act expended brings
one its precise equivalent in return. . . .

September 28.

Still nothing to report.

I am astonished at the false impression these entries give
of myself.   The picture is incomplete anyhow.   It repre-
sents the cloud of forebodings over my inner self but does
not show the outward front I present to others.   This is
one of almost constant gaiety—unforced and quite natural.
Ask E——, who said yesterday I was like a schoolboy.

> ' Camerade, I give you my hand !
> I give you my love more precious than money,
> I give you myself before preaching or law;
> Will you give me yourself ?   Will you come, travel with me ?
> Shall we stick by each other as long as we live ?'

She cut this out of her copy of Walt Whitman and gave
it me soon after our engagement.   It is very precious
to me.

(On Sept. 29th, on the Doctor's advice I went away by the sea alone, my nerves being all unstrung. For an account of the miseries of this journey, see Dec. 12th *infra*.)

October 3.

A wire to say Susan arrived 2.15 p.m.   All well.

October 5.

Home again with my darling.   She is the most wonderful darling woman.   Our love is for always.   The Baby is a monster.

October 23.

The fact that I can't write, finally bottles me up.[1] Damn! Damn! Damn! If only I can get my Essay on Journal Writers done.   E—— goes on well.   I have a thousand things to say.

October 27.

Still awaiting a reprieve.   I hate alarming the Doctor —he's such a cheerful man so I conceal my symptoms, quite a collection by now.

The prospect of breaking the news to her makes me miserable.   I hide away as much as possible lest she should see.   I *must* speak when she is well again.

October 28.

Life has been very treacherous to me—this, the greatest treachery of all.   But I don't care.   I exult over it.   Last nigl t I lay awake and listened to the wind in the trees and was full of exultation.

Now I can only talk, but nobody to talk to.   Shall hire a row of broomsticks.   More and more, the War appears to me a tragic hoax.

---

[1] The handwriting is painfully laboured, very large across a page and so crooked as to be almost undecipherable in places.

November 1.

E—— has had a set-back and is in bed again.   However sclerotic my nerve tissue, I feel as flaccid as a jelly.

My God ! how I loathe the prospect of death.

November 3.

I must have some music or I shall hear the paralysis creeping.   That is why I lie in bed and whistle.

' My dear Brown, what am I to do ?'[1]   (I like to drama-tise myself like that—it is an anodyne.)

I feel as if I were living alone on Ascension Island with the tide coming up continuously, up and up and up.

November 6.

She has known *all* from the beginning !   M—— warned her *not* to marry me.   How brave and loyal of her !   What an ass I have been.   I am overwhelmed with feelings of shame and self-contempt and sorrow for her.   She is quite cheerful and an enormous help.

November 12.

What a wreck my existence has become and—dragging down others with me.

If only I could rest assured that after I am dead these Journals will be tenderly cared for—as tenderly as this blessed infant !   It would be cruel if even after I have paid the last penalty, my efforts and sufferings should continue to remain unknown or disregarded.   What I would give to know the effect I shall produce when pub-lished !   I am tortured by two doubts—whether these MSS. (the labour and hope of many years) will survive accidental loss and whether they really are of any value. I have no faith in either.

November 14.

In fits of panic, I keep saying to myself: ' My dear Brown, what am I to do ?'   But where is Brown ?   Brown, you devil ! where are you ?

[1] This is from a letter written by the dying Keats in Naples to his friend Brown.

. . . To think how I have acted the Prince to her when really I am only a beggar !

November 16.

A little better and more cheerful: altho' my impregnable colon still holds out.

It would be nice if a physician from London one of these days were to gallop up hotspur, tether his horse to the gate post and dash in waving a reprieve—the discovery of a cure !

. . . I was in an impish mood and said: ' Oh ! dear, I'm full of misery.'

' Don't be silly,' she said, 'so am I.'

November 17.

E—— has been telling me some of her emotions during and after her fateful visit to my Doctor just before our marriage. He did not spare her and even estimated the length of my life after I had once taken to my bed—about 12 months. I remember his consulting room so well—all its furniture and the photograph of Madame Blavatsky over the door, and I picture her to myself sitting opposite to him in a sullen silence listening to the whole lugúbrious story. Then she said at last: ' All this won't make any difference to me.' She went home to her mother in a dream, along the streets I have followed so often. I can follow all her footsteps in imagination and keep on retracing them. It hurts, but I do so because it seems to make her some amends for my being childishly unconscious at the time. Poor darling woman—if only I had known ! My instinct was right—I felt in my bones it was wrong to marry, yet here was M—— urging me on. ' You marry,' her mother said to her, ' I'll stand by you,' which was right royal of her. There followed some trying months of married life with this white hot secret in her bosom as a barricade to perfect intimacy; me she saw always under this cloud of crude disgusting pathos making her say a hundred times to herself: ' He doesn't know;' then Zeppelin raids and a few symptoms began to grow obvious, until what before she

had to take on trust from the Doctor came diabolically
true before her eyes. Thank God that's all over at last.
I know her now for all she is worth—her loyalty and devotion, her courage and strength. If only I had something to give her in return ! something more than the dregs
of a life and a constitutional pessimism. I greatly desire
to make some sacrifice, but I am so poor these days, so
very much a pauper on her charity, there is no sacrifice I
can make. Even my life would scarcely be a sacrifice in
the circumstances—it is hard not to be able to give when
one *wants* to give.

November 20.

In the doldrums. Tired of this damnable *far niente*,—I
am being gently smothered under a mountain of feathers.
I should like to engage upon some cold, hard, glittering
intellectualism.

'I want to read Kant,' I said. The Baby slept, E——
was sewing and N—— writing letters. I leaned back in
my armchair beside the bookshelf and began to read out
the titles of my books in a loud voice.

'My dear !' E—— said.

'I am caressing my past,' I answered. 'Wiedersheim's
Comparative Anatomy of Vertebrates, Smith Woodward's
Vertebrate Palæontology—why it's like visiting old prospects
and seeing how the moss has grown over the stones.'

I hummed a comic song and then said: 'As I can't burn
the house down, I shall go to bed.'

N——: 'You can talk if you like, it won't interfere.'

E——: 'He's talking to his besoms.'

'Certainly,' I said to N——, absent-mindedly.

E——: 'You ought to have said "Thank you."'

I blew out my cheeks and E—— laughed.

N——: 'How do you spell "regimental"?'

I told her—wrongly, and E—— said I was in a devilish
mood.

'If we say that we have no sin' I chanted in reply, 'we
deceive ourselves and the truth is not in us.' I next gave

a bit out of a speech by Disraeli with exaggerated rhetorical gestures.

E—— (with pity): ' Poor young man.'

Presently she came over and in a tired way put her arms around my neck so I immediately began to sing ' Rock of Ages, cleft for me,' in the bass, which immediately reminded me of dear old Dad, whose favourite hymn it was. . . . Then I imitated the Baby. And then to bed fretful and very bitter.

November 27.

. . . I wish I could die of heart failure—and at once ! What a luxury that would be as compared with my present prospect !

A Tomtit on the fence this morning made me dissolve in tears:—self-pity I believe. I remember Tomtits in ——shire. Put on a gramophone record and—ugh ! but I'm too sick to write.

November 28.

The shock I gave my spinal column in 1915 up in the Lakes undoubtedly re-awakened activity among the bacteria. Luck for you ! I, of all persons to concuss my spine ! !

. . . I listen to the kettle singing, l look at the pictures in the fire, read a bit, ask what time it is, see the Baby ' topped and tailed,' yawn, blow my nose, put on a gramophone record—I have the idea of ceasing on the midnight with no pain to the tune of some healing ragtime.

November 29.

The anniversary of our engagement day two years ago. How mad the idea of marriage seemed to me—and my instinct was right: if only I had known ! Yet she says she does not regret anything.

.   .   .   .

This morning I turned to read with avidity accounts of the last hours of Keats, Gibbon, Oscar Wilde and Baude-

laire.   I gained astonishing comfort out of this, especially
in the last . . . who died of G.P.I. in a Brussels Hospital.

. . . . . .

E—— is awfully courageous and, —— as usual ready to
do everything in her power.   How can I ever express
sufficient gratitude to these two dear women (and my wife
above all) for casting in their lot knowingly with mine ?

December 1.

I believe I am good for another 12 months without abnormal worries.   Just now, of course, the Slug ain't exactly
on the thorn—on the cabbage in fact as E—— suggested.
The Grasshopper is much of a burden and the voice of the
Turtle has gone from my land (where did all these Bible
phrases come from ?).   The first bark of the Wolf (God save
us, 'tis all the Animal Kingdom sliding down my penholder)
was heard with the reduction in her work to-day, and I
suspect there's worse to come with a sovereign already only
worth 12s. 6d.

December 4.

The Baby touch is the most harrowing of all.   If we
were childless we should be merely unfortunate, but an
infant . . .

December 11.

Am receiving ionisation treatment from an electrical
therapeutist—a quack ! He is a sort of electrician—
still, if he mends my bells I'll kiss his boots.   As for ——,
he is no better than a byreman, and I call him Hodge.
This is not the first time I have felt driven to act behind
the back of the Profession.   In 1912, being desperate, and
M—— worse than a headache, I greedily and credulously
sucked in the advice of my boarding-house proprietor and
went to see a homœopathist in Finsbury Circus.   He
proved to be a charlatan at 10s. 6d a time, and tho' I
realised it at once, I religiously travelled about for a month
or more with tinctures and drop-bottle.

I could write a book on the Doctors I have known and the blunders they have made about me. . . . The therapeutist took me for 33. I feel 63. I am 27. What a wreck I am, and . . .

December 12.

It is so agreeable to be able to write again that I write now for the sheer physical pleasure of being able to use a pen and form letters.

An Adventure in Search of Health

About the end of September, I began to feel so ill that Nurse went for the Doctor who assured me that E—— was all right—I need not worry—' You go away at once and get some fresh air,' and so forth. ' I feel quite ill,' I said, struggling to break the news.

' Sort of nervous ?' he enquired good-naturedly, ' run down ? I should get right away at once.'

I began tentatively. ' Well, I have a rather long medical history and perhaps . . . you . . . might care to read the certificate of my London Doctor ?'

I went to my escritoire and returned with M——'s letter addressed to ' The M.O. examining Mr B.' [1]

Hodge pulled out the missive, studied the brief note carefully and long, at the same time drawing in his breath deeply, and gnawing the back of his hand.

' I know all about it,' I said to relieve him.

' Is it quite certain ? about this disease ?' he said presently. ' You are very young for it.'

' I think there is no doubt,' and he began to put me thro' the usual tricks.

' I should go right away at once,' he said, ' and go on with your arsenic. And whatever you do—don't worry—your wife is all right.'

After beseeching him to keep silence about it as I thought she did not know, I shewed him out and locked up the certificate again.

Next morning I felt thoroughly cornered: I was not

---

[1] I had destroyed the first certificate (see p. 225), but it was necessary to obtain another when conscription came in.

really fit enough to travel; my hand and leg were daily
growing more and more paralysed and J—— wired to say
she could not put me up as they were going away for the
week end. So I wired back engaging rooms, as with the
nurse in the house and E—— as she was, I simply could not
stay at home. . . .

On the way to the Station I was still in two minds
whether or not to pull the taxi up at the Nursing Home
and go inside, but harassing debate as it was, our rapidly
diminishing bank balance finally drove me on.

—— came up to London with me and sought out a
comfortable corner seat, but by the time the train left, a
mother and a crying child had got in and everywhere else
was full. A girl opposite who saw —— hand me a brandy
flask and knew I was ill, looked at me compassionately.

At Reading, another woman with a baby got in and both
babies cried in chorus, jangling my nerves to bits !—until
I got out into the corridor, by a miracle not falling down,
with one leg very feeble and treacherous. All seats were
taken, excepting a first-class compartment where I looked
in enviously at a lucky youth stretched out asleep full
length along the empty seat.

All the people and the noise of the train began to make
me fret, so I sought out the repose of a lavatory where I
remained eating sandwiches and an apple for the best
part of an hour. It was good to be alone.

Later on, I discovered an empty seat in a compartment
occupied by persons whose questionable appearance my
short sight entirely failed to make me aware of until I got
inside with them. They were a family of Sheenies, father,
mother and three children, whose joint emanations in a
closed-up railway carriage made an effluvium like to kill
a regiment of guards. They were E. end pawnbrokers or
dealers in second-hand clothes.

I was too nervous to appear rude by immediately with-
drawing, so I said politely to the man clad in second-hand
furs: ' Is that seat taken ?'

He affected to be almost asleep. So I repeated. He
stared at me and then said:

'Oh! yes . . . but you can have it for a bit if you like.'

I sat down timorously on the extreme edge of the seat and stared at, but could not read, my newspaper out of sheer nervous apprehension. My sole idea was to get out as soon as I decorously could. Out of the corner of my eye, I observed the three children—two girls and a boy— all garbed in black clothes and wearing large clumsy boots with nails and scutes on the soles. The girls had large inflorescences of bushy hair which they swung about as they turned their heads and made me shudder. The mother's face was like a brown, shrivelled apple, topped with a black bonnet and festooned on each side with ringlets of curly dark hair. Around her neck a fur tippet: as I live—second-hand clothes dealers from Whitechapel.

The man I dare not look at: I sat beside him and merely imagined.

At ——, I got a decent seat and arrived at T—— jaded, but still alive, with no one to meet me. Decent rooms on the sea-front.

Next morning J—— went away for the week end and I could not possibly explain how ill I was lest she stayed at home.

To preserve my sanity, Saturday afternoon, took a desperate remedy by hiring a motor-car and travelling to Torquay and back *via* Babbacombe. . . .

On the Sunday, feeling suddenly ill, I sent for the local medico whom I received in the drab little room by lamplight after dinner. 'I've a tingling in my right hand,' I said, 'that drives me nearly silly.'

'And on the soles of your feet?' he asked at once.

I assented, and he ran thro' at once all the symptoms in series.

'I see you know what my trouble is,' I said shyly. And we chatted a little about the War, about disease, and I told him of the recent memoir on the histology of the disease —— in the *Trans. Roy. Soc.,* Edin. which interested him. Then he went away again—very amiable, very polite —an obvious *non possumus.* . . .

On Monday at 4 went up to —— to tea as previously arranged, but found the house shut up so returned to my rooms in a rage.

After tea, having read the newspapers inside out, sat by the open window looking out on to the Marine Parade. It was dusk, a fine rain was falling, and the parade and seafront were deserted save for an occasional figure hurrying past with mackintosh and umbrella. Suddenly as I sat looking out on this doleful scene, a dirge from nowhere in particular sounded on my ears which I soon recognised as ' Robin Adair,' sung very *lento* and very *maestoso* by a woman, with a flute obligato played by some second person. The tide was right up, and the little waves murmured listlessly at long intervals: never before I think have I been plunged into such an abyss of acute misery.

Next day the wire came. But it was too late. The day after that, I was worse, a single ray of sunshine being the rediscovery of the second-hand-clothes family from Whitechapel taking the air together on the front. This dreary party was traipsing along, the parents in their furs giving an occasional glance at the sea uncomfortably, as if they only noticed it was wet, and the children still in black and still wearing their scuted boots, obviously a little uncomfortable in a place so clean and windswept. I think they all came to the seaside out of decorum and for the satisfaction of feeling that they could afford it like other folk, and that old-clothes was as profitable a business as another.

On Thursday, returned home as I was afraid of being taken ill and having to go into the public hospital. Arrived home and went to bed and here we are till Jan. 1st on 3 months' sick leave. However, the swingeing urtication in my hands and feet has now almost entirely abated and to-day I went out with E—— and the perambulator, *which I pushed.*

December 13.

A Baby-Girl

Walked down the bottom of the road and hung over some wooden railings. A little village baby-girl aged not more than 3 was hovering about near me while I gazed abstractedly across the Park at the trees. Presently, she crawled through the railings into the field and picked up a few dead leaves—a baby picking up dead leaves! Then she threw them down, and kicked them. Then moved on again—rustling about intermittently like a winter Thrush in the shrubbery. At last, she had stumbled around to where I was leaning over the railings. She stood immediately in front of me and silently looked up with a steady reproachful gaze: ' Ain't you 'shamed, you lazy-bones ?' till I could bear her inquisitorial gaze no longer, and so went and hung over some more railings further on.

Service

He asked for a Tennyson. She immediately went upstairs in the dark, lit a match and got it for him.

He asked for a Shakespeare. And without a moment's hesitation, she went upstairs again, lit another match and got that for him.

And I believe if he had said ' Rats,' she would have shot out silently into the dark and tried to catch one for him. Only a woman is capable of such service.

Hardy's Poetry

> ' You did not come,
> And marching time drew on and wore me numb—
> Yet less for loss of your dear presence there
> Than that I thus found lacking in your make
> That high compassion which can overbear
> Reluctance for pure loving-kindness' sake
> Grieved I, *when, as the hope-hour stroked its sum,*
>   You did not come.''

I thoroughly enjoy Hardy's poetry for its masterfulness, for his sheer muscular compulsion over the words and sentences. In his rough-hewn lines he yokes the recalcitrant words together and drives them along mercilessly with something that looks like simple brute strength. Witness the triumphant last line in the above where the words are absolute bondslaves to his exact meaning, his indomitable will. All this pleases me the more for I know to my cost what stubborn, sullen, hephæstian beasts words and clauses can sometimes be. It is nice to see them punished. Hardy's poetry is Michael Angelo rather than Greek, Browning not Tennyson.

December 14.

What a day ! After a night of fog signals, I awoke this morning to find it still foggy and the ground covered with a grey rime. All day the fog has remained: I look out now thro' the yellowish atmosphere across a field which is frosted over, the grass and brambles stiff and glassy. My back is aching and the cold is so intense that unless I crouch over the fire hands and feet become immediately stone-cold. All day I have crouched over the fire, reading newspapers, listening to fog signals and the screaming of the baby. . . . I have been in a torpor, like a Bat in a cavern— really dead yet automatically hanging on to life by my hind legs.

December 15.

' To stand upon one's guard against Death exasperates her malice and protracts our sufferings.' W. S. Landor.

December 19.

The Parson called, over the christening of the baby. I told him I was an agnostic. ' There are several interesting lines of thought down here,' he said wearily, passing his hand over his eyes. I know several men more enthusiastic over Fleas and Worms than this phlegmatic priest, over Jesus Christ.

December 20.

The reason why I do not spend my days in despair and my nights in hopeless weeping simply is that I am in love with my own ruin. ' I therefore deserve no sympathy, and probably shan't get it: my own profound self-compassion is enough. I am so abominably self-conscious that no smallest detail in this tragedy eludes me. Day after day I sit in the theatre of my own life and watch the drama of my own history proceeding to its close. Pray God the curtain falls at the right moment lest the play drag on into some long and tedious anticlimax.

We all like to dramatise ourselves. Byron was drama-
tising himself when, in a fit of rhetorical self-compassion,
he wrote:

' Oh ! could I feel as I have felt or be what I have been,
  Or weep as I could once have wept o'er many a vanished scene.'

Shelley, too, being an artist could not stand insensible
to his own tragedy and Francis Thompson suggests that
he even anticipated his own end from a passage in *Julian
and Maddalo*, '. . . if you can't swim, Beware of Providence.' ' Did no earthly *dixisti*,' Thompson asks, ' sound
in his ears as he wrote it ?'

In any event, it was an admirable ending from the
dramatic point of view; Destiny is often a superb drama-
tist. What more perfect than the death of Rupert Brooke
at Scyros in the Ægean ?[1] The lives of some men are
works of art, perfect in form, in development and in climax.
Yet how frequently a life eminently successful or even
eminently ruinous is also an unlovely, sordid, ridiculous
or vulgar affair ! Every one will concede that it must be
a hard thing to be commonplace and vulgar even in
misfortune, to discover that the tragedy of your own
precious life has been dramatically bad, that your life even
in its ruins is but a poor thing, and your own miseries
pathetic from their very insignificance; that you are only
Jones with chronic indigestion rather than Guy de Maupassant mad, or Coleridge with a great intellect being
slowly dismantled by opium.

If only I could order my life by line and level, if I could
control or create my own destiny and mould it into some
marble perfection ! In short, if life were an art and not
a lottery ! In the lives of all of us, how many wasted efforts,

[1] Contrast with it Wordsworth rotting at Rydal Mount or
Swinburne at Putney.
    Napoleon regretted that he had not died at Borodino. At St.
Helena he is reported to have said : ' To die at Borodino would have
been to have died like Alexander : to be killed at Waterloo would have
been a good death : perhaps Dresden would have been better : but
no, better at Waterloo.'

how many wasted opportunities, false starts, blind grop-
ings—how many lost days—and man's life is but a paltry
three score years and ten: pitiful short commons indeed.

Sometimes, as I lean over a five-barred gate or gaze
stupidly into the fire, I garner a bitter-sweet contentment
in making ideal reconstructions of my life, selecting my
parents, the date and place of my birth, my gifts, my
education, my mentors and what portions out of the infinity of knowledge shall gain a place within my mind—
that sacred glebe-land to be zealously preserved and
enthusiastically cultivated.   Whereas, my mind is now a
wilderness in which all kinds of useless growths have
found an ineradicable foothold.   I am exasperated to find
I have by heart the long addresses of a lot of dismal business correspondents and yet can't remember the last
chapters of Ecclesiastes: what a waste of mind-stuff there !
It irks me to be acquainted even to nausea with the spot
in which I live, I whose feet have never traversed even
so much as this little island much less carried me in triumph
to Timbuctoo, Honolulu, Rio, Rome.

December 21.

This continuous preoccupation with self sickens me—as
I look back over these entries.   It is inconceivable that I
should be here steadily writing up my ego day by day in
the middle of this disastrous war. . . .   Yesterday I had
a move on.   To-day life wearies me.   I am sick of myself
and life.   This beastly world with its beastly war and hate
makes me restless, dissatisfied, and full of a longing to be
quit of it.   I am as full of unrest as an autumn Swallow.
'My soul,' I said to them at breakfast with a sardonic grin,
' is like a greyhound in the slips.   I shall have to wear
heavy boots to prevent myself from soaring.   I have such
an uplift on me that I could carry a horse, a dog, a cat, if
you tied them on to my homing spirit and so transformed
my Ascension into an adventure out of Baron Munchausen.'
With a gasconnade of contempt, I should like to turn on
my heel and march straight out of this wretched world at
once.

December 22.

Gibbon's Autobiography

This book makes me of all people (and especially just now) groan inwardly. ' I am at a loss,' he says, referring to the *Decline and Fall,* ' how to describe the success of the work without betraying the vanity of the writer. . . . My book was on every table and almost on every toilette.' It makes me bite my lip. Rousseau and his criticism of ' I sighed as a lover; I obeyed as a son,' and Gibbon on his dignity in reply make one of the most ludicrous incidents in literary history. ' . . . that extraordinary man whom I admire and pity, should have been less precipitate in condemning the moral character and conduct of a stranger !' Oh my giddy Aunt ! Isn't this *rich ?* Still, I am glad you did not marry her: we could ill spare Madam de Staël, Madam Necker's daughter, that wonderful, vivacious and warmhearted woman.

' After the morning has been occupied with the labours of the library, I wish to unbend rather than exercise my mind ; and in the interval between tea and supper, I am far from disdaining the innocent amusement of a game of cards.' How Jane Austen would have laughed at him ! The passage reminds me of the Rev. Mr Collins saying:

' Had I been able I should have been only too pleased to give you a song, for I regard music as a harmless diversion and perfectly compatible with the profession of a clergyman.'

'When I contemplate the common lot of mortality,' Gibbon writes, ' I must acknowledge I have drawn a high prize in the lottery of life,' and he goes on to count up all his blessings with the most offensive delight—his wealth, the good fortune of his birth, his ripe years, a cheerful temper, a moderate sensibility, health, sound and peaceful slumbers from infancy, his valuable friendship with Lord Sheffield, his rank, fame, etc., etc., *ad nauseam.* He rakes over his whole life for things to be grateful for. He intones his happiness in a long recitative of thanksgiving that his lot was not that of a savage, of a slave, or a peasant;

he washes his hands with imaginary soap on reflecting on the bounty of Nature which cast his birth in a free and civilised country, in an age of science and philosophy, in a family of honourable rank and decently endowed with the gifts of fortune—sleek, complacent, oleaginous and salacious old gentleman, how I would love to have bombed you out of your self-satisfaction !

Masefield's ' Gallipoli '

It amused me to discover the evident relish with which the author of *In the Daffodil Fields* emphasises the blood and the flowers in the attack on Achi Baba. It's all blood and beautiful flowers mixed up together to Masefield's great excitement.

> ' A swear word in a city slum
> A simple swear word is to some—
> To Masefield something more.'
>   MAX BEERBOHM.

Still, to call Gallipoli ' bloody Hell ' is, after all, only a pedantically exact description. You understand, tho', a very remarkable book—a work of genius.

December 23.

To be cheerful this Xmas would require a *coup de théâtre*—some sort of psychological sleight of hand.

I get downstairs at 10 and spend the day reading and writing, without a soul to converse with. Everything comes to me second-hand—thro' the newspapers, the world of life thro' the halfpenny *Daily News*, and the world of books thro' the *Times Literary Supplement*. For the rest I listen to the kettle singing and make symphonies out of it, or I look into the fire to see the pictures there. . . .

December 24.

Everyone I suppose engaged in this irony of Xmas. What a solemn lunatic the world is.

Walked awhile in a beautiful lane close by, washed hard

and clean and deeply channelled by the recent rain. On
the hill-top, I could look right across the valley to the uplands, where on the sky line a few Firs stood in stately
sequestration from common English Oaks, like a group of
ambassadors in full dress. In the distance a hen clucked,
I saw a few Peewits wheeling and watched the smoke
rising from our cottage perpendicularly into the motionless
air. There was a clement quiet and a clement warmth,
and in my heart a burst of real happiness that made me
rich even beside less unfortunate beings and beyond what I
had ever expected to be again.

December 26.

'In thus describing and illustrating my intellectual
torpor, I use terms that apply more or less to every part
of the years during which I was under the Circean spells
of opium. But for misery——'

(Why do I waste my energy with this damned Journal ?
I stop. I hate it. I am going out for a walk in the fog.)

December 31.

Reminiscences

For the past few days I have been living in a quiet
hermitage of retrospect. My memories have gone back
to the times—remote, inaccessible, prehistoric—before
ever this Journal was begun, when I myself was but a
jelly without form and void—that is, before I had developed
any characteristic qualities and above all the dominant
one, a passion for Natural History.

One day a school friend, being covetous of certain stamps
in my collection, induced me to 'swop' them for his collection of birds' eggs which he showed me nestling in the bran
at the bottom of a box. He was a cunning boy and thought
he had the better of the bargain. He little realised—nor
did I—the priceless gift he bestowed when his little fat
dirty hands, decorated, I remember, with innumerable
warts, picked out the eggs and gave them to me. In fact,
a smile momentarily crossed his face, he turned his head
aside, he spat in happy contemplation of the deal.

I continued eagerly to add to the little collection of Birds'
eggs, but for a long time it never occurred to me to go out
into the country myself and collect them,—I just *swopped*,
until one day our errand boy, who stuttered, had bandy
legs, and walked on the outside of his feet with the gait of
an Anthropoid, said to me, ' I will sh-show you how to
find Birds' n-nests if you like to come out to the w-woods.'
So one Saturday, when the backyard was cleaned down
and the coal boxes filled, he and I started off together to
a wood some way down the river bank, where he—my
good and beneficent angel—presently showed me a Thrush's
nest in the fork of a young Oak tree. Never-to-be-forgotten
moment ! The sight of those blue speckled eggs lying so
unexpectedly, as I climbed up the tree, on the other side
of an untidy tangle of dried moss and grass, in a neat little
earthenware cup, caused probably the first tremor of real
emotion at a beautiful object. The emotion did not last
long ! In a moment I had stolen the eggs and soon after
smashed them—in trying to blow them, schoolboy fashion.

Then, I rapidly became an ardent field naturalist. My
delight in Birds and Birds' eggs spread in a benignant in-
fection to every branch of Natural History. I collected
Beetles, Butterflies, Plants, Birds' wings, Birds' claws, etc.
Dr Gordon Stables in the *Boy's Own Paper*, taught me
how to make a skin, and I got hold of a Mole and then a
Squirrel (the latter falling to my prowess with a catapult),
stuffed them and set them up in cases which I glazed myself. I even painted in suitable backgrounds, in the one
case a mole-hill, looking, I fear, more like a mountain, and
in the other, a Fir tree standing at an impossible angle of
45°. Then I read a book on trapping, and tried to catch
Hares. Then I read Sir John Lubbock's *Ants, Bees and
Wasps*, and constructed an observation Ants' nest (though
the Ants escaped).

In looking back to these days, I am chiefly struck
by my extraordinary ignorance of the common objects
of the countryside, for although we lived in the far
west country, the house, without a garden, was in the
middle of the town, and all my seniors were as ignorant

as I. Nature Study in the schools did not then exist, I had no benevolent paterfamilias to take me by the hand and point out the common British Birds; for my father's only interest was in politics. I can remember coming home once all agog with a wonderful Bird I had seen—like a tiny Magpie, I said. No one could tell me that it was, of course, only a little Pied Wagtail.

The absence of sympathy or of congenial companionship, however, had absolutely no effect in damping my ardour. As I grew older my egg-collecting companions fell away, some took up the law, or tailoring, or clerking, some entered the Church, while I became yearly more engrossed. In my childhood my enthusiasm lay like a watch-spring, coiled up and hidden inside me, until that Thrush's nest and eggs seized hold of it by the end and pulled it out by degrees in a long silver ribbon. I kept live Bats in our upstairs little-used drawing-room, and Newts and Frogs in pans in the backyard. My mother tolerated these things because I had sufficiently impressed her with the importance to science of the observations which I was making and about to publish. Those on Bats indeed were thought fit to be included in a standard work—Barrett-Hamilton's *Mammals of Great Britain and Ireland*. The published articles served to bring me into correspondence with other naturalists, and I shall never forget my excitement on receiving for the first time a letter of appreciation. It was from the author of several natural history books, to

'W. N. P. Barbellion, Esq.,
Naturalist,
Downstable,'

and illustrated with a delightful sketch of Ring Plovers feeding on the saltings. This letter was carefully pasted into my diary, where it still remains.

After all, it is perhaps unfair to say that I had no kindred spirit with me in my investigations. Martha, the servant girl who had been with us for 30 years, loved animals of all sorts and—what was strange in a country girl—she had no fear of handling even such things as Newts and Frogs. My Batrachia often used to escape from their pans in the yard into Martha's kitchen, and, not a bit scandalised, she would sometimes catch one marching across the rug or squeezing underneath a cupboard. ' Lor' !' would be her comment as she picked the vagrant up and took it back to its aquarium, ' can't 'em travel ?' Martha had an eye for character in animals. In the long dynasty of cats we possessed one at length who by association of opposite ideas we called Marmaduke because he ought to have been called Jan Stewer. ' A chuff old feller, 'idden 'ee ?' Martha used to ask me with pride and love in her eyes. ' He purrs in broad Devon,' I used to answer. Marmaduke need only wave the tip of his tail to indicate to her his imperative desire to promenade. Martha knew if no one else did that every spring ' Pore 'Duke,' underneath his fur, used to come out in spots. ' 'Tiz jus' like a cheel —'e gets a bit spotty as the warm weather cums along.' Starlings on the washhouse roof, regularly fed with scraps, were ever her wonder and delight. ' Don' 'em let it down, I zay ?' In later years, when I was occupied in the top attic, making dissections of various animals that I collected, she would sometimes leave her scrubbing and cleaning in the room below to thrust her head up the attic stairs and enquire, ' 'Ow be 'ee gettin' on then ?' Her unfeigned interest in my anatomical researches gave me real pleasure, and I took delight in arousing her wonder by pointing out and explaining the brain of a Pigeon or the nervous system of a Dog-fish, or a Frog's heart taken out and still beating in the dissecting dish. She, in reply, would add reflections upon her own experiences in preparing meat for dinner—anecdotes about the ' maw ' of an old Fowl, or the great ' pipe ' of a Goose. Then, suddenly scurrying downstairs, she would say, ' I must be off or I shall be all be'ind like the cow's tail.' Now the dignified interest of the average educated man would have chilled me.

By the way, years later, when he was a miner in S. Wales, that historic errand-boy displayed his consciousness of the important rôle he once played by sending me on a postcard congratulations on my success in the B. M. appointment. It touched me to think he had not forgotten after years of separation.

1917

January 1.

The New Year came in like a thief in the night—noiselessly; no bells, no sirens, no songs by order of the Government. Nothing could have been more appropriate than a burglarious entry like this—seeing what the year has come to filch from us all in the next 12 months.

January 20.

I am over 6 feet high and as thin as a skeleton; every bone in my body, even the neck vertebræ, creak at odd intervals when I move. So that I am not only a skeleton but a badly articulated one to boot. If to this is coupled the fact of the creeping paralysis, you have the complete horror. Even as I sit and write, millions of bacteria are gnawing away my precious spinal cord, and if you put your ear to my back the sound of the gnawing I dare say could be heard. The other day a man came and set up a post in the garden for the clothes' line. As soon as I saw the post I said ' gibbet '—it looks exactly like one, and I, for sure, must be the malefactor. Last night while E—— was nursing the baby I most delightfully remarked: ' What a little parasite—why you are Cleopatra affixing the aspic —" Tarry good lady, the bright day is done, and we are for the dark." '

The fact that such images arise spontaneously in my mind, show how rotten to the core I am.

. . . The advent of the Baby was my *coup de grâce*. The little creature seems to focus under one head all my personal disasters and more than once a senseless rage has clutched me at the thought of a baby in exchange for my ambition, a nursery for the study. Yet, on the whole, I find it a good and satisfying thing to see her, healthy, new, intact on the threshold: I grow tired of my own dismal life just as one does of a suit of dirty clothes. My life and person are patched and greasy; hers is new and without a single blemish or misfortune. . . . Moreover, she makes her mother happy and consoles her grandmother too.

January 21.

Death

What a delightful thing the state of Death would be if the dead passed their time haunting the places they loved in life and living over again the dear delightful past—if death were one long indulgence in the pleasures of memory! if the disembodied spirit forgot all the pains of its previous existence and remembered only the happiness! Think of me flitting about the orchards and farm-yards in —— birdsnesting, walking along the coast among the seabirds, climbing Exmoor, bathing in streams and in the sea, haunting all my old loves and passions, cutting open with devouring curiosity Rabbits, Pigeons, Frogs, Dogfish, *Amphioxus*; think of me, too, at length unwillingly deflected from these cherished pursuits in the raptures of first love, cutting her initials on trees and fences instead of watching birds, day-dreaming over *Parker and Haswell* and then bitterly reproaching myself later for much loss of precious time. How happy I shall be if Death is like this: to be living over again and again all my ecstasies, over first times—the first time I found a Bottle Tit's nest, the first time I succeeded in penetrating into the fastnesses of my El Dorado—Exmoor, the first time I gazed upon the internal anatomy of a Snail, the first time I read Berkeley's *Principles of Human Understanding* (what a soul-shaking epoch that was!), and the first time I kissed her! My hope is that I may haunt these times again, that I may haunt the places, the books, the bathes, the walks, the desires, the hopes, the first (and last) loves of my life all transfigured and beatified by sovereign Memory.

January 26.

Out of doors to-day it's like the roaring forties ! Every tree I passed in the lane was a great wind instrument, bellowing out a passionate song, and the sky was torn to ribbons. It is cold enough to freeze the nose off a brass Monkey, but very exhilarating. I stood on the hill and squared my fists to the wind and bade everything come on. I sit writing this by the fire and am thoroughly scourged and purified by this great castigating wind. . . . I think I will stick it out—I will sit quite still in my chair and defy this skulking footpad—let the paralysis creep into every bone, I will hang on to the last and watch it skulking with my most hideous grimace.

January 27.

Still freezing and blowing. Coming back from the village, tho' I was tired and hobbling badly, decided to walk up the lane even if it meant crawling home on hands and knees.

The sky was a quick-change artist to-day. Every time you looked you saw a different picture. From the bottom of the hill I looked up and saw above me—it seemed at an immense and windy height—a piece of blue, framed in an irregular edge of white woolly cloud seen thro' the crooked branches of an Oak. It was a narrow crooked lane, sunk deep in the soil with large smooth surfaces of stone like skulls bulging up in places where the rain had washed away the soil.

Further on, the sun was lying low almost in the centre of a semi-circular bend in the near horizon. It frosted the wool of a few sheep seen in silhouette, and then slowly disappeared in mist. On the right-hand side was a cottage with the smoke being wrenched away from the chimney top, and on the left a group of stately Firs, chanting a requiem like a cathedral choir.

January 28.

Still blowing and bitterly cold. Along the path fields in the Park I stopped to look at a thick clump of Firs

standing aloof on some high ground and guarded by an
outside ring of honest English Oaks, Ashes and Elms. They
were a sombre mysterious little crowd intent, I fancied, on
some secret ritual of the trees. The high ground on which
they stood looked higher and more inaccessible than it
really was, the clump was dark green, almost black, and
in between their trunks where all was obscurity, some
hardy adventurer might well have discovered a Grand
Lama sitting within his Penetralia. But I had no taste
for any such profanity, and even as I looked the sun came
out from behind a cloud very slowly, bringing the picture
into clearer focus, chasing away shadows and bringing
out all the colours. The landscape resumed its homely
aspect: an English park with Firs in it.

January 29.

Last night, I pulled aside the window curtain of our
front door and peeped out. Just below the densely black
projecting gable of the house I saw the crescent moon
lying on her back in a bed of purple sky, and I saw our
little white frosted garden path curving up towards the
garden gate. It was a delicious *coup d'œil*, and I shewed
it to E——.

January 31.

Showers of snow at intervals, the little flakes rocking
about lazily or spiralling down, while the few that eventually reached the ground would in a moment or so be
caught up in a sudden furious puff of wind, and sent driving
along the road with the dust.

My usual little jaunt up the lane past the mossy farm-
house. Home to toasted tea-cakes and a pinewood fire,
with my wife chattering prettily to the baby. After tea,
enchanted by the reading of a new book—*Le Journal de
Maurice de Guérin*—or rather the introduction to it by
Sainte-Beuve. I devoured it! I have spent a devouring
day; under a calm exterior I have burnt up the hours;
all of me has been athrob; every little cell in my brain has
danced to its own little tune. For to-day, Death has been

an impossibility. I have felt that anyhow to-day I could not die—I have laughed at the mere thought of it. If only this mood would last! If I could feel thus always, then I could fend off Death for an immortality of life.

But suddenly, as now, the real horror of my life and future comes on me in a flash. For a second I am terrified by the menace of the future, but fortunately only for a second. For I've learnt a trick which I fear to reveal; it is so valuable and necessary to me that if I talked of it or vulgarised it my secret might be stolen away. Not a word then!

Later. I have just heard on the gramophone some Grieg, and it has charged my happiness with disrupting voltage of desire. Oh! if only I had health, I could make the welkin ring! I shall leave so little behind me, such a few paltry pages beside what I have it in me to do. It shatters me.

February 1.

Looking back, I must say I like the splendid gusto with which I lived thro' yesterday: that mettlesome fashion in which I took the lane, and at the top, how I swung around to sweep my gaze across to the uplands opposite with snow falling all the time. Then in the evening, the almost complete absorption in the new book when I forgot everything *pro tem.* It was quite like the old days.

February 2.

Crowd Fever

After four months' sick leave, returned to work and London.

An illness like mine rejuvenates one—for the time being! A pony and jingle from the old 'Fox and Hounds Inn' took me to the Station, and I enjoyed the feel of the wheels rolling beneath me over the hard road. In the train, I looked out of the window as interested as any schoolboy. On the Underground I was delighted with the smooth, quiet way with which the 'Metro' trains glide into the

Station. I had quite forgotten this.   Then, when my hand
began to get better, I rediscovered the pleasures of pen-
manship and kept on writing, with my tongue out.   And I
re-enjoyed the child's satisfaction in coaxing a button to
slip into its hole: all grown-up people have forgotten how
difficult and complex such operations are.

This morning how desirable everything seemed to me !
The world intoxicated me.   Moving again among so many
human beings gave me the crowd-fever, and started again
all the pangs of the old familiar hunger for a fuller life,
that centrifugal élan in which I feared for the disruption
and scattering of my parts in all directions.   Temporarily
I lost the hegemony of my own soul.   Every man and
woman I met was my enemy, threatening me with the
secession of some inward part.   I was alarmed to discover
how many women I could passionately love and with how
many men I could form a lasting friendship.   Within, all
was anarchy and commotion, a cold fright seized me lest
some extraordinary event was about to happen: some
general histolysis of my body, some sudden disintegration
of my personality, some madness, some strange death.
. . . I wanted to crush out the life of all these men and
women in a great Bear's hug, my God ! this sea of human
faces whom I can never recognise, all of us alive together
beneath this yellow catafalque of fog on the morning of
the announcement of world famine and world war ! . . .

.   .   .   .

To-night, I have lost this paroxysm.   For I am home
again by the fireside.   All the multitude has disappeared
from my view.   I have lost them, every one.   I have lost
another day of my life and so have they, and we have lost
each other.   Meanwhile the great world spins on unrelentingly, frittering away lightly my precious hours
(surely a small stock now ?) while I sit discomfited by the
evening fire and nurse my scraped hands that tingle because the spinning world has wrenched itself out of my
feeble grasp.

February 3.

This morning on arriving at S. Kensington, went straight to a Chemist's shop, but finding someone inside, I drew back, and went on to another.

' Have you any morphia tabloids ?' I asked a curly-haired, nice-looking, smiling youth, who leaned with both hands on the counter and looked at me knowingly, as if he had had unlimited experience of would-be morphinomaniacs.

' Yes, plenty of them,' he said, fencing.   And then waited.

' Can you supply me ?' I asked, feeling very conscious of myself.

He smiled once more, shook his head and said it was contrary to the Defence of the Realm Act.

I made a sorry effort to appear ingenuous, and he said :
' Of course, it is only a palliative.'

With a solemn countenance intended to indicate pain I answered :

' Yes, but palliatives are very necessary sometimes,' and I walked out of the hateful shop discomfited.

February 6.

Am busy re-writing,[1] editing and bowdlerising my journals for publication against the time when I shall have gone the way of all flesh.   No one else would prepare it for publication if I don't.   Reading it through again, I see what a remarkable book I have written.   If only they will publish it !

February 7.

Chinese Lanterns

The other morning as I dressed, I could see the sun like a large yellow moon rising on a world, stiff, stark, its contours merely indicated beneath a winding-sheet of snow.   Further around the horizon was another moon— the full moon itself—yellow likewise, but setting.   It was

[1] John Wesley *rewrote* his journals from entries in rough draft.

the strangest picture I ever saw. I might well have been
upon another planet; I could not have been more surprised
even at a whole ring of yellow satellites arranged at regular
intervals all around the horizon.

In the evening of the same day, I drove home from the
Station in a little governess-cart, over a snow-clogged road.
The cautious little pony picked out her way so carefully in
little strides—pat-pat-pat—wherever it was slippery, and
the Landlord of the Inn sat opposite me extolling all the
clever little creature's merits. It was dusk, and for some
reason of the atmosphere the scraps of cloud appeared as
blue sky and the blue sky as cloud, beneath which the full
moon like a great Chinese lantern hung suspended so low
down it seemed to touch the trees and hills. How have
folk been able to ' carry on ' in a world so utterly strange
as this one during the past few days ! I marvel that
beneath such moons and suns, the peoples of the world
have not ceased for a while from the petty business of
war during at least a few of our dancing revolutions around
this furnace of a star. One of these days I should not be
surprised if this fascinated earth did not fall into it like
a moth into a candle. And where would our Great War
be then ?

February 28.
The Strangeness of my Life

Consider the War: and the current adventures of millions
of men on land, sea and air; and the incessant labours of
millions of men in factory and workshop and in the field;
think of the hospitals and all they hold, of everyone hoping,
fearing, suffering, waiting—of the concentration of all
humanity on the one subject—the War. And then think
of me, poor little me, deserted and forgotten, a tiny fragment sunk so deep and helplessly between the sheer
granite walls of my environment that scarce an echo
reaches me of the thunder among the mountains above. I
read about the War in a ha'penny paper, and see it in the
pictures of the *Daily Mirror*. For the rest, I live by

counting the joints on insects' legs and even that much effort is almost beyond my strength.

That is strange enough. But my life is stranger still by comparison. And this is the marvel: that every day I spend by the waters of Babylon, weeping and neglected among enthusiasts, enthusiastically counting joints, while every evening I return to Zion to my books, to Hardy's poems, to Maurice de Guérin's Journals, to my own memoirs. Mine is a life of consummate isolation, and I frequently marvel at it.

The men I meet accept me as an entomologist and *ipso facto*, an enthusiast in the science. That is all they know of me, and all they want to know of me, or of any man. Surely no man's existence was ever quite such a duplicity as mine. I smile bitterly to myself ten times a day, as I engage in all the dreary technical jargon of professional talk with them. How they would gossip over the facts of my life if they knew ! How scandalised they would be over my inner life's activities, how resentful of enthusiasm other than entomological !

I find it very irksome to keep up this farce of concealment. I would love to declare myself. I loathe, hate and detest the secrecy of my real self: the continuous restraint enforced on me ulcerates my heart and makes harmonious social existence impossible with those who do not know me thoroughly. 'On dit qu'au jugement dernier le secret des consciences sera révélé à tout l'univers; je voudrais qu'il en fût ainsi de moi dès aujourd'hui et que la vue de mon âme fût ouvert à tous venants.' Maurice de Guérin.

March 1.

It is curious for me to look at my tubes and microscope and realise that I shall never require them again for serious use. Life is a dreadful burden to me at the Museum. I am too ill for any scientific work so I write labels and put things away. I am simply marking time on the edge of a precipice awaiting the order, ' Forward.'

It is excoriating to be thus wasting the last few precious

days of my life in such mummery merely to get bread to
eat. They might at least let me die in peace, and with
fitting decorum. It is so ignoble to be tinkering about
in a Museum among Scarabees and insects when I ought
to be reflecting on life and death.

I ask myself what ought to be my most appropriate
reaction in such circumstances as the present? Why, of
course, to carry on as if all were normal, and the future
unknown: why, so I do, to outward view, for the sake of
the others. Yet that is no reason why in my own inward
parts I should not at times indulge in a little relaxation.
It is a relief to put off the mailed coat, to sit awhile by the
green-room fire and have life as it really is, all to myself.
But the necessity of living will not let me alone. I must
be always mumming.

My life has been all isolation and restriction. And it
now appears even my death is to be hedged around with
prohibitions. Drugs for example—how beneficent a little
laudanum at times in a case like mine! and how happy I
could be if I knew that in my waistcoat pocket I carried a
kindly, easy means of shuffling off this coil when the time
comes as come it must. It horrifies me to consider how
I might break the life of E—— clean in two, and sap her
courage by a lingering, dawdling dying. But there is the
Defence of the Realm Act. It is a case of a Scorpion in a
ring of fire but without any sting in its tail.

March 2.

I ask myself: what are my views on death, the next world,
God? I look into my mind and discover I am too much of
a mannikin to have any. As for death, I am a little bit of
trembling jelly of anticipation. I am prepared for anything, but I am the complete agnostic; I simply don't
know. To have views, faith, beliefs, one needs a backbone.
This great bully of a universe overwhelms me. The stars
make me cower. I am intimidated by the immensity
surrounding my own littleness. It is futile and pre-
sumptuous for me to opine anything about the next world.
But I *hope* for something much freer and more satisfying

after death, for emancipation of the spirit and above all
for the obliteration of this puny self, this little, skulking,
sharp-witted ferret.

A Potted Novel

(1)

He was an imaginative youth, and she a tragedy queen.
So he fell in love with her because she was melancholy and
her past tragic. 'She is *capable* of tragedy, too,' he said,
which was a high encomium.

But he was also an ambitious youth and all for dalliance
in love. 'Marriage,' said he sententiously, 'is an economic trap.' And then, a little wistfully: 'If she were a
bit more melancholy and a bit more beautiful she would
be quite irresistible.'

(2)

But he was a miserable youth, too, and in the anguish
of loneliness and lovelessness a home tempted him sorely.
Still, he dallied. *She* waited. Ill-health after all made
marriage impossible.

(3)

Yet love and misery drove him towards it. So one day
he closed his eyes and offered himself up with sacrificial
hands. . . . 'Too late,' she said. 'Once perhaps . . .
but now. . . .' His eyes opened again, and in a second Love
entered his Temple once more and finally ejected the money
changers.

(4)

So they married after all, and he was under the impression she had made a good match. He had ill-health perhaps,
yet who could doubt his ultimate fame ?

Then the War came, and he had the hardihood to open a
sealed letter from his Doctor to the M.O. examining recruits.
. . . Stars and staggers ! ! So it was she who was the
victim in marriage ! That harassing question: Did she
know ? What an ass he had been all through, what
superlative egoism and superlative conceit !

(5)

Then a baby came.   He broke under the strain and
daily the symptoms grew more obvious.   Did she know ?
. . . The question dazed him.

Well, she *did* know, and had married him for love,
nevertheless, against every friendly counsel, the Doctor's
included.

(6)

And now the invalid's gratitude is almost cringeing, his
admiration boundless and his love for always.   It is the
perfect *rapprochement* between two souls, one that was
honeycombed with self-love and lost in the labyrinthine
ways of his own motives and the other straight, direct,
almost imperious in love and altogether adorable.

Finis

March 5.

At home ill again.   Yesterday was a day of utter dreari-
ness.   All my nerves were frozen, my heart congealed.
I had no love for anyone . . . no emotion of any sort.   It
was a catalepsy of the spirit harder to bear than fever or
pain. . . . To-day, life is once more stirring in me, I
am slowly awaking to the consciousness of acute but almost
welcome misery.

March 6.

An affectionate letter from H—— that warmed the
cockles of my heart—poor frozen molluscs.   A—— has
written only once since August.

March 7.

I am, I suppose, a whey-faced, lily-livered creature . . .
yet even an infantry subaltern has a chance. . . .

My dear friend —— —— has died and a *Memorial*
Exhibition of his pictures is being held at the Goupil
Gallery.   The most fascinating man I ever met.   I was
attracted by him almost as one is attracted by a charming

woman: by little ways, by laughing eyes, by the manner of speech. And now he is dead, of a lingering and painful disease.

March 8.

Death

Have been reading Sir Oliver Lodge's *Raymond*. I do not deny that I am curious about the next world, or about the condition of death. I am and always have been. In my early youth, I reflected continually on death and hated it bitterly. But now that my end is near and certain, I consider it less and am content to wait and see. As, for all practical purposes, I have done with life, and my own existence is often a burden to me and is like to become a burden also to others, I wish I possessed the wherewithal to end it at my will. With two or three tabloids in my waistcoat pocket, and my secret locked in my heart, how serenely I would move about among my friends and fellows, conscious that at some specially selected moment—at midnight or high noon—just when the spirit moved me, I could quietly slip out to sea on this Great Adventure. It would be well to be able to control this: the time, the place, and the manner of one's exit.. For what disturbs me in particular is how I shall conduct myself; I am afraid lest I become afraid, it is a fear of fear. By means of my tabloids, I could arrange my death in an artistic setting, say underneath a big tree on a summer's day, with an open Homer in my hand, or more appropriately, a magnifying glass and Miall and Denny's *Cockroach*. It would be stage-managing my own demise and surely the last thing in self-conscious elegance !

I think it was De Quincey who said Death to him seemed most awful in the summer. On the contrary the earth is warm then, and would welcome my old bones. It is on a cold night by the winter fire that the churchyard seems to me the least inviting: especially horrible it is the first evening after the funeral.

March 10.

Have had a relapse. My hand I fear is going. Food
prices are leaping up. Woe to the unfit and the old and
the poor in these coming days! We shall soon have
nothing left in our pantries, and a piece of Wrigley's chewing gum will be our only comfort.

.   .   .   .

When I come to quit this world I scarcely know which
will be the greater regret: the people I have never met,
or the places I have never seen. In the world of books, I
rest fairly content: I have read my fair share.

To-day I read down the column of to-morrow's preachers
with the most ludicrous avidity, ticking off the Churches I
have visited: St. Paul's and the Abbey, the Ethical Church
in Bayswater and Westminster Cathedral. But the Uni-
tarians, the Christadelphians, the Theosophists, the Church
of Christ Scientist, the Buddhist Society, the Brompton
Oratory, the Church of Humanity, the New Life Centre;
all these adventures I intended one day to make. . . . It
is not much fun ticking off things you have done from a
list if you have done very little. I get more satisfaction
out of a list of books. But Iona and the Hebrides, Edinburgh, Brussels, Buenos Ayres, Spitzbergen (when the
flowers are out), the Niagara Falls (by moonlight), the
Grindelwald, Cairo—these names make me growl and
occasionally yelp like a hurt puppy, although to outward
view I am sitting in an armchair blowing smoke-rings.

March 11.

The Graph of Temperament

In this Journal, my pen is a delicate needle point, tracing
out a graph of temperament so as to show its daily fluctua-
tions: grave and gay, up and down, lamentation and revelry,
self-love and self-disgust. You get here all my thoughts
and opinions, always irresponsible and often contradictory
or mutually exclusive, all my moods and vapours, all the
varying reactions to environment of this jelly which is I.

I snap at any idea that comes floating down, particularly
if it is gaudy or quixotic, no matter if it is wholly incom-
patible with what I said the day before. People unpleasantly refer me back, and to escape I have to invent
some sophistry. I unconsciously imitate the manner-
isms of folk I am particularly taken with. Other people
never fail to tell me of my simulations. If I read a book
and like it very much, by a process of peaceful penetration,
the author takes possession of my whole personality just
as if I were a medium giving a sitting, and for some time
subsequently his ideas come spurting up like a fountain
making a pretty display which I take to be my own. Other
people say of me, ' Oh ! I expect he read it in a book.'

I am something between a Monkey, a Chameleon, and
a Jellyfish. To any bully with an intellect like a blunder-
buss, I have always timidly held up my hands and afterwards gnashed my teeth for my cowardice. In conversation with men of alien sentiment I am self-effacing to my
intense chagrin, often from mere shyness. I say, ' Yes
. . . yes . . . yes,' to nausea, when it ought to be ' No
. . . no . . . no.' I become my own renegade, an amiable dissembler, an ass in short. It is a torture to have a
sprightly mind blanketed by personal timidity and a feeble
presence. The humiliating thing is that almost any strong
character hypnotises me into complacency, especially if
he is a stranger; I find myself for the time being in really
sincere agreement with him, and only later, discover to
myself his abominable doctrines. Then I lie in bed and
have imaginary conversations in which I get my own back.

But, by Jove, I wreak vengeance on my familiars, and
on those brethren even weaker than myself. They get my
concentrated gall, my sulphurous fulminations, and would
wonder to read this confession.

Cynicism

For an unusually long time after I grew up, I main-
tained a beautiful confidence in the goodness of mankind.
Rumours did reach me, but I brushed them aside as

slanders. I was an ingénu, unsuspecting, credulous. I
thoroughly believed that men and women and I were much
better than we actually are. I have not come to the end
of my disillusions even now. I still rub my eyes on occasion. I simply can't believe that we are such humbugs,
hypocrites, self-deceivers. And strange to say it is the
'good' people above all who most bitterly disappoint me.
Give me a healthy liar, or a thief, or a vagabond, and he
arouses no expectations, and so I get no heart-burning.
It is the good, the honest, the true, who cheat me of my
boyhood's beliefs. . . . I am a cynic then, but not a
reckless cynic—a careworn unhappy cynic without the
cynic's pride. 'It is easy to be cynical,' someone ad-
monished me. 'Unfortunately it is,' I said.

We are so cold, so aloof, so self-centred even the warmest
friends. Men of piety love God, but their love for each
other is so commonly but a poor thing. My own affections
are always frosted over with the Englishman's reserve.
I hesitate as if I were not sure of them. I am afraid of
self-deception, I hate to find out either myself or others.
And yet I am always doing so. Mine is a restlessly analytical brain. I dissect everyone, even those I love, and
my discoveries frequently sting me to the quick. 'To the
pure all things are pure,' whence I should conclude I
suppose that it is the beam in my own eye. But I would
not tolerate being deceived concerning either my own
beam or other people's motes.

March 12.

Archæopteryx and Mudflats

Yesterday I collected two distinct and several twinges
and hereby save them up. They were more than that—
they were pangs, and pangs that twanged.

(Why do I make fun of my suffering ?)

One was when I saw the well known figure of the *Archæopteryx* remains in the slab of Lithographic sandstone of
Bavaria : a reproduction in an illustrated encyclopædia.
the other was when someone mentioned mud, and I thought

of the wide estuary of the T——, its stretches of mudflats
and its wild-fowl. We were turning over some pages and
she said:

'What's that?'

'*Archæopteryx*,' said I.

'Whatever is *Archæopteryx*?'

'An extinct bird,' l answered mournfully.

Like an old amour, my love of palæontology and anatomy,
and all the high hopes I entertained of them, came smarting
to life again, so I turned over the page quickly.

But why need I explain to you, O my Journal? To
others, I could not explain.   I was tongue-tied.

'I used to get very muddy,' I remarked lamentably,
'in the old days when stalking birds on the mudflats.'

And they rather jeered at such an occupation in such a
place, just as those beautiful sights and sounds of zostera-
covered mud-banks, twinkling runnels, swiftly running
thin-legged waders, their whistles and cries began to steal
over my memory like a delicate pain.

To my infinite regret, I have no description, no photograph or sketch, no token of any sort to remember them
by. And their doom is certain. Heavens! how I wasted
my impressions and experiences then! Swinburne has
some lines about saltings which console me a little, but I
know of no other descriptions by either pen or brush.

March 15.

How revolting it is to see some barren old woman love-
sick over a baby, bestowing voluptuous kisses on its nose,
eyes, hands, feet, utterly intoxicated and chattering incessantly in the 'little language,' and hopping about like
an infatuated cock grouse.

May 5.

The nurse has been here now for over five weeks. One
day has been pretty much the same as another. I get
out of bed usually about tea-time and sit by the window
and churn over past, present, and future. However, the
Swallows have arrived at last, though they were very late,

and there are also Cuckoos, Green Wood-peckers, Moor-hens, calling from across the park.   At night, when the moon is up, I get a great deal of fun out of an extremely self-inflated Brown Owl, who hoots up through the breadth and length of the valley, and then I am sure, listens with satisfaction to his echo.   Still, I have much sympathy with that Brown Owl and his hooting.

What I do (goodness knows what E—— does), is to drug my mind with print.   I am just a rag-bag of Smollett, H. G. Wells, Samuel Butler, the *Daily News*, the Bible, the *Labour Leader*, *Joseph Vance*, etc., etc.   Except for an occasional geyser of malediction when some particularly acrid memory comes uppermost in my mind, I find myself submitting with a surprising calm and even cheerfulness. That agony of frustration which gnawed my vitals so much in 1913 has disappeared, and I, who expected to go down in the smoke and sulphur of my own fulminations, am quite as likely to fold my hands across my chest with a truly Christian resignation.   Joubert said, ' Patience and misfortune, courage and death, resignation and the inevitable, generally come together.   Indifference to life generally arises with the impossibility of preserving it '—how cynical that sounds !

May 8.

This and another volume of my Journal are temporarily lodged in a drawer in my bedroom.   It appears to me that as I become more static and moribund, they become more active and aggressive.   All day they make a perfect uproar in their solitary confinement—although no one hears it.   And at night they become phosphorescent, though nobody sees it.   One of these days, with continued neglect they will blow up from spontaneous combustion like diseased gunpowder, the dismembered diarist being thus hoist upon his own petard.

June 1.

We discuss post mortem affairs quite genially and without restraint.   It is the contempt bred of familiarity, I suppose.

E—— says widows' weeds have been so vulgarised by the
war widows that she won't go into deep mourning. 'But
you'll wear just one weed or two for me?' I plead, and
then we laugh. She has promised me that should a suitable chance arise, she will marry again. Personally, I
wish I could place my hand on the young fellow at once,
so as to put him thro' his paces—shew him where the
water main runs and where the gas meter is, and so on.

You will observe what a relish I have for my own
macabre, and how keenly I appreciate the present situation.
Nobody can say I am not making the best of it. One
might call it pulling the hangman's beard. Yet I ought,
I fancy, to be bewailing my poor wife and fatherless child.

June 15.

I sit all day in my chair, moving 8 feet to my bed at
night, and 8 feet from it to my chair in the morning—and
wait. The assignation is certain. 'Life is a coquetry
of Death that wearies me, Too sure of the amour.'

July 5.

It is odd that at this time of the breaking of nations,
Destiny, with her hands so full, should spare the time to
pursue a non-combatant atom like me down such a labyrinthine side-track. It is odd to find her determined to
destroy me with such tremendous thoroughness—one
would have thought it sufficient merely to brush the dust
off my wings. Why this deliberate, slow-moving malig-
nity? Perhaps it is a punishment for the impudence of
my desires. I wanted everything so I get nothing. I gave
nothing so I receive nothing. I am not offering up my life
willingly—it is being taken from me piece by piece, while I
watch the pilfering with lamentable eyes.

I have tendered my resignation and retire on a small
gratuity.

July 7.

My hand gets a little better. But it's a cat and mouse
game, and so humiliating to be the mouse.

. . . Parental affection comes to me only in spasms, and if they hurt, they do not last long. Curiously enough, as in the case of very old people, my consciousness reverts more easily to conditions long past. I seem unable to apprehend all the significance of having a nine-months old daughter, but some Bullfinches or Swallows seen thro' the window rouse me more. No one can deny I have loved Birds to intoxication. In my youth, birds' eggs, and little nestlings and chicken sent me into such raptures I could never tell it to you adequately. . . . I am too tired to write more.

July 23.

Reading Pascal again. If Shelley was 'gold dusty from tumbling among the stars,' Pascal was bruised and shaken. The one was delighted, and the other frightened. I like Pascal's prostration before the infinities of Time, Space and the Unknown. Somehow, he conveys this more vividly than the uplift afforded him by religion.

July 25.

I don't believe in the twin-soul theory of marriage. There are plenty of men any one of whom she might have married and lived with happily, and simpler men than I am. Methinks there are large tracts could be sliced off my character and she would scarcely feel the want of them. To think that she of all women, with a past such as hers, should be swept into my vicious orbit ! Yet she seems to bear Destiny no resentment, so I bear it for her and enough for two. At our engagement I gave her my own ring to wear as a pledge—we thought it nicer than buying a new one. It was a signet ring with a dark smooth stone. Strange to say it never once occurred to me till now that it was a mourning ring in memory of a great-uncle of mine, actually with an inscription on the inside.

July 26.

As long as I can hold a pen. I shall, I suppose, go on trickling ink into this diary !

I am amusing myself by reading the *Harmsworth Encyclopædia* in 15 volumes, *i.e.*, I turn over the pages and read everything of interest that catches my eye.

I get out of bed about ten, wash and sit by the window in my blue striped pyjama suit. It is so hot I need no additional clothing. E—— comes in, brushes my hair, sprinkles me with lavender water, lights my cigarette, and gives me my book-rest and books. She forgets nothing.

From my window I look out on a field with Beech hedge down one side and beyond, tall trees—one showing in outline exactly like the profile of a Beefeater's head, more especially at sunset each evening when the tree next behind is in shadow. The field is full of blue Scabious plants, Wild Parsley and tall grass—getting brown now in the sun. Great numbers of White Butterflies are continually rocking themselves across—they go over in coveys of four or five at a time—I counted 50 in five minutes, which bodes ill for the cabbages. Not even the heaviest thunder showers seem to debilitate their kinetic ardour. They rock on like white aeroplanes in a hail of machine-gun bullets.

Then there are the Swallows and Martins cutting such beautiful figures thro' the air that one wishes they carried a pencil in their bills as they fly and traced the lines of flight on a Bristol board. How I hanker after the Swallows! so free and gay and vigorous. This autumn, as they prepare to start, I shall hang on every twitter they make, and on every wing-beat; and when they have gone, begin sadly to set my house in order, as when some much loved visitors have taken their departure. I am appreciating things a little more the last few days.

August 1.

A Jeremiad

When I resigned my appointment last month, no one knows what I had to give up. But *I* know. Tho' if I say what I know no one is compelled to believe me excepting out of charity. It will never be discovered whether what I am going to state is not simply despairing bombast. My few intimate friends and relatives are entirely inno-

cent of science, not to say zoology. and all they realise is
the significant fact that I am prone to go extravagant
lengths in conversation. But you may take it or leave it:
I was the ablest junior on the staff and one of the ablest
zoologists in the place—but my ability was always muffled
by the inferior work they gave me to do. My last memoir
published last December was the best of its kind in treatment, method and technique that ever issued from the
institution—I do not. say the most important. It was
trivial—my work always was trivial because they put me
in a mouldy department where all the work was trivial
and the methods used as primitive, slipshod and easy as
those of Fabricius, the idea being that as I had enjoyed no
academic career I was unsuited to fill other posts then
vacant—one, work on the Cœlenterates and another on
Vermes, both rarely favoured by amateurs and requiring
laboratory training. Later, I had the mortification of
seeing these posts filled by men whose powers I by no means
felt inclined to estimate as greater than my own. Meanwhile, I who had been dissecting for dear life up and down
the whole Animal Kingdom in a poorly equipped attic
laboratory at home, with no adequate instruments, was
bitterly disappointed to find still less provision made even
in a so-called Scientific Institution so grandly styled the
British Museum (N.H.). On my first arrival I was presented with a pen, ink, paper, ruler, and an enormous instrument of steel which on enquiry I found to be a paper
cutter. I asked for my microscope and microtome. I
ought to have asked what Form I was in.

So I had to continue my struggle against odds, and only
within the last year or so began to squeeze the authorities
with any success. In time I should have revolutionised
the study of Systematic Zoology, and the anonymous paper
I wrote in conjunction with R—— in the *American
Naturalist* was a rare *jeu d'esprit*, and my most important
scientific work.

    ·   ·   ·   ·   ·

In the literary world I have fared no better. My first
published article appeared at the age of 15 over my father's

name, my motive being not so much modesty as cunning
—if the literary world (!) ragged it unmercifully, there was
still a chance left for me to make good.

My next achievement of any magnitude was the unexpected printing of a story in the *Academy* after I had
unsuccessfully badgered almost every other newspaper.
This was when I was 19. No proof had been sent me and
no intimation of its acceptance. Moreover, there were two
ugly printer's errors. I at once wrote off to correct them
in the next issue. My letter was neither published nor
acknowledged. I submitted, but presently wrote again,
politely hinting that my cheque was overdue.   But—
screams of silence, and I thought it wise not to complain
in view of future printing favours. I soon discovered that
the journal had changed hands and was probably on its
last legs at the time of my success. As soon as it grew
financially sound again no more of my stories were accepted.

A more recent affair I had with the American *Forum*,
which delighted me by publishing my article, but did not
pay—tho' the Editor went out of his way to write that
'payment was on publication.' I did not venture to
remonstrate as I had another article on the stocks which
they also printed without paying me.   In spite of uniform
failure, my literary ambition has never flagged.[1] `I have
for years past received my rejected MSS. back from every
conceivable kind of periodical, from *Punch* to the *Hibbert
Journal*. At one time I used to file their rejection forms
and meditated writing a facetious essay on them. But I
decided they were too monotonously similar. My custom
was when the ordinary avenues to literary fame had failed
me—the half-crown Reviews and the sixpenny Weeklies—
to seek out at a library some obscure publication—a Parish
Magazine or the local paper—anything was grabbed as a
last chance. On one of these occasions I discovered the
Westminster Review and immediately plied them with a
manuscript and the usual polite note. After six weeks,

---

[1] I once received from an editor a very encouraging letter which
gave me a great deal of pleasure and made me hope he was going
to open the pages of his magazine to me. But three weeks after
he committed suicide by jumping out of his bedroom window.

having no reply, I wrote again and waited for another six weeks. My second remonstrance met with a similar fate, so I went into the City to interview the publishers, and to demand my manuscript back. The manager was out, and I was asked to call again. After waiting about for some time, I left my card, took my departure and decided I would write. The same evening I told the publishers that the anonymous editor would neither print my article nor return it. Would they kindly give me his name and address so that I could write personally. After some delay they replied that although it was not the custom to disclose the editor's name, the following address would find her. She was a lady living in Richmond Row, Shepherd's Bush. I wrote to her at once and received no answer. Meanwhile, I had observed that no further issues of the review had appeared on the bookstalls, and the booksellers were unable to give me any information. I wrote again to the address—this time a playful and facetious letter in which I said I did not propose to take the matter into court, but if it would save her any trouble I would call for the MS. as I lived only a few minutes' walk distant. I received no answer. I was busy at the time and kept putting off executing my firm purpose of visiting the good lady until one evening as I was casually reading the *Star* coming home in the 'bus, I read an account of how some charitably disposed woman had recently visited the Hammersmith Workhouse and removed to her own home a poor soul who was once the friend of George Eliot, George Henry Lewes, and other well-known literary persons of the sixties and had, until it ceased publication a few months before, edited the once notable *Westminster Review*.

Recently, however, there has been evidence of a more benevolent attitude towards me on the part of London editors. A certain magnificent quarterly has published one or two of my essays, and one of these called forth two pages of quotation and flattering comment in *Public Opinion*, which thrill me to the marrow. I fear, however, the flood-tide has come too late.

.   .   .   .

If this achievement impressed me it did not seem to impress anyone else. A—— regarded it as a joke and laughed incredulously when someone told him of ' P.O.'s ' eulogy. You see I am still his foolish little brother. I am secretly very nettled too because E—— treated the whole matter very indifferently. She did not even take the trouble to read the paper's critique, and tho' she volunteered to buy several copies to send to friends, she never remembered to do so, and the whole affair has passed out of her mind.

Now a pleasant paragraph that appeared in the press noticing some drawings of a friend of her friend, she read twice and marched off to Francesca with it in great glee. Another successful young person got his photo into the picture papers—a man we know only by hearsay, and yet it impressed her until I recalled, what strange to say she had quite forgotten, how the photographers wished to publish her own photograph in the picture papers at the time of our marriage. But she scornfully refused. (And so did I.)

But what a queer woman! . . . [And I, too, a queer man, drunken with wormwood and gall.]

August 6.

E—— and I were very modern in our courtship. Our candour was mutual and complete—parents and relatives would be shocked and staggered if they knew. . . . You see I am a biologist and we are both freethinkers. *Voilà!* . . . I hate all reticence and concealment. . . . There is a good deal of that ass, Gregers Werle, in my nature.

August 7.

My Gastrocnemius

I become dreadfully emaciated. This morning, before getting off the bed I lifted my leg and gazed wistfully along all its length. My flabby *gastrocnemius* swung suspended from the *tibia* like a gondola from a Zeppelin. I touched it gently with the tip of my index finger and it oscillated.

August 17.

My beloved wife comes home this evening after a short, much needed holiday.

August 27.

My gratuity has turned out to be unexpectedly small. I hoped at least for one year's salary.   And the horrible thing is I might live for several years longer !   No one was ever more enthusiastic for death than I am at this moment. I hate this world with its war, and I bitterly regret I never managed to buy laudanum in time.   There are only E——— and. dear R——— and one or two others—the rest of the people I know I hate *en bloc*.   If only I could get at them. I hate to have to leave them to themselves without getting my own back.

August 31.

My darling sweetheart, you ask me why I love you.   I do not know.   All I know is that I *do* love you, and beyond measure.   Why do *you* love me?—surely a more inscrutable problem.   You do not know.   No one ever knows.   ' The heart has its reasons which the reason knows not of.'   We love in obedience to a powerful gravitation of our beings, and then try to explain it by recapitulating one another's characters just as a man forms his opinions first and then thinks out reasons in support.

What delights me is to recall that our love has *evolved*. It did not suddenly spring into existence like some beautiful sprite.   It developed slowly to perfection—it was forged in the white heat of our experiences.   That is why it will always remain.

September 1.

Your love, darling, impregnates my heart, touches it into calm, strongly beating life so that when I am with you, I forget I am a dying man.   It is too difficult to believe that when we die true love like ours disappears with our bodies.   My own experience makes me feel that human love is the earnest after death of a great reunion of souls in God who is love. When as a boy I was bending the knee to Haeckel, the saying 'God is Love' scarcely interested me. I am wiser now. You must not think I am still anything but an infidel (as the Churchmen say),—I should hate not to be taken for an infidel—and you must not be surprised that an embittered, angry, hateful person like myself should believe in a Gospel of Love. I am embittered because an intense desire to love has in many instances[1] been baulked by my own idealising yet also analytical mind. I have wanted to love men blindly, yet I am always finding them out, and the disappointment chills the heart. Hence my malice and venom: which, dear, do not misconstrue. I am as greedy as an Octopus, ready out of love to take the whole world into my inside—that seat of the affections!—but I am also as sensitive as an Octopus, and quickly retract my arms into the rocky, impregnable recess where I live.

September 2.

But am I dying? I have no presentiments—no conviction—like the people you read of in books. Am I, after all, in love? ' I dote yet doubt; suspect yet strongly love.' It is all a matter of degree. Beside Abélard and Héloïse, our love may be just glassy affection. It is a great and difficult question to decide. I love no one else but E——, that, at least, is a certainty, and I have never loved anyone more.

September 3.

My bedroom is on the ground floor as I cannot mount the stairs. But the other day when they were all out, I determined to clamber upstairs if possible, and search in the bedrooms for a half-bottle of laudanum, which Mrs —— told me she found the other day in a box—a relic of the time when —— had to take it to relieve pain.

I got off the bed on to the floor and crawled around on

---

[1] The Egoist explains himself again.

hands and knees to the door, where I knelt up straight,
reached the handle and turned it.   Then I crawled across
the hall to the foot of the stairs, where I sat down on the
bottom step and rested.   It is a short flight of only 12
steps and I soon reached the top by sitting down on each
and raising myself up to the next one with my hands.

Arrived at the top, I quickly decided on the most likely
room to search first, and painfully crawled along the passage and thro' the bathroom by the easiest route to the
small door—there are two.   The handles of all the doors
in the house are fixed some way up above the middle, so
that only by kneeling with a straight back could I reach
them from the floor.   This door in addition was at the
top of a high but narrow step, and I had to climb on to
this, balance myself carefully, and then carefully pull
myself up towards the handle by means of a towel hung on
the handle.   After three attempts I reached the handle
and found the door locked on the inside.

I collapsed on the floor and could have cried.   I lay on
the floor of the bathroom resting with head on my arm,
then set my teeth and crawled around the passage along
two sides of a square, up three more steps to the other
door which I opened and then entered.   I had only examined two drawers containing only clothes, when a key
turned in the front door lock   and E—— entered with
—— and gave her usual whistle.

I closed the drawers and crawled out of the room in
time to hear E—— say in a startled voice to her mother:
' Who's that upstairs ?'   I whistled, and said that being
bored I had come up to see the cot: which passed at that
time all right.

Next morning my darling asked me why I went upstairs
I did not answer, and I think she knows.

September 4.

I am getting ill again, and can scarcely hold the pen.
So good-bye Journal—only for a time perhaps.

.   .   .   .   .   .   ,

Have read this blessed old Journal out to E——. It required some courage, and I boggled at one or two bits and left them out.

September 5.

Leap-frog

Some girls up the road spent a very wet Sunday morning playing leap-frog in their pyjamas around the tennis lawn. It makes me envious. To think I never thought of doing that! and now it is too late. They wore purple pyjamas too. I once hugged myself with pride for undressing in a cave by the sea and bathing in the pouring rain, but that seems tame in comparison.

Liebestod

A perfect autumn morning—cool, fine and still. What sweet music a horse and cart make trundling slowly along a country road on a quiet morning! I listened to it in a happy mood of abstraction as it rolled on further and further away. I put my head out of the window so as to hear it up to the very last, until a Robin's notes relieved the nervous tension and helped me to resign myself to my loss. The incident reminded me of the Liebestod in ' Tristan,' with the Robin taking the part of the harp.

For days past my emotions have been undergoing kaleidoscopic changes, not only from day to day but from hour to hour. For ten minutes at a time I am happy or miserable, or revengeful, venomous, loving, generous, noble, angry, or murderous—you could measure them with a stop-watch. Hell's phantoms course across my chest. If I could lie on this bed as quiet and stony as an effigy on a tomb! But a moment ago I had a sharp spasm at the sudden thought that never, never, never again should I walk thro' the path-fields to the uplands.

September 7.

My 28th birthday.

Dear old R—— (the man I love above all others) has been in a military hospital for months. It is a great hardship to have our intercourse almost completely cut off.

Dear old Journal, I love you! Good-bye.

September 29.

I could never have believed so great misery compatible with sanity. Yet I am quite sane. How long I or any man can remain sane in this condition God knows. . . . It is a consummate vengeance this inability to write.[1] I cannot help but smile grimly at the astuteness of the thrust. To be sure, how cunning to deprive me of my one secret consolation! How amusing that in this agony of isolation such an aggressive egotist as I should have his last means of self-expression cut off. I am being slowly stifled.

Later. (*In E.'s handwriting.*)

Yesterday we shifted into a tiny cottage at half the rental of the other one, and situated about two miles further out from the village. . . . A wholly ideal and beautiful little cottage you may say. But a 'camouflaged' cottage. For in spite of the happiness of its exterior it contains just now two of the most dejected mortals even in this present sorrow-laden world.

September 30.

Last night, E—— sitting on the bed by me, burst into tears. It was my fault. 'I can stand a good deal but there must come a breaking point.' Poor, poor girl, my heart aches for you.

I wept too, and it relieved us to cry. We blew our noses. 'People who cry in novels,' E—— observed with detachment, 'never blow their noses. They just weep.' . . . But the thunder clouds soon come up again.

[1] Writing difficult to decipher.

October 1.

The immediate future horrifies me.

October 2.

Poushkin (as we have named the cat) is coiled up on my bed, purring and quite happy.   It does me good to see him.

But consider: A paralytic, a screaming infant, two women, a cat and a canary, shut up in a tiny cottage with no money, the war still on, and food always scarcer day by day.   'Give us this day our daily bread.'

I want to be loved—above all, I want to love. My great danger is lest I grow maudlin and say petulantly, 'Nobody loves me, nobody cares.'   I must have more courage and more confidence in other people's good-nature. Then I can love more freely.

October 3.

I am grateful to-day for some happy hours plucked triumphantly from under the very nose of Fate, and spent in the warm sun in the garden.   They carried me out at 12, and I stayed till after tea-time.   A Lark sang, but the Swallows—dear things—have gone.   E—— picked two Primroses.   I sat by some Michaelmas Daisies and watched the Bees, Flies, and Butterflies.

October 6.

In fits of maudlin self-compassion I try to visualise Belgium, Armenia, Serbia, etc., and usually cure myself thereby.

October 12.

It is winter—no autumn this year. Of an evening we sit by the fire and enjoy the beautiful sweet-smelling wood-smoke, and the open hearth with its big iron bar carrying pot-hook and hanger. E——knits warm garments for the Baby, and I play Chopin, César-Franck hymns, Three Blind Mice (with variations) on a mouth-organ called 'The Angels' Choir,' and made in Germany. . . .   You would pity me, would you?   I am lonely, penniless, paralysed, and just turned twenty-eight. But I snap my fingers in your face and with equal arrogance I pity you. I pity you your smooth-running good luck and the stagnant serenity of your mind. I prefer my own torment. I am dying, but you are already a corpse. You have never really lived. Your body has never been flayed into tingling life by hopeless desire to love, to know, to act, to achieve. I do not envy you your absorption in the petty cares of a commonplace existence.

Do you think I would exchange the communion with my own heart for the toy balloons of your silly conversation? Or my curiosity for your flickering interests? Or my despair for your comfortable Hope? Or my present tawdry life for yours as polished and neat as a new three-penny bit? I would not. I gather my mantle around me and I solemnly thank God that I am not as some other men are.

I am only twenty-eight, but I have telescoped into those few years a tolerably long life: I have loved and married, and have a family; I have wept and enjoyed, struggled and overcome, and when the hour comes I shall be content to die.

October 14 *to* 20.
Miserable.

October 21.
Self-disgust.

FINIS.

[Barbellion died on December 31.]

A LAST DIARY

'We are in the power of no calamity while
Death is in our own.' *Religio Medici*.

March 21.

Misery is protean in its shapes, for all are indescribable. I am tongue-tied. Folk come and see me and conclude it's not so bad after all—just as civilians tour the front and suppose they have seen war on account of a soldier with a broken head or an arm in a sling. Others are getting used to me, though I am not getting used to myself.

Honest British jurymen would say ' Temporarily insane ' if I had a chance of showing my metal. I wish I could lapse into permanent insanity—'twould be a relief to let go control and slide away down, down. Which is the farthest star ? I would get away there and start afresh, blot out all memory of this world and its doings. Here, even the birds and flowers seem soiled. It makes me impatient to see them— they are indifferent, they do not know. Those that do not know are pathetic, and those knowing are miserable. It is ghostly to live in a house with a little child at the best of times—now at the worst of times a child's innocence haunts me always.

March 25.

I shall not easily forget yesterday (Sunday). It was just like Mons Sunday. The spring shambles began on Thursday in brilliant summer weather. Yesterday also was fine, the sky cloudless, very warm with scarcely a breeze. They wheeled me into the garden for an hour : primroses, violets, butterflies, bees ; the song of the chaffinches and thrushes— otherwise silence. With the newspaper on my knee, the beauty of the day was oppressive. Its unusualness at this time of year seemed of evil import. Folk shake their heads, and they say in the village there is to be an earthquake on account of the heat. In rural districts simple souls believe it is the end of the world coming upon us.

At such times as these my isolation here is *agonising*. I write the word, but itself alone conveys little. I spend hours by myself unable to talk or write, but only to think. The war news has barely crossed my lips once, not even to the bedpost—in fact, I have no bedpost.   And the cat and canary and baby would not understand.   It is hard even to look them in the face without shame.   All the while I hear the repeated ' kling ' in my ears as the wheel of my destiny comes full circle—not once but a hundred superfluous times. When am I going to die ?   This is a death in life.

I intended never to write in this diary again.   But the relief it affords could not be refused any longer.   I was surprised to find I could scribble at all legibly.   Yet it is tiring.

March 26.

In reply to a query from me if there were any fresh news in the village this afternoon, my mother-in-law thus (an *obiter dictum*, while dandling the babe) : ' No, not good news anyway.   Still, when there's a thorough assault, we're bound to lose some. . . .   Dancy, dancy, poppity pin,' etc.

But we are all moles, in cities as in villages, burrowing blindly into the future.   These enormous prospects transcend vision; we just go on and go on—following instinct, nursing babies, and killing our enemies.   How unspeakably sorrowful the whole world is !   Poor men, killing each other. Murder, say, of a rival in love, is comparatively a hallowed thing because of the personal passion.   Liberty ?   Freedom ?   These are things of the spirit.   Every man is free if he will.   Yet who is going to lend an ear to the words of a claustrated paralytic ?   I expect I'm wrong, and I am past hammering out what is right.   I must anæsthetise thought and accept without comment.   My mind is in an agony of muddle, not only about this world but the next.

May 29.

Publication of the Journal

This journal in part is being published in September (D.V.).   In the tempest of misery of the past three weeks, this fact at odd intervals has shone out like a bar of stormy white light.   By September I anticipate a climax as a set-off to the achievement of my book.   Perhaps, like Semele, I shall perish in the lightning I long for !

My dear E—— has had a nervous breakdown—her despairing words haunt me.   Poor, poor dear—I cannot go on.

June 1.

A fever of impatience and anxiety over the book.   I am terrified lest it miscarry.   I wonder if it is being printed in London ?   A bomb on the printing works ?

When it is out and in my hands I shall believe.   I have been out in a beautiful lane where I saw a white horse, led by a village child ; in a field a sunburnt labourer with a black wide-brimmed hat lifted it, smiling at me.   He seemed happy and I smiled too.

Am immensely relieved that E—— is better.   I cannot, *cannot* endure the prospect of breaking her life and health. Dear woman, how I love you !

Regard these entries as so many weals under the lash.

June 3.

When it is still scalding, grief cannot be touched.   But now after twenty-five days, I look back on those dreadful pictures and crave to tell the story.   It would be terrible. . . . I scorn such self-indulgence, for the grief was not mine alone, nor chiefly, and I cannot desecrate hers.

The extraordinary thing is that all this has no effect on me.   The heart still goes on beating.   I am not shrivelled.

June 15.

I get tired of these inferior people drawn together to look after me and my household.   If, as to-day, I utter a witticism, they hastily slur it over so as to resume the more quickly the flap-flap monotone of dull gossip.   I had a suspicion once that my fun was at fault.   I was ill and perhaps had softening of the brain and delusions.   So I made an experiment: I foisted off as my own some of the acknowledged master-strokes of Samuel Foote and Oscar Wilde, but with the same result. So I breathed again.

However, I except the old village woman come in to nurse me while E—— is away. She is a dear, talks little and laughs a lot, is mousy quiet if I wish, has lost a son in the war, has another an elementary-school master who teaches sciences—' a fine scientist.' She keeps on feeling my feet and says, ' They're *lovely* warm,' or else is horrified because they are cold. Penelope she calls ' little miss ' (I like this), and attempts to caress her with, ' Well, my little pet.' But P—— is a ruthless imp and screams at her.

I sat up in my chair to tea yesterday. It was all very quiet, and two mice crept out of their holes and audaciously ate the crumbs that fell from my plate. It is a very old cottage. In the ivy outside a nest of young starlings keep up a clamour. The Doctor has just been (three days since) and says I may live for thirty years. I trust and believe he is a damned liar.

The prospect of getting the proofs makes me horribly restless. The probability of an air raid depresses me, as I am certain the bombs will rain on the printers. Oh! do hurry up! These proofs are getting on my mind.

June 16.

Malignant Fate

I'm damned; my malignant fate has not forsaken me; after the agreement on each side has been signed, and the book partly set up in type, the publishers ask to be relieved of their undertaking. The fact is, the reader who accepted the MS. has been combed out, and his work continued by a member of the firm, a godly man, afraid of the injury to the firm's reputation as publishers of school-books and bibles! H. G. Wells, who is writing an Introduction, will be amused! At the best, it means an exasperating delay till another publisher is found.

June 17.

E—— comes home on Thursday.

A robin sits warming her eggs in a mossy hole in the woodshed. A little piece of her russet breast just shows, her bill lies like a little dart over the rim of the nest, and her beady eyes gleam in a fury at the little old nurse in her white bonnet and apron who stands about a yard away, bending down with hands on her knees, looking in and laughing till the tears run down her face : ' Poor little body, poor little body—she's got one egg up on her back.' They were a pretty duet. She is Flaubert's ' Cœur simple.'

July 1.

Turning out my desk I found the other day :

> ' 37, WEST FRAMBES AVE.,
> ' COLUMBUS, OHIO.
> ' *September* 30*th*, 1915.

' MR. BRUCE CUMMINGS, ENGLAND.

' DEAR SIR,

' I wonder if you will pardon my impertinence in writing to you. You see I haven't even your address ; I am doing this in a vague way, but I wanted to tell you how much I appreciated your ' Crying for the Moon ' which I read in the April *Forum*. You have expressed for me, at least, most completely the insatiable thirst for knowledge. I can't live enough in the short time allotted to me, but I've seldom found anyone so eager, so desirous as you to secure all that this word has to offer in the way of knowledge. My undergraduate work was done at Ohio State University. Then for two years following I was a Fellow in English at the same school, and at present I am here as a laboratory assistant in psychology. Always I am taking as much work as possible to secure as varied a knowledge as possible. I am working now for my doctor's degree ; I have my master's.

' I have had the idea of trying only *so* much ; I can't get

away from the Greek idea of Nemesis, but your article gave
me the suggestion that one should try everything; better to
be scorched than not to know anything about everything.
And so this year I am trying to lead a fuller life.   The
article has inspired and helped me to attain a clearer vision
of the meaning of Life.   As one of your readers, allow me to
thank you for the splendid treat you gave us.   Pardon
please this long message.

' Respectfully,

' (MISS) VERONA MACDOLLINGER.'

On its receipt, I was slightly flattered but chiefly scornful.
I know the essay deserved better criticism.   But *now*, I am
touched—beggars can't be choosers—and grateful.   Dear
Miss Verona Macdollinger! thank you so much for your
sympathy, and your truly wonderful name.   Perhaps you
are married now and have lost it—perhaps there is a baby
Verona.   Perhaps . . . I don't know, but I am curious
about you.

August 7.

Four Weeks of Happiness

In the cottage alone with E—— and nurse.   Four weeks
of happiness—with the obvious reservation.   I am in love
with my wife!   Oh! dear woman, what agony of mind, and
what happiness you give me.   To think of you alone struggling against the world, and you are not strong, you want
a protector, someone's strong arm.   But we are happy,
these few weeks—I record it because it's so strange.   I am
deeply in love and long to have something so as to sacrifice
it all with a passion, with a vehemence of self-abnegation.

August 15.

The Bishops are very preoccupied just now in justifying
the ways of God to man.   I presume it an even harder task
to justify the ways of man to God.   Why does not God stop
the war? the people are asking—so the Bishops complain.

But why did man make it ?   Man made the war and we
know his reasons.   God made the world, but He keeps His
own counsel.   Yet if man, who aspires to goodness and
truth, can sincerely justify the war, I am willing to believe—
this is my faith—that God can justify the world, its pain
and suffering and death.   We *made* the war and must assume responsibility.

Yet why is not the world instantaneously redeemed by a
few words of reproach coming from a dazzling figure in the
Heavens, revealed unmistakably at the same instant to
every man, woman, and child in the world ?   Why *not* a
sign from Heaven ?

September 1.

Eighteen months ago I refused to take any more rat
poison, with food so dear, and I refused to have any more
truck with doctors.   I insist on being left alone, this grotesque disease and I.   Meanwhile I must elaborately observe it getting worse by inches.   But I scoff at it.   It's
so damned ridiculous, and I only give ground obstinately,
for I have two supreme objects in life which I have not yet
achieved, tho' I am near, oh ! so very near the victory.   The
days creep past shrouded in disappointment ; still I cling to
my spar—if not to-day, why then to-morrow, perhaps, and
if not to-morrow it won't be so bad—not so very bad because
The Times Literary Supplement comes then ; that lasts for
two days, and then the *Nation.* . . .   My thoughts move
about my languid brain like caterpillars on a ravaged tree.
All the while I am getting worse—and they are all so slow :
if they don't hurry it will be too late—oh ! make haste.
But I must wait, and the caterpillars must crawl.   They
are ' Looper ' caterpillars, I think, which span little spaces.

September 2.

A Splendid Dream

It was a brilliantly fine day to-day, with the great avenue
of blue sky and sunlight thro' groups of clouds ranged on

each side. I rolled along a very magnificent way bordered by tall silvered bracken and found two tall hedges. It irked me to remain on the hard road between those two high hedges fending me off from little groups of desirable birch-trees in the woodlands on each side. Suddenly I sprang from my chair, upset it, dumbfounded the nurse, and dis-appeared thro' the hedge into the woods. I went straight up to the birches and they whispered joyously ' Oh ! he's come back to us.' I pressed my lips against their smooth, virginal cheeks. I flung myself down on the ground and passionately squeezed the cool soft leaf-mould as a man presses a woman's breasts. I scraped away the surface leaves and, bending down, drew in the intoxicating smell of the earth's naked flesh. . . . It was a splendid dream. But I wonder if I *could* do it if absent-mindedly I forgot myself in an immense desire !

September 3.

Passed by the birches again to-day. Their leaves rustled as I approached, thrilling me like the liquefaction of Julia's clothes. But I shook my head and went by. Instantly they ceased to flutter, and no doubt turned to address themselves to prettier and more responsive young men who will pass along that road in the years to come.

September 4.

Still no news. I have to reinforce all the strength of my soul to be able to sit and wait day by day, impotent and idle and alone. . . .

September 7.

Goodness the Chief Thing

During the past twelve months I have undergone an up-heaval, and the whole bias of my life has gone across from the intellectual to the ethical. I know that Goodness is the chief thing.

September 24.

Thatching: A Kodak Film

Two brown men on a yellow round rick, thatching; in the background, a row of green elms; above, a windhover poised in mid-air; perpendicular silver streaks of rain; bright sunlight, and a rainbow encircling all. It was as simple as a diagram. One could have cut out the picture with a pair of scissors. I looked with a cold detached eye, for all the world as if the thatchers had no bellies nor immortal souls, as if the trees were timber and not vibrant vegetable life; I forgot that the motionless windhover contained a wonderful and complex anatomy, rapidly throbbing all the while, and that the sky was only a painted ceiling.

But this simplification of the universe was such a relief. It was nice for once in a way not to be teased by its beauty or over-stimulated by its wonder. I merely received the picture like a photographic plate.

September 25.

Saw a long-tailed tit to-day. Exquisite little bird! It was three years since I saw one. I should like to show one to Hindenburg, and watch them in juxtaposition. I wonder what would be their mutual effect on each other. I once dissected a ' specimen '—God forgive me—but I didn't find out anything.

September 26.

Emily Brontë

It was over ten years ago that I read *Wuthering Heights*. Have just read it again aloud to E—— and am delighted and amazed. When I came to the dreadfully moving passages of talk between Cathy and Heathcliff——

' " Let me alone, let me alone," sobbed Catherine. " If I have done wrong, I'm dying for it. It is enough ! You left me too ! But I won't upbraid you for it ! I forgive you ! Forgive me !"

' " It is hard to forgive, and to look at those eyes and feel those wasted hands," he answered. " Kiss me again, and don't let me see your eyes ! I forgive you what you have done to me. I love my murderer—but yours ? How can I ?" '——

I had to stop and burst out laughing, or I should have burst into tears. E—— came over and we read the rest of the chapter together.

I can well understand the remark of Charlotte, a little startled and propitiatory—that having created the book, Emily did not know what she had done. She was the last person to appreciate her own work.

Emily was fascinated by the *beaux yeux* of fierce male cruelty, and she herself once, in a furious rage, blinded her pet bulldog with blows from her clenched fist. *Wuthering Heights* is a story of fiendish cruelty and maniacal love passion. Its preternatural power is the singular result of three factors in rarest combination—rare genius, rare moorland surroundings, and rare character. One might almost write her down as Mrs. Nietzsche—her religious beliefs being a comparatively minor divergence. However that may be, the young woman who wrote in the poem ' A Prisoner ' that she didn't care whether she went to Heaven or Hell so long as she was dead, is no fit companion for the young ladies of a seminary. ' No coward soul is mine,' she tells us in another poem, with her fist held to our wincing nose. I, for one, believe her. It would be idle to pretend to love Emily Brontë, but I venerate her most deeply. Even at this distance, I feel an immediate awe of her person. For her, nothing held any menace. She was adamant over her ailing flesh, defiant of death and the lightnings of her mortal anguish—and her name was Thunder !

October 4.

Raskolnikoff and Sonia

This evening, E—— being away in Wales for a few days, sat with Nurse, who with dramatic emphasis and real under-

standing read to me in the firelight St. Matthew's account of
the trial of Jesus. It reminded me, of course, of Raskol-
nikoff and Sonia, in *Crime and Punishment*, reading the
Bible together, though my incident was in a minor key.
Nurse told me of the wrangle between Mr. P. and Miss B.
over teaching the Sunday School children all about hell.

October 5.

Some London neurologist has injected a serum into a
woman's spine with beneficial results, and as her disease is
the same as mine, they wish me to try it too. I may be
able to walk again, to write, etc., my life prolonged !

They little know what they ask of me. Whatever the
widow may have expressed, I doubt not Jesus received scant
gratitude from the widow's son at Nain for his resurrection
—and I have been dead these eighteen months. Death is
sweet. All my past life is ashes, and the prospect of beginning anew leaves me stone cold. They can never understand—I mean my relatives—what a typhoon I have come
through, and just as I am crippling into port I have no
mind to put to sea again ! I am too tired now to shoulder
the burden of Hope again. This chance, had it been earlier,
had been welcome, but in this present mood Life seems more
of a menace than Death ever did. At the best it would be
whinings and pinings and terrible regrets. And how could
I endure to be watching her struggles, and, if further misfortune came, how could I meet her eyes ?

In short, you see, I funk it, yet I am sure the best thing
for her would be to wipe out this past, forget it and start
fresh. Memory even of these sad years would lose its outline in course of time. My pity merely enervates; and
sympathy takes on an almost cynical appearance where
help is needed.

November 2.

The war news is fine ! For weeks past I have gained full
possession of my soul and lived in dignity and serenity of

spirit as never before.   It has been a gradual process, but I am changed, a better man, calm, peaceful, and, by Jove ! top dog.   May God forgive me all my follies.   My darling E——, I know, is secretly travelling along the same mournful road as I have travelled these many years, and am now arrived at the end of, and I must lend her all the strength I can.   But it is hard to try to undo what I have done to her. Time is our ally, but it moves so slowly.

November 3 to November 26.

Posterity will know more about these times than we do. Men are now too preoccupied to digest the volume of history in each day's newspaper.

On the 11th my newspaper never came at all, and I endured purgatory.   Heard the guns and bells and felt rather weepy.   In the afternoon Nurse wheeled me as far as the French Horn, where I borrowed a paper and sat out in the rain reading it.

Some speculators have talked wildly about the prospect of modern civilisation, in default of a League of Nations, becoming extinct.   Modern civilisation can never be extinguished by anything less than a secular cataclysm or a new Ice Age.   You cannot analogise the Minoan civilisation which has clean vanished.   The world now is bigger than Crete, and its history henceforward will be a continuous development without any such lacuna as that between Ancient Greece and our Elizabethans.   Civilisation in its present form is ours to hold and to keep in perpetuity, for better, for worse.   There can be no monstrous deflection in its evolution at this late period any more than we can hope to cultivate the pineal eye on top of our heads—useful as it would be in these days of aeroplanes.   But the chance is gone—evolution has swept past.   Perhaps on some other planet mortality may have had more luck.   There are, peradventure, happy creatures somewhere in this great universe who generate their own light like glow-worms, or can see in the dark like owls, or who have wings like birds.

Or there may be no mortality, only immortality, no stomachs, no 'flu, no pills—and no kisses, which would be a pity ! But it's no good we earth-dwellers repining now. It is too late. Such things can never be—not in our time, anyhow ! So far as I personally am concerned, I am just now very glad man is only bipedal. To be a centipede and have to lie in bed would be more than even I could bear.

If the civilisations of Ancient Greece or Ancient Rome had permeated the whole world they would never have become extinct.

We are now entered on the kingless republican era. The next struggle, in some ways more bitter and more protracted than this, will be between capital and labour. After that, the millennium of Mr Wells and the Spiritistic age. After the aeroplane, the soul. Few yet realise what a transformation awaits the patient investigations of the psychical researchers. We know next to nothing about the mind force and spirit workings of man. But there will be a tussle with hoary old materialists like Edward Clodd.

November 26.

The Old Lady Shows her Coins

My old nurse lapses into bizarre malapropisms. She is afraid the Society for the *Propagation* of Cruelty to Animals will find fault with the way we house our hens; for boiling potatoes she prefers to use the camisole (casserole) ! She says *Mr. Bolflour, arminstance, von Tripazz*, and so on. Yesterday, in the long serenity of a dark winter's night, with a view to arouse my interest in life, she went and brought some heirloom treasures from the bottom of her massive trunk—some coins of George I. ' Of course, they're all obsolute now,' she said. ' What ! absolutely obsolute ?' I enquired in surprise. The answer was in the informative.

In spite of physical difficulties surrounding me in a mesh-work, I have now unaided corrected my proofs in joyful triumph—an ecstatic conqueror up to the very end. I take

my life in homœopathic doses now.   I am tethered by but
a single slender thread—curiosity to know what Mr. Wells
says in the Preface—a little piece of vanity that deserves to
be flouted.

November 29.

O all ye people ! the crowning irony of my life—where is
the sacred oil ?—is my now cast-iron religious convictions
shortly summarised as *Love and Unselfishness*.   These, my
moral code, have captured the approval, not only of my
ethical but my intellectual side as well.   Undoubtedly, and
dogmatically if you like, a man should be unselfish for the
good of the soul and also to the credit of his intellect.   To be
selfish is to imprison in a tiny case the glorious ego capable
of penetrating to the farthest confines of the universe.   As
for love, it is an instinct and the earnest, like all beauty,
physical as well as moral, of our future union into One.
' One loving heart sets another on fire.'—St. Augustine
(*Confessions*).

December 1.

What I have always feared is coming to pass—love for my
little daughter.   Only another communication string with
life to be cut.   I want to hear ' the tune of little feet along
the floor.'   I am filled with intolerable sadness at the
thought of her.   Oh ! forgive me, forgive me !

December 3.

The ' Puggilist '

' My word ! you do look a figure !' the old nurse exclaimed
to me to-day in the course of one of the periodical tetanuses
of all my muscles, when the whole body is contorted into a
rigid tangle.   ' I shall never make a *puggilist* ' (the word is
her own), I said.

I was rather impressed, though, for she is one of those
who, like Mr. Saddletree, I believe, in *The Heart of Mid-*

lothian, never notice anything. She would not notice if she came into my room, and I was standing on my head as stiff as a ferule. ' You may observe,' I should say, ' I am standing upside down—would you turn me round ?' ' With pleasure,' is her invariable reply to *every* request I proffer.

December 23.

Victory at Christmas

It is strange to hear all this thunderous tread of victory, peace, and Christmas rejoicings above ground, all muffled by the earth, yet quite audible. They have not buried me deep enough. Here in this vault all is unchanged. It is bad for me, for, as to-day, a faint tremor passes along my palsied limbs—a tremor of lust—lust of life, a desire to be up and mingling in the crowd, to be soaked up by it, to feel a sense of all mankind flooding the heart, and strong masculine youth pulsing at the wrists. I can think of nothing more ennobling than the sense of power, unity, and manhood that comes to one in a sea of humanity, all animated by the same motive—to be sweeping folk off their feet and to be swept off oneself ; that is to be man, not merely Mr. Brown.

Christmas Day.

Death

Surely, I muse, a man cannot be accounted a failure who succeeds at last in calling in all his idle desires and wandering motives, and with utter restfulness concentrating his life on the benison of Death. I am happy to think that, like a pilot hard aport, Death is ready at a signal to conduct me over this moaning bar to still deep waters. After four years of war, life has grown cheap and ugly, and Death—how desirable and sweet ! Youth now is in love with Death, and many are heavy-hearted because Death flouts their affection—the maimed, halt, and blind. How terrible if Life had no end !

With how splendid a zest the young men flung themselves
on Death—like passionate lovers !   A magnificent slaughter
—for indifference to Life is the noblest form of unselfishness,
and unselfishness is the highest virtue.

Victurosque Dei celant ut vivere durent, Felix esse mori.
Lucan, with Sir Thomas Browne's rendering:

> We're all deluded, vainly searching ways
> To make us happy by the length of days;
> For cunningly, to make 's protract this breath,
> The gods conceal the happiness of death.

This mood, not permanent, but recurring constantly,
equals the happiness and comfort of the drowning man
when he sinks for the third time.   A profound compassion
for my dear ones and friends, and all humanity left on the
shore of this world struggling, fills my heart.   I want to say
genially and persuasively to them as my last testament:
Why not die ?   What loneliness under the stars !   It is
only bland, unreflecting eupepsia that leads poets to dithy-
rambs about the heavenly bodies, and to call them all by
beautiful names.   Diana !   Yet the moon is a menace and
a terrible object-lesson.   Despite Blanco White, it were well
if the night had never revealed the stars to us.   Suppose a
man with the swiftness of light touring through the darkness
and cold of this great universe.   He would pass through
innumerable solar systems and discover plenty of pellets
(like this earth, each surging with waves of struggling life,
like worms in carrion).   And he would tour onwards like
this for ever and ever.   There would be no end to it, and
always he would be discovering more hot suns, more cold
and blasted moons, and more pellets, and each pellet would
be in an internal fatuous dance of revolutions, the life on it
blind and ignorant of all other life outside its own atmosphere.

But out of this cul-de-sac there is one glorious escape—
Death, a way out of Time and space.   As long as we go on
living, we are as stupid and as caged as these dancing rats
with diseased semicircular canals that incessantly run round

and round in circles.   But if we be induced to remain in
this cul-de-sac, there is always an alleviative in communication and communion with our fellows.   Men need each other
badly in this world.   The stars are crushing, but mankind
in the mass is even above the stars—how far above, Death
may show, perhaps to our surprise.

But if I go on, I shall come round to the conviction that
life is beer and skittles.   Cheerio ! . . .   This is not written
in despair—' despair is a weakening of faith, hope in God.'
But I am tired and in need of relief.   Death tantalises my
curiosity, and sometimes I feel I could kill myself just to
satisfy it.   But I agree that Death, save as the only solution, is merely a funk-hole.

Boxing Day.

James Joyce is my man (in the *Portrait of the Artist as a
Young Man*).   Here is a writer who tells the truth about
himself.   It is almost impossible to tell the truth.   In this
journal I have tried, but I have not succeeded.   I have *set
down* a good deal, but I cannot *tell* it.   Truth of self has to
be left by the psychology-miner at the bottom of his boring.
Perhaps fifty or a hundred years hence Posterity may be
told, but Contemporary will never know.   See how soldiers
deliberately, from a mistaken sense of charity or decency,
conceal the horrors of this war.   Publishers and Government aid and abet them.   Yet a good cinema film of all the
worst and most filthy and disgusting side of the war—
everyone squeamish and dainty-minded to attend under
State compulsion to have their necks scroffed, their sensitive
nose-tips pitched into it, and their rest on lawny couches
disturbed for a month after—would do as much to prevent
future wars as any League of Nations.

It is easy to reconcile oneself to man's sorrows by shutting
the eyes to them. But there is no satisfaction in so easy a
victory. How many people have been jerry-building their
faith and creed all their lives by this method !   One breath
of truth and honest self-dealing would blow the structure

down like a house of cards.   The optimist and believer must bear in mind such things as the C.C.S. described by M. Duhamel, or this from M. Latzko's *Men in Battle:*

' The captain raised himself a little, and saw the ground and a broad dark shadow that Weixler cast.   Blood ?   He was bleeding ?   Or what ?   Surely that was blood.   It couldn't be anything but blood.   And yet it stretched out so peculiarly, and drew itself up like a thin thread to Weixler, up to where his hand pressed his body as though he wanted to pull up the roots that bound him to the earth.

' The captain had to see.   He pulled his head farther out from under the mound—and uttered a hoarse cry, a cry of infinite horror.   The wretched man was dragging his entrails behind him.'

The reviewer suggests that the book should be *read by school-children* in every school in the world !   I should like to take it (and I hope it is large and heavy) and bring it down on the heads of the heartless, unimaginative mob, who would then have to look at it, if only to see what it was that cracked down on their skulls so heavily.

Certainly Joyce has chosen the easier method of transferring his truth of self to a fictional character, thus avoiding recognition.   I have failed in the method urged by Tolstoi in the diary of his youth : ' Would it not be better to say ' (he asks), ' " This is the kind of man I am ; if you do not like me, I am sorry, but God made me so " ? . . .   Let every man show just what he is, and then what has been weak and laughable in him will become so no longer.'   Tolstoi himself did not live up to this.   He confessed to his diary, but he kept his diary to himself.   Some of my weaknesses I publish, and no doubt you say at once ' self-advertisement.'   I agree more or less, but believe *egotism* is a diagnosis nearer the mark.   I do not aspire to Tolstoi's *ethical* motives. Mine are *intellectual*.   I am the scientific investigator of myself, and if the published researches bring me into notice, I am not averse from it, though interest in my work comes first.

Did not Sir Thomas Browne say ever so long ago: ' We carry within us the wonders we seek without us ; there is all Africa and her prodigies in us . . . ' ?

1919

January 1.

My dear Arthur !—if it's a boy, call him Andrew Chatto Windus. Then perhaps the firm will give him a royalty when he is published at the font.

My life here has quite changed its orientation. I am no longer an intellectual snob. If I were, E—— and I would have parted ere now. I never liked to take her to the B.M. (in my petty way) because there all the values are intellectual.

I write this by candlelight in bed. In the room above E—— is in bed with 'flu. We have had days of cold rain, and just now it drips drearily off the roof, and the wind blows drearily in gusts round the cottage as if tired of blowing, and as if blowing prospects were nothing to be roaring about.

Wilson

President Wilson in my hero. I worship him. I could ask him to stamp across my prostrate body to save getting his feet wet in a puddle. But I know nothing about him save what I read in the *Nation*, and I don't want to. Supposing I discovered traits . . . ? I have had enough of disenchantment to last me a lifetime. If he is not the greatest figure in modern history, then there's no money in Wall Street.

January 3.

She taxes me with indifference, says my sympathy is cold. By God ! this is hard to bear. But she is so desperate, she is lunging out right and left at all. I fear for her mental balance. What's going to happen to us ? Why does everyone seem to have forsaken us ? Ah ! it is almost too hard for me to bear. And I can't break down. I am like ice. I can't melt. I had a presentiment of evil awaiting us about now. I don't know why, unless long experience of it produces a nose for it, so that I can smell it in advance.

January 4.

I have talked of being *in love with one's own ruin*, Bash-kirtseff of liking to suffer, to be in despair. Light, frivolous talk. At the most, such moods are only short lulls between the spasms of agony of suffering ; one longs to be free of them as of acute physical pain, to be unconscious. I look forward to night, to darkness, rest, and sleep. I sleep well between twelve and six and then watch the dawn, from black (and the owl's hoot) to grey (and the barncock's crow) to white (and the blackbirds' whistle). The oak beam on my ceiling, the Japanese print on the wall come slowly into view, and I dread them. I dread the day with my whole soul. Each dawn is hopeless. Yes, it is true, they have not buried me deep enough. I don't think I am buried at all. They have not even taken me down from the tree. And my wife they are just nailing up. I can never forget, wherever I may be, in Heaven or Hell, her figure in dressing-gown and shawl drawn up erect—but swaying because she is so weak—before me at the fireside (she had just been bending over me and kissing me, hot cheeks and hot tears that mingled and bound us together to that moment for ever), her head tilted towards the ceiling, and her poor face looking so ill and screwed up as she half-whispered : ' Oh, God ! it's so hopeless.' I think that picture is impressed even on the four walls of the room, its memory is photo-graphed on the air to haunt those who may live here in the time to come. I said : ' Fight it out, dear. Don't give in. I believe in a personal devil. The human spirit is un-conquerable. You'll come through if you fight.' It was but a few weeks ago that she came home one evening, dug out from a drawer her beautiful dance dress, got into it, and did a *pas seul* for my pleasure round the little cottage room. That ogre Fate was drawing out her golden wing and mocking her loss of liberty. Ah ! the times we *intended* to have together !

January 8.

I lie stiff and contorted till Nurse arrives at nine-thirty. She straightens me out and bolsters me up. Breakfast at nine. Cigarettes while I listen with ravenous ears for the postman. No letter for me, then *plop* right down into the depth among the weeds and goblins of the deep sea for an hour. There usually is no letter for me.

My chief discovery in sickness and misfortune is the callousness of people to our case—not from hard-heartedness (everyone is kind), but from absence of sympathetic imagination. People don't know the horrors and they can't imagine them—perhaps they are unimaginable. You will notice how suicides time and again in farewell notes to their closest and dearest have the same refrain, ' I don't believe even you can realise all I suffer.' Poor devil ! of course not. Beyond a certain point, suffering must be borne alone, and so must extreme joy. Ah ! we are lonely barks.

January 13.

All the postman brought me to-day was an income-tax form !

Last night: Nurse (having put me back to bed). : ' Shall I shut up your legs ?'

B.: ' No, thank you. They've been bent up all the evening, and it's a relief to have them out straight.'

Later: B.: ' Before you go you might uncross my legs.'

(She pulls bed-clothes back, seizes my feet, one in each hand, and forces them apart, chanting humorously: ' Any scissors to grind ?' As I have pointed out to her, the *sartorius* muscle, being on the inside of the thigh and stronger than the others, has the effect of crossing my legs when a tetanic spasm occurs.)

N.: ' There, good-night.'
B.: ' And a good-night to you.'
N.: ' I'll come in first thing in the morning.'
(Exit.)

I lie on my back and rest awhile. Then I force myself on to the left side by putting my right arm over the left side of the bed beneath the wood-work and pulling (my right arm is stronger than any of the other limbs). To-night, Nurse had not placed me in the middle of the bed (I was too much over on the right side), so even my long arm could not reach down beneath the woodwork on the left. I cursed Nanny for a scabby old bean, struggled, and at last got over on my left side. The next thing was to get my legs bent up —now out as stiff and straight as ferrules. When lying on the left side I long ago found out that it is useless to get my right leg up first, as it only shoots out again when I come to grapple with the left. So I put my right arm down, seized the left leg just above the knee and pulled ! The first result is always a violent spasm in the legs and back. But I hang on and presently it dies away, and the leg begins to move upward a little. Last night Nanny uncrossed my legs, but was not careful to separate them. Consequently, knee stuck side by side to knee, and foot to foot, as if glued, and I found, in pulling at my left, I had the stubborn live weight of both to lift up. I would get them part way, then by a careless movement of the hand on a ticklish spot both would shoot out again. So on for an hour—my only relief to curse Nanny.

And thus, any time, any week, these last eighteen months. But I have faith and hope and love in spite of all. I forgive even Nanny !

January 19.

The situation is eased. E—— is at Brighton for a change, and has P—— with her (she came up from Wales with the nurse after seven months' visit). But I am heart-sore and unhappy.

January 20.

If I were to sum up my life in one word I should say
suffocation.   R—— has been my one blow-hole.   Now I
look forward to a little oxygen when my Journal is published !   I am delighted and horrified at the same time.
What will my relatives say ?   'Twill be the surprise of their
lives.   I regard it as a *revanche*.   The world has always gagged and suppressed me—now I turn and hit it in the belly.

January 22.

Am now lodging alone under one roof with Nanny !
Makes me think of some of Sterne's adventures in the
Sentimental Journey, only I must shut my eyes very tight
to see the likeness and imagine very hard.   This is a selec-
tion from last night's conversation (remember she is deaf,
old, and obstinate ; she hates to be instructed or corrected ;
hence her ignorance and general incapacity) :

Ornithology

N.: ' I think a sparrow out at the back has young birds,
by the way she carries off the food.'

B.: ' It's too early for young sparrows.   A sparrow is too
worldly wise to encumber himself with a young family in
January, or in February or March for that matter.'

N.: ' I've seen young sparrows in March.'

B.: ' Why didn't you write to the papers about it ?'

N.: ' There wasn't so much writing to the papers in my
days.   But there were things I could have written about.
Young plovers, for example, I used to catch and hold in my
lap.   You know the plover ?   It's called the lapwing
sometimes; only a few young at a time——'

B.: ' Four.'

N.: ' Yes.   Now Charlie used to show me partridges' nests
with as many as twenty-four.'

B.: ' Yes, but laid probably by more than one hen.'

N.: ' Charlie said it was all one bird.   The prettiest nest
he ever showed me was a greenfinch's.'

B.: ' What was that like ?'

N.: ' It was swung underneath the bough of a fir-tree right at the end.'

B.: ' That was not a greenfinch's.'

N.: ' Well, Charlie said it was, and he showed it to all of us; we all saw it.'

B.: ' It was the nest of a goldcrest.'

N.: ' Yes ?   Charlie had a wonderful collection of eggs. He could name them all, and labelled the names on them. They would cover the table when all set out.'

B.: ' Yes ?'

N.: ' Oh, I forgot, another nest he showed me—a king-fisher's.'

B.: ' What was that like ?'

N.: ' It was right down among some reeds of a stream.'

B.: ' What were the eggs like ?'

N.: ' There were no eggs in it when I saw it.   Another pretty——'

B.: ' That was not a kingfisher's nest.   A kingfisher nests at the end of a hole in the bank of the stream.'

N.: ' Charlie said it was.   Another pretty nest was the robin's.'

B.: ' The prettiest nest of all, I think, is the long-tailed tit's.'

N : ' Oh, yes, I know that.'

B.: ' What's it like ?'

N.: ' I can't recollect.'

B.: ' All arched over with sticks and lined with green leaves ?'

N.: ' Oh, yes.'

I suspect ' Charlie ' (whoever he was) could not tell a hawk from a handsaw, even when the wind was southerly. Now what a stupid old woman not to make better use of me !

January 23.

Have been sustaining a hell of tedium by reading a sloppy novel—sentimental mucilage—called *Conrad in Quest of*

His Youth, which sent me in quest of mine. I see now that my youth was over before I came to London. For never after did I experience such electric tremors of joy and fear as,. *e.g.*, over ——. As a small boy I knew her, and always lifted my hat. But one day at the age of sixteen, with a heart like nascent oxygen (though I did not know it), I lifted my hat and, in response to her smile, fell violently in love. During country rambles I liked to pause and carve her initials on the bark of a tree. It pleased me to confide my burning secret to the birds and wild things. I knew it was safe in their keeping. And I always hoped she might come along one day and see the letters there, and feel curiosity, yet she couldn't find out. . . . I daresay they are still legible in places, some of them of exquisite rural beauty ; though the letters themselves probably now look obscured and distorted by the evergrowing bark, the trees and locality doubtless are still as beautiful :

> ' Upon a poet's page I wrote
> Of old two letters of her name ;
> Part seemed she of the effulgent thought
> Whence that high singer's rapture came.
> When now I turn the leaf the same
> Immortal light illumes the lay,
> But from the letters of her name
> The radiance has waned away.'

For a whole year I was in agony, meeting her constantly in the town, but never daring to stop and speak. I used to return home after a short cap-lifting encounter with an intolerable ache that I did not understand. Even in subsequent miseries I do not believe I suffered mental pain equal to this in acuteness. I used to lift my cap to her in the High Street, then dart down a side-street and around, so as to meet her again, and every time I met her came a raging stormy conflict between fear and desire. I wanted to stop —my heart always failed me. How I cursed myself for a poltroon the very next moment !

I always haunted all the localities—park, concerts, skating-rink—where I thought to see her. In church on

Sundays I became electrified if she was there. One afternoon at a concert in company with my sister, I determined
on a bold measure: I left before it was over—saw my sister
home, and at once darted back to the hall and met my
paragon coming out. She was with her friend (how I hated
her !) and her friend's mother (how I feared her !) I was
seventeen, she was seventeen, and of ravishing, virginal
beauty. I spoke. I said (obviously) : ' How did you enjoy
the concert ?'

While the other two walked on, she replied ' Very much.'
That was all. I could think of nothing more, so I left her,
and she rejoined her friends. It had been a terrible nervous
strain to me. At the crucial second my nose twitched and I
felt my face contorted. But I walked home on air and my
soul sang like a bird. It was the beautiful rhapsody of a
boy. There was nothing carnal in it. Indeed, the poor
girl was idealised aloft into something scarcely human.
But that at the moment of speaking to her I was in the
power of an unprecedented emotion is obvious if I write that
neither before nor after has anything ever caused facial
twitching. It is evidence of my ardour and youth.

Our acquaintance remained tenuous for long. I was shy
and inexperienced. I was too shy to write. I heard
rumours that she was staying by the sea, so I went down
and wandered about to try to see her. In vain. I went
down another day, and it began to pour with rain. So I
spent all my time sheltering under doorways and shop awn-
ings, cursing my luck, and groaning at the waste of my
precious time. ' There was a large halibut on a fishmonger's
stall,' I posted in my diary, ' but not caught, I think, off
this coast.' Then follows abruptly :

> ' A daughter of the gods she walked,
> Divinely tall, and most divinely fair.'

I bought a local paper in the High Street, and, examining
the ' Visitors' List,' I went through hundreds of names, and
at the end saw ' The most recent arrivals will be found on

page 5.' I turned to page 5 and found nothing there. I complained to the manager. ' Ah, yes, I know, an unfortunate oversight, sir. If you will leave your name and address, I will see it appears in next week's issue.' I felt silly, and slunk off, saying : ' Oh, never mind. I don't care much about it.'

' It is the more worrying to me because I know—

(1) It is wasting good time.

(2) A common occurrence to others, and they all get over it.

(3) There is no comfort in study or reading. Knowledge is dull and dry. Poetry seems to me to be more attractive.'

Then immediately follows a description of a ring snake with notes on its anatomy. Then a few days later : ' Have not seen my beloved all the week. Where on earth has she been hiding herself ?' And again : ' I cannot hope ever to see more wonderful eyes—of the richest, sweetest brown-amber, soft, yet bright.' At length we became friends, wrote letters to one another (her first one was an event), and went for walks.

Of course, the next stage was kissing her. It took me over another twelve months to kiss her. I must have been close on nineteen. We had been walking in the woods all the afternoon, then had tea in the garden tea-rooms. We sat in the green arbour till after dark. I was in a terrible state. Restlessness and fever were exhausting me. Desire struggled with pride. What if she smacked my face ? Then I lit a cigarette for her (I used to buy her little heliotrope boxes of cigarettes labelled in gold ' My Darling '). Greatly daring, I put my left arm round her neck, and holding the matchbox, struck a light and kissed her at the same moment. She said, ' I ought not to let you really,' quite calm. I was in too much of a turmoil to answer, but kissed her again.

I kissed her many times after that. One wet afternoon we had spent kissing in a linhay by a country lane. Coming home, we met her sister's baby, and she stopped to lean over

the pram, and crow. This irritated me, and I strolled on.
' Do you like babies ?' I asked when she came up. ' Yes,'
she answered, ' do you ?' ' Not much,' said I with dryness,
and changed what I felt to be almost an indelicate subject.
After all, a baby is only a kiss carried to a rational conclusion, in natural sequence, sometimes arithmetical, sometimes geometrical. It depends on the length of the engagement.

But it was curious how this kissing destroyed my ideal.
I soon knew I was not in love. With callous self-possession
I was investigating a new sensation, and found it very
enjoyable. ' I kiss *you*,' I said to her one night in the park,
' but you never kiss me.' She at once gave me a passionate
token on my lips, and having exacted thus much tribute, I
sank into complacency, self-adulation, and, ultimately,
indifference. I had been *surcharged*. The relief was too
complete. After exchanging impassioned verses (oh, such
tosh !), each other's photographs, and plenty of letters, my
romance died a natural death. My agony and sweat became a trifle, and one I wished to blot from my memory out
of boyish sense of shame.

Doubtless I broke her heart. She had left the town,
when one morning I received a last pathetic appeal. I
remember now the nausea that love-letter caused me. I
put it on the fire, and thought, ' Heavens what a fool the
girl is !' In 1913 I met her again, and had the effrontery to
go to her home and have dinner with her people. (See
May 31st and June 3rd, 1913.)

Now, in my old age, I like to gaze back on this flashing
gem of youth. It still reflects the light, and she is a princess
again. ' Love in the Valley ' becomes a personal memory
instead of someone else's poem.

Ah ! what a heart I had in those days ! a nascent oxygen
with an affinity for every pretty girl who smiled at me. I
fell in love with a post-office girl, a silversmith's daughter, a
grocer's daughter, the daughter of a judge. For months I
worshipped ——, and bought every kind of photograph of

her. But I've never seen her in my life, and now she's Dead Sea fruit. I had never set eyes on any beautiful women until I came to London. Then I was dazzled by them all— in every rank or station, in the street or on the street, in the Café de l'Europe or the Café Royal—pretty, laughing girls, handsome women, or beautiful pieces of mere flesh only. . . . I was doomed to destruction from the first. If I had not developed disease, if I had come up from the country a healthy, lusty youth, I must soon have got on the rocks. Now that the blood is slow, it is difficult to recall the anguish. That I only succumbed twice is a marvel to me and a joy. My situation at one time was fraught with dire possibilities. My secret life was a tumult. I never went skylarking with jaunty pals in the West End. I crept along the streets alone . . . all this time I was alone, in dirty diggings, by myself. I am consumed with self-pity at the thought.

I cannot understand how saints like Augustine and Tolstoi confess how they went with women in their youth, but recall no sense of nausea. They just deplore their *moral* lapse. When St. Augustine's mother enjoined him never to lie with his neighbour's wife, he laughed at the advice as womanish !

For myself, I never received any parental instruction. I first learned of the wonder of generation through the dirty filter of a barmaid's nasty mind.

I remember —— telling me in sardonic vein that the only advice his father ever gave him on leaving home was to keep his bowels open. The present generation has altered all that.

Birds' eggs were another electrifying factor in my youth. I can remember tramping to and fro all one warm June afternoon over a bracken-covered sandy waste, searching for a nightjar's eggs. H—— and I quartered out the ground systematically, till presently, after two hours' search, the hen goat-sucker flipped up at my feet and fluttered away like a big moth across the silvery bracken out of sight. Lying before me on the ground were two long, grey eggs, marbled like pebbles. I turned away from this

intoxicating vision, flicking my fingers as if I had been
bitten. Then I turned, approached slowly, and gloated.

It was just such an effect on me as a girl's beautiful face
used to make—equally tantalising and out of reach. I
stared, fingered them, put one to my lips. Then it was
over. I had to leave them, and an equal thrill at goat-
suckers' eggs could never return again.

January 24.

The Cottage on the Shore

It was as mysterious as Stevenson's Pavilion on the
Links. For a long time I never noticed any indication of
its being inhabited, save a few chickens at the back which
no one seemed to feed. I could see it from miles around, as
it was situated in a desolate, treeless waste, thousands of
acres of marshes and duckponds (known as the *Mires*) on
the one side, and on the other a wilderness of sandy links
and sandhills swarming with rabbits (known as the *Bur-
rows*). Immediately in front, the waters of a broad tidal
estuary came up almost to the door during spring tides.
The nearest human habitation was the lighthouse, a mile
away round the corner on the sands near the harbour bar.
In my rambles in search of bird or beast, I used occasionally,
while eating sandwiches at midday on a sandhill top, to
turn my field-glasses on the cottage idly. For long I saw
no one. Then one spring, while thousands of lapwings
circled above my head, calling indignantly at me ' Little
boo-oy,' and larks dotted the blue sky everywhere in little
white-hot needle-points of song, I saw a tiny man—a
manikin—come out of this tiny cottage—a doll's house—
and throw some corn to the chickens. He was three miles
away, and by the time that I arrived at the cottage, the
little man had disappeared. It was a little four-roomed
cottage, with no path leading up to it, no garden, no enclo-
sure, only a few hardy shrubs to keep the sandy soil from
drifting. For a long time I never saw him again, and began

to think he had been an hallucination. But the desolate cottage was still there and the chickens were still alive, so they must have been fed. Then one day I ran up against him on the Mires, and we exchanged greetings. He was a round, tubby, short man with a stubble of beard. Devon folk would have called him bungy, stuggy. His face bore a ludicrous resemblance to the monkey in the ' Monkey Brand ' advertisement, only fatter and rounder. We discussed birds (he was the gamekeeper) and became fast friends. He would take me the round of his duckponds, and sometimes he sent me a postcard when there were wild swans or geese ' in over,' or when he had discovered a ' stranger ' on his water.

But this did not dispel the mystery of the cottage. For he had a woman inside whose presence was never suspected until I had occasion to knock at the door. There was no answer and no sound. All the windows were shut. I knocked again, and heard a distant noise. Then there were long, preparatory noises, as if someone were climbing up from an underground cellar or cave, or wandering down a long, dark passage. Bolts were drawn (and powerful enough they sounded to make fast a portcullis), and I watched the door opening with curiosity ; a tall, fat, middle-aged woman stood their blinking at me like an owl unaccustomed to daylight. Her eyes were weak blue, and her face puffy and red.

' Oh ! is Fedder about ?' I enquired.

Without changing a muscle of her face, she replied mechanically :

' No, but Fedder said if the young gentleman called, I was to say that the shovellers brought off their brood all right.'

I thanked her and departed, as she was obviously embarrassed. In her moping countenance I detected a startled look—Robinson Crusoe, as it were, discovering Friday all at once without any advertising Friday. I heard her bolting the door again, as I strolled off down by the waterside to examine the tide-wrack. It was almost eerie to hear the cackle of herring gulls overhead. They seemed to be laughing at the stupidity of human nature.

There are some things the imagination boggles at. For example, what did that woman in that desolate cottage do ? What did she think about ? What were her wants, her grievances? Where were her relatives ? Did she ever love, or want little babies ? Did murder stories interest her at all ? Drugs ? That is an easy explanation—to jump at some horrible vice. Theatrical. In reality I should have found, I expect, the answer would be just *nothing at all*. She did nothing, thought nothing, perhaps only feared a little, so she always bolted the door and hid herself away. I suppose if one saw nothing bigger than a kingplover or a seagull during the twelve months, and heard no noises other than the trumpet of wild swans and the cries of Fedder's wild fowl, a tall man six feet high, with a voice like a human being's, must seem a little disconcerting.

January 26.

Here is some arithmetic which ought to please me. But it doesn't. I wrote:

> 12 papers in the *Zoologist* in the years 1905–1910; 6 in the *P.Z.S.* (1912–1916) ; 7 in the *Annals and Magazine of Natural History* (1912–1916); 3 in *Bulletin of Entomological Research* ; 2 B.M. pamphlets, in addition to 18 literary efforts (some in newspapers and some not published), and other old scientific papers in different periodicals such as *British Birds*, the *Journal of Animal Behaviour*, etc. In all 65 publications.

Further, in my locker lie:

> 6 unpublished literary MSS.
> 17 volumes of Journal post quarto, pre-war 1s. thickness.
> 12 smaller volumes written in boyhood.
> 6 volumes (post quarto 1s.) of abstracted entries from the Journal.

$2\frac{1}{2}$ post quarto volumes of abstract, abstracted from the volumes of abstract for publication purposes.

In vulgar parlance, *cacoëthes scribendi*.

January 27.

Have you ever considered what a fever of anticipation must be raging in me as I sit by the fire, day after day, awaiting the constantly delayed publication of this my Journal; how I strain to hold it, to smell the fresh ink, to hear the binding crackle as I open it out, and above all to read what one of the foremost literary men thinks about me and my book.

I wait with head on the block for my child to be brought to receive my farewell blessings.

Will it come in time? I nearly died last month of 'flu, and get worse almost daily. I am running a neck-and-neck race up the straight with my evil genius on the black horse. It is touch and go who wins; and if I do, I expect some horrible forfeit will be exacted of me, a penalty will have to be paid—*lèse-majesté*—for my audacity in challenging the stars in their courses and defeating them.

My life has certainly been an astonishing episode in human story. To me, it appears as a titanic struggle between consuming ambition and adverse fortune. Behold a penniless youth thirsting for knowledge introduced into the world out of sheer devilment, hundreds of miles from a university, with a towering ambition, but cursed with ill-health and a twofold nature—pleasure-loving as well as labour-loving. The continuous, almost cunning frustration of my endeavours long ago gave me a sense of struggle with some evil genius. Think of the elaborate precautions I took of my MSS. during the air-raids! I saw each bomb labelled ' Barbellion's contemptible ambition.' Consider the duplication of abstracts—I saw an army of housemaids prowling round to throw them on the fire after Carlyle's *French Revolution*. I have been consciously contesting with an

incendiary, a bomber from Hunland, a wicked housemaid,
a whole world of wicked folk, in league with a hostile spirit
decided on killing and obliterating me and my ambition—a
grotesque couple, a monkey astride a hippogriff, an ass with
a Jabberwock ! True, he has ruined me ; yet the struggle
is not over. With demoniac determination, I am *getting on*
still, crawling on all fours, with the dagger between my
teeth. I am mauled, battered, scorched, but not slain.
The dagger I hope to see published by Messrs. Chatto and
Windus next month.

You can search all history and fiction for an ambition
more powerful than mine and not find it. No, not Napoleon,
nor Wilhelm II, nor Keats. No, I am not proud of it, not
at all. The wonder is that I remain sane, the possessed of
such a demon. I am sane or I could not make fun of it as
I do. Ah ! my God ! it is a ridiculous weakness, but the
leopard cannot change his spots, and I feel just as hopelessly spotty as a leopard.

January 28.

' The rest is silence '—I should like this inscribed at the
end of this garrulous Journal, an inscription for the base of
my self-erected monument.

January 30.

Rowbotham, the Modern Homer

The Human Epic; *The Twelfth Epic Poem of the World*;
The Story of the Universe and Prehistoric Man; *The Vanished
Continent in the Atlantic*; *The Ice Age*; *The Anemones,
Corals, and Population of the Primeval Ocean* (' These latter
cantos have been made the subject of interesting lectures '
—*The Bard*); *Other Epics by Rowbotham, the Modern
Homer*; *God and the Devil*; *The Swiss Lake Dwellers*; *The
Epic of the Empire*; *London*; *Charlemagne*. Each Epic
2s. 6d. Foyle, 121, Charing Cross Road.

Who is ' The Bard ' ? What a safe remark to make

about the anemones and corals ! Who is Rowbotham ? I wish someone would lecture to me on him. What are the ' other epics of the world ' ? The twelfth has the suggestion of quack verse sold as a green liquid from a four-wheeled vehicle at a country fair. But I can't run to 2s. 6d., though I ache to read and know you, O Rowbotham ! Rowbotham, *the late Mr Homer*, I suppose. Say, though, who is this Rowbotham ?

Snow lies on the ground outside. All the morning it was too dark in my vault to read. Even had it been light, my eyesight had become temporarily too deranged for me to see the print. Had my eyes been all right, it was so cold that I had to keep my hands under the bedclothes.

All the afternoon I dozed. In the evening I sat by the fire and read *Urn-burial*. During the day, at long intervals, Nanny comes in, and I shout out fatuities—*e.g.*, ' Still snowing,' or ' Colder than ever.'

There are some days when I give up, surrender voluntarily every earthly desire, when every thread binding me to life is cut. I long to be free, and hack and cut in a frenzy— frenzies in which I curse and swear out loud to myself, alternating with fits of terrible apathy, when I am indifferent to everything and everybody, when the petty routine of my existence, washing, eating, and sitting out, goes on and carries me along with it mechanically. And I wonder all the time why on earth I trouble about it. I look at human life and human affairs with inhuman detachment, yet not from the side of the angels. I am neither one thing nor the other, neither dead nor alive, a nondescript creature in a No-Man's Land, and, like all who keep a middle course, not claimed with any enthusiasm by either side. The living must be tired of me, and the dead don't seem eager for my reception. Yet I must go somewhere, and by heavens ! I will not choose willingly, God knows, the bare heath of this world. The bare bodkin is an alluring symbol to lonely paralytics, meaning liberty, fraternity, peace. Ever since I came into it, I have felt an alien in this life—a refugee by

reason of some pre-natal extradiction. I always felt alien
to my father and mother. I was different from them. I
knew and was conscious of the detachment. They seemed
the children and I was a very old man. My father's youth,
which continued to flower past middle-age and in the midst
of adversity and terrible affliction, and his courage and
happiness of soul I admired greatly. But we were very far
from one another. I was proud and irritable. My mother
I loved, and she loved us all with an instant love and
tenderness such as I have never seen in any mother since. I
did not realise this at the time, alas ! Her love helped to
wear her out. She never parted from me for however short
a period without tears—tears certainly of weakness—
especially later, of sheer inability to stand steady any longer
against the buffetings of a hard lot. But we had little in
common. I was a queer duckling, self-willed and determined at the water's edge, heedless of her frantic ' clucks.'
Dear soul ! ' If you behave so,' she would warn me sorrow-
fully, ' no one, you know, will like you when you go out into
the world.' ' I don't care,' I would answer. ' I don't
want them to like me. I shan't like them. Theirs would
be the greater loss.' Ours was a family—not uncommon I
imagine, at any time—in which the parents were under the
tolerant surveillance and patronage of the children.

I was a little alien among my school-fellows. I knew I
was different, and accepted my ostracism as a quite natural
consequence. I never played games with them, but after
afternoon school hurried home, gobbled down an early tea
(prepared for me in the kitchen by Martha), and went off
on a long solitary ramble till nightfall (and later sometimes), through orchards of very old crooked trees ; the air
reeking of garlic or humming with the scoldings of tits whose
nests I was after in the holes in trees ; through gorse-covered
thickets, over streams, in woods, disturbing the game—I
went across country, avoiding lanes, roads, and footpaths
as if they were God-forsaken.

I never entered into any intimacy with my masters.

They and the boys regarded me quizzically with a menacing
' Now then, Barbellion, where are you sloping off to ? '   I
would flush, and parry with them with ' I've got to be home
early to-night.'   It was a lie.   I knew it was a lie.   They
knew it was a lie.   But I presented such an invertebrate,
sloppy, characterless exterior, that no one felt curious
enough to probe further into my way of life.   And I was
content to leave it at that.

It was the same in London.   I was alien to my colleagues
and led a private life, totally outside their imaginings.
Among them only R., dear fellow, has ventured to approach
my life, and seek a communion with me.   And I can't
believe he has suffered any hurt.   I am not a live wire.
Now at all events my power station is dismantled, my career
a cinder-path.   I wish I could think that others who have
come near me are similarly immune.   My wife and child
seem at a remote distance from me.   Strange to say, I am
calmer in mind when they are away, as now.   Would that
they could go on with their lives as if I had never been.
E—— is a dear woman.   I love her, and she, I hope, loves me
a little.   She is my wife, and it is my child, and my dreamy
ineffectual existence, poised between earth and heaven,
cannot annul the physical contact.   They may be dream
figures, but I created them, and am responsible.   Forgive
me, forgive me, and try to think well of me.   I am weak,
and this great universe is a bully.   This disease has
weakened the fibre of my life.   Existence blows me about
anywhere.   I am possessed by any idle devil who cares to
take me, give me a shake, and pass on : forebodings and evil
visions, imaginary pictures of horrible accidents, cata-
clysms, fears—fears that the earth may drop into the sun.

February 3.

Suffering does not only insulate.   It drops its victim on
an island in an ocean desert where he sees men as distant
ships passing.   I not only feel alone, but very far away
from you all.   But what is my suffering ?   Not physical

pain. I have none. Pain brings clusters of one's fellows—
a toothache is intelligible. But when I say I am grown
tired of myself, have outlived myself, am unseasonable and
' mopy ' like a doomed swallow in November, it is something that requires a John Galsworthy to understand. The
world to me is but a dream or mock show; and we all
therein but Pantalones and Anticks to my severe contempla-
tions. This used to be a transitory impression that amused
my curiosity. But it hurts and bewilders now that it has
become the permanent complexion on my daily existence,
when I long for real persons and real things. Tinsel and
pictures are melancholy substitutes to anyone heart-hungry
for the touch of real hands, and the sound of real voices.
Acute mental pain at intervals seizes me with pincers and
casts me helpless into the whirlpool—it may be E——'s
despair, or the failure to find a home for me to go to. But
these are spasms of reality, the momentary opening and
closing of a shutter on Life. As soon as they are over, I at
once relapse into the dull monotone of misery and picture-
show.

I have not left my room since November 11th. I eat
well, sleep well, am in possession of all my higher faculties—
those for feeling and thinking. But I can't get out.

I think sometimes folk do not come to see me because I
am such a gruesome object. It is not pleasant to feel you
are gruesome. I have outstayed my welcome. I know
everyone will be relieved to hear of my death—no doubt for
my sake, as they will eagerly point out, but also for their
own sake, as I believe. Yet now and then in selfish and
ignoble moods, I, being an egotist, fancy I would like some
loving hands to clutch at me, in a blind, ineffectual effort to
save me in any condition if only alive.

February 4.

The last part of yesterday's entry was maudlin tosh—
entirely foreign to my nature. I hereby cancel it.

The Day's Life

I woke at seven, when my desk, the Japanese print on the wall, the wooden chair with my basin on it, the chest of drawers were emerging out of a grey obscurity. I had tetanuses of my legs (which alternately shot out straight and contracted up to my chin) till eight-thirty, when Nanny came in and drew the blinds, letting in a foggy light. It is bitterly cold. I hear noises in the kitchen—a dull mewing sound (this is the tap being turned on), then a scrape, scrape (she is buttering my toast).

Then breakfast arrives (two pieces of toast and two cups of tea), for which I am set up in bed with pillows. Through the window on my left I can see the branch of a walnut-tree and beyond, a laurel. The little squares of ancient glass are so loosely fixed in the leads (one is broken and covered over with a piece of cardboard) that the draught pours through and sometimes makes wind enough to blow out my match for a cigarette. As I eat comes a heavy scrunch, scrunch, right up the front door, which is only a few feet away from me, concealed behind a curtain. It is the postman, who puts the letters in the porch, gives a resounding knock, and goes away again. As I smoke my cigarette there is another scrunch, scrunch, but this one goes round to the back door. There is a hammering on the door (they all know Nanny is deaf) and I hear a rough, throaty voice, saying, ' Nearly copped him that time,' and Nanny replying, ' Yes, 'tis cold this morning.' It is the newspaper man, who always shies half a brick at a rat that haunts our garden.

While reading the *Daily News* I hear every now and then a distant rattle, which comes nearer, increases to a roar and passes off again in a furious rattle of sound—it is a motor-car along the Oxford Road. Then I hear the clock at the Manor strike twelve, sparrows chattering, or a scolding tit in the garden.

Presently a smell of dinner comes through from the kitchen, and while it cooks, N—— comes in with the hot

water and helps me to wash.   All the afternoon I sleep or
doze.   At four-thirty I get up, by a little careful arrangement get into my wheeled chair, and am taken to the fireside.   My legs having shot out in a tetanus meanwhile,
they have to be bent up before I can climb into my armchair.   As soon as I have tricked myself into the chair they
shoot out again, and have to be bent up, and feet placed on
the hot bottle.

Then tea !   N—— sits opposite—a short, fat little
woman, who always on all occasions wears large black boots,
which she says are necessary on account of her varicose veins.
Her white apron above the waist is decorated with an
embroidered design—a large red ' O ' with green leaves
around it.   She always eats with her mouth open, otherwise, I suspect, she has discovered the noise of her mastica-
tion drowns every other sound.

After tea I read Gogol.   After supper, Gogol.   Then, my
eyes aching, I stop and gaze into the fire.   Nanny reads me
a lot of funny stories out of *Answers*.   I listen with a set
smile, still gazing into the fire.   I do not mind in the least,
for to me it is all a mock show.   Then came a biographical
study of Charlie Chaplin—his early struggles, his present
tastes and habits, what his Japanese chauffeur said of him
(in the pidgin English of a Chinaman), his favourite holiday
retreat, how he reads voraciously and always carries with
him when he travels a trunk full of books (ah ! my God, it
did not give their titles !), etc.   There was a ridiculous
likeness in all this to a ' critique ' of, say, George Moore in
the *Bookman*.   It aroused my slumbering brain.   It interested me.   (N—— was absorbed.)   This flashlight into
a strange new world where the life, thoughts, habits of Mr
Chaplin were of transcendent interest recalled me to reality.
I had been floating in a luxury of dream.   Now I flouted
Circe, and struggled back into full possession of my personality.   I was tickled, amused, amazed.

Then N—— read me a series of informative snippets :
how to make your lamp burn brighter (by putting a spoon-

ful of sugar in the oil-well) ; how black beetles were not really *beetles* at all ; how Alfred Noyes was a great poet ; what a red bargee meant ; what a Blue Peter signified.

At this my gorge rose at last. In the tones of a puff-breasted pedagogue addressing a small boy, I said : ' Oh, don't you know the famous line of R. L. S. about climbing into a sea-going ship when the Blue Peter is floating aloft ? '

Now this was a contemptible piece of pride, for I only wanted to demonstrate to this scabby old bean that I knew all about a Blue Peter, and it was like her cheek to suppose I didn't. I experience the same irritation when she explains to me how to go from Paddington to Victoria, or where the British Museum is. Of a truth I am no dream figure then. The veritable W. N. P. B. shows his bristling pelage from every opening in the wires of the cage.

How petty ! Intellectual pride has been the bane of my life. Yet I must be fair to myself. Who, I should like to know, has received greater incentive to this vice ? Have not inferior types all my life choked me, bound me, romped over me ? But what a beautifully geometrical Nemesis it all is ! Here I am in the last scene of the last act, the ruthless, arrogant intellectual, spending the last days of his ruined life alone, in the close companionship of an uneducated village woman who reads *Answers*.

February 8.

100,000 copies of Marie Bashkirtseff's Journal were sold in America alone. If 100,000 copies of my book are sold, that will mean £5,000 for E——. Then I have a second volume for posthumous publication, the remainder of my diary from March, 1918, to the end, under the sensational and catchpenny title of *The Diary of a Dying Man*, beginning with Sir Thomas Browne's ' We are in the power of no calamity while Death is in our own,' and finishing up with Hamlet's last worst words : ' The rest is silence.' Another £5,000, eh ? and E—— a rich woman ? Time will show.

The Icons

Every man has his own icon. Secreted in the closet of
each man's breast is an icon, the image of himself, concealed
from view with elaborate care, treated invariably with great
respect by means of which the Ego, being self-conscious,
sees itself in relation to the rest of mankind, measures itself
therewith, and in accordance with which it acts and moves
and subsists. In the self-righteous man's bosom, it is a
molten image of a little potentate who can do no wrong.
In the egoist's, an idol loved and worshipped by almost all
men, addressed with solemnity and reverence, and cast in
an immutable brazen form. Only the truth-seeker preserves his image in clay-covered, damp rags—a working
hypothesis.

A man towards his icon is like the tenderness and secretive-
ness of a little bird towards its nest, which does not know
you have discovered its heart's treasure. For everyone
knows the lineaments of your image and talks about them
to everyone else save you, and no one dare refer to his own—
it is bad form—so that in spite of the gossip and criticism
that swirl around each one's personality, a man remains
sound-tight and insulated.

The human comedy begins at the thought of the ludicrous
unlikeness, in many cases, of the treasured image to the real
person—as much verisimilitude about it as, say, about a
bust by Gaudier-Brzeska.

Heavens ! what a toy-shop it will be at the Last Day,
when all our little effigies are taken from their cupboards,
unwrapped and ranged along beside us, shivering and nude.
In that day how few will be able to say that they ever
cried ' God be merciful to me, a sinner,' or ' a fool,' or ' a
humbug.'

The human tragedy begins as soon as one feels how often
a man's life is ruined by simple reason of this disparity
between the image and the real—the image (or the man's
mistaken idea of himself) like an *ignis fatuus* leading him

through devious paths into the morass of failure, or worse, of sheer laughing-stock silliness. The moral is γνῶθι σεαυτόν.

(My dear chap, quoting Greek at your time of life !)

February 11.

At 9 a.m. I heard the garden gate being forced open (it was frozen to the post) and the postman's welcome footsteps up the path. He dropped a parcel on the porch seat, knocked and went away again. I could not get at my parcel, though I was only a few feet away from it. So I lay and reflected what it might be. Surely not the book ordered at Bumpus's ? Too soon. H——'s promised cigarettes ? It sounded too heavy. My own book ? An early advance copy ? Perhaps.

Nanny came in and settled it. It was the book from B——'s. I was so interested I let her go away without cutting the string. I struggled, but could not tear off the cover, and had to sit with the book on my lap, wondering. She came in to light the fire, and I asked for a knife. She picked the parcel up, took it to the kitchen, and brought the book back opened. I did not like this. I like opening my own parcels.

It was James Joyce's *Portrait of the Artist*—a book which the mob will take fifty years to discover, but having once discovered it will again neglect.

It was cold enough to freeze a brass monkey. I had had some diary to post up. The diary seemed to lose all interest and attraction. It was a sore temptation, but I decided to be a Stoic, and wrote till eleven-thirty, though my hands were blue and my nose ran.

Then I read Joyce. An amazing book. Just the book I intended to write—had started it, in fact, when the crash came. He gives the flow of the boy's consciousness—rather the trickle of one thing after another—almost as well as Bashkirtseff. I have never read anything so extraordinary as the latter's pages wherein she plumbs to the bottom and the dregs of current consciousness. Her brain runs syn-chronously with her pen. She eviscerates her current thoughts and records them exactly with a current pen.

It is difficult to do. I've tried it in this Journal and failed. I am trying it now, but it's not coming very easily. What I like is Joyce's candour and verisimilitude. I have tried that, but it's no good. The publishers rejected two splendid entries about prostitutes and other stuff. That is why I think, in truth, 100,000 copies will not be sold. My diary is too unpleasant for popularity. It is my passion for taking folk by the nose and giving them a wigging, my fierce contempt for every kind of complacency. Stephen *Daedalus*. Butler started the fashion with Edward *Pontifex*. Then there is Wells' George *Ponderevo*. Pontifex is a good name.

On the wall in front of me is a pattern of ivy-leaves. In odd moments of listlessness I am always counting them: there are 30 perpendicular rows with 47 leaves in each row —that's 1,410 leaves in all. You'd never think there were so many, to look at the wall. I know to nausea that there are 40 little panes of glass in the window on my left—really only 39, as one is broken and stopped with cardboard. There are 7 bars (5 thin and 2 thick) in the back of the wooden chair. There were 17 degrees of frost this morning, and I have to stop constantly to wipe my nose and warm my hands on a water-bottle. There is also a water-bottle at my feet. KLIM—that is MILK backwards—printed on a

wooden box I use as a book-rest and now lying upside down. YLIAD SWEN—this is the *Daily News* backwards. I am for ever reading it backwards as it lies about on my bed upside down. Then there are faces on the morris-patterned curtain and in the fire. I saw a face like this last night. It was like me, but with a big hole excavated in the top of the skull, carrying red-hot coals and giving off a black smoke. The face was coal-black, too. I might have been some evil genie stoking the fires of hell.

Heavens! I wish I could discuss James Joyce with someone. I must write to R——.

'DEAR OLD LAD,

'Have you ever read James Joyce? *Literature*, my boy; the most vivid book, living, obviously autobiographical, candid, such realism, beauty of style. Am so pleased I have found him out! I am quite exultant. He is one of us!'

Our sukie is an old copper one, and sings sometimes in splendid imitation of an orchestra tuning up. I can hear very clearly the oboes and violins. It makes me thirsty.

My hand has gone too cold and stiff to write more.

My Canary

The jacket is put over his cage at nightfall, and all night he roosts on a table close to my bed. When I wake in the silence of the night, it is difficult to believe that close to me there is a little heart incessantly pumping hot red blood. I have a sense of companionship at the thought. For I, too, silent, concealed in my bed, possess a heart pumping incessantly, though not so fast. I, too, am an animal, little bird, and we must both die.

A Gasconade

I owe neither a knee nor a bare gramercy to any man. All that I did, I did by my own initiative. To this sweeping assertion I make one exception—R——, if for no other reason than that he taught me to love music.

February 13.

I had a letter from H. G. Wells this morning. He says: ' You will have seen my Preface by this time.' (I haven't.)

' Prefaces always devastate relationships. But I hope you didn't think it too horrible. I had to play up to your standard of frankness.' I knew he would be rude. But I'm afire to see what he says.

I am going to be quite fond of this old Nanny. She is always cheerful and ready to do any mortal thing for me. Across the frightful abyss that separates our two several existences I throw this thin line of attachment and appreciation.

The difference between a highly developed human—say, like Meredith—and his housemaid is greater than the difference between the highest ape and the housemaid.

February 16.

The publishers this morning sent me a proof of Mr Wells' Introduction. It is excellent, and not rude at all. I devoured it with avidity—can't you see me? The book won't be ready till about the end of March.

The Bankruptcy of Imagination

Mr. Lloyd George, at the Peace Conference, said that he was persuaded to the League of Nations idea when recently he saw in France the innumerable graves of the fallen covering acres.

Perpend. The statement is worth considering. Note that it is at the end of the war he is speaking, that it is the *number* of graves he is moved by, and that what moves him to realise the horrors of war is the graves of *dead* men. What was Mr Lloyd George's imagination doing before he went to France and saw the graves? Would it help on the League, think you, if someone took his child by the hand and showed him all the acres of all the graves in Europe; or all the mutilated in the hospitals when their wounds are being dressed; or all the asylums when the madmen are having their morning rave; or all the St Dunstan's in the world; or all the dying and dead babies?

The war has beggared the imagination. If a woman
loses five sons, she is not smitten five times as much as if she
lost only one. All suffering has limits beyond which the
heart is insensible. We are no more appalled at the death
of ten million men than at that of ten thousand, or, indeed,
if it be under our eyes, ten or one. It is a fact that we are
forgetting the war already—those who weren't in it.
Skating, dancing, political squabbles are all the go—pigs
over their pannage. If a woman has lost a son, compensations are manifold—*e.g.*, some gewgaw from the King's
hands at Buckingham Palace. What the son thought or
suffered no one knows, because he's dead. If he survives
he wants to remain dumb, or lacks capacity to express his
thought about the hell and damnation of war. If he had
such a capacity, his hearers would lack the imaginative
sympathy to be scalded by his boiling ink.

In this week's *Times Literary Supplement* is a cringing
review of a rotten book, *Notebooks of a Spinster Lady*—
obviously a nob—say, an earl's daughter. True, the
reviewer deferentially refers to some of the stories as *old*,
but hastens to explain that all he means is *old to him*. In
the same issue is another snobbish review on the life of
Meredith, excellent according to other reviewers. It is
headed ' Small Talk about George Meredith '—from which
one knows what to expect. The reviewer knew Meredith
personally, and explains with delightful *naïveté* that the
reason why Meredith would not go to see his first wife on her
death-bed, though she asked him to come, was his sensitive
horror of death-bed scenes. As for Meredith being ashamed
of being a tailor's son, the idea is scouted. Yet, he was,
and I hate him for it.

February 17.

Reading the Introduction was like reading my own
obituary notice. It rather moved me. All day yesterday
I buzzed over it like a famished bee. Streaks of it at
intervals would shoot through my mind. I weighed sen-

tences, measured them, tested them. I was curious over
' a certain thread of unpremeditated and exquisite beauty
that runs through the story this diary tells.' Lord in
heaven, what is it ?

Mr Wells is sympathetic and almost too generous.
Characteristically he concentrates on me as a biologist,
whereas I like to look at myself posthumously as a writer.

He is a good fellow, and I am most grateful and most
pleased.

It's milder to-day, and the chaffinches are sweetly singing
outside my window.

Nurse said to me after breakfast:

' Well, what are you going to do ?'

I replied apologetically:

' Oh, writing, I suppose.'

' This everlasting writing.' She shrugged her shoulders,
and I felt it was most unsociable in me not to satisfy her
curiosity.

February 15.

Legs

B.: (to Nurse stepping on his toes) : ' Seemingly either my
feet or yours are very large.'

N.: ' Oh, but you see it's my legs are so short. I can't
step across easily. It will be all right if you go to Eastbourne. Nurse —— has long legs.'

B.: ' But what's the use of her long legs if she can't get
a house ?'

N.: ' Aunt Hobart's legs were so bent up that though she
was six feet long, her coffin was only four feet.'

B.: ' Why were Aunt Hobart's legs bent up ?'

N.: ' Rheumatism. She was buried at the same time as
her grand-daughter.'

B.: ' But *her* legs were not bent up ?'

N.: ' Oh, no. Bessie was only sixteen, and died of
scarlet fever.'

The Water Ousel's Song

A Memory

I leaned over the parapet of an old stone bridge covered with great, old, branching, woody tangles of ivy, and leading from an oak wood across a stream into a meadow. I leaned over the parapet, and gazed long at the rushing water below. ' I will look,' I said, ' as if I am never going to see this picture again.' And so I looked, and now I am glad I looked like that, for the memory of the picture in every detail comes back, and indeed has never left me.

Along each bank margin grew a row of alders, and in the bed of the river were scattered great slabs of rock jutting out of the water, and spotted white with the droppings of water ousels. and kingfishers that loved to pause on them. A great body of swift, strong and silent water came sweeping down to the falls, then dropping over in a solid green bar into a cauldron of roaring, hissing liquid below, churning the surface waters into soapy foam of purest white—the white of the summer cloud and the water ousel's breast. Outside the foam-belt the water of this salmon pool ripples away gently in oily eddies and circles. After the rough passage over the falls, some of the water rests awhile in little recesses on the periphery of the pool. But gradually it works round into the current which, like the wake of a steamer, cuts diametrically across the pool, and swishes everything—leaves, twigs, dead insects—on to the hurtling shallows. ' Watch how the vault of water first bends unbroken in pure polished velocity over the arching rocks at the brow of the cataract covering them with a dome of crystal, twenty feet thick, so swift that its motion is unseen, except when a foam globe from above darts over it like a fallen star.'

This is from Ruskin's description of the Falls of Schaffhausen. But note that it is equally applicable to my little falls—if we banish the phantom Size.

It may be only sour grapes for my part, but—

> ' Why go gallivanting
> With the nations round ?
> Leave to Robert Browning
> Beggars, fleas, and vines—
> Leave to mournful Ruskin
> Popish Apennines.
> Where's the mighty credit
> In admiring Alps ?
> Any goose sees glory
> In their snowy scalps.'

A water ousel alighted on a boulder and bowed to me. He and his little white shirt-front, continually bobbing, were like a concert-room artist acknowledging the plaudits of an enthusiastic audience. I was pleased with him, but his excess of ecstasy at sight of me made my own pleasure seem dull and lethargic.

Then he hopped a little higher on to the stump of an alder, and being twilight now, and the day's food hunt over, he poured out his quivering soul in an ecstasy of song. Like a solo violin with orchestra accompaniment, it blended in harmony with the voluminous sound of the water, now rising above it, now overwhelmed by it. Then, as if suddenly shy and nervous of his self-revelation, the little bird gave one or two short bobs, and flew swiftly away upstream. Such spiritual ecstasy made me feel very poor indeed in soul, and I went home with a sense of humiliation.

February 20.

My beloved wife spent the night here, then returned to Brighton. ' Do you feel my heart on my lips ?' ' Dear, I love you,' and her tears trickled on to my beard.

Two poor grief-stricken things. She shook with the anguish of the moment, withdrew, and again flung herself on my breast. I sat motionless in my chair. Ah! my God! how I longed to be able to stand and pick up, press to me, and hide away in the shelter of strong arms that sweet, dear, fluttering spirit. It is cruel—cruel to her and cruel to me. I thought my heart must break. There comes a time when evil circumstances squeeze you out of this world.

There is no longer any room. Oh! Why did she marry
me? They ought not to have let her do it.

February 21.

I sometimes fancy I am not weaned from life even now.
Pictures in the paper make me agonise. Oh, for a little
happiness for her and me together, just a short respite.
What agony it is to have a darling woman fling herself into
your arms, press you to her dear bosom and ask you desperately to try to get well, when you know it is hopeless.
She knows it is hopeless, yet every now and then. . . . She
pictures me in a study in her flat (all her own), walking on
two sticks. And already the tendons of my right leg are
drawing in permanently.

I am not weaned because my curiosity is not dead.
When I think of dying, I am tantalised to know all that will
happen after. I want to be at my funeral, and see who's
there and if they are very sorry, who sheds a friendly tear,
what sort of service, etc. Oh! I wish I were dead and
forgotten.

February 22.

Mr. Wells, in his Preface, refers to my watching bats in a
cave (they were deserted manganese mine borings) and the
evening flights of starlings, which were described in separate
articles I sent him. Herewith is my adventure among the
bats. A first-class field naturalist who has made some
remarkable studies in the habits of that elusive and little
known animal the mole, said to me at the conclusion of his
investigations: ' Yes, I have lived two years with the
mole, and have arrived only on the fringe of the subject.'
He was a melancholy fellow and too absorbed in his studies
even to shave his face of a morning. I arrived only on the
outside of the fringe in my study of the habits of the Greater
Horseshoe Bat, but I got a lot of enjoyment out of the risky
adventure of exploring the disused mines. The wooden
struts were rotten, and the walls and roofs of the galleries

had fallen in here and there. So we had sometimes to crawl on hands and knees to get past. All the borings were covered with a red slime, so we wore engineers' overalls, which by the time we had finished changed from blue to red, speckled with grease dropping from our candles. Occasionally, in turning a corner, a sudden draught would blow the candles out, and in one rather lofty boring we were stopped by deep water, and, boy-like, meditated the necessity of removing clothes and swimming on with candles fastened on our foreheads. One boring opened into the side of a hill by a small, insignificant, and almost invisible hole at the bottom of a steep slide. We slid down with a rope, and once inside the little hole at the bottom, found a big passage with a narrow-gauge line and abandoned truck—great excitement ! Another entrance to the mines was by way of a shaft no bitter than an ordinary man-hole in a drain pipe, its mouth being overgrown with brambles. We fixed a rope round the trunk of a tree, and went down, hand over hand. We crawled along a narrow passage—three of us, leaving no one at the top to guard the rope—and at intervals espied our game, hanging to the roof by the hind legs. We boxed three altogether, gently unfixing the hind legs, and laying the little creatures in a tin carefully lined with wool. The Horseshoe Bat is the strangest sight in the world to come upon in a dark cave hanging upside down from the roof like an enormous chrysalis in shape. For when roosting, this bat puts its two thin hind legs and feet very close together, making a single delicate pedicle, and wraps its body entirely in its wings, head and ears included. When disturbed, it gently draws itself up a little by bending its legs. When thoroughly awakened, it unfolds its wings and becomes a picture of trembling animation : the head is raised, and it looks at you nervously with its little beady dark, glittering eyes, the large ears all the while vibrating as swiftly as a tuning-fork. These with the grotesque and mysterious leaf-like growth around its nose—not to mention the centrepiece that stands out like a door-knocker—

make a remarkable vision by candle-light in a dark cave.

February 23.

Despite the unfathomable ennui and creeping slowness of the hours in the living through of each day, the days of the past month or two, by reason of their dull sameness, seem, when viewed in retrospect, like the telegraph poles on a railway journey.   And always rolling through my head is the accompaniment of some tune—Shepherd Fennel's Dance, Funeral Marches.

I want to hear Berlioz's Requiem.   Poor Berlioz!   How I sympathise with you.

February 25.

Am feeling rather queer these last few days, and am full of forebodings.   Dear E——'s struggles harrow me, and worst of all, I anticipated this as from December, 1915. When I showed my terrible gloom then, one person laughed gaily.   Too much imagination—the ability to foresee in detail and preconstruct—is a curse.   For I have lived through all this time before; yet the actual loses none of its poignancy.

February 26.

The doctor came to-day and recommended petroleum. All right.   He is a decent sort and knows his business.   Am feeling muzzy.   *Horas non numero nisi serenas.*   This should make us nineteen-nineteeners smile !

February 27.

A little easier in mind.   Posted proofs of my Journal to R——.   Am much perturbed.   Will he shrink from me, or merely tolerate me as a poor wretched manikin ?   I fear it will not bring me any increase of affection from anyone, and some ——

A load of sadness settled on me this afternoon.   As I lay

resting down in bed, for no reason I can discover, the memory of the evening prayers my mother taught me flashed over my mind, and because steeped in memory seemed very beautiful.   Here they are:

> ' Gentle Jesus, meek and mild,
> Look upon a little child,
> Pity my simplicity,
> Suffer me to come to Thee.'

Then the Lord's Prayer.   Then:

> ' Keep us faithful, keep us pure,
> Keep us ever more Thine own,
> Help, O help us to endure,
> Fit us for the promised crown.'

Then I hopped into bed and was asleep in a moment.

I went on mechanically saying these prayers when I was grown to a big boy, and subconsciously felt that the first verses were quite unsuitable.   But I never had, like some, an instinct for prayer.   I don't suppose I ever prayed, only raced through some rhymed requests learnt by rote !

I can remember very clearly the *topography* these addresses to the Almighty assumed in my brain.   Thus:

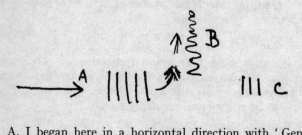

A. I began here in a horizontal direction with ' Gentle Jesus,' the successive verses being so many hurdles to leap over.   Then I turned abruptly to the left and ran up a tall, narrow, squiggly piece like a pagoda—the Paternoster (B) finishing off with the tail-piece (C), the single verse of 4 lines.

I never had till recently any religious sense at all.   I was a little sceptic before I knew it.   With no one to direct me,

I had a nose for agnostic literature, and when I found
Haeckel and Hume I whooped with satisfaction. ' I
thought so,' I said to myself.

' Beautiful,' did I say ? Why, no. Sottish doggerel.
The pathos of an innocent child repeating it !

February 28.

I thirst, I thirst for a little music—to replenish my jaded
spirit. It is difficult to keep one's soul alive in such an
atmosphere.

March 10.

Analysis of the ' Journal of a Disappointed Man '

1. Ambition.
2. Reflections on Death.
3. Intellectual Curiosity.
4. Self Consciousness.
5. Self Introspection.
6. Zest of Living.

I wonder if any reviewer will bring out these points:

7. Humour.
8. Shamelessness.

My confessions are shameless. I confess, but do not
repent. The fact is, my confessions are prompted, not by
ethical motives, but intellectual. The confessions are to
me the interesting records of a self-investigator.

If I live to read the review notices, I shall probably
criticise them. I shall be criticising the criticisms of my
life, putting the reviewers right, a long lean hand stretching
out at them from the tomb. I shall play the part of
boomerang, and ' cop ' them one unexpectedly. There
will be a newspaper discussion : Is Barbellion dead ? And
I shall answer by a letter to the Editor :

' DEAR SIR,
'　' Yes, I am dead. I killed myself off at the end of my

book, because it was high time.   Your reviewer is incorrect in saying I died of creeping paralysis.   It was of another kindred but different disease.

' P.S.—It may interest your readers to know that I am not yet buried.'

Or,

' DEAR SIR,

' There is an inaccuracy in your reviewer's statement. I was not in the Secret Service.   It should have been the Civil Service, of which I was a member up to within eighteen months of my decease.'

Or,

' DEAR SIR,

' I should be glad if you would correct the impression generated by one of your correspondents that *Barbellion* is the name of an evil spirit appearing on Walpurgis night. As a matter of fact, my forbears were simple folk—tallow chandlers in B——'

March 12.

> ' Out of the day and night
> A joy has taken flight.
> Fresh spring and summer and winter hoar
> Fill my faint heart with grief, but with delight
>   No more, O nevermore.'

These sobbing words bring a catch in my breath and tears to my eyes.   Dear Shelley, I, too, have suffered.

> ' No more, O nevermore !
> No more, O nevermore !'

March 15.

The first peep of the chick: among the publishers' announcements in *The Times*: ' *The Journal of a Disappointed Man*, a genuine confession of thwarted ambition and disillusionment.'

Am reading another of James Joyce's—*Ulysses*—running

serially in that exotic periodical, *The Little Review*, which announces on its cover that it makes ' no compromise with the public taste.' *Ulysses* is an interesting development. Damn ! it's all my idea, the technique I projected. According to the reviews, Dorothy Richardson's *Tunnel* is a novel in the same manner—intensive, netting in words the continuous flow of consciousness and semi-consciousness. Of course the novelists are behind the naturalists in the recording of minutiæ: Edmund Selous and Julian Huxley and others have set down the life of some species of bird in exhaustive detail—every flip of the tail, every peck preceding the grand drama of courtship and mating. But this queer comparison lies between these naturalists and novelists like William de Morgan rather than Joyce.

March 16.

I am getting rapidly worse. One misery adds itself to another as I explore the course of this hideous disease.

March 17.

Here is Hector Berlioz in his amazing Memoirs writing to a friend for forgiveness for causing him anxiety: ' But you know how my life fluctuates. One day, calm, dreary, rhythmical; the next, bored, nerve-torn, snappy and surly as a mangy dog; vicious as a thousand devils, sick of life and ready to end it, were it not for the frenzied happiness that draws ever nearer, for the odd destiny that I feel is mine; for my staunch friends; for music, and lastly for *curiosity*. My life is a story that interests me greatly.' This *verfluchte* curiosity ! I could botanise over my own grave, attentively examine the maggots out of my own brain.

March 18.

Mother (she liked me to call her Moth. Hubbard, Lepidopterous Hubbard, and she used to sign her letters *Hubbard*) had a pretty custom, which she hated anyone to detect, of putting every letter she wrote to us when stamped, directed and sealed, into her Bible for a minute or two, ostensibly to sanctify the sealing up.

Memories like these lurk in corners of my dismantled brain like cobwebs. I fetch them down with a pen for a mop.

I've had such a dear and beautiful letter from H—— this morning.

March 19.

> ' While all alone
>   Watching the loophole's spark
>   Lie I, with life all dark,
>   Feet tethered, hands fettered
>   Fast to the stone.
>   The grim walls, square lettered
>   With prisoned men's groan,
>   Still strain the banner poles,
>   Through the wind's song ;
>   Westward the banner rolls
>   Over my wrong.'

For all C.O.'s and paralytics (selected by E——).

March 20.

A letter from H. G. Wells. My book, he says, interested him personally as he once ' tried hard ' to get into the B.M. (in Flower's time), but failed. ' I don't think I should have found it very suitable.' No ! He would have promptly finished on the gallows for murdering the keeper.

March 21.

Another cobweb : an illustrated book of miscellanies called *The World of Wonders* in our ancient bookcase at home alongside Eliza Cook's poems, Howitt's *Visits to Remarkable Places*, an immense green volume of Hogarth's drawings, a Dictionary of Dates, Roget's *Thesaurus*, etc. I remember distinctly the pictures of the Man in the Iron Mask, freak tubers, and carrots like human heads in a row across a page, snow crystals, Indian jugglers, two Amazons of heroic girth carrying swords, striding along sands; the swords were curved, and one lady was much stouter than the other. I used to stare at these pictures before I could read, and invented my own legends. I always thought the potatoes and carrots were a species of savage, and many pictures I can recall, but do not know what they represent even now.

March 26.

Time lures me forward. But I've dug my heels in awaiting those two old tortoises, Chatto and Windus.

March 27.

I've won! This morning at 9 a.m. the book arrived. C. and W. thoughtfully left the pages to be cut, so I've been enjoying the exquisite pleasure of cutting the pages of my own book. And nothing's happened. No earthquake, no thunder and lightning, no omen in a black sky. In fact, the sun is shining. Publication next week.

March 28.

Having stabbed my arm and signed the contract, now when the clock strikes, I'd like to stay:

> ' O lente, lente, currite noctis equi !
> The stars move still, time runs, the clock will strike,
> The devil will come, and Faustus must be damned.'

But I asked for it, have got it—and to the full—and must fulfil my undertaking. My feelings see-saw. To-day I want to live in Hell's despite. The day before yesterday I had my back to the wall in a feat of sheer endurance.

March 30.

Now that I have spurred my hippogriff to the journey's end, now that I have wreaked my will on that very obtuse gentleman, my Lord Destiny, who failed to take due measure of his man, now as soon as I have freed myself from the

hard cocoon of my environment, and can sweeten and soothe
my warped frame with a little of the delicious honey of kindly
recognition, I can rest in the sun a while, soak up the
warmth and sweetness into this tortured spirit and crave
everyone's pardon before the end comes.   For I know that
the Journal will mean horror to some.   I realise that a
strong-minded man would by instinct keep his sufferings to
himself—the Englishman above all—(but I doubt if I am
an Englishman really.   My true home I guess is further
east).   I have been recklessly self-willed and inconsiderate,
and I have no sort of excuse except the most unprecedented
provocation.   I have been in the grip of more than one
strong passion, and my moral strength has been insufficient
to struggle with them and throw them off.   I have been
overcome, and the publication of my Journal is really the
signal of my defeat.

Ah, but it takes a terrific lot of energy to set about
putting one's moral house in order !   It is too late, and I am
too weakened.   You must take me as I am and remember
that with a longer life, just as I might have done better
things intellectually, so also morally.   Give me your love if
you can.   I love you all, and because I love you comfort my
self-despondency with the thought that there *must* be some
grain of goodness in me overlaid.

April 1.

I love my hair to be combed—it makes one realise what
an avenue for self-expression was closed when man lost his
tail.   I bitterly regret the loss of my tail ; I love the benison
of hot water for my urticating hands ; the tick-tack of our
cottage clock ; a cigarette—many cigarettes ; letters—these
are all my pleasures ; pills, the air-cushion, hot bottle, a
cramped leg straightened—these are my reliefs ; sleep—this
my refuge.

April 5.

R. and I at the B.M.

What friends we were ! The mutual sympathy between us was complete, so that our intercommunication was telegraphic in its brevity, frequently telepathic and wordless, yet all-sufficing. He had an extraordinary faculty for apt quotations: he loved Admiral Buzza, Mr Middleton, and similar cronies. Shakespeare was a never-failing reservoir. Together we passed along the street to our rendezvous, coats flapping, hands waving, tongues wagging, two slim youths, bespectacled, shoulders bent, bright-eyed.

We used to lunch at Gloucester Road, sometimes in Soho, and in the summer in Kensington Gardens. Our luncheon talks were wild and flippant. It was in the evenings after dinner at his rooms or at mine that we conversed seriously far into the stilly night, serious and earnest as only youth can be. During the course of a year our discussions must have several times passed in stellar transit through the whole zodiac of intellectual, moral, and social arcs. God ! how we talked ! I took charge of metaphysics and literature; R—— of art and sociology.

His room and mine at the British Museum were near one another on opposite sides of the same corridor, and one of my vivid memories of those days is R—— coming in the course of the morning, gently opening my door, stealing in and advancing slowly up towards my table on tip-toe, eyebrows raised as far as he could possibly get them right up under his scalp, arms down straight at the sides, hands raised at the wrists and performing continuous circular movements outwards while he softly whistled some beautiful melody we'd heard the night before. I would drop my dissections, turn and ask ' How does that piece go that starts —— ?' (I whistled a fragment.)

At lunch-time, whoever was first ready would visit the other's room, and should the occupant's head be still bent over his work, the same kind of remark was regularly made : ' Come, come ! I don't like to see this absorption in the

trivial round. Remember the man with the muckrake.
The sun shines: be heliotropic. Let gallows gape for dog,
let man go free.'

Our intimacy nettled some of our colleagues. ' What are
you two conspirators up to? ' (R—— in a black billycock,
and I in a brown one, were tête-à-tête in the corridor.)
' Discussing the modern drama ' (said to annoy, of course).

' Damon and Pythias,' sneered one, and we laughed
aloud.

We carried our youth like a flag through those dusty
galleries, and our warm friendship was a ringing challenge
to all those frosty pows.

April 8.

Went out yesterday for the first time for nearly five
months. A beautiful April day, warm, a full bird chorus,
the smell of violets, of wood-smoke—and the war was over.
I felt I could as an honourable human being look a Long-
tailed Tit in the feathers now and not blench. The sky was
above me—scores of white eyots floating in the sea of blue
—and my heart fluttered a little, and for a moment my
bood ran wine, until the inevitable reflection settled like a
blight. I should have preferred not to be reminded, but the
realisation how beautiful the world is swept over me all
unready in a mighty flood. ' Women are pretty things
really,' said E—— as she looked at photos in a picture
paper: it was reborn in her mind in a flash of delight.

April 10.

A quiet day with my heart full of loving-kindness for all.
Given time, I could change myself into something better.
You may not believe it, but even in my worst days I once
had a big desire for self-sacrifice. I was thrilled to find that
I was making someone happy by my love and deeply longed
to surrender all for love.

April 11.

An Enigma

In 1915 I received a p.c. which has puzzled me ever since. It is an enigma to me as baffling as a piece of Coptic text. It was in an uneducated hand asking for a museum pamphlet I had written on the louse, signed ' T. Wood (*Boggeria princeps*).' Any suggestions ?

Nurse and I have lived here alone for over a month, and she is kindness itself, cheerful, willing to fetch and bring, never impatient with me or irritable—a good soul.

April 14.

The Rabbits' Golgotha

Those sand dunes ! Their characteristic feature was rabbits' skulls, rabbits' scapulæ, ribs, pelvises, legs, bleached, white and dry; rotting rabbits being mined and gradually buried by gaudy red-marked carrion beetles; pieces of rabbits' fluff and fur ; rabbits' screams in the teeth of a stoat (a common sound); and the little round dry pellets of rabbits, more numberless than the snail shells.   And lastly, rabbits—rabbits hopping, racing, slinking, disappearing down holes, always and everywhere showing the intruder fleeting glimpses of the little white patches on the underside of the stumpy tail, the signal to disperse or dive into the sand.

The dunes are always associated in my mind with burning hot, cloudless, summer days, during the whole long course of which without ceasing Lapwings flopped around my head, uttering their crazy wails, circuses of scimitar-winged Swifts swished by and screamed hysterically, the face of the blue sky was dotted at regular intervals with singing Larks, singing all day long without intermittence, poised menacingly overhead, so that the white-hot needle points of their song seemed likely at any moment to descend perpendicularly and penetrate the skull.   Occasionally, a dazzlingly white Herring Gull would sail slowly, majestically in

from the cliffs, and from a much greater height than all the
rest of us, cry in a deep voice ' ha-ha-ha,' like some supreme
being in sardonic amusement at the vulgar whirligig of life
below him.

A still summer day, say you ?   The air was charged with
sound, had you the ears to hear.   It is not merely the
birds' cries, it is their dangerous living, feverish and intense,
that contributes to this uproar of life.   The heart-muscles
and wing-muscles give out a note as they contract (this is a
physiological fact).   The interior of, say, a Falcon's body
is a scene of dark-sounding romance and incessant activity,
with the blood racing through the vessels, and the glands
secreting, and the muscles contracting.   Just here at my
feet is an avalanche, jagged boulders of silica are descending
and spreading out in a fan-shaped talus—only sand grains,
so I cannot hear the crash of the boulders, but matter—
atomic solar systems—colossal !

And behind all, behind every sight and every other sound,
is the sound of the great sea, the all-powerful creator of the
dunes, who in a single evening (for a thousand ages are but
an evening in his calculations) could sweep them away or
sweep up another area of sand and marram grass as big.
One church is already obliterated.   That was yesterday.
To-morrow, maybe, the village further inland will have
vanished too.

That is the secret of the fascination of the dunes.   Super-
ficially, all seems dead and dull.   Reflection brings the
deeper understanding of myriad forms of life, creeping,
running, springing, burrowing—of noisy, screaming, struggling life, dominated by the august, secular movements of
the great sea.

Sometimes, towards the end of the afternoon, I would
grow tired, the brilliance would become garish.   Then,
leaving the thyme, the eyebright, the wild pansies, the
viper's bugloss (in clusters), an occasional teazle, after
boxing every sort of insect and every sort of plant that I had
not collected before (the birds' eggs I had long ago swept

into my cabinet), I would hurry out to the shore, take off
my clothes, and be rebaptised in the sea.   A hundred yards'
run up the cool sands and back, and I was dry, and dallied
awhile in the sand-hills before putting on my shirt that
smelled of stale sweat.

It was so good to divest myself of particularities that
clung like the burrs on my stockings, and plunge into the
universality of the sea! Subconsciously that was my
motive and the cause of my delight.

April 16.

I am still miserable, especially on E——'s account, that
dear brave woman.   But I have undergone a change.   My
whole soul is sweetened by the love of those near and dear
to me, and by the sympathy of those reading my book.

April 21.

Nurse was cutting my beard, and handed me the mirror
to report progress.   ' The right moustache,' I said critically,
' seems to droop down a lot.'   She twisted up the left
between finger and thumb, and then in a flash, before I had
time to scream, damped her finger with her tongue, and
gave a powerful screw to the right !

April 22.

Beauty

Under the lens of scientific analysis, natural beauty disappears.   The emotion of beauty and the spirit of analysis
and dissection cannot exist contemporaneously.   The sunset becomes waves of light impinging on atmospheric dust ;
the most beautiful pearl, the encysted itch of a mollusc.

And not natural beauty alone, but all beauty—all the
furniture of earth, and all the choir of heaven at the
intellect's beck must shed their beautiful vestments,
although their aureoles in the interim shall remain safe in
the keeping of man's soul.   For just as man's scientific

analysis destroys beauty, so his synthetic art creates it, and man creates beauty, Nature supplying the raw materials.

Nature is the clay, man the potter. Everyone feeling the emotion of beauty becomes a creative artist. If the world were as ugly as sin, the artist would recreate it beautiful in the image of his own beautiful spirit, just as Frank Brangwyn and Joseph Pennell are actually now doing with those industrial hideousnesses. But man's generous nature, because there is beauty in his own heart, naïvely assumes its possession by others, and so projects it into Nature. But he sees in her only the truth and goodness that are in himself. Natural beauty is everyone's mirror.

Similarly, as I believe, man creates the world itself after his own mind. Consult the humanists, in whose system of philosophy I have a profound intuitive belief.

Certainly there are many times when Nature, by pure accident, having other aims than our delight, produces the finished article. Helen of Troy, I suppose, required no emendation from the artist's hand. Nor does the Watersmeet, Lynton. Occasionally a human drama completes itself perfectly in five acts, observing all the unities.

It may be claimed by the moralists that there must be some very definite inherent direction in Nature's processes towards the light of beauty, if in the ordinary course of producing, say, a blue flower to attract insects, a thing of rare beauty at the same time emerges therefrom. But this is putting the cart before the horse. For man's own ideas of beauty are necessarily based on the forms and colour he finds in Nature, the only world he knows. So that we may say roughly that for our purposes we love blue flowers, for instance, because bees first loved them ! The bees were the original artists who created and educated our taste—they and the blue sky above us, that is. As a fact it is impossible to imagine the physical world ' as ugly as sin '—unless at the same time you imagine man's soul as being ' as ugly as sin.' You can imagine the world *different*—*e.g.*, with fewer forms and colours, say uniformly flat and brown, a desert.

But that would mean that, not only art would be poorer, but man himself as such would cease to exist. Instead we should have evolved as glorified sand.

Art has to take its cue from Nature, though Nature, whatever its chance form in any sort of planet, would always be emended by Art provided man were the same, because Mind is above Matter, Art above Nature.

April 25.

My beloved's birthday.

April 26.

Here is the nucleus of a sordid newspaper tragedy. I sleep on the ground floor in the front. Nurse sleeps at the back, upstairs. She is very deaf and I am helpless. Her father and mother both died of heart failure. One sister has heart disease and another heart weakness. Her heart too is weak, and my electric bell won't ring. If it did, she can only hear it when awake. We live alone, and each morning I endure suspense till I hear her coming down the stairs.

Overheard in the World Outside

In the road, *en passant.*

A Patrician's Voice: I was staying at Lord Burnham's place over the week-end. Very jolly.

Second Voice: I can never understand why he . . . (They passed.)

Two countrymen meeting in the road. I cannot see them, but quite well know how they have drawn up like railway engines standing on their metals, one on the right side and the other on the left of the road, converse a moment across the intervening middle space:

' How is it then ?'

' Oh, pretty middling.'

' They 'aven't shot your dog yet then, I see ' (rabies reported in the district).

' I'll watch it.'

And they steam slowly onwards.

April 28.

Yes, there *are* compensations. Few can appreciate a sunny morning and a blackbird's contralto from the walnut-tree.

The ' happy and comfortable ' like to hear about the compensations. They always thought things were never so bad as they seem. ' You must pull your socks up and make the best of things.' But you shouldn't have the impudence to tell him so.

Last night, a blizzard, a gale !

April 29.

Having cast my bread upon the waters, it amuses me to find it returning with the calculable exactitude of a tidal movement—*e.g.*, in my Journal I stroked *Public Opinion* and it now purrs to the tune of two and half pages of review : the *Saturday Review* I cursed with bell, book, and candle and—*voilà*! they mangle me in their turn.

For the most part the reviewers say what I have told them to say in the book. One writes that it is a remarkable book. I told him it was. Another says I am a conceited prig. I have said as much more than once. A third hints at the writer's inherent madness. I queried the same possibility. It is amusing to see the flat contradictions. There is no sort of unanimity of opinion about any part of my complex character. One says a genius, another not a genius ; witty—dull ; vivacious—dismal ; intolerably sad— happy ; lewd—finicky ; ' quiet humour '—' wild and vivacious wit.' As a whole, I am surprised and delighted with the extraordinary kindness and sympathy meted out to it, more than I deserve or it deserves, while one or two critics, with power that amazes, penetrate to the wretched Barbellion's core. To Mr Massingham I feel I can only murmur, ' Too kind, too kind,' like the aged Florence

Nightingale when they came to present her with the O.M.
But what sympathetic understanding! Compare one man
who said I was a social climber; another that I was ' finicky '
on sexual matters (Ha! ha! ha! pardon my homeric
laughter); another—or was it the same?—that I *shrank*
from life—yes, shrank! Give me more life, to parody
Goethe: I have shouted thus for years. Poor old reviewers!
Friends and relatives say I have not drawn my real self.
But that's because I've taken my clothes off and they can't
recognise me stark! The book is a self-portrait in the nude.

May 1.

What a sad, intractable world! Will human love and
goodness *ever* overcome it?

May 2.

I long to see my little daughter again. Yet I fear it
horribly, I am ashamed to meet her gaze. She will be
frightened at me. Better she should have no memory of
me at all to take through life.

May 16.

On the 14th at 2 p.m. a well-appointed ambulance took
me to a nursing home at Eastbourne, where I arrived at
7 p.m., exhausted but cheerful. It was like being raised
from the dead. We travelled *via* Acton and Ealing and
Shepherd's Bush, where we turned down H—— road past
my old rooms, across Kensington Road, and down Warwick
Gardens, where one dark November night E—— and I
plighted our troth beneath a lamp-post. We passed the
lamp-post! Then to West Cromwell Road, to Fulham,
Wandsworth, Tooting, to Tunbridge Wells, where at four-
thirty we drew up at an inn and a servant-maid put a tray
of tea and cakes on the bench beside me, and I ate and
smoked while the driver in the road compared notes with the
landlord on war adventures.

' Where were you then? '

' Messines.'

' Ah ! I didn't go so far north as that.'

It was so hot, I lay on my couch with my rugs, etc., off. But the street boys were so curious over my pyjama suit, I pulled the blinds. Then they moved round and looked in through the door. Nurse closed it. They moved round to the other side, so Nurse drew those blinds too. Then they capered off.

After that across Crowborough Forest, the car running at an even pace uphill and down. I lay happy and triumphant, and watched the country speeding by. We passed picnic parties—someone should have given them a warning and an exhortation; a dreadful thing for them, thought I, if they are not aware fully of their magnificent good fortune. The sky was cloudless. It was an amusing thing to me to feel so happy. Then I became displeased at my mood, on E——'s account, as I recollected the picture of her and baby in the road waving me goodbye.

May 17.

This egotism business: the Journal is more egoism than egotism, especially the latter part. And ought not Meredith to have called it ' The Egotist ' ?

May 18.

In the Journal I can see now that I made myself out worse than I am, or was. I even took a morbid pleasure in intimating my depravity—self-mortification. If I had spoken out more plainly I should have escaped all this censure. The reviewers are only too ready to take me at my word, which is but natural. I don't think on the whole my portrait of myself does myself justice.

A beautiful morning. At the bottom of my bed two French windows open out on to the garden, where a black-bird is singing me something more than well. It is a magnificent flute obligato to the tune in my heart going ' thub-dup ' ' thub-dup ' wildly as if I were a youth again

in first love.　He shouted out his song in the evening, the
very moment I arrived here.　What fine spirits these blackbirds are !　I listen to him and my withered carcase soaks
up his song with a sighing sound, like a dry sponge taking
up water.

May 20.

Pompa Mortis

If I could please myself, I should have my coffin made and
kept under my bed.　Then if I should die they could just
pull the old box out and put me in it.　It is the orthodox
pompa mortis that makes death so ugly and terrible.　I like
the idea of William Morris, who was taken to the cemetery
in an old farm-cart.

Ludicrous Impotence

I often laugh loud at the struggles of Nurse with my perfectly ludicrous, impotent body.　If you saw us, you would
certainly believe in a personal devil ; but when you saw what
a devil he is, you would also see in him a most fantastic
clown.　My right leg is almost completely anæsthetised—
curious experience this.　You could poke the fire with it,
and I shouldn't feel anything out of the way.　I could
easily emulate Cranmer's stoical behaviour.　It is so dead
that if you put my body out in the sun, the flies in error
would come and lay their eggs on me.　Yes, Satan was the
first and chiefest of Pantaloons.　Everyone who desires to
possess a complete knowledge of the world should read
Duhamel, Latzko, Barbusse, and consult the illustrations in
a textbook of tropical medicine.

The Idealist

The ultimate detection of a few bad faults in a good man
most unfairly discounts his goodness in the idealist's judgment.　For the idealist can be a stern, implacable task-

master. So a few good points unexpectedly coming to light in a bad man are enough to make the ever sanguine idealists forget the fellow's general badness. For the man of ideals must snatch at a straw. This is not justice, but it's human nature.

Those Nurses Again

Nurse No. 1 (helping her colleague to put away her books, examining a lapful): 'Ah, French novels ! Tum-ti-tum-tum !'

Nurse No. 2 (scandalised): ' French *classics* !'

Nurse No. 1: ' Oh, I beg your pardon—I thought they were French novels.'

May 22.

The reviewers say I am introspective—they mean self-introspective. I am really both.

May 24.

My legs have to be tied down to the bed with a rope. A little girl staying here lends me her skipping rope.

The Peace Treaty

After those bright hopes of last autumn Justice will be done only when all power is vested in the people. Every liberal-minded man must feel the shame of it.

This is the end. I am not going to keep a diary any more.

June 1.

The Brightest Thing in the World

Rupert Brooke said the brightest thing in the world was a leaf with the sun shining on it. God pity his ignorance ! The brightest thing in the world is a Ctenophor in a glass jar standing in the sun. This is a bit of a secret, for no one knows about it save only the naturalist. I had a new sponge

the other day and it smelt of the sea till I had soaked it.
But what a vista that smell opened up !—rock pools, gobies,
blennies, anemones (crassicorn, dahlia—oh ! I forget).   And
at the end of my little excursion into memory I came upon
the morning when I put some sanded, opaque bits of jelly,
lying on the rim of the sea into a glass collecting jar, and to
my amazement and delight they turned into Ctenophors—
alive, swimming, and iridescent !   You must imagine a tiny
soap bubble about the size of a filbert with four series of
plates or combs arranged regularly on the soap bubble from
its north to its south pole, and flashing spasmodically in
unison as they beat the water.

June 3.

To-morrow I go to another nursing home.

.   .   .   .

The rest is silence.